Principles of Administrative Law
A Comparative Study

SECOND EDITION

Principles of Administrative Law

A Comparative Study

SECOND EDITION

HAMID KHAN

OXFORD
UNIVERSITY PRESS

OXFORD
UNIVERSITY PRESS

Oxford University Press is a department of the University of Oxford.
It furthers the University's objective of excellence in research, scholarship,
and education by publishing worldwide. Oxford is a registered trade mark of
Oxford University Press in the UK and in certain other countries

Published in Pakistan by
Oxford University Press
No. 38, Sector 15, Korangi Industrial Area,
PO Box 8214, Karachi-74900, Pakistan

© Oxford University Press 2012

First Edition published in 2012
Second Edition published in 2020

ISBN 978-0-19-070394-3

Second Impression 2022

Typeset in Adobe Garamond Pro
Printed on 63gsm Offset Paper

Printed by Kagzi Packages, Karachi

Dedicated to the Memory of

Justice A.R. Cornelius
Chief Justice of Pakistan
(1960-68)

who had advocated the study and introduction of the system of
administrative law and administrative courts in Pakistan,
a system prevalent in France and other European Countries
since the nineteenth century.

Contents

Table of Cases

Preface to the Second Edition

Administrative law, as a subject of study, assumed great importance during the twentieth century, especially after the Second World War. With the expansion of governmental functions, particularly in the social and economic fields, makes its importance further enhanced during the twenty-first century. This is the reason that a formal study of this subject was introduced all over the world in the middle of twentieth century. All law schools in USA, UK and other countries that practice common law have been offering 'Administrative Law' as course of study at the Bachelor's (LL.B.) and Master's (LL.M.) levels. In the days of Professor Dicey, Britain regarded 'Administrative Law' repugnant to the 'Rule of Law'. Subsequently, Britain recognized the importance of this field of law and some of the leading British authors like H.W.R. Wade, J.F. Garner, J.A.G. Griffith produced outstanding textbooks on the 'Administrative Law' which are widely recommended for study in the law schools in USA and UK and other Commonwealth countries.

The law schools and colleges in India have been offering this subject in their LL.B. and LL.M. curricula since 1950s and 1960s. Renowned Indian Law Professors like I.P. Massey, S.P. Sathe, M.P. Jain, and others have greatly contributed on the subject. This subject has gained much importance and in 1995, it was introduced in the the LL.B. and LL.M. course of studies.

In early 1980s, I under took a study and research in 'Administrative Law' with the intention of writing a textbook for law students in Pakistan. Since 'administrative law' as a body of knowledge is still a developing field of law in Pakistan, therefore, such a textbook had to be a comparative study, relying heavily on English and Indian case law and textbooks with some input from American law as well. However, I have included the case law developed by the courts and tribunals in Pakistan.

The first edition of this book was published in 2000 by PLD Publishers, Lahore. It was well received by the law schools and colleges in Pakistan. The universities in Pakistan adopted it as recommended textbook for the paper on 'Administrative Law' in the LL.B. examinations.

The book was accepted for publication by the Oxford University Press (OUP), Karachi. I revised the book thoroughly and enlarged it keeping in mind that being the only textbook available in Pakistan on the subject, it may also be used by the students at the LL.M. level. The first revised and updated paperback edition was published by OUP in 2012. About a hundred pages were added to the text of the original work.

For the second edition, I have thoroughly revised the text of the first edition to update and include new laws in Pakistan, India and Britain and the latest case law on the subject in these countries. The book is written as a textbook on 'administrative law' for the students of LL.B. and LL.M. courses in Pakistan. It is also designed to be useful for the legal practitioners, law professors, law students and the members of the administrative services in Pakistan at the federal and provincial levels. Every effort has been made to explain complex concepts of 'administrative law'.

I am grateful to Mr. Asghar Baig and Mr. Ishtiaq Ahmed for preparing soft copies of the entire manuscript of the book. I am deeply indebted to Mr. Samuel Ray of OUP for his attention to detail and complete co-operation for its publication.

Hamid Khan
Lahore
11 June 2020

CHAPTER I

Introduction to Administrative Law

1.1 INTRODUCTION

While studying any branch of law, it is essential to define the scope and field of study. Administrative law, or the law relating to administration, has no precise definition or limitation. In the nineteenth century, the British jurist A.V. Dicey[1] stated that there was no administrative law in Britain, in the sense that there does not exist a concise and separate system of administrative law[2] as it was to be found in many Continental (European) countries.[3] He was, to a certain extent, right but it was not entirely true to say that there was no law relating to administration. However, if administrative law is simply considered to be the law relating to the administration of government, then there must be a large body of administrative law in Britain today, since there is an extensive system of public administration and a vast corpus of rules relating to that administration.[4]

Law defies definition, but perhaps the most satisfactory description of law (in a legal, and not in the scientific sense) is that it is a body of rules recognized by the courts of the country as the law. Logically, of course, this is not a valid definition, for 'courts' can themselves be defined only by reference to law. As a description, however, theories of the realist school[5] are perhaps the most acceptable for the English legal system. 'Administrative law' can therefore be described as those rules which are recognized by the courts as law, and which relate to and regulate the administration of government. Before evaluating this definition, the following three points need to be clarified:

(I) THE DISTINCTION BETWEEN ADMINISTRATIVE LAW AND CONSTITUTIONAL LAW

This distinction is important when delimiting the subject, but is not essential or fundamental; constitutional law does not differ in essence from administrative law, or indeed from other branches of law. The sources of both are the same and are concerned with the functions of government. Both are a part of what is sometimes known as 'public law', but perhaps the best description of the thin line that separates the two is that constitutional law is concerned with the organization and functions of government at rest, whilst administrative law is concerned with organization and functions in motion.[6] However, this is not entirely correct, as the law relating to the electoral system, and the organization of certain administrative bodies at a level below the central government, such as the local authorities and independent statutory corporations, is commonly regarded as being within the scope of administrative law. The distinction between the two is one of convenience and custom than logic. Administrative law and constitutional law together may be said to amount to the *jus publicum* or public law of a modern state, although modern lawyers also recognize specialized branches of public law, such as the law of taxation and military law, which are not considered a part of administrative or constitutional law.

Dr F.J. Port, the author of the first book to be published in Britain titled *Administrative Law*,[7] gave up attempting to define administrative law and contented himself with the following description:[8]

'Administrative law' is made up of all those legal rules—either formally expressed by statutes or implied in the prerogative[9]—which have as their ultimate object the fulfilment of public law. It touches firstly the legislature, in rules that are formally expressed which are laid down by that body; and secondly the judiciary where (a) there are rules (both statutory and prerogative) which govern judicial actions that may be brought by or against administrative persons, and (b) administrative bodies that are sometimes permitted to exercise judicial powers; thirdly, it is, of course, essentially concerned with the practical application of the law.

(II) ADMINISTRATIVE LAW IS NOT CONCERNED ONLY WITH LAW

Other subjects in law, such as tort, industrial law, the law of property, etc. are concerned solely with 'lawyers' law', with law as understood by the realist school. The sources of all these branches of law will be found exclusively in statutes, judicial precedent, and perhaps in custom. When studying administrative law, however, the student—and more so the practitioner—is concerned with these[10] and also with rules which are strictly not law. Administrative 'law' is also concerned with ministerial circulars and memoranda, decisions of local authorities or public corporations, or *la jurisprudence constante* (in the French sense)[11] of several administrative tribunals, none of which would be recognized or applied by the 'ordinary' courts as law. Even the internal structure of the various government agencies is of interest to the administrative lawyer and it has been suggested that there are common practices observed by local authorities which would seem in some respects comparable with the conventions of the constitution.

(III) THE MEANING OF ADMINISTRATION

Administrative law is concerned with administration; what then is meant by this concept or expression? 'Administration' is different because it is used to signify the government of the day or the body of persons who, for the time being, carry on the government. Herman Finer[12] has defined administration as being 'the governmental machine by which policy is implemented'. Unfortunately, this definition introduces another difficulty, as distinction has to be made between 'administration' and 'policy'. Policy means the formation of a general line or course of action— the idea of leadership, and the taking of a major decision on a matter of discretion, whereas administration involves the execution or implementation of that policy formulated in accordance with general principles.

Administrative law, it seems, deals with rules, most but not all of which are less of law in a strict sense, because they are concerned with the conduct of general business of the government of the country, within the broad principles laid down by the policymakers. It is concerned with various kinds of government agencies, both at the centre and locally, with the interplay of ideas and control between these several agencies, and the relationship between these agencies and the general public or the private citizen. It is concerned with the preservation of order, the welfare of the citizen and the rights of the individual as against the government of the country, and also with the machinery by which such matters are protected.

1.2 DEFINITION OF ADMINISTRATIVE LAW

As the discussion in the preceding section shows, it is probably impossible to give a precise definition of administrative law. Nevertheless, attempts have been made over the years by various renowned writers to define 'administrative law' as precisely as possible.

In 1887–8, F.W. Maitland, in his *Lectures on the Constitutional History of England*, discussed the definitions of constitutional and administrative law. He examined first the views of John Austin to whom constitutional law merely determined what sovereign powers a person or classes of persons have, while administrative law determined the ends and the measure in which the sovereign powers were exercised. Maitland regarded this definition of constitutional law as too narrow. Here, the idea of 'sovereignty' is treated as being more within the scope of a course on jurisprudence rather than on constitutional law and the 'rules' which determine who is sovereign—that are found more in the pages of historical works and in works on political theory than in statutes and constitutional conventions. Maitland next turned to some statements by Holland whose views he summarized by saying: 'I think we catch his idea if we say that, while constitutional law deals with structure, administrative law deals with function', although Holland included within his definition of constitutional law what Maitland calls 'the broader rules which regulate function', such as many of the King's prerogatives and the privileges of the Parliament. Sir Ivor Jennings wrote: 'Administrative law is the law relating to administration. It determines the organization, powers and duties of administrative authorities'.[13] This is the most commonly accepted definition today but it does not attempt to distinguish constitutional law which, in its usual meaning, has a great deal to say concerning the organization of administrative authorities. In another sense also, this is a very wide definition, for the law which determines the powers of these authorities must include, for example, the provisions of Acts relating to public health, housing, town and country planning, the National Coal Board, and personal health services. Indeed, almost every statute affects, to some extent, the powers and duties of administrative authorities.

According to Professor H.W.R. Wade, a first approximation to a definition of administrative law is to say that it is the law relating to the control of governmental power and as a second approximation to a definition, administrative law may be said to be the body of general principles which govern the exercise of powers and duties by public authorities.[14] K.C. Davis defined administrative law as the law concerning the powers and procedures of administrative agencies, including especially the law governing judicial review of administrative action. In his view, emphasis of administrative law is on procedures for formal adjudication and for rule-making and also on matters such as investigation, prosecution, negotiation, settlement or informal actions.[15]

The truth is, as all these writers (with the possible exception of Austin) would themselves point out, that any definitions of constitutional or administrative law and any distinctions drawn between them are arbitrary and based on the convenience of the particular writer.[16] There is, however, more to the question of the definition of administrative law than convenience. The study of administrative law in Britain did not recover fully for a long time from Dicey's denial of its existence. This denial arose in his comparison of English rules with those of the French over a very limited field, for Dicey dealt with *droit administratif* as though it related solely to the problem of judicial remedies. His misunderstanding of the French system was twofold. In the first place, he misunderstood and feared the idea of special courts which dealt with cases to which the administration was a party. This misunderstanding has been revealed; the true position in France explained and the fear shown to be groundless. It does not, therefore, today have any appreciable influence. But, in the second place, Dicey, by confining his examination to that part of the *droit administratif* which deals with remedies, gave to the meaning of 'administrative law' in Britain a similarly restricted interpretation. As a result, an undue emphasis has been placed on two problems in particular. The first problem is that of subordinate or delegated legislation, which means the statutory practice whereby Parliament empowers the administration in Britain (generally a Minister or the Queen in Council) to make rules and regulations. The second problem is that of administrative adjudication which means the statutory power of the administration to decide issues that arise between individuals and the administration, or, occasionally, between two parts of the administration itself. These are important problems, but they do not comprise the whole of the law relating to administration. As previously discussed, this law contains the rules relating to the organization and powers of the administration. Focusing on these two problems not only tends to blur the background of organization and powers, but makes a proper appreciation of these problems very difficult. Moreover, this focusing tends to divert attention from other developments which are taking place in that more important background. Organization and powers, as well as liabilities and duties, must, therefore, be dealt with in part.[17]

A book on administrative law is primarily concerned with the following questions:

(i) What is the structure of the administration?
(ii) What sort of powers and procedures does the administration exercise or adopt?
(iii) What are the limits of these powers and procedures?
(iv) How fairly are such powers and procedures exercised?
(v) What are the ways in which the administration is kept within these limits?
(vi) How are the contents of these exercised powers examined or reviewed?

(vii) What mechanism can be provided to check maladministration or excessive use of powers by the administration?

1.3 NATURE AND SCOPE OF ADMINISTRATIVE LAW

Administrative law is general in nature and governs the administration of any public programme. While it is necessary to understand administrative, legal, and policy contexts within which questions may arise regarding, for example, procedural fairness, abuse of discretion, and the interpretation of legislation, the focus of administrative law is not a detailed study of the law of particular programmes. Courses on labour relations, planning of land use, securities, broadcasting and communications, human rights, and immigration, for example, fulfil this function.[18]

In order to determine the nature and scope of administrative law, it is imperative to know what it deals with. Administrative law deals with:

  (i) the structure, powers and functions of the organs of administration,
 (ii) the limits of their powers and functions,
(iii) the methods and procedures followed by the organs of administration in exercising their powers and functions, and
(iv) the methods by which their powers are controlled, including the legal remedies available to any persons when their rights are infringed by their operation.[19]

This statement has four features. The first deals with the composition and powers of the administrative organs. The study of these powers comes under the purview of constitutional law. The second refers to the limits on the powers of the administrative authorities. The third refers to the procedures used in exercising those powers. The study of current administrative law seeks to emphasize not only the extraneous control but also the processes and procedures which administrative authorities follow in the exercise of their powers. Evolving of fair procedures is a way of minimizing the abuse of vast discretionary powers conferred on the administration. The fourth refers to the control of administration through judicial and other means. This is very important because in the modern day onslaught of administration, the individual is affected in many ways in the name of 'public good' and 'public interest'. The individual is in a weak and defensive position against the mighty power of the administration. It is, therefore, an important function of administrative law to ensure that the government's powers are exercised according to law, on proper legal principles, according to the rules of reason and justice, and not on the mere caprice or whim of the administrative officers, and that the individual has adequate remedies when his rights are infringed upon by the administration.

1.4 HISTORICAL DEVELOPMENT

Administrative law has been characterized as one of the most outstanding legal developments of the twentieth century. It does not, however, mean that there was no administrative law in any country before the twentieth century. Being related to public administration, administrative law should be deemed to have been in existence in some form or the other in every country having some form of government.[20] It is as ancient as administration itself and, as concomitant of organized administration. In India, administrative law can be traced to the well-organized and centralized administration under the Mauryas and the Guptas, several centuries before Christ. This period was followed by the administrative system introduced by the Mughals to the administration under the East India Company, the precursor of the modern administrative system. However, administrative law has developed quantitatively and qualitatively having relative significance in the twentieth century and has become articulate and definitive as a system in democratic countries like England and United States of America. It has assumed a more recognizable form in the present century, so much so that it is identified as a branch of public law by itself, distinct and separate from constitutional law, a subject of independent study and investigation in its own right.

1.4.1 THE RAPID GROWTH OF ADMINISTRATIVE LAW

In modern times, law is partly attributed to the critical international and internal situation that leads to a sense of insecurity. This insecurity compels the government to acquire vast powers to provide for the defence of the country, particularly in an emergency, and to maintain law and order within the country. The main growth of administrative law can be attributed to a change in the philosophy on the role and function of the state. The ruling political gospel of the nineteenth century was *laissez faire* which manifested itself in the theories of individualism, individual enterprise, and self help. This philosophy envisaged minimum government control, maximum free enterprise, and contractual freedom. The state was characterized as a 'law and order' state and its role was perceived to be negative because its interest extended primarily to defending the country from external aggression, maintaining law and order within the country, dispensing justice to its subjects, and collecting taxes to finance these activities. It was an era of free enterprise during which there was a minimum of government's responsibility and functions. The management of social and economic life was not regarded as the government's responsibility. However, the *laissez faire* doctrine resulted in human misery with the realisation that the bargaining position of every person was not equal and the uncontrolled contractual freedom led to the exploitation of the weaker by the stronger; for example, of the labour by the management in industries. On the one hand the Industrial Revolution led to slums, unhealthy and dangerous conditions of work, child labour, widespread poverty, and exploitation of masses, and on the other hand, there was a concentration of wealth in a few hands that became the order of the day. Thus the plea taken at that time was that the state should take more responsibility for ameliorating the conditions of the poor, and the general public opinion favoured state intervention, and social control and regulation of individual enterprises. The state started to act in the interest of social justice and assumed a 'positive' role. During the course of time, the concept of a 'social welfare state' emerged—a state in which the socio-economic welfare of the people was promoted.

The emergence of the social welfare concept profoundly affected the democracies. It led to state activism. There also occurred a phenomenal increase in the area of state operation; it took over a number of functions which were previously left to private enterprise. The state today pervades every aspect of human life; it runs buses, railways and postal services; it undertakes planning of social and economic life of the community with a view to raising the living standards of the people and reducing the concentration of wealth; it plans and improves urban and rural life, manages health, education, transport and communications, important key industries and the energy sectors. The state acts as an active agent of socio-economic policy; regulates individual life and freedom to a large extent, provides benefits to its citizens, and imposes social control and regulation over private enterprises. The functions of a modern state may broadly be placed into five categories: the state as protector, provider, entrepreneur, economic controller, and arbiter. The ideals of a social welfare state are being translated into practice through state planning of economic resources and social control of private enterprise with a view to creating a socio-economic pattern of society which involves improving the economic condition of the people keeping in view the demands of social justice. A large number of government enterprises have thus come into existence, some key industries, financial institutions, and transport services have been nationalized; increasing provision is being made by the state for such social services as education, housing and health; the state is required to arrange food-stuffs for the people; a rigorous system of state control and regulation of private enterprise has been created. Thus, the state plays a major role in promoting socio-economic welfare of labour by regulating the employer–employee relationship by other means.

Historically ancient Indian polity was characterized by the existence of a self-sufficient village as the basic economic unit which survived till the advent of British rule, in spite of all political convulsions, religious upheavals and devastating wars. It stood impregnable in the face of all foreign invasions, dynastic changes and violent territorial re-locations in inter-state struggles. Through all the upheavals during which kingdoms rose and collapsed, the self-sufficient village continued to survive. Village communities were like little republics having almost everything they needed and generally independent of any central control. They seemed to survive by themselves when nothing else lasted.[21]

The administrative unification of the Subcontinent was accomplished by British rule. Through successive reforms, it erected a hierarchy of central, provincial, and subordinate services which formed the executive branch of the unified state. British rule also established a uniform reign of law. It enacted and codified laws which were enforced throughout the country by a hierarchical graded system of lower courts, district courts, and high courts, finally culminating in the Federal Court and Privy Council. By 1935, when the new Constitution Act came into force, the responsibilities of the government were much greater than those initially envisaged, i.e. collection of revenue, defence of the territory and maintenance of law and order. In many parts of India, the government controlled rents of agricultural land, prevented the transfer of agricultural land to non-cultivators, took over the management of estates if their proprietors were incapable, maintained registration offices for transactions affecting immovable property, set up co-operative departments to encourage mutual assistance in economic activities, supplied food and started relief works during famine, managed vast areas of forest, manufactured salt and opium, owned or managed the greater part of the railway system, constructed and maintained irrigation works, roads and buildings, operated post and telegraph services, acted as a banker issuing notes and coins, regulating the balance of trade and rate of exchange, controlled the manufacture, sale and consumption of liquor and narcotics by short-term licences, supplied educational and medical services on a modest scale, and enforced a uniform system of audit of accounts of all public receipts and expenditures. After independence, India embarked upon an extensive programme of development through economic planning—a task which the state undertook to contribute the lion's share through the public sector by participating in trade, industry, agriculture, welfare activities, and all other works covered by the Five-Year Plans. As a direct impact of the process of economic development carried out through successive Five-Year Plans, the structure and powers of the administrative authorities are undergoing rapid changes. Functions are increasing and new ministries and departments are coming into existence to deal with special problems.[22]

Pakistan also introduced economic planning in order to achieve economic growth—a process in which the state is directly taking part through the public and semi-public sectors. This necessitated reorganisation and expansion of the administrative machinery to meet the requirements of its expanding role. Thus, in response to the needs for economic developments, changes in the administrative organization of the Government of Pakistan have taken place from time to time.[23] Many functions of the central government have been transferred to the provincial government. Some ministries like the Ministry of Food and Agriculture were reconstituted; some functions have been separated and embodied in self-contained units such as the Ministry of Works. New ministries like the Ministry of Fuel, Power and Natural Resources were created to deal specifically with urgent problems.

The powers of local authorities at various levels have also expanded as a result of this development. In India, the expansion of functions and powers of the local authorities was due to the community development programmes and demands for administrative decentralisation. The community development programmes cover the broad aspects of agriculture, animal husbandry, irrigation, and reclamation, health and rural sanitation, education, social education, communication, rural arts, crafts, industries, and housing. Local self-government has, therefore, to deal with problems and exercise jurisdiction of a kind that is unprecedented in its history.

The net result of this development has been a massive state intervention in economic activities. In some spheres, the intervention has taken the form of regulation under the specific statutes of trade and industry; while in other spheres, it has been more direct either in the form of nationalisation (as in the case of railways, irrigation works, communication and broadcasting, electricity undertakings etc.), or through the creation of public corporations.[24]

1.5 THE ADMINISTRATIVE PROCESS

State activism has led to one inevitable result—the quest to improve physical, moral and economic welfare of the people. In doing so, the state has assumed more and more powers and functions. A state consists of three organs—legislature, judiciary and executive. While increase in state activities has meant increased work for all organs, yet the largest extension in depth and range of functions and powers has taken place at the level of executive-cum-administrative organ. Thus in an administrative age, the administrative organ has become predominant and is on the rise; its functions and powers have grown vastly over a period of time. Administration is now an all-pervading feature of life today. It makes policies, provides leadership to the legislature, executes and administers the law, and takes manifold decisions. It exercises today not only the traditional functions of administration, but all other varied types of functions as well. The administrative organ exercises legislative power and issues a plethora of rules, bye-laws, and orders of a general nature which are designated as delegated or subordinate legislation.

Delegated legislation has assumed more importance, quantitatively and qualitatively, even more so than the legislation enacted by the legislature itself. The administration has also acquired powers of adjudication over disputes between itself and private individuals, and private individuals *inter se*, and thus has emerged a plethora of tribunals (apart from innumerable quasi-judicial bodies), diversified in structure, jurisdiction, procedures and powers, connected with the administration in varying degrees, and pronouncing binding decisions like the courts, whose powers have been diluted or excluded in several areas. The administration has secured extensive powers to grant, refuse or revoke licences, impose sanctions, and take action of various kinds in its discretion or subjective satisfaction. To enable the administration to discharge effectively its rule-making, adjudicating, and other discretionary and regulatory functions, it has been given vast powers of inquiry, inspection, investigation, search and seizure, and supervision. The truth is that in modern democratic societies, the administration has acquired immense power and discharges functions which are varied and multifarious in scope, nature and consequence. In the words of Robson, the hegemony of the executive is now an accomplished fact.[25] The modern administration impinges more and more on the individual rights and it has assumed a tremendous capacity to affect the rights and liberties of the people.

Extension in functions and powers of the administration has led to the contemporary complex socio-economic problems which could be tackled best, from a practical point of view, only by an administrative process instead of the normal legislative or judicial process. A legislative body is best suited to determining the direction of major policy, but it lacks time, technique and expertise to handle the mass of detail. The legislature has to content itself with laying down broad policies and to leave the rest to the administration. Thus the need has arisen practice of delegated legislation. Administrative adjudication has arisen largely because a multitude of cases arising for adjudication under the modern legislation needs to be decided expeditiously with the least formality and technicality, at the minimum cost, and by persons having specialized skills to handle such cases. The courts are not in a position to fulfil these conditions. Thus, the administrative tribunals were established.

Another advantage of the administrative process is that it could evolve new techniques, processes, and instrumentalities, and acquire expertise and specifications to meet and handle new complex problems of modern society. Administration has become a highly complex job requiring a depth of technical knowledge and expertise. Continuous refining and adjustment of detail has become an essential requisite of modern administration. If a certain rule is found to be impracticable, a new rule can be enacted incorporating the lessons learned from experience. Even a time-tested rule may have to be revised due to the rapid changes in a developing or a developed society. The administration can do so without much delay. When dealing with a problem case by case (as in a court of law), the Administration can change its approach according to the exigency of the situation and the requirements and demands of justice. Such flexible approach is not possible in the legislative or judicial process. In a judicial process the decisions are made after hearing lengthy arguments and on the basis of evidence on record, and is not suited to decide matters involving wide discretion that may be exercised on the basis of a particular departmental policy, position of finance, priorities and allocations between competing claims. In many cases, preventive administrative action may prove to be more effective and useful than punishing a person later on for a breach of law. Thus, inspection and grading of foodstuffs by the state would satisfy the consumer's needs more adequately than prosecuting the seller for adulteration after injury has been done to the consumers by purchase of unwholesome food.

The establishing of the administrative process in Indo-Pak Subcontinent was precipitated by a rapid expansion of the government's activities in various fields during British rule. In the post-Independence era, this administrative process was accepted by the constitution makers in both India and Pakistan. Thus, Article 19 of the Indian Constitution, while guaranteeing all citizens the right 'to practise any profession, or to carry on any occupation, trade or business', subjects this right to 'reasonable restrictions' which may be imposed by the state in the interests of the general public under Article 19(6). The Constitution of Pakistan similarly authorises (a) the regulation of any trade or profession by a licensing system; (b) the regulation of trade, commerce or industry in the interest of free competition therein; and (c) the carrying on by the central or provincial government or by a corporation controlled by any such government, of any trade, business industry or service to the exclusion, complete or partial, of other persons.[26] Article 39 of the Indian Constitution in the chapter on 'Directive Principles of State Policy', enjoins the state to direct its policy towards securing the ownership and control of material resources of the community are so distributed that best to sub-serve the common good and also ensures that the economic system does not result in the concentration of wealth and means of production to the common detriment. These constitutional provisions thereby sanction the operation of administrative adjudicatory authorities which have been set up under specific statutes.[27]

The post-Independence years have seen the emergence of a plethora of administrative tribunals, boards, and agencies, widely differing from one another in their constitution, powers, and procedures—some closely similar to the courts in the strict sense of the term, others bearing a closer resemblance to informal committees or interviewing boards. There are statutory bodies like the Railway Board, Mining Boards, Transport Authority, Central Board of Revenue, Regional Transport Authorities, Industrial Tribunal, Employees' Insurance Court, Court of Survey, Railway Rates Tribunal, Compensation Tribunals, and the Tax Appellate Tribunal, all enjoying varying degrees of autonomy and independence. There are also departmental authorities like the Income Tax Authorities, the Estate Duty Controller, the Customs Authorities, the Rent Controller, the Custodian of Evacuee Property, the Controller of Import and Export, the Controller of Essential Commodities, the Wage Board, the Registrar of Copyright, the Registrar of Trade Marks, the Controller General of Patents and Designs, the Central Board of Film Censure, Central Road Traffic Board, etc. All Commissions of Inquiry are set up by the government under the provisions of different statutes for the purpose of making a full and complete investigation into the circumstances of various cases that involve the general question of public importance with a view to framing policies. In India and Bangladesh, administrative tribunals have been established to adjudicate upon matters arising out of terms and conditions of persons in the service of the government. There are also provisions to deal with corruption. Again, departmental inquiries are conducted against the public servants under the Public Servants (Inquiries) Act 1850, and other statutes. The direct result of this has been the growth of administrative adjudication of claims or rights of private individuals which is in some way 'a technique of adjudication' that is better suited to respond to the social requirements of time than the elaborate and costly system of decision provided by litigation in the courts of law.[28]

1.6 IMPORTANCE OF ADMINISTRATIVE LAW

In this context, the study of administrative law becomes greatly significant. As explained in the preceding section, the rapid increase in administrative functions has created a vast new complex of relations between the administration and the citizen. Most citizens come into contact with the administration directly or indirectly. The prevailing circumstances at any given time pose certain basic and critical questions for the administrative lawyers. Does giving the administration increased powers uphold the interests of the individual supreme? Have adequate precautions been taken to ensure that the administration does not misuse or abuse its powers? Do the administrative agencies while discharging their functions follow procedures that are reasonable and consistent with the rule of law, democratic values and natural justice? Has an adequate control mechanism been developed to ensure that the administrative powers are kept within the limits of law and that it would not act as a power-seeking entity, but would act only after independently weighing carefully the various issues involved and balancing the individual's interest against the needs for social control? It is increasingly important to control the administration, consistent with the demands of efficiency, in a way that does not interfere with impunity rights of the individual. There is an old adage containing a lot of truth that 'power corrupts and absolute power corrupts absolutely'. Between individual liberty and the powers of the government, there is an age-old conflict. Thus there is a need to constantly monitor and evaluate the relationship between the government and the governed so that a proper balance may be evolved between private and public interests. Prudence demands that while sweeping powers may be conferred on administrative organs, there should be an adequate control mechanism to ensure that the officials do not use their powers in an undue manner or for an unwarranted purpose. It is the task of administrative law to ensure that the government's functions are exercised according to law, on proper legal principles and according to rules of reason and justice; that adequate control mechanism, judicial and otherwise, exists to check administrative abuses without unduly hampering the administration in the discharge of its functions efficiently. Therefore, the objectives of administrative law are to ensure legal control of administrative power and to provide protection to the individual against abuse of such power.[29] Administrative law seeks to adjust the relationship between public power and personal rights.[30] Of course, in securing this balance the needs of an efficient administration are to be duly respected. However, the efficiency of administration, though desirable, cannot be the only yard stick by good administration is measured. Fair and just treatment to the individual concerned are important values that must be achieved along with efficient administration. A fair and just administration is good administration. In Australia, the Kerr Committee emphasized that '. . . although administrative efficiency is a dominant objective of the administrative process, nevertheless the achievement of that objective should be consistent with the attainment of justice to the individual.'[31] This makes the study of administrative law important in every country. A strong desire for rapid development creates its own dangers and pitfalls. A country in which the roots of democracy are not very deep, a strong bureaucracy may have the tendency to undermine the rights of people. The vast administrative powers if exercised properly, may lead to the formation of a welfare state; but if abused, they may lead to administrative despotism. A careful and systematic study and development of administrative law may help to keep the administration in check while working towards the larger public interest.

1.7 THE RULE OF LAW AND ADMINISTRATIVE LAW

In 1885, Dicey stated that the 'rule of law' means 'the absolute supremacy or predominance of regular law as opposed to the influence of arbitrary power, and excludes the existence of arbitrariness, of prerogative or even wide discretionary authority on the part of the government.'[32] Dicey claimed that the Englishmen were ruled by law and law alone; he denied that in England the government was based on exercise in authority by persons having wide, arbitrary or discretionary powers. While in many countries the executive exercised wide discretionary powers and authority, it was not so in England. Dicey asserted that wherever there was discretion there was room for arbitrariness which led to insecurity of legal freedom of the citizens.

Another significant point which Dicey attributed to the concept of 'rule of law' was the 'equality before the law or the equal subjection of all classes to the ordinary law of the land administered by the ordinary law Courts.'[33] In England, he maintained, every person was subject to one and the same body of law. He criticized the system of *droit administratif* prevailing in France where there were separate administrative tribunals for deciding cases between the government and the citizens. He went on to state that in England there was no administrative law. The idea of having separate bodies to deal with disputes in which government is concerned, and keeping such matters out of the purview of the common Courts, asserted Dicey, was unknown to the law of England, and indeed was fundamentally inconsistent with the English traditions and customs.

Dicey's thesis has had a tremendous impact on the growth of administrative law in England where people were not ready till very recently to accept that anything like administrative law had come into being. But Dicey was factually wrong in his analysis even in 1885. He ignored the privileges and immunities enjoyed by the Crown (and thus the whole government) under the cover of the constitutional maxim that 'the king can do no wrong'. Even in his days, many statutes had conferred discretionary powers on the executive which could not be called into question in ordinary courts. He also ignored the growth of administrative tribunals, quite a few of which had come into existence by 1885. He also misunderstood and misconstrued the real nature of the French system and thought that this system was designed to protect officials from liability for their acts, but as later studies have revealed, it is in certain respects more effective in controlling the administration than the common law system.[34] It is interesting to note that while Dicey was denying the existence of administrative law in England, his contemporary Maitland perceived its emergence.[35] However, by 1915, after the famous *Rice*[36] and *Arlidge* cases[37] Dicey himself became conscious of the emergence of administrative law in England and performance of the judicial and quasi-judicial powers being conferred on officials of the government which earlier had not been regarded as its concern. But even then, Dicey asserted, that as long as the courts dealt with a breach of law by an official, there could be no *droit administratif* in England and the rule of law would be preserved.[38]

Dicey thus reluctantly recognized the beginning of administrative law in England under force of circumstances. However, since then, things have changed rather drastically. In 1929, alarmed by the large-scale assumption of power by the executive, Lord Hewart, in his book *The New Despotism*, made a scathing attack on the expansion of administrative powers of legislation and adjudication, and warned that vast opportunities had come to exist for misuse of powers of officials. He claimed that bureaucracy had become the true rulers of the country. As a result of this, the Committee on

Ministers' Powers (also known as the Donoughmore Committee) was appointed in 1929 'to consider the powers exercised by or under the direction of (or by persons or bodies appointed specially by) Ministers of the Crown by way of: (a) delegated legislation, (b) judicial or quasi-judicial decision, and to report what safeguards are desirable or necessary to secure the constitutional principles of the sovereignty of Parliament and the supremacy of the Law.' In the words of Carr, the questions posed for the committee were whether Britain had gone off the Dicey standard and, if so, what was the quickest way back.[39] In 1932, the committee submitted its report. It found nothing fundamentally wrong in the developments which were taking place. It accepted, however, that there were opportunities for misuse of powers by the administration and, therefore, made a number of suggestions to improve the control and supervisory mechanism. The report called attention to three main defects in the existing system of administrative law: (a) the inadequate provision made for publication and control of subordinate legislation; (b) the lacuna in the law caused by the inability of a subject to sue the Crown in tort; and (c) the extent to which the control and supervision of administrative decisions were passing out of the hands of the courts and were being entrusted by the parliament to specialist tribunals and enquiries. As a result of these findings, in 1944, the House of Commons established a Committee on Statutory Instruments. In 1946, the Statutory Instruments Act was enacted to tidy up, to some extent, matters relating to subordinate legislation. This Act has been characterised as purporting to enact a 'comprehensive procedural code for the making of subordinate legislation.' It formulates rules for publication of statutory instruments and also regulates the laying of procedures before Parliament. In 1947, Parliament enacted the Crown Proceedings Act to liberalise the law relating to civil proceedings against the Crown. The report of the Donoughmore committee represents the first attempt made in England at systemisation of administrative law.

In 1954, the British political 'Crichel Down Affair' occurred.[40] The Air Ministry had compulsorily purchased a piece of land for use as a bombing range during the Second World War. After the war, the original owner wanted to repurchase the land as it was no longer required by the Air Ministry, but the latter transferred the land to the Ministry of Agriculture for use as a model farm. The claim of the original owner was handled by the various officials with little care and consideration which was later considered as bad administration. The affair led not only to the resignation of the Minister of Agriculture, but also to the setting up of the Franks Committee to look into the system of adjudication by the administration. As a result of the Committee's findings and recommendations, the Tribunals and Inquiries Act was enacted in 1958. It led to the appointment of a Council on Tribunals and the making of various procedural improvements in the working of the tribunals and inquiries in the country.

Till 1958, the areas of delegated legislation and administrative adjudication had been investigated and some reforms introduced therein, but the area of other administrative powers had been left untouched. This task was performed by Justice, the English branch of the International Commission of Jurists, which published a report in 1961 (known as the Whyatt Report) suggesting the appointment of an ombudsman in England.[41] In 1967, England adopted the ombudsman system.

Dicey's concept of 'rule of law' has had its advantages and disadvantages. Although, the complete absence of discretionary powers, or absence of inequality, are not possible in this administrative age, yet the concept of the rule of law has been used to spell out many propositions and deductions to restrain an undue increase in administrative powers and to create controls over it. The rule of law has given to the countries following the common law system, a philosophy to curb the government's power and to keep it within bounds; it has provided touchstone or standard to judge and test administrative law prevailing in the country at a given time. Traditionally, rule of law denotes absence of arbitrary powers, and, therefore, one can denounce increase of arbitrary or discretionary powers of the administration and advocate controlling it through procedures and other means. Similarly, rule of law is also associated with the supremacy of courts, and therefore, in the ultimate analysis, courts should have the power to control administrative action and any overt diminution of that power is to be criticized and objected to. Judicial control of administrative action has become the pivot of administrative law in England. *Principle implicit* in the rule of law states that the executive must act under the law, and not by its own decree or *fiat,* is still a cardinal principle of the English system of law. The executive is regarded as not having any inherent powers of its own but all its powers flow and emanate from the law, a principle which plays a vital role in all democracies. It also serves as the basis of judicial review of administrative action for the judiciary sees to it that the executive keeps itself within the limits of law and not overstep the same. In many investigations into the various aspects of administrative law in England, the concept of rule of law has been invoked. In reality, viewed as a system of control of administrative power, it can be asserted that administrative law does not infringe but promotes the rule of law.[42]

But there has been a negative side of the concept of rule of law as well. For long, Dicey's thesis generated a sense of complacency in the English people so that they failed to see the growth and emergence of administrative law as such till they were rudely shaken by some powerful voices. The result of this has been that administrative law as a subject of study became well known recently. But, perhaps the greatest defect of the concept has been the misplaced trust in the efficacy of judicial control as a panacea for all evils, and somewhat irrational attitude generated towards the French system. People still believe that so long as are there courts, they can control the administration in all its actions. Faith in the courts has stood in the way of adopting other more efficacious means of controlling the administration outside the judiciary. After a careful study of the French system, many scholars have come to the conclusion that the executive is controlled much more effectively in France than in England[43] and that a better safeguard against the excesses of the administration can be found in adopting some kind of an administrative court on the lines of the French and German models. The Whyatt Report issued by Justice in 1971 suggested the setting up of an administrative division in the High Court.[44] In New Zealand, a country with the common law system, a separate administrative division has been established in the Supreme Court.[45] This division has replaced a large number of ad hoc administrative appeal authorities. In Australia, the Commonwealth Administrative Committee[46] in its report published in 1971, suggested the establishment of an Administrative Review Tribunal to provide a review of administrative decisions involving discretions on merits. The tribunal's key concern would be a fact finding review of whether there had been an improper or unjust exercise of discretionary powers. The Administrative Review Tribunal has been established in Australia.

It is thus clear that there is widespread thinking in common law countries on how to improve administrative law. There is disenchantment now with Dicey's rule of law. It is widely believed that a mere court review cannot be an effective control mechanism on activities of the administration, and furthermore, some principles of *droit administratif* should be incorporated within the common law system in order to have an effective control-mechanism over the administration.

Overall, it can be said that while the concept of rule of law helped in safeguarding and preserving the traditions of basic freedoms of the people, and the independence of the judiciary, nevertheless it also generated an irrational mental attitude for people who do not want to face the ground realities of the situation and look for corrective measures to problems encountered in administrative law.[47]

1.8 THE SEPARATION OF POWERS AND ADMINISTRATIVE LAW

While the 'rule of law' created obstacles in the recognition of administrative law in England, the doctrine of 'separation of powers' had a significant impact on the growth of administrative process and administrative law in the United States.[48] The doctrine of separation of powers is implicit in the American Constitution. It emphasises the mutual exclusiveness of the three organs of the government: (a) the legislature cannot exercise executive or judicial power; (b) the executive cannot exercise legislative or judicial power; and (c) the judiciary cannot exercise legislative or executive powers. Thus the government of the United States of America is characterised as a presidential form of government and is based on the theory that there should be a separation between the executive and the legislature. This is different to the parliamentary form of government in England or other countries, where the government is based on the coordination between the executive and the legislature. Of course, the doctrine of separation of powers does not apply rigorously even in the United States and some exceptions to it are recognized in the constitution. For instance, a bill passed by the Congress may be vetoed by the President, and to this extent, the President may be said to be exercising legislative functions. Again, certain appointments of high officials are to be approved by the Senate, and any treaty agreed by the President does not take effect until it is approved by the Senate; to this extent, the Senate may be said to be exercising executive functions. This exercise of some functions of one organ by the other is justified as checks and balances, i.e. the functioning of one organ being checked to some extent by the other.

The doctrine of separation has influenced, and has itself been influenced by, the growth of administrative law. In the face of new demands on the government to solve many complex socio-economic problems of modern society, new institutions have been created and new procedures evolved by which the doctrine of 'separation' has been largely diluted. But the character of administrative law has been influenced and conditioned to some extent by this doctrine.

The strict separation theory was dented to some extent when the courts conceded that legislative power could be conferred on the executive and thus introduced the system of delegated legislation in the USA. But because of the separation theory, courts have laid down that the Congress cannot confer an unlimited amount of legislative power on an administrative organ, and that it must itself lay down the policy which administration is to follow while making the rules. The lack of development of legislative control over delegated legislation in the United States through a legislative committee, similar to legislative control in England is partly due to the constitutional doctrine of separation of powers.[49] A further encroachment was made on the separation theory when the power of adjudication was conferred on the executive which was recognized and a few administrative tribunals, like the Tax Court, were established in the country. A much more serious dent in the separation theory was made with the development of independent statutory commissions that were established to handle and regulate new areas of activities and empowered with the triple functions of legislation, execution, and adjudication along with powers of investigation and prosecution. For long, it continued to be debated whether such bodies were constitutional or not.[50] But such bodies have been in existence for long, and new bodies are being created from time to time.

The aim of the doctrine is to guard against tyrannical and arbitrary power of the state. The rationale underlying the doctrine has been that if all power is concentrated in one and the same organ, there would be the danger that tyrannical laws might be enacted and executed in a despotic manner, and their interpretation could be in an arbitrary fashion without any external checks. In the face of the complex socio-economic problems demanding a solution in a modern welfare state it may no longer be possible to apply the separation theory strictly. Nevertheless, it has not become completely redundant and its chief value lies in emphasizing that it is essential to develop adequate checks and balances to prevent administrative arbitrariness. Its object is the preservation of political safeguards against the capricious exercise of power and it lays down the broad lines of an efficient division of functions. Its logic is the logic of polarity rather than strict classification. The great end of the theory is, by dispersing in some measure the centres of authority, to prevent absolutism. Thus, it may not be practical, by strictly adhering to the doctrine, to separate completely the adjudicatory function from other functions, but it may be possible to have some internal separation of the function of investigation and prosecution from that of adjudication within the same agency. This the Administrative Procedure Act, 1946 seeks to achieve.

By force of circumstances, administrative law has inevitably grown in the United States, but the separation doctrine did not generate an attitude of indifference towards it, as happened in England under the spell of the Dicean concept of rule of law. The attitude in the US was that of examination and criticism of the advisability and propriety of the new development. Many people criticized the growth of administrative process as doing violence to the concept of separation of powers. There was an insistent demand that a full fledged investigation be carried out in the new trends and that due safeguards against abuse of powers be devised. As a result of this, the US Attorney-General appointed a committee to review the entire administrative process and to recommend improvements therein. In 1941, the committee presented its report. It conducted a thorough probe into the administrative procedures followed by the various agencies of the federal government and came up with a number of recommendations to reduce the chances of abuse of power. No progress was made during the Second World War, and thereafter no immediate progress could be made to give legal effect to these recommendations. After sometime the most tangible result was the enactment of the Administrative Procedure Act of 1946. This Act lays down the minimum procedures to be followed by administrative agencies. The statute has been characterized as one which represents a compromise between two contending ideas. The one, mainly propagated by the legal profession, was to seek to restrain the administrative power, to provide for greater uniformity and certainty in administrative procedures, and to expand the role of judiciary in controlling the exercise of administrative powers. On the other side, there were the administrative agencies who wanted to retain flexibility and diversity in the administrative process and were not in favour of expanding the scope of judicial review. The Administrative Procedure Act 'represents a moderate adjustment on the side of fairness to the citizens in the never ending quest for the proper balance between the government's efficiency and individual freedom.'[51] It contains many compromises and generalities. In several aspects it is simply a declaratory document on existing law and its practice. In others, it has affected changes and has extended judicial review while adhering to the needs of flexibility and diversity in administrative process.

The Administrative Procedure Act, 1946 was amended subsequently and the main purpose of these amendments was to remove secrecy in the functioning of administrative agencies. Thus the amendment to the statute in 1967[52] makes it obligatory on an agency to publish orders, opinions, statements of policy, interpretations, etc. Another amendment[53] requires an agency where it consists of a body composed of two or more members to hold open meetings which are open to public observations with certain exceptions. Another innovation in the US has been the establishment of the Administrative Conference of the United States which carries on continuous research into the problems of administrative law and initiates proposals for reform.[54]

Notes

1. 'The words "administrative law", which are its [*droit administratif*] most natural rendering, are unknown to English judges and counsel, and are in themselves hardly intelligible without further explanation.' [A.V. Dicey, *Law of the Constitution* (10th edn.) 330.]
2. 'We do not have a developed system of administrative law—perhaps, because until fairly recently, we did not need it.' (*per* Lord Reid, in *Redge* v. *Baldwin*, [1963] 2 All ER 66, 76; [1964] AC 40).
3. In particular, in France.

4. Garner's *Administrative Law* (6th edn., London: Butterworths, 1985) 3–4.

5. For example, 'For any particular lay person, the law, with respect to any particular set of facts, is a decision of a court with respect to those facts so far as that decision affects that particular person.' (Jerome Frank, *Law and the Modern Mind*, 46)

6. Hood Phillips *Constitutional and Administrative Law* (3rd edn.) 13, citing Holland in *Jurisprudence*. Robson, on the other hand, points out that whilst constitutional law emphasizes individual rights, administrative law lays equal stress on public need [*Justice and Administrative Law* (3rd edn.) 429].

7. Longman (1929), now out of print.

8. Ibid. p. 13.

9. Port does not mention the influence of precedent, the other important modern source of law, but this should not be overlooked.

10. Custom is not relevant, so far as administrative law is concerned, but of course delegated legislation is very important.

11. The general effect or trend of a series of decisions; in French law this is the only extent to which decided cases become a definitive source of law, the English doctrine of precedent and the binding effect of the *ratio decidendi* of a single case being unknown. The decisions of administrative tribunals in Britain do not have the weight of precedents, but a series of decisions to the same effect tend to establish a practice to be followed in future cases. This tendency is strengthened in some cases where 'reports' of decided cases are published by the department responsible for the particular tribunal.

12. *The Theory and Practice of Modern Government*. In his *English Local Government*, the same writer describes government as being 'the system of functions and machinery established by any society for the supreme and ultimate control of all individuals and groups within its territory.' See p. 3 thereof.

13. *The Law and the Constitution* (5th edn.) 217.

14. H.W.R. Wade, *Administrative Law* (4th edn., 1977) 5–6.

15. K.C. Davis, *Administrative Law* (Text edn., 1971) 1–3.

16. J.A.G. Griffith, and H. Street, *Principles of Administrative Law* (4th edn., London: Sir Isaac Pitman and Sons Ltd, 1967) 3.

17. Ibid. p. 4

18. J.M. Evans, H.N. Janisch, and Multan Daood, J, *Administrative Law* (Toronto: Edward Montgomery Publications Ltd, 1995) 4.

19. M.P. Jain and S.N. Jain, *Principles of Administrative Law* (3rd edn., N.M. Tripathi Private Ltd, 1979) 12.

20. 'Since administrative law is the law that governs, and is applied by, the executive branch of government, it must be as old as that branch.' Parker, 'The Historic Basis of Administrative Law' [1958] 1 Rutg. LR 449.

21. A.R. Desai, *Social Background of Indian Nationalism* (Popular Book Depot, 1959) 7.

22. M.A. Fazal, *Judicial Control of Administrative Action in India, Pakistan and Bangladesh* (3rd edition, New Delhi: Butterworths, 2000) 3–4.
23. Ibid., p. 4.
24. Ibid., pp. 4–5.
25. Robson, *Justice and Administrative Law* (1951), 34.
26. The Constitution of Pakistan 1973, Fundamental Right No. 18. See also Article 47 of the Constitution of Bangladesh.
27. Supra Note 21, pp. 8–9.
28. Ibid., pp. 9–10.
29. H.W.R. Wade, *Administrative Law*, Supra Note 14, pp. 1–3.
30. Griffith and Street, *Principles of Administrative Law*, Supra Note 16, p. 2.
31. M.P. Jain and S.N. Jain, *Principles of Administrative Law*, Supra Note 19, pp. 7–8.
32. *The Law of Constitution* (8th edn.) 198.
33. Ibid.
34. Brown and Garner, *French Administrative Law* (1973); Schwertz, *French Administrative Law and the Common Law World* (1954).
35. Maitland, *Constitutional History of England 501* (1908)
36. *Board of Education* v. *Rice* [1911] AC 179.
37. *Local Government Board* v. *Arlidge* [1915] AC 129.
38. Dicey, 'The Development of Administrative Law in England' (1915) 31 LQR 148.
39. Cecil Carr, *Concerning English Administrative Law* (1941).
40. Crichel Down Enquiry (1954) Cmd 9176.
41. Justice, *The Citizen and the Administration*.
42. Harry W. Jones, 'The Rule of Law and the Welfare State' (1958) 58 Col. LR 143.
43. For instance, see Brown and Garner, *French Administrative Law* (1973) 161–62.
44. Justice, *Administration Under Law*.
45. See Paterson, 'First Report of the Public and Administrative Law Reform Committee (1968)' [1968–69] 3 NZULR 351; Northey, 'A Decade of Change in Administrative Law' [1974–5] 6 NZULR 25.
46. Known as the Kerr Committee.
47. Jain and Jain, Supra Note 19.
48. Thus Davis says: 'Probably the principal doctrinal barrier to the development of the administrative process has been the theory of separation of powers.' *Administrative Law Treatise* (1958) 64.
49. See Jaffe and Nathanson, *Administrative Law: Cases and Materials 109–115* (1961); Schwatz, 'Legislative Control of Administrative Rules and Regulations: The American Experience' [1955] 30 NYULR 1031.
50. See I. Davis, *Administrative Law Treatise* (1958) 65.
51. Byse, 'The Federal Administrative Procedure Act' [1958] IJILI 82, 107.

52. Through the Freedom of Information Act, 1967. See Erid Cambell, 'Public Access to Government Documents' [1967–68] Aus. LJ 41, 73.

53. Through the government in the Sunshine Act, 1976.

54. Wozencraft, 'The Administrative Conference of the United States' [1968–69] Business Lawyer 915, 24.

CHAPTER II

Administrative Action

2.1 ADMINISTRATIVE ACTION OR ACT

Administrative action or act is a comprehensive term which may defy exact definition. It is a term of wide import which means many things at the same time. Administrative actions may include administrative directions, administrative instructions, and administrative functions. Hence all transactions arising out of administrative process, whether in the form of administrative directions, instructions or functions, can be broadly described as administrative actions. However, the concept of administrative action can be better explained by its various classifications.

2.1.1 CLASSIFICATION OF ADMINISTRATIVE ACTION

In modern times, the administrative process is a by-product of the intensive form of government, which cuts across the traditional classification of the government's powers and combines into one, all the powers which were traditionally exercised by the three different organs of the state. This presents difficulties in defining a strict classification. Nevertheless, administrative action can be classified into the following broad categories:[1]

   (i)   Rule-making action or quasi-legislative action
  (ii)   Decision-making action or quasi-judicial action
 (iii)   Rule application action or administrative action
 (iv)   Finality of administrative action

2.1.2 DIFFICULTY OF CLASSIFICATION

The classification of administrative action as quasi-judicial generally presents a difficult problem. There are a number of administrative tribunals such as the Industrial Relations Commission, the Income Tax Appellate Tribunal, etc. which, though part of the administration, act in a judicial manner for all practical purposes. They have all the trappings of a court. There are, however, many other authorities which do not have such manifest judicial trappings but have to act judicially. It is with regard to such authorities that the classification becomes difficult. Before undertaking any formulation of the tests of classification, it should be remembered that different tests are applicable for different purposes[2] as discussed below.

(i) Where *certiorari* and prohibition are sought on grounds of excess of jurisdiction, the tendency is to classify all actions as 'judicial', unless they are purely legislative or ministerial in character or where they entail the exercise of a wide policy discretion by a body which has neither the trappings of a court or tribunal nor is required to decide *lis inter partes*.

(ii) Where classification is required for deciding whether a body is required to act in accordance with the principles of natural justice, the courts tread more warily. For this purpose, the courts use the word 'judicial' to describe the quasi-judicial functions performed by the administrative bodies or persons in contrast with what may be purely ministerial acts.[3]

(iii) Where classification is required for determining whether an act or decision is judicial so as to attract the competent authority and immunity from tortious liability, provided the litigant has acted in good faith, the interpretation of judicial function can be very extensive.

(iv) Where classification is required for determining whether absolute privilege in respect of defamatory statements and reports is attached to such bodies, it may be sufficient to establish the judicial character of the tribunal, to show either that it decides issues of a nature normally decided by the ordinary courts or that its constitution and procedures closely resemble that of the ordinary courts.[4]

(v) Where classification is required for the purpose of determining whether the previous proceedings before an administrative authority bar subsequent proceedings in a court of law on the ground of 'double jeopardy', the courts take a restricted view of the judicial function. Thus it was held that the sea customs authorities acting to confiscate smuggled goods under the Sea Customs Act were not 'judicial tribunals' and if the persons charged of smuggling were subsequently prosecuted under the Foreign Exchange Regulation Act before an ordinary court, they could not successfully raise the plea of double jeopardy.[5] However, in a different context, it was held that the customs authorities acted judicially while deciding upon the question of confiscation.[6] Similarly, it was also held that a departmental enquiry being held against a public servant is not in the nature of judicial process so as to bar the subsequent prosecution of those alleged to be guilty before the ordinary court.[7] For the purpose of observance of the rules of natural justice, however, such proceedings are considered to be quasi-judicial.[8]

2.1.3 RULE-MAKING ACTION OR QUASI-LEGISLATIVE ACTION

It is the legislature which is the law-making organ of any state. In most written constitutions the law-making power is expressly stated to vest in the legislature. It is the intention of all constitution makers that law-making must be exercised by those bodies alone in which this power is vested by the constitution.[9] In the twentieth century and even today these legislative bodies cannot give that quality and quantity of laws which is required for the efficient functioning of a modern intensive form of government. Therefore, the delegation of law-making power to administration is a compulsive necessity. When any administrative authority exercises the law-making power delegated to it by legislature, it is known as a rule-making action of the administration or quasi-legislative action.

Rule-making action of the administration is characterized by a normal legislative action. Such characteristics may include generality; prospectivity, and a behaviour pattern based on policy considerations that extends a right or creates a disability. These characteristics are not without exception. In some cases, administrative rule-making action may be particularized, retroactive and based on evidence.[10] The Indian Supreme Court held that (1) where the provisions of a statute provides for legislative activity like making of a legislative instrument or promulgation of a general rule of conduct or a declaration by a notification; (2) where the power exercised by the authority under a statute does not concern the interest of an individual but relates to the public in general, or concerns a general direction of a general character and is not directed against an individual or to a particular situation and (3) lays down a future course of action, such action would generally be held to be quasi-legislative action of the authority.[11]

Based on these characteristics a differentiation between quasi-legislative and quasi-judicial action can be made. A quasi-judicial action in contradistinction to a quasi-legislative action is specifically based on the facts of a case and declares a pre-existing right. However, in certain situations, like wage or rate fixing, it is not capable of easy differentiation. The Supreme Court of India left the question open on whether the function of the Wage Commission under the Working Journalists (Conditions of Service) Act, 1956 is quasi-judicial or quasi-legislative.[12]

In the same manner, the Committee on Ministers' Power which was appointed in England in 1928 to differentiate between administraive and quasi-legislative action on the ground that whereas the former is a process of performing particular acts or of making decisions involving the application of general rules to particular cases, the latter is the process of formulating general rules of conduct without reference to particular cases and are usually meant for future operation.[13]

Administrative rule-making action is generally controlled by the parliament and the courts through legislature and judicial review respectively.

2.1.4 DECISION-MAKING ACTION OR QUASI-JUDICIAL ACTION

Today, a large number of decisions that affect a private individual are not handed down by the courts but are given by the administrative agencies who exercise adjudicatory powers. The reasoning seems to be that since administrative decision-making is also a by-product of the intensive form of government, the traditional judicial system cannot give to the people that quantity and quality of justice which is required in a welfare state.

In some jurisdictions the term 'quasi-judicial' is used to denote administrative adjudicatory or decision-making process. Since the term 'quasi-judicial' is vague and difficult to define, it is hardly used anymore. Administrative decision-making may be defined as the power to perform acts, administrative in character, but requiring incidentally some characteristics of judicial dispensation.

2.1.5 Attributes of administrative decision-making action or quasi-judicial action and the distinction between judicial, quasi-judicial and administrative action

The administrative power and quasi-judicial power with public authorities is differentiated on the basis of the nature of power conferred on a person and framework of law under which such power is conferred as well as the manner of exercise of power and the consequential order passed in a matter. In civilized societies, all organs of the state are supposed to be regulated and controlled by rule of law. The concept of rule of law may lose its vitality if the state functionaries are not charged with the duty of discharging their functions in a fair and just manner thus showing that administrative actions were taken justly and fairly and were not arbitrary and capricious. The dividing line of 'administrative' and 'quasi-judicial' power is that in quasi-judicial decisions, the procedural formalities of law are considered inherent for exercise of power. These formalities are almost merely facilities of law which may have no substantive effect on the ultimate decision but any violation of these procedural formalities may create doubt in respect of the transparency of the decision. Consequently, any executive authority while exercising administrative powers under statutory law or exercising the quasi-judicial power is required to pass an order in respect of the rights of a person in judicious manner so that not only the rule of propriety but also the principles of natural justice are not in any manner offended.[14]

The Donoughmore Committee on Ministers' Powers (1932) analysed the characteristics of a 'true judicial decision' and summed up the attributes the presence or absence of which stamped a decision as administrative decision-making or quasi-judicial action. The committee was of the view that a true judicial decision presupposes a *lis* between two or more parties and then involves four requisites:

(i) Presentation of the case.

(ii) Ascertainment of questions of fact by means of evidence given by the parties.

(iii) Ascertainment of questions of law on the basis of submission of legal arguments.

(iv) A decision which disposes of the whole matter by applying the law to the facts.

The committee reported that a quasi-judicial decision involves the first two determinants, though it may or may not involve the third, but never involves the fourth determinant, because instead of applying law to the facts, the administrative agencies apply policy, expediency or discretion to it.

This approach of the committee was misunderstood because even the judges take into consideration the policy, socio-economic and political philosophy, expediency, and discretion while deciding a case. Judiciary is like any other branch of the government because litigation like legislation and administration is a stage in the accommodation of interests. On the other hand, in certain areas of administrative adjudication, like tax, the administration applies law to the facts in the same manner as the judges. Therefore, it is wrong to suggest that any admixture of policy in virgin purity of a judicial determination immediately reduces it to the rank of quasi-judicial decision.[15]

As the English 'law and policy' determinant is devoid of sufficient classification, in the same manner, the American 'position of the judge' approach is not without exception. In the American approach, a court is where a judge sits as arbiter—impartial and with no interest in the suit between the two parties. The institution and presentation are the responsibilities of the parties. In an administrative decision, on the other hand, the judge is rarely one who is disinterested in the case and sits detached. One may be tempted to argue and rightly so, that this classification matrix would also fail in the case of independent tribunals where the presiding officer does sit in judge-like detachment.

Therefore, only that classification of determinant can be called reasonable which is institutional rather than functional. There are separate and distinct administrative agencies that exercise adjudicatory powers like the courts, though it is only the will of the legislature that these are not classified as courts. However, it does not mean that administrative decision-making action is required to follow the elaborate judicial procedure. It is sufficient if, in the absence of any statutory requirement, the action is rendered by following the minimum requirements of natural justice.

There was a time when the view prevailed that the rules of natural justice have application to a quasi-judicial proceeding as distinct from an administrative proceeding. The distinguishing feature of a quasi-judicial proceeding in this behalf is that the authority concerned is required by law under which it is functioning to act judicially. Duty to act judicially was spelt out in *Rex* v. *Electricity Commissioners*[16] by Lord Atkins thus:

> Whenever a body of persons having legal authority to determine questions affecting the rights of the subjects, and having the *duty to act judicially,* act in excess of its legal authority, they are subject to the controlling jurisdiction of the King's Bench Division.

Lord Hewart, CJ, in *Rex* v. *Legislative Committee of the Church Assembly,*[17] read this observation of Lord Atkins to mean that the duty to act judicially should be an additional requirement existing independently of the 'authority to determine questions affecting the rights of the subjects'—something super-added to it. This gloss placed by Lord Hewart, CJ, on the dictum of Lord Atkins, bedevilled the law for a considerable period of time and stultified the growth of the doctrine of natural justice.[18] The court was constrained, in every case that came up before it, to make a search for the duty to act judicially, sometimes from tenuous material and sometimes from the service of the statute and this led to over-subtlety and over-refinement resulting in confusion and uncertainty in the law.[19]

In India, the judicial search for the duty to act judicially was sometimes made within the four corners of the statute[20] under which the authority exercised power, and sometimes in the tenuous material, remote and extraneous, such as *lis inter partis* including proposition and opposition,[21] implications arising from the nature of the functions, and the rights affected thereby.[22]

This doctrinal approach of the courts in England and India not only made the law confused and uncertain but also eluded justice in many cases.

However, in England, a turning point came with *Ridge* v. *Baldwin*[23] when Lord Reid pointed out that the gloss of Lord Hewart was based on misunderstanding of the observations of Lord Atkins. Lord Reid observed: 'If Lord Hewart meant that it is never enough that a body has a duty to determine what the rights of the individual should be, but that there must always be something more to impose on it a duty to act judicially, then that appears to me impossible to reconcile with the earlier authorities.' Lord Reid held that the duty to act judicially must arise from the very nature of the function intended to be performed and it need not be shown to be superadded. Professor Clark in his article 'Natural Justice, Substance, and Shadow' expressed the view that the observation of Lord Reid has restored light to an area 'benighted by the narrow conceptualism of the previous decade'.

This development of law is traceable in India also where the Supreme Court even earlier than *Ridge* v. *Baldwin* was of the view, that if there is power to decide and determine the prejudice of a person, the duty to act judicially is implicit in the exercise of such power.[24] In *A.K. Kraipak* v. *Union of India*[25] the judicial behaviour in India became still more striking. In this case the Supreme Court held that though the action of making selection for government services is administrative, yet the selection committee is under a duty to act judicially. The court observed that the dividing line between an administrative power and quasi-judicial power is almost negligible and is being gradually obliterated. Moving a step further, the Supreme Court of India clearly held[26] that it is not necessary to classify an action of the administrative authority as quasi-judicial or administrative because the administrative authority is bound to follow the principles of natural justice in any case. In this case, the question was whether the power to fix a minimum wage under the Minimum Wages Act is quasi-judicial or administrative.[27]

For determining whether a power is quasi-judicial or administrative, due care must be taken to determine (1) the nature of the power conferred; (2) the authority on whom the power is conferred; (3) the framework of the law conferring that power; (4) the consequences that ensue from the exercise of that power; and (5) the manner in which that power is expected to be exercised.[28] The Supreme Court defined the meaning and attributes of a quasi-judicial function. In this case the question was whether the function of the Election Commission to register a political party is quasi-judicial or administrative? The court held that the legal principle as to when an act of a statutory authority would be a quasi-judicial act is where (1) a statutory authority is empowered under a statute to undertake any act; (2) which would prejudicially affect the subject; (3) although there is no *lis* or two contending parties and the contest is between the authority and the subject, and (4) the statutory authority is required to act judicially under the statute, the decision of the said authority shall be quasi-judicial.[29] The court further elaborated that where the law requires that an authority before arriving at a decision must make an enquiry, such a requirement of law makes the authority quasi-judicial authority. In other words if an authority is required to act according to rules, its functions will be quasi-judicial. Therefore, if the authority has power to summon witnesses, enforce their attendance, examine them on oath and requires discovery and production of documents, its functions will be quasi-judicial.[30]

Elaborating the law further, the court identified three characteristics of a quasi-judicial action:[31]

(1) It is in substance a determination upon investigation of a question by the application of objective standards to facts found in the light of pre-existing legal rules;

(2) It declares rights or imposes upon parties obligations affecting their civil rights ; and

(3) That the investigation is subject to certain procedural attributes contemplating an opportunity of presenting its case to a party, ascertainment of facts by means of evidence if dispute is on questions of fact, and if the dispute be on question of law on the presentation of legal argument, and a decision resulting in the disposal of the matter on findings based upon those questions of law and fact.

Applying the above characteristics, the court concluded that the power exercised by the Chief Justice of the Allahabad High Court under paragraph 14 of the United Provinces High Courts (Amalgamation) Order, 1948 to transfer a writ petition from Lucknow Bench to Allahabad Bench in administrative capacity is quasi-judicial power subject to review by the higher forum. The court observed that the Chief Justice could not have allowed the plea without hearing the affected party and without determining on objective criteria and upon investigation whether the case is transferable and should be transferred. The decision of the Chief justice would have direct bearing on the right of the appellant to choose "forum convenience", hence the action is quasi-judicial subject to review by the higher forum.[32]

2.1.6 RULE APPLICATION ACTION OR ADMINISTRATIVE ACTION

Though the distinction between quasi-judicial and administrative action has become unclear, however, it does not mean that there is no distinction between the two. The difference between quasi-judicial and administrative action may not be of much practical consequence today but it may still be relevant in determining the measure of natural justice applicable in a given situation.

In *A.K. Kraipak* v. *Union of India*[33], the court was of the view that in order to determine whether the action of the administrative authority is quasi-judicial or administrative, one has to see the nature of power conferred, to whom power is given, the framework within which power is conferred and the consequences. In *State of AP* v. *S.M.K. Parasurama Gurukul*,[34] replying to the question whether the power of the government to appoint trustees under a statute was quasi-judicial or administrative, the court held the function as administrative and laid down that if there is *lis* (a dispute) between the parties, and the opinion is to be formed on objective satisfaction, the action is quasi-judicial, otherwise it is administrative. In the same manner in *G.G. Patel* v. *Gulam Abbas*,[35] the court came to the conclusion that since there is nothing in the Act to show that the collector has to act judicially or in conformity with the recognised judicial norms and as there is also nothing requiring the collector to determine questions affecting the right of any party, the function of the collector in giving or withholding permission of transfer of land to a non-agriculturist under Section 63(1) of Bombay Tenancy and Agricultural Lands Act, 1947 is administrative. The Delhi High Court, while applying the same parameters, held that the function of the Company Law Board in granting authority to shareholders to file a petition in the High Court is an administrative function and not a quasi-judicial function.[36]

Therefore, administrative action is the residuary action which is neither legislative nor judicial. It is concerned with the treatment of a particular situation and is devoid of generality. It has no procedural obligations of collecting evidence and weighing argument. It is based on subjective satisfaction where a decision is based on policy and expediency. It does not decide a right though it may affect a right.

No exhaustive list of such actions may be drawn; however, a few may be noted for the sake of clarity:

   (i) Issuing directions to subordinate officers, not having the force of law.[37]

 (ii) Making a reference to a tribunal, for adjudication under the law of industrial relations.[38]

(iii) Preventive detention, internment, externment, and deportation.[39]

(iv) Granting or withholding sanction to file a suit under Section 55(2) of the Muslim Wakf Act, 1954.[40]

 (v) Granting or withholding sanction by the Advocate-General under Section 92 of the Civil Procedure Code.[41]

(vi) Fact-finding action.[42]

(vii) Requisition, acquisition and allotment.[43]

An administrative action may either be statutory, i.e. having the force of law, or non-statutory, i.e. devoid of such legal force. The major part of administrative action is statutory because a statute or the constitution gives it a legal force, but in some cases it may be non-statutory, i.e. issuing directions to subordinates not having the force of law, but its violation may result in disciplinary action. Though by and large, administrative action is discretionary and is based on subjective satisfaction, but nevertheless, administrative authority is required to act in a fair, impartial, and reasonable manner.

A further distillate of administrative action is ministerial action. Ministerial action being that action of the administrative agency, which is taken as a matter of duty, imposed upon it by the law, devoid of any discretion or judgment. Therefore, a ministerial action involves the performance of a definite duty in which there is no choice. The collection of revenue may be one such example of ministerial action. However, the area of such actions is highly limited because any efficient discharge of a governmental function presupposes at least some discretion vested in the administrative authority.

2.1.7 FINALITY OF ADMINISTRATIVE ACTION

The subject of finality of administrative action is extremely complex with intricate ramifications because the courts have often shifted their positions on the subject. The grasp of general principles may be simple, yet their application to a particular situation demands flexibility and subtlety. The increasing powers of the administration are a cause for concern but the powers assuming a finality are a cause for greater concern. Generally, a clause is inserted in the statute by which the actions of an administrative authority are considered final. Such a clause has been given various names, i.e. finality clause, exclusion clause, ouster clause, conclusive clause etc.

No specific generalization is possible as to the manner in which administrative actions are made final. However, there may be three usual modes of conferring finality on any administrative action:

(i) Sometimes the finality clause in a statute may make the administrative action final by expressly barring the jurisdiction of the court.

(ii) Sometimes the finality clause in a statute does not expressly bar the jurisdiction of the courts but otherwise states that the administrative action is final.

(iii) Sometimes the statute neither expressly bars the jurisdiction of the courts nor confers finality on the administrative action, yet the finality of the administrative action may be inferred by necessary implication. Such inference may be drawn when the statute is a self-contained code which gives a right and also provides mechanism for the vindication of such rights.

The question of conferring finality on administrative action can be studied under the following headings:

Constitutional modes of judicial review and administrative finality

No finality clause contained in any statute and expressed in any language can bar the judicial review available under the constitution. In *Deokinandan Prasad* v. *State of Bihar*,[44] the Supreme Court held that Section 23 of the Pension Act, 1871 which provided that the suits relating to matters mentioned therein cannot be entertained in any court does not bar the constitutional modes of judicial review. In the same manner the High Court of Andhra Pradesh quashed Section 6(a) of the A.P. Preventive Detention Act, 1970 which provided that the order of detention would not be invalidated on the ground that it contained some vague and irrelevant grounds, as violative of Article 22(5) of the Constitution.[45]

Even in cases where the constitution itself makes the action of an administrative authority final, the constitutional modes of judicial review cannot be barred by any necessary implication. In another case,[46] the Supreme Court of India held that even in the face of Article 217(3) of the constitution which makes the order of the President final, in cases of dispute relating to the age of a Judge, the constitutional mode of judicial review is not barred.

Sticking to the same kind of judicial behaviour, the Indian Supreme Court again held in Indira *Nehru Gandhi* v. *Raj Narain*[47] that clause (4) of Article 329A (inserted by the Constitution Thirty-ninth Amendment Act, 1975) which frees the disputed election of the Prime Minister and the Speaker from the restraints of all election laws, does not bar the constitutional modes of judicial review.

Non-constitutional modes of judicial review and administrative finality

The non-constitutional mode of judicial review is exercised by the civil courts. Section 9 of the Civil Procedure Code, 1908 states that the courts shall have jurisdiction to try all suits of a civil nature excepting suits of which their cognizance is barred either expressly or by necessary implication.

The approach of the court in cases of express exclusion of the jurisdiction of the civil courts has been to strictly interpret the clause and if the words are clear and the statute is a self-contained code, to refrain from exercising jurisdiction. In *Firm of Illuri Subbayya Chetty* v. *State of Andhra Pradesh*,[48] the Supreme Court held that Section 18-A of the Madras General Sales Tax Act, 1939, which provided that no suit can be instituted in any civil court to set aside or modify the assessment made under the Act, did bar the jurisdiction of the civil court. In this case a suit had been filed in a civil court on the ground that the administrative authority instead of taxing sale has taxed purchases also. However, in *Government of Madras* v. *Basappa*,[49] Justice Hidayatullah took a contrary view on more or less similar facts, and held that the word 'final' means final for the purpose of the Act only. But this view of the court was soon reversed in *State of Kerala* v. *Ramaswami Iyer*[50] and the Supreme Court held that the finality clause contained in Kerala Sales Tax Act barred the jurisdiction of the civil courts in entertaining any suit for the recovery of excess tax collected by the sales tax authority.

The implied exclusion of the jurisdiction of the civil courts may be inferred if the statute containing the finality clause is in itself a self-contained code. The inference of implied exclusion may also be drawn when the action is left to the subjective satisfaction of the administrative authority by using expressions such as 'if satisfied' or 'if in the opinion of the administrative authority it is just and proper'. In view of such an implied exclusion, if the civil courts decline jurisdiction, it may be a case of self-limitation and not inherent lack of power. However, if the statute creates a new right and also provides a mechanism for the vindication of such right, the jurisdiction of the civil court shall be deemed to have been barred by necessary implication. In *Premier Automobiles Ltd* v. *K.S. Wadke*,[51] the Supreme Court of India held that the jurisdiction is impliedly barred as the Industrial Disputes Act is a self-contained code and the subject matter could form an industrial dispute and thus the remedy would lie under the Industrial Disputes Act.

However, the law relating to administrative finality as discussed above does not cover the cases of *ultra vires* acts of the administrative authority or the unconstitutionality of law under which the authority exercises power. A finality clause does not bar the jurisdiction of the courts if the action is *ultra vires* the powers of the administrative authority. In *Munni Devi* v. *Gokal Chand*[52] the Supreme Court held that the UP (Temporary Control of

Rent and Eviction) Act, 1947 which gives power to the District Magistrate to allot a vacant shop and also makes the decision of the District Magistrate final, does not bar the jurisdiction of the court in cases where the authority commits a jurisdictional error and allots a shop which is not vacant. Therefore, not only in the cases of substantive *ultra vires*, but in cases of procedural *ultra vires* also, the finality clause is not to be deemed final. In *Pabbojan Tea Co. v. Dy. Commr.*[53] The Supreme Court held that the finality clause as laid down under Section 24 of the Minimum Wages Act, 1941 does not bar the jurisdiction of the civil courts if the authority has violated the mandatory procedure of hearing before fixing the minimum wages for the tea plantation workers.

In the same manner, it is also not the implication of the finality clause that void laws be enforced without a remedy. This view was expressed by the Supreme Court in *Dhulabhai* v. *State of MP*.[54] In this case certain notifications issued by the government under the Madhya Bharat Sales Tax Act, 1950 were declared *ultra vires*. Thereafter, a suit was filed for the recovery of tax charged under these unconstitutional notifications. Section 17 of the Act contained a finality clause which provided that the orders made under the Act should not be called in question in any court. The Supreme Court upholding the maintainability of the civil suit in the face of a finality clause held that it is not the implication of the finality clause that void laws be enforced without any remedy.

2.1.8 Delegatee cannot further delegate its powers

It is settled law that a delegatee cannot further delegate its powers unless expressly authorized under the law. It is also settled law that in order to enable a person to delegate the power or functions, there must be an authority, expressed or implied, to delegate,[55] When power is conferred on a particular person, then that person alone has to exercise the power and cannot transfer its exercise to another person. The Supreme Court of Pakistan, while examining the power of appointment of Commissioners vested in the Federal

Government under the Securities and Exchange Commission of Pakistan Act 1997, observed and held that it was well settled law that a statutory delegatee could not sub-delegate his or her powers.[56] De Smith in his book 'Judicial Review of Administrative Actions' (7th edn.2013) states:

> "A discretionary power must, in general, be exercised only by the public authority to which it has been committed. It is a well-known principle of law that when a power has been conferred to a person in circumstances indicating that trust is being placed in his individual judgment and discretion, he must exercise that power personally unless he has been expressly empowered to delegate it to another"

The Indian Supreme Court[57] has held as follows:-

> "By now it is almost settled that the legislature can permit any statutory authority to delegate its powers to any other authority, of course, after the policy has been indicated in the statute itself within the framework of which such delegatee is to exercise the power. The real problem or the controversy arises when there is a sub-delegation. It is said that when Parliament has specifically appointed authority to discharge a function, it cannot be readily presumed that it had intended that its delegate should be free to empower another person or body to act in its place."

2.2 ADMINISTRATIVE INSTRUCTIONS

In any modern government, the desirability and efficacy of administrative instructions issued by the superior administrative authorities to their subordinates cannot be overemphasised. 'Administrative instruction' is an efficacious technique for achieving some uniformity in administrative discretion, and to regulate in an area which is new and dynamic. Such instructions also give a desired flexibility to administration without adhering with the technicalities of the rule-making process.

Administrative instructions may be specific or general and directory or mandatory. The nature of instruction depends largely on the provisions of the statute which authorises the administrative agency to issue instructions. The instructions which are generally issued not under any statutory authority but under the general power of administration are considered as directory, and hence are unenforceable. They do not have the force of law. In *Fernandez* v. *State of Mysore*,[58] the court held the Mysore PWD Code of instructions as not having the force of law because this is issued under non statutory authority but in exercise of general administrative power. Nevertheless, the determination of statutory or non-statutory source of administrative direction is always a very complex question.[59]

In situations where administrative instructions have a statutory source, their binding character depends on multiple factors. In *Raman* v. *State of Madras*[60], the Supreme Court came to the conclusion that the administrative instructions, despite their issuance under the Motor Vehicles Act, 1939, did not have the force of law. However, the Supreme Court in *Jagjit Singh* v. *State of Punjab*[61] held that if the administrative instructions do not run counter to the statutory rules, they are binding and their violation can be enforced through a court of law. Undoubtedly, the government in exercise of its executive authority cannot supersede a statutory rule or regulation but it can certainly effectuate the purpose of a regulation by supplementing it.[62]

However, no specific instructions can be issued to any administrative authority exercising quasi-judicial power or any other statutory power, laying down the manner in which this power is to be exercised. It has always been considered as an interference with the independent exercise of power by the agency and is also opposed to the principles of administrative due process.[63]

If administrative instructions are construed as making a representation to the people then anyone who acts on such representation, can hold the administrative agency bound by it on the grounds of equitable estoppel.[64]

2.3 ADMINISTRATIVE FUNCTION

The term 'administrative function' is widely used to denote administrative actions of various kinds and general nature of rule-making, quasi-judicial or administrative. It is a generic expression and is difficult to compartmentalize. An attempt has been made above to point out the distinguishing features of administrative action, i.e. legislative, quasi-judicial, and administrative. Although there are no clear definitions of the term, yet the nature of an administrative function is determined by looking to its purport, by evaluating its implications for the person against whom it is taken and by looking at its general background including the wording of the relevant statutory provisions. The classification often poses serious difficulty because of the complex combination of these functions in one agency. It is generally determined by examining the most dominant features of the proceeding. The purpose of such classification is only to analyse an administrative action or function with a view to determining how far the legality of judicial review is possible and which remedy will best serve the need of the litigant. The recent trend is towards liberalising the availability of remedies, as is seen in the decisions which made rules of natural justice applicable even to purely administrative actions. Since the functions of modern governments are becoming more widespread and complex, the chances of friction between individual liberty and state action become more and more frequent. Therefore, administrative law will have to keep pace with this new development by evolving new concepts of judicial control of various administrative functions.

2.4 ADMINISTRATIVE DIRECTIONS

2.4.1 DIRECTIONS AS DISTINGUISHED FROM RULES

In addition to rules and other forms of delegated legislation, there is an increasing trend of issuance of directions or instructions by the administration. Directions are issued for varying purposes. Administrative authorities mechanically issue directions through letters, circulars, orders, memoranda, pamphlets, public notices, press notes, etc. At times, directions may even be published in the government gazette.

A direction may be specific, being applicable to a particular purpose, or a particular case, or it may be of a general nature, stating general principles, policies, practices, or procedures to be followed in similar cases only. The directions of a general nature are discussed below.

Superficially, a 'direction' of a general nature may resemble a rule or delegated legislation, in form, as both are of general applicability. But, the two differ basically in concept and essence. To underline the difference between directions and delegated legislation, at times, directions are designated as 'administrative quasi-laws' or 'administrative quasi-legislation'.[65] Delegated legislation can be issued only when the authority concerned has statutory power to do so. But statutory power is not necessary for the purpose of issuing directions. Generally, directions are issued under the general administrative power of the government[66] although, at times, statutory power may also be conferred to issue administrative directions. The basic distinguishing feature between administrative direction and delegated legislation is that while delegated legislation is binding on both administration and the individual and is enforceable through a court of law at the instance of either, a direction generally speaking is not so binding and enforceable.[67] Barring certain exceptions, a direction does not confer any enforceable right on an individual, or impose an obligation on administration or the individual. Even if a direction is misapplied or ignored by administration, the affected individual can rarely claim a remedy through a court of law against administration. On a parity of reasoning, a direction cannot jeopardize a right of an individual and administration cannot enforce it against him. The absence of requisite statutory provisions or Rules and Regulations cannot be filled through administrative standing orders.[68]

Although directions may not be enforceable legally, it does not follow from this that administrative authorities may disregard them with impunity. The authorities are expected to follow the directions and their breach by them may lead to disciplinary or other appropriate action against them. There may be an administrative remedy available to an individual concerned for enforcing directions, i.e. the litigant may go to a higher authority in the administrative hierarchy and plead for enforcing a direction in his favour issued by the concerned department. The point still remains valid that the remedy available to the individual in such a case is intra-departmental or administrative in nature and not through a court of law. A breach of a direction by an officer is mostly a matter between him and his superiors and not for the courts to take cognisance of, barring some exceptional situations.

2.4.2 DETERMINATION OF THE NATURE OF DIRECTIONS

A government is continuously engaged in the process of 'legislation'—laying down general norms for public behaviour or administrative behaviour. As discussed in the preceding section, government 'legislation' may be classified as either delegated legislation or administrative directions. However, this differentiation leads to significant results. It is, therefore, very important to identify whether a piece of government 'legislation' is direction or delegated legislation. This may, at times, be a complex exercise. In doing so, at the threshold, an administrative lawyer may be faced with a problem arising from incorrect terminology. Expressions like 'code', 'rules', and 'regulations', which are appropriate for being used in the area of delegated legislation, are also used haphazardly and indiscriminately used for administrative directions, and, therefore, the appellation by which a particular piece of government 'legislation' is called is not always determinative of its true character. For example, the Madhya Pradesh Pre-Medical Examination Rules, 1972, regulating admission to medical colleges, although called 'rules' were held in reality not to be rules—but merely executive directions.[69]

The difficulties in this area are further compounded by the fact that the one and same government issues pronouncements that may be held partly as constituting directions and partly as delegated legislation. Thus, a chapter of the UP Police Regulations dealing with disciplinary proceedings in the police force has been held to constitute rules,[70] another chapter of the same document empowers the police to interfere with the personal liberty of a person,[71] or lays down the method of investigation by the police—criminal charges have been held to be merely directions.[72] The latter were held to be based on no statutory foundation, and contain injunctions merely for the guidance of police officers in the discharge of their work. However, in another case, similar provisions in the Madhya Pradesh Police Regulations have been held to have statutory force.[73] The later view appears to be more accurate because such provisions of police regulations that provide safeguards against wanton interference with the personal liberties of citizens should be given statutory force.

Usually, directions are issued by the administration in exercise of its general administrative powers conferred by the constitution on the central or provincial governments. These constitutional provisions describe the extent and scope of the executive power of the central or a provincial government and do not confer any legislative power.[74] When the government issues a pronouncement under a statutory provision or some specific constitutional provision conferring legislative power, then the same would be regarded as a rule. Where the constitution or a law does not confer any rule-making power on the concerned government, the directions issued by a government do not have the status or force of a rule. Thus, in *Fernandez* v. *State of Orissa*[75] the Supreme Court characterised the Mysore PWD Code as containing only 'executive instructions' as the code had been issued by the government not under any statutory authority but under its general administrative powers. This is the broad distinction between rules and directions.

A statute may delegate to the administration, power to promulgate and delegate legislation. The administration may then seek to issue an instrument under its general administrative power rather than under its statutory power. Such an instrument will amount to a direction and not delegated legislation. But here the crucial problem would be to ascertain whether the government instrument in question has been issued under the general administrative power or the statutory rule-making power, particularly when it does not indicate the source of the power under which it is being issued. If it says that it is being issued under the statutory power, then it is easy to identify it as a rule. But when it does not indicate its source, then the problem of identification of its nature becomes complicated. There appears to be no definitive test to ascertain the nature of a government pronouncement or instrument in such a situation.

This can be illustrated by reference to service matters. Article 309 of the Indian Constitution empowers the president, or the governor, as the case may be, to make rules to regulate the recruitment and conditions of service of persons appointed to the public services and posts in connection with the affairs of the Union or the state. Here the attitude of the courts has been that it is not always necessary for the government to make rules under Article 309 to regulate service matters. In the absence of rules, the concerned government could, under its administrative powers, issues directions concerning service matters. The courts have argued that the executive power of a government is co-extensive with its legislative power and, therefore, in the absence of a statute, or rules made under Article 309, administrative instructions can be issued to regulate service matters.[76] This interpretation has given rise to a great deal of confusion and the uncertainty in a number of cases, the courts have been called upon to decide whether the norms laid down by the government regarding a particular service matter would constitute as rules under Article 309, or only to give directions under its general administrative power. In a few cases the principles laid down for promoting officers from a lower to a higher grade have been held as only administrative instructions and not rules under Article 309.[77] It has been held that the government can issue instructions for reservation of posts for scheduled castes and backward classes.[78] The Railway Establishment Code,[79] and a portion of the UP Police Regulations dealing with police disciplinary matters,[80] have been held to be rules and not directions.

An idea of the uncertainty prevailing in service matters can be measured by the Supreme Court's treatment of government memoranda for fixing the retirement age of civil servants. In *I.N. Saxena* v. *Madhya Pradesh,*[81] the question asked was whether a memorandum issued by the Government of Madhya Pradesh fixing the age of retirement of civil servants should be characterised as a rule, having been issued under Article 309, or only as a direction, having been issued under the administrative power of the government. The court upheld that it was merely an executive direction and not a rule on the following considerations; the memorandum in question had not been published in the gazette; it was in the form of a letter issued by the government to the collectors; its form (it began with the words that 'The Government has decided') showed that the government was conveying an executive decision to the collectors to be followed by them. After some time, a similar question arose regarding the central services. Rule 56 of the Fundamental Rules fixed the age of retirement at 55 years. Subsequently an office memorandum was issued by the central government raising the retirement age to 58 years subject to certain exceptions. The date on which the memorandum was to be effective was mentioned therein. Thereafter, Rule 56 was amended to incorporate the substance of the office memorandum. The court ruled[82] that the memorandum must be held to have been issued under Article 309 and to have become effective on the date mentioned therein. There was nothing in the memorandum to suggest that it was not to be effective until Fundamental Rule 56 was subsequently amended. The court made no reference to the Saxena case. But in *Assam* v. *B.K. Das,*[83] an office memorandum issued by the Assam Government on the same subject was held to be merely an executive instruction and not a rule under Article 309.

These cases show how the courts may take different views about the nature of parallel and similar documents.

Administrative instructions or directions can be treated as 'rules' if they have certain visible characteristics of statutory rules. A rule is required to be expressed with precision and yet to possess generality so as to be capable of application to a large number of cases.[84] Departmental instructions are capable of creating legal rights and of possessing a binding effect if they are expressed in precise terms and yet possess generality in order to be capable of being applied with exactness in all relevant cases and are issued by the rule-making authority.[85] Such administrative or departmental instructions assume the status of statutory rules. The absence of formal embodiment in the shape of a rule and of publication in the Government Gazette does not operate to render these instructions any less than obligatory upon the government.[86] In *Habibur Rahman* v. *West Pakistan Public Service Commission*,[87] it was held that instructions embodied in the relevant letters issued by the Provincial Governor (the rule-making authority) to the Public Service Commission are in the nature of statutory service rules and would ordinarily be binding on the Public Service Commission in the matter of assessing the merit of the competing candidates and formulating its recommendations on the basis of oral interviews for recruitment to high technical posts. Where the letters containing administrative instructions do not have the attributes described above, then they cannot take the place of properly framed rules and cannot override any general rules of the service that had relevance.[88]

Where the Act confers rule-making powers on the government, it may issue some 'rules', but the court may hold these rules not to be rules but merely directions because of certain lacunae therein. A case in point is *Kumari Regina* v. *St. A.H.E School*.[89] Here, the government laid down certain norms for recognition of schools and called them 'rules'. The court, however, declared that these were not rules but merely administrative instructions for the following reasons: (a) the rules under the relevant statute could be made for carrying out the purposes of the Act which was the condition precedent, but the so-called 'rules' in question could be related to no purpose or provision of the concerned statute; (b) the government did not claim to have made these 'rules' under its statutory power; and (c) under the Act, pre-publication of the rules was necessary but the so-called 'rules' in question had not been pre-published. The so-called 'rules', therefore, could not be related to the statutory authority as these were *ultra vires* the Act. The 'rules' were treated as having been issued under the general administrative power and so characterised as directions.

A statute may confer a general power to pass orders. Such a power may authorise passing of orders that are both administrative and legislative in character and, at times, the courts may be hard put to delineating the nature of an order. Confusion is sometimes created because the government often issues public notices or circulars, outside of the statutory provision, under its general administrative power. For example, the government periodically announces its import control policy, which has been held by the Indian Supreme Court to be non-statutory,[90] i.e. only a direction which can be changed, rescinded or altered by mere administrative instructions issued at any time.[91] The judicial view is that the import policy published from time to time is only guidance to the concerned administrative officers and the principles contained therein have no statutory force whatsoever. This view is based on the premise that the imports require foreign exchange and so they need to be constantly controlled. In granting import licences for an item, the concerned authorities have to keep in view various flexible factors which may have an impact on imports of other more important items and overall the economy of the country has to be the key consideration.[92] Therefore, the principles stated therein cannot be held binding on the government.

Apart from the import policy, the central government issues from time to time public notices concerning regulation of imports and exports. The question would arise as to what is the nature of these public notices even if they were published in the official gazette. In *East India Commercial Co. v. Collector of Customs*,[93] the Supreme

Court of India held such public notices not to be statutory in nature because a perusal of the public notice showed that it was intended to give information to the public as regards the procedure to be followed in the matter of filing of applications by different categories of applicants and it not only did not on its face purport to be a statutory order but also the internal evidence furnished by it clearly showed that it could not be issued under the statute. The statutory orders regulate rights of the parties; the public notice in question did not do any such thing but only gave information to the public regarding principles governing the issue of licences. The court thus ruled that the public notice in question was a policy statement administratively made by the government for public information. In this case, the court relied solely on the form of the public notice to hold it to be non-statutory in nature.

In a series of cases, the Anglo-Afghan Agencies case[94] constitutes a significant pronouncement. The Supreme Court was called upon to decide the nature of an export scheme giving inducements to exporters and it was published in the gazette. The court held that as the scheme was of a general nature, was published in the gazette, and issued under the Imports and Exports (Control) Act, 1947 it could not merely be assumed that it would be of statutory character. Both 'legislative' and 'executive' (or administrative) orders could be issued under the Act, and furthermore, the court held that the import trade control policy containing the scheme was 'executive or administrative instructions' and not legislative in character. In its judgment, the court also stated that, 'It is neither the form of the order, or the method of its publication or the source of its authority, but its substance, which determines its true character.'

Therefore, 'the source of power' is the crux of the matter. The form of an order in question, its substance, method of its publication are all relevant factors to determine the source from which the order under question may have emanated which would ultimately determine whether the order is a direction or not. Whether an instrument is informational or procedural, or whether it deals with the mechanism of administration, are also the considerations that are helpful in deciding whether it can be related to a statutory power or not. Similarly, publication of the instrument in the gazette may be relevant for a specific purpose. If a statutory provision envisages making of rules by publication in the gazette, and the instrument has been published, this may be a strong indication that the rule may have been issued under a statutory provision, but if it is not published then it may not be related to a statutory provision.

On the basis of the foregoing discussion, the following propositions may be stated for the purpose of identifying whether a government pronouncement is a direction or a rule:

(i) When the rule mentions the statutory provision under which it has been issued, it should be treated as a rule if the specific statutory provision authorises the making of rules; the rule should be treated as a direction, if the specific statutory provision authorises the issue of directions;

(ii) When the government issues some norms (howsoever designated—notification, public notice, etc.) under its rule-making power, and all the prescribed formalities have been complied with, these should invariably be treated as rules and not directions;

(iii) Difficulties in identification arise when a government instrument is silent on the source of power under which the rule/direction has been issued. It may be related either to statutory or general administrative power. In such a case, it may be helpful to ask the following questions:

(a) Does the instrument in question impose obligations on individuals?
(b) Is it merely informative or procedural in content or deals only with matters of administration?
(c) Does it impose obligations on the administration?
(d) Does it confer rights and privileges on the individuals?

With regard to questions (a) and (b), it may be held as non-statutory and hence it is a direction. Here it is prudent to hold an instrument that imposes obligations on individuals as direction so that interests of the affected individuals may be protected. In questions (c) and (d), it may be treated as a rule as in all other conditions prescribed, the relevant statutory provision for rule-making have been fulfilled so that the concerned individuals may assert their rights or bind the administration to its self-imposed obligation.

That the source of power is decisive of the nature of a government order finds support in another pronouncement of the Indian Supreme Court. In *Jayantilal Amratlal* v. *F.N. Rana*[95], a notification issued by the president under Article 258(1) of the Constitution entrusting to the commissioners in a state, the powers of the central government under the Land Acquisition Act, 1894, concerning acquisition of land for the centre, was held to have the force of law to the extent of *pro tanto* amending the Act in question so that instead of the word 'appropriate government' in the Act, the words 'appropriate government or the commissioners' were to be read. The court clarified the position in the following words:

> This is not to say that every order issued by the executive authority has the force of law. If the order is purely administrative or is not issued in exercise of any statutory authority it may not have force of law. But where a general order is issued even by an executive authority which confers power exercisable under a statute, and which thereby in substance modifies or adds to the statute, such conferment of powers must be regarded as having the force of law.

The case also indicates that an instrument laying down norms of procedure, or containing a mechanism for provision or giving instructions to officers may not always be regarded as a direction. It will be so, if it is not issued under any specific statutory powers; it will not be so if it is issued under a statutory power or a constitutional power.

Then there are interpretative rules, i.e. rules issued by the administration to clarify statutory provisions. Here the administration gives its own interpretation of a statutory provision. The system of interpretative rules is widespread in the United States. Where administrative agencies freely issue interpretations, rulings, or opinions upon the laws they administer, without any specific authorisation to do so. Such 'rules' can only be regarded as directions and not rules as these are issued not under any statutory provision but under the general administrative power.

Rules, regulations or bye-laws made by a private association, or any other body incorporated or registered under a statute are not regarded as 'law' or to have the force of law. Therefore, the bye-laws made by a cooperative society in pursuance of statutory provisions do not have the force of law. Such bye-laws may be binding on the person's party to them, but they do not have the force of a statute. These bye-laws are similar in nature to the articles of association of a company which do not have the force of law. The bye-laws of a society laying down conditions of service of the employees would be binding between the society and the employees just like conditions of service laid down by contract between the parties.[96] But there may be situations when even bye-laws made by private bodies may be treated by the courts as having statutory force. The Forward Contracts (Regulation) Act, 1952 provides for regulation of certain matters relating to forward contracts. It empowers a recognized association to make bye-laws for the regulation and control of forward contracts subject to the previous approval of the central government. The Act also provides that any forward contract in goods which is in contravention of any of the bye-laws 'shall be void'. The Supreme Court of India held in *Megna Mills* v. *Ashoka Marketing*[97] that the bye-laws made by the recognised association are mandatory and any contract entered into in contravention of these bye-laws would be invalid. The court has relied for this view, on a provision in the Act stating that any contract in contravention of the bye-laws would be void and illegal. It is not clear whether the bye-laws of the recognised association would have been treated as being similar to those of a cooperative society in the absence of such a statutory declaration.

On the other hand, the position taken by a body set up by a statute is different from that of a private body registered or incorporated under a statute. The rules, bye-laws, and regulations made by a statutory body under statutory power conferred on it for the purpose are treated as having legal force.[98] However, on the other hand the Indian Supreme Court held in *Indian Airlines Corporation* v. *Sukhdeo Rai*[99] that service regulations made by a statutory corporation were only directions and not rules in the real sense of the term. It implied that the regulations made by the corporation affecting the public (other than its employees) would be regarded as having statutory force. The decision of the court was very debatable. The Indian Airlines case has, however, been overruled in *Sukhdev Singh* v. *Bhagatram*.[100] The Supreme Court has later ruled that regulations made by a statutory body under a statutory power constitute delegated legislation, that there is no difference between rules and regulations, and that regulations (even those applying to employees) are statutory in nature.[101]

Some statutes confer powers on the administration to issue directions. Usually, these statutes also confer powers to make rules. In such statutes there may be two provisions, one to enable the making of rules and the other to authorise the issuance of directions.

2.4.3 ENFORCEABILITY OF DIRECTIONS

A basic rule is that a direction is not enforceable in a court of law against either an individual or the administration. The rule of non-enforceability of directions is well established.[102] Misconstruction or misapplication of a direction does not amount to an error of law. Even when a direction is couched in mandatory terms and *prima facie* seeks to impose an obligation either on the individual or the administration, the non-compliance of the direction leads to no action by the court. The validity of an administrative action taken in breach of a direction cannot be challenged and the court could refuse to issue any writ even when there is a patent breach of an administrative direction.[103] Thus, in *S.K. Aggarwal* v. *State*,[104] the court held that non-compliance by the concerned officers of the Orissa Forest Code does not confer any right on the petitioner, and it is not a justifiable matter, for the code is merely administrative in nature and has been issued by the government under its executive power to give instructions to its servants as to how they should act in certain circumstances. Similarly, a breach of an executive instruction laying down the procedure to be followed by government officers in the matter of granting leases of forest lands for cultivation confers no right on a person seeking to quash the administrative action.[105] As the important policy is a direction, no person can claim an enforceable right to the grant of an import licence merely on the basis of the import policy.[106] On a parity of reasoning, if the right to an import licence has accrued to an individual, it cannot be denied to him merely on the basis of a change in the import policy.[107] When conditions of service of the employees are prescribed by a co-operative society in its bye-laws, an industrial tribunal can vary the same as bye-laws do not have the force of law.[108]

The principle of non-enforceability of directions is applied even when the same are issued under a statutory provision. The Motor Vehicles Act, 1939 (as applicable to Madras) authorised the state government to issue such orders and directions of a general nature as it might consider necessary, in respect of any matter relating to road transport, and the transport authority concerned 'shall give effect to all such orders and directions'. The Supreme Court held in *Raman and Raman* v. *State of Madras*[109] that the directions issued under this statute did not have the status of law or rules as it conferred 'administrative and not legislative' power. The main ground for the court's view was that the statute provided not only for the issue of directions but also for the making of rules and that for rule-making, certain formalities, like pre-publication of the draft rules, consultation of interests, laying them before legislature, publication of the rules in the gazette, were required to be observed. All these salutary precautions could be ignored if directions issued under the statute were also treated as law for no such formalities were prescribed for issuing directions. It would also create an incongruity if the government could issue directions in respect of those very matters for which it could make rules under some restrictions. Rules and directions could not thus be equated otherwise the rule-making power would become redundant.

However, the rule of non-enforceability of directions is not immutable and is subject to some exceptions. In some cases, the courts have enforced directions on certain grounds. Under another provision of the Motor Vehicle Act, 1939 a regional transport authority, while considering an application for a stage carriage permit, was enjoined to have regard, *inter alia*, to the 'interests of public generally'. The state government issued a direction prescribing 'place of business' on the route for which a permit was applied for as one of the considerations for issuing the permit. In *K.M. Shanmugam* v. *SRVS Ltd*[110] the Supreme Court reiterated the position as laid down in Raman that directions could not add to, or subtract from, the considerations prescribed under the law but could only afford a reasonable guidance for exercising the jurisdiction by the authority. The existence of a 'branch office place of business' in the case of the applicant was, however, held a relevant fact for deciding the issue of 'interests of public generally'. In this case, the court took pains to emphasise that it was seeking to enforce not a direction, but the law itself.

The Central Board of Revenue could issue instructions and directions to all officers employed in the implementation of the Income Tax Act, where in the instructions it was provided that all officers 'shall observe and follow the orders, instructions and directions of the Central Board of Revenue'. However, under the Income Tax Rules an option was given to all income tax officers to tax income of foreign concerns accruing in India 'in such other manner as the income tax officer may deem suitable'. The Board issued instructions and laid down the basis on which an income tax officer could apply for the purpose. Where the assessee claimed the benefit of instructions but the income tax officer denied it to him, the Supreme Court of India in *Ellerman Lines* v. *Commissioner of Income Tax*[111] ruled that the circular was binding on all officers and persons employed in the execution of the Income Tax Act.

Another example of directions being held enforceable in some situations is furnished by *Union of India* v. *K.P. Joseph*.[112] The government issued an office memorandum providing for fixation of salary of re-employed personnel. The respondent wanted the memorandum enforced in his case. The government contended that the memorandum being an administrative direction conferred no justiciable and enforceable right upon the respondent. The Supreme Court of India ruled otherwise. It observed:

> Generally speaking, an administrative order confers no justiciable right, but this rule, like all other general rules is subject to exceptions. . . . To say that an administrative order can never confer any right would be too wide a proposition. There are administrative orders which confer rights and impose duties.

In *Juthika* v. *State of Madhya Pradesh*,[113] a provision in the memorandum issued by the government as regards the qualifications of the staff of higher secondary schools run by the government was held binding. The court did not go into the question whether the memorandum was to be treated as a direction of rule.

Courts may issue *certiorari* to quash the decisions of a body established under a non-statutory scheme if its proceedings or determination are tainted by defects which would justify the issue of *certiorari* against a statutory body.[114]

From the cases stated above, it appears that generally speaking, directions are non-enforceable. But this rule is subject to some exceptions. In theory, interpretative rules issued by the administration to clarify statutory provisions do not have any final effect for what are binding on the courts are the statute itself and not any interpretation put on it by the administration. These 'rules' are in reality directions, but in actual practice, the interpretation placed by the administration on a statutory provision for a considerable length of time has some value and the courts may be guided by it, though courts may put their own meaning on the provision without being bound by the administrative view. In *Oudh Sugar Mills* v. *State of Madhya Pradesh*,[115] the court rejected the administrative interpretation of a rule as being 'an untenable interpretation, which is opposed to common sense interpretation and which in effect would amount to rioting with common sense'.

Where the departmental practice has followed a course in the implementation of the relevant rule whether right or wrong, it would be extremely unfair to make a departure from it after a lapse of many years and disturb rights that have been settled by a long and consistent course of practice.[116] As regards 'departmental constructions', the construction which is placed in practice on the provisions of a statute or rules by the administrative authorities who are charged with the execution of the statute or the rules, Crawford thus observed:

> Where the executive construction has been followed for a long time, an element of estoppels seems to be involved. Naturally, many rights will grow up in reliance upon the interpretation placed upon a statute by those, whose duty it is to execute it. Often grave injustices would result should the courts reject the construction adopted by the executive authorities.[117]

The position of directions is secondary to the rules. While directions can be used to fill in the gaps in the rules and supplement them, they cannot amend, supplant or supersede the rules. A rule can only be amended by a rule and not a direction.[118] A direction inconsistent with a rule cannot be issued and statutory rules cannot be modified or amended by administrative instructions or directions.[119] When service rules laid down certain conditions and qualifications for promotion, the government would not be competent to add to these qualifications through instructions or directions as these will be inconsistent with the rules.[120] Where the telephone department by administrative directions had adopted the practice of categorisation of applications for telephone connections into OYT, special category and general category there was no provision to this effect in the Telegraph Act or the rules made thereunder, the directions were challenged as unauthorised. The court, however, rejected the argument and held that when the rules are silent, directions can be issued for carrying out the functions under the Act subject to the rider that the directions should not conflict with or defeat any provisions in the parent Act or the rules. As the directions in question were held to be not inconsistent with the Act or the rules, they were not beyond the powers of administration and were not invalid or inoperative.[121]

Directions conflicting with the parent statute could not be operative and have to be ignored even though they have been followed for a number of years, have been found to be convenient, and have worked well. Where under the relevant statute, power to grant licences vested in the licensing authority subject to 'control' of the government, the government issued directions practically ousting the licensing authority and concentrating the entire power to grant licences in its own hands. The court ruled that the direction was not justified. The power of 'control' cannot be exercised so as to completely oust the licensing authority and usurp its function. The court pointed out that to hold that the control of the government contemplated by the statute would justify government's taking away the entire jurisdiction and authority from the licensing authority, 'is to permit the Government by means of its executive powers to change the statutory provision in a substantial manner; and that position clearly is not sustainable.'[122] Even the notifications granting exemptions are not beyond the reach of law and the courts can interfere with them if found to be against the principles of law.[123]

Directions cannot undermine the exercise of statutory powers and the courts have struck down attempts made by the administration to superimpose through directions some additional consideration over and above those laid down in the law in question. Where the government directed the licensing authorities to grant licences only to a specified co-operative society and no other person, the

Supreme Court of India held that when a licensing authority acted under the government's directions to refuse licences to anybody else, there was discrimination against him. Under the order, the licensing authority could prefer a co-operative society in granting a licence if it was of the view that it would fulfil the objectives of the statutory provision in question. But to refuse a licence to anyone else only to create monopoly in favour of one co-operative society alone amounted to discrimination in the administration of the law.[124] The autonomous bodies have to function as such under the provisions of the laws establishing them. They cannot act merely as agents to the government and import considerations extraneous to the law in deciding applications. They are under legal obligation to deal with all applicants before them fairly, justly, and equitably. An applicant has a legal right to demand that the administrative body should determine the matter in accordance with the law.[125]

An administrative instruction or direction cannot be permitted to interfere with, or prevail over statutory provisions. Provisions of the law cannot be circumvented or overridden by directions. What law must legitimately do, the same cannot be undone by administrative directions. Article 21 of the Indian Constitution permits restrictions on personal liberty of an individual through 'procedure established by law'. As departmental instructions without statutory foundation do not constitute 'law', no restraints can validly be put on anyone's personal liberty through directions.[126]

In order to safeguard and protect impartiality, independence, and objectivity of quasi-judicial bodies, the courts have evolved the principle that directions cannot be issued to such bodies so as to restrict or control their discretion and best judgement. The government should not issue directions to such bodies so as to interfere with their independent exercise of judgement in matters entrusted to them under the statute. The Supreme Court of India declared[127] that, as it is of the essence of fair and objective administration of law that quasi-judicial bodies should be left unfettered by any extraneous guidance by the executive, the law should be so interpreted as to take out of its purview the issuing of directions relating to matters of adjudication by quasi-judicial bodies. The court emphasised that exercise of judicial powers should be regulated by law and rules and not by administrative directions.

A direction as such is not binding on a quasi-judicial body as stated above, but, if it lays down a relevant fact, and is not directly addressed to the quasi-judicial body itself, and the tribunal takes it into consideration in deciding a matter, then its decision is not questionable.

Even to a body exercising administrative or legislative function, no directions can be issued by an authority superior to it or by the government, if it is an authority designated by the statute and there is no provision in the statute to issue directions to it.[128] This is on the ground that by specifying the authority the legislature has placed trust in that authority and it should act without any dictation from anyone.

Notes

1. I.P. Massey, *Administrative Law* (Lucknow: Eastern Book Company, 1980) 31.
2. S.P. Sathe, *Administrative Law* (2nd edn., Bombay: N.M. Tripathi Private Ltd, 1974) 29–31.
3. *Basappe* v. *Nagappa*, AIR 1954 SC 440.
4. S.A. de Smith, *Judicial Review of Administrative Action* (2nd edn., 1968) 76.
5. *Maqbool Hussain* v. *State of Bombay* [1953] AIR, SC 325.
6. *F.N. Roy* v. *Collector of Customs*, AIR 1957 SC 648; *Sewpujaura* v. *Collector of Customs*, AIR 1958 SC 845; *Indo-China Steam Navigation Co.* v. *Jasjit Singh*, AIR 1964 SC 1140.
7. *Venkatraman* v. *Union of India*, AIR 1954 SC 375.
8. *D.L. Board* v. *Zafar Imam*, AIR 1966 SC 282.
9. *Re The Delhi Law Act*, AIR 1951 SC 332.
10. *Union of India* v. *Cynamide India Ltd.*, (1987)2 SCC 720.
11. *State of Punjab* v. *Tehal Singh*, (2002) 2 SCC 7.
12. *Express Newspapers* v. *Union of India*, AIR 1958 SC 578.
13. [1948] Cmd 4060, 20.
14. *Fahim Haider* v. *Government of Pakistan*, 2010 GBLR 467.
15. 49 LQR, 94.

16. [1924] 1 KB 171.
17. [1928] 1 KB 411.
18. *Maneka Gandhi* v. *Union of India* [1978] 1 SCC 248.
19. Ibid.
20. *Province of Bombay* v. *Khushaldas Advani*, AIR 1950 SC 222; *Radeshyam* v. *State of MP*, AIR 1959 SC 107.
21. *G. Nageswara Rao* v. *APSRTC*, AIR 1959 SC 308.
22. *Babul Chandra* v. *Chief Justice, H.C. Patna*, AIR 1954 SC 524; *Raman and Raman Ltd* v. *State of Madras*, AIR 1959 SC 694; *Board of High School and Intermediate Education* v. *Ghanshyam Das*, AIR 1962 SC 1110; *Shivoji Nathubhai* v. *Union of India*, AIR 1960 SC 606; *Board of Revenue* v. *Vidyawati*, AIR 1962 SC 1217; *Dwarka Nath* v. *ITO*, AIR 1966 SC 81; *Lakhanpal* v. *Union of India*, AIR 1967 SC 1507; *Rampur Distillery* v. *Co. Law Board* [1969] 2 SCC 774; *Indian Sugar and Refineries Ltd* v. *Amarvathi Service Co-operative Society* [1976] 1 SCC 318.
23. [1964] AC 40.
24. *Board of High School* v. *Ghanshyam*, AIR 1962 SC 1110.
25. [1969] 2 SCC 262.
26. *CB Boarding and Lodging House* v. *Mysore* [1969] 3 SCC 84.
27. See also *DFO South Kheri* v. *Ram Sanehi Singh* [1971] 3 SCC 864.
28. *Automotive Tyre Manufacturing* v. *Designated Authority*, (2011)2 SCC 258.
29. *Indian National Congress* v. *Institute of Social Welfare*, (2002) 5 SCC 685.
30. *State of Maharashtra* v. *M.F. Desai*, (2002) 2 SCC 318.
31. *Manju Varma* v. *State of U.P.*, (2005) 1 SCC 73.
32. Massey, I.P Administrative Law (9th edn, 2017), Delhi, pp. 54–55.
33. [1969] 2 SCC 262.
34. [1973] 2 SCC 232.
35. [1977] 3 SCC 179.
36. *Krishna Tiles & Potteries (P) Ltd* v. *Company Law Board* [1979] ILR 1, Delhi 435, per V.S. Deshpande, CJ.
37. *Nagarajan* v. *State of Mysore*, AIR 1966 SC 1942.
38. *State of Madras* v. *C.P. Sarathy*, AIR 1953 SC 53.
39. *Gopalan* v. *State of Madras*, AIR 1950 SC 27.
40. *Abdul Kasim* v. *Mohd. Dawood*, AIR 1961 Mad. 244.
41. *A.K. Bhaskar* v. *Advocate-General*, AIR 1962 Ker. 90.
42. *Narayanlal* v. *Mistry*, AIR 1961 SC 29.
43. *Province of Bombay* v. *Khushaldas Advani*, AIR 1950 SC 222.
44. [1971] 2 SCC 330. See also *Durga Shankar* v. *Raghuraj*, AIR 1954 C 520, wherein the SC held that Section 105 of the Representation of the People Act which made every order of the Election Tribunal final and conclusive does not bar constitutional modes of judicial review.
45. [1972] ILR, Andh Pra. 1025.
46. *Union of India* v. *J.P. Mitter*, AIR 1971 SC 1093. See also *Election Commission* v. *V. Rao*, AIR 1953 SC 210.

47. [1975] SCC Supp 1.
48. AIR 1964 SC 322. See also *Secretary of State* v. *Mask & Co.*, AIR 1940 PC 105.
49. AIR 1964 SC 1873.
50. AIR 1966 SC 1738. See also *Kamala Mills* v. *State of Bombay*, AIR 1965 SC 1942.
51. [1976] 1 SCC 496.
52. [1969] 2 SCC 879.
53. AIR 1968 SC 271.
54. AIR 1969 SC 78. See also *Vekataraman* v. *Madras*, AIR 1966 SC 1089, in which *Raleigh Investment Co.* v. *Governor-General-in-Council*, AIR 1947 PC 78 was overruled.
55. *Oil and Gas Development Company Ltd.* v. *Federal Board of Revenue*, 2016 PTD 1675 (Islamabad High Court).
56. *Muhammad Ashraf Tiwana v. Pakistan*, 2013 SCMR 1159.
57. *Sahni Silk Mills Ltd.* v. *Employee's State Insurance Corporation*, (1994) 5 SCC 346.
58. AIR 1967 SC 1753.
59. *I.N. Saksena* v. *State of MP*, AIR 1967 SC 1264; *Kumari Regina* v. *AHE School* [1972] 4 SCC 188.
60. AIR 1959 SC 694.
61. [1978] 2 SCC 196. See also *Jayantilal Amratlal* v. *F.N. Rana*, AIR 1964 SC 648; *Ellerman Lines* v. *CIT* [1972] 4 SCC 474; *Indian Airlines Corpn.* v. *Sukhdeo Rai* [1971] 2 SCC 192; AIR 1971 SC 1828.
62. *Gurdial Singh Fijji* v. *State of Punjab* [1979] 2 SCC 368.
63. *Rajagopala Naidu* v. *State Transport Appellate Tribunal*, AIR 1964 SC 1573; *Sri Rama Vilas Service* v. *Road Traffic Board*, AIR 1948 Mad. 400.
64. *Union of India* v. *Anglo-Afghan Agencies Ltd*, AIR 1968 SC 718.
65. Megarry, 'Administrative Quasi-Legislation' [1944] 60 LQR 125; Allen, *Law and Orders* (1965) 192; Benjafield and Whitmore, *Principles of Administrative Law* (1971) 116.
66. See Articles 73 and 162 of the Constitution of India; Jain, *Indian Constitutional Law* (1978) 309.
67. M.P. Jain and S.N. Jain, *Principles of Administrative Law* (3rd edn., Bombay: N.M. Tripathi Pvt Ltd, 1979).
68. *Punjab Healthcare Commission v. Mushtaq Ahmad Chaudhry*, PLD 2016 SC 237
69. *S.P. Manocha* v. *State*, AIR 1973 MP 84.
70. *Uttar Pradesh* v. *Babu Ram*, AIR 1961 SC 751.
71. *Kharak Singh* v. *Uttar Pradesh*, AIR 1963 SC 1295.
72. *Niranjan Singh* v. *Uttar Pradesh*, AIR 1957 SC 142.
73. *Govind* v. *Madhya Pradesh*, AIR 1975 SC 1378.
74. *Nagarjan* v. *Mysore*, AIR 1966 SC 1942.
75. AIR 1967 SC 1753.

76. *Sant Ram Sharma* v. *Rajasthan*, AIR 1967 SC 1910.

77. *Hari Prasad* v. *State*, AIR 1972 Pat 4; *Lalit Mohan Deb* v. *India*, AIR 1972 SC 995.

78. *Balbir Singh* v. *Punjab*, AIR 1975 P and H 83.

79. *Southern Railway* v. *Raghavendrachar*, AIR 1966 SC 1529.

80. *Uttar Pradesh* v. *Babu Ram*, AIR 1961 SC 751.

81. AIR 1967 SC 1264.

82. *E.V. Naidu* v. *India*, AIR 1973 SC 698.

83. AIR 1973, SC 1252. The judgment in *Naidu* was delivered on 09 January 1973 and that in *Das* on 22 December 1972. Vaidialingam, J participated in both the decisions and yet *Naidu* does not take note of *Das* nor does it suggest as to why it takes a different view from *Das*. A view similar to *Das* was adopted by the Supreme Court in *Assam* v. *Premadhar*, AIR 1970 SC 1314.

84. *Pakistan* v. *Sheikh Abdul Hamid*, PLD 1961 SC 105.

85. *Province of West Pakistan* v. *Ch. Din Muhammad*, PLD 1964 SC 21; *Faizullah Khan* v. *Government of Pakistan*, PLD 1974 SC 291; *Muhammad Afzal* v. *Government of Balochistan* [1995] PLC (CS) 567.

86. *Government of West Pakistan* v. *Dr A.A. Aziz*, PLD 1966 SC 188.

87. PLD 1973 SC 144.

88. *Government of West Pakistan* v. *Nasir M. Khan*, PLD 1965 SC 106.

89. AIR 1971 SC 1920.

90. The Supreme Court of India has dilated upon the nature of the Import Policy in *India* v. *Anglo-Aghan Agencies*, AIR 1968 SC 718 as follows: It may be possible to pick out paragraphs which appear in isolation to be addressed generally and have direct impact upon the rights of the people, but by and large it deals with matters of procedure; it gives advice to the persons engaged in the business of import and export and gives instructions to departmental officers. It deals with such heterogeneous matters as forms of applications, application fee, designation of licensing officers, classification of importers, etc. 'There is no pattern or order or logical sequence in the policy statement, it is a jumble of executive instructions and matters which impose several restrictions on the rights of citizens.' The policy facilitates the mechanism of the Imports Act and the Orders issued thereunder.

91. *Dy. Asst. Iron and Steel Controller* v. *Manickchand*, AIR 1972 SC 935; *AI Works* v. *Chief Controller Imports*, AIR 1974 SC 1539.

92. *Sha Poosafi Magilal* v. *Ministry of Commerce*, AIR 1976 Mad. 86.

93. AIR 1962 SC 1893.

94. *Union of India* v. *Anglo-Afghan Agencies*, AIR 1968 SC 718.

95. AIR 1964 SC 648.

96. *Co-operative Credit Bank* v. *Industrial Tribunal, Hyderabad*, AIR 1970, SC 245; *National ICC Federation* v. *Delhi Administration*, AIR 1971 Del 141; *BS Co-op. Bank* v. *Registrar, Co-operative Societies*, AIR 1975 Pat. 187.

97. AIR 1971 SC 166.

98. *Trustees, Port of Bombay* v. *Premier Automobiles*, AIR 1971 Bom. 317; *Prabhakar Ram Kishan Jodh* v. *A.L. Pande* [1965] 2 SCR 713; *Dr I.P. Gupta* v. *W.R. Nathu*, AIR 1963 SC 274; *Mafatlal Barot* v. *Div. Controller, State Transport, Mehsana*, AIR 1966 SC 1364; *Sirsi Municipality* v. *C.K.F. Tellis*, AIR 1973 SC 855.

99. AIR 1971 SC 1828.

100. AIR 1974 SC 1331.

101. M.P. Jain, 'The Legal Status of Public Corporation and their Employees' [1976] 18 JILI 1; [1975] XI ASIL 464, 527.

102. *Fernandez* v. *State of Mysore*, AIR 1967 SC 1753; *Nagendra Nath Bora* v. *Commissioner of Hills Division*, AIR 1958 SC 398.

103. *Abdulla Rowther* v. *STA Tribunal*, AIR 1959 SC 896; *General Electrical & Engineering Co., Trichur* v. *Chief Engineer*, AIR 1974 Ker. 23; *S.P. Manocha* v. *State* [1973] AIR, MP 84.

104. AIR 1973 Orissa 217.

105. *I. Co-op. Society* v. *K. Service Co-op. Bank*, AIR 1975 Ker. 4.

106. *Dy. Asstt. Iron & Steel Controller* v. *L. Manikchand*, AIR 1972 SC 935; *AI Works* v. *Chief Controller*, AIR 1974 SC 1539.

107. *JCC Imports & Exports* v. *Aminchand*, AIR 1966 SC 478.

108. *Co-op. Credit Bank* v. *Industrial Tribunal, Hyderabad*, AIR 1970 SC 245.

109. AIR 1959 SC 694.

110. AIR 1963 SC 1626.

111. AIR 1972 SC 524.

112. AIR 1973 SC 303.

113. AIR 1976 SC 2534.

114. *R.* v. *Criminal Injuries Compensation Board, ex p. Lain* [1967] 2 QB 864; *R.* v. *Cr. Inj. Comp. Board, ex p. Schofield* [1971] 1 WLR 926.

115. AIR 1975 MP 125.

116. *Nazir Ahmad* v. *Pakistan*, PLD 1970 SC 453; *Radaka Corporation* v. *Collector of Customs* [1989] SCMR 353.

117. Crawford's *Statutory Construction* (1940 edn.) 399.

118. *Sant Ram Sharma* v. *State of Rajasthan*, AIR 1967 SC 191.

119. *Muhammad Riaz Akhtar* v. *Sub-Registrar*, PLD 1996 Lahore 180.

120. *State of Haryana* v. *Shamsher Jang Shukla*, AIR 1972 SC 1546.

121. *P.M. Mohamed Ali* v. *Union of India*, AIR 1974 Ker. 157.

122. *State of Punjab* v. *Hari Kishan*, AIR 1966 SC 1081.

123. *Ittefaq Foundry* v. *Federation of Pakistan*, PLD 1990 Lahore 121.

124. *Mannalal Jain* v. *State of Assam*, AIR 1962 SC 386.

125. *Ikram Bus Service* v. *Board of Revenue*, PLD 1963 SC 564.

126. *Kharak Singh* v. *Uttar Pradesh*, AIR 1963 SC 1295.

127. *B. Rajgopala Naidu* v. *State Transport Ltd*, AIR 1964 SC 1573.

128. *Shri Ram Viias Service* v. *Road Traffic Board*, AIR 1948 Madras 400.

CHAPTER III

Delegated Legislation

3.1 INTRODUCTION

In all democratic countries today, only a relatively small part of the total legislative output emanates directly from legislature, and extensive law-making is undertaken by the executive which is known as 'delegated legislation'. Usually, the legislature enacts a law covering only the general principles and policies relating to the subject matter in question, and confers rule-making power on the government or other administrative agencies. This technique of delegated legislation is commonly and extensively resorted to, so that now there is hardly a statute passed by the legislature which does not delegate some power of legislation to the executive. Delegated legislation is so multitudinous that a statute book will not only be incomplete but even misleading unless it is read along with the delegated legislation which enhances it.[1] In no democratic country does the legislature monopolize the whole of the legislative power; it shares this power with the government and other administrative agencies.

The term 'delegated legislation' is generally given two meanings: (a) the exercise by a subordinate agency of the legislative power delegated to it by the legislature, or (b) the subsidiary rules which are made by the subordinate agency in pursuance of the power that is delegated to it. An administrative lawyer would be more interested in the 'technique', rather than the actual rules made and so the term 'delegated legislation' is used here in the first sense. Sometimes the term 'subordinate legislation' is used to convey the idea that the authority enacts the legislation is subordinate to the legislature.

The technique of delegated legislation is extensively used in Pakistan and India. The Imports and Exports (Control) Act, 1947 is a small piece of legislation containing a few sections. The central government has introduced a vast mechanism of import and export licensing through delegated legislation promulgated under the statute.

Delegated legislation, as mentioned above, is given several names such as, rules, regulations, bye-laws, orders, etc., though the term 'rules' is more commonly used. The terms 'regulations' and 'bye-laws' are usually used with respect to the legislation framed by statutory corporations under delegated legislative power. Generally, in these corporations there are two levels of delegated legislation: the government itself has power to promulgate 'rules' and, accordingly, to distinguish the government-made 'rules' from those which the corporation may make. A different terminology ('regulations') is used for the latter. At times, a statute may use different terms to confer the power of delegated legislation. For instance, in the income tax law, powers to issue orders, notifications, and rules are spread over a number of sections, and a general power to make rules for several matters is conferred on the Central Board of Revenue. The distribution and allocation of work to be performed by various tax authorities may be made through orders by the central government through a 'notification' in the official gazette, which may take away an exemption granted under a section from certain newly established undertakings.

Delegated legislation has been defined by Salmond as 'that which proceeds from any authority other than the sovereign power and is therefore dependent for its continued existence and validity on some superior or supreme authority.'[2] Such authority may be the central government or the provincial government depending upon whether the statute is a central or a provincial law. Sometimes central laws delegate legislative power to the provincial government. At other times both the central and provincial governments receive law-making power from the same Act.[3] Other bodies on which power of delegated legislation is conferred are:

   (i) the Central Board of Revenue, under Section 8 of the Income Tax Ordinance 1979 and Section 85 of the Indian Estate Duty Act, 1953;
   (ii) the Central Electricity Board, under Section 37 of the Electricity Act, 1910; and
   (iii) the Pakistan Bar Council, under Section 55 of the Legal Practitioners and Bar Councils Act 1973.

The power to make regulations is given to bodies such as the Indian Nursing Council under Section 16 of the Indian Nursing Council Act, 1947; the Industrial Finance Corporation under Section 43 of the Industrial Finance Corporation Act, 1948; and the Pakistan Engineering Council under Section 25 of the Pakistan Engineering Council Act, 1976.

The power to make bye-laws is conferred on bodies such as the State Bank of Pakistan under the State Bank of Pakistan Act, 1956. Bye-laws are usually enacted to govern the internal working of autonomous institutions. For example, co-operative societies make bye-laws to regulate the conduct of their members. In addition to the rules, regulations, and bye-laws there are some other forms of delegated legislation that are schemes, orders, etc. In India, Schemes are issued under Section 3 of the Dock Workers' (Regulation of Employment) Act, 1948, and Orders are issued under Section 3 of the Essential Commodities Act, 1955. The orders mentioned here are general in application as distinguished from executive orders which are particular. Thus an order asking a person to evacuate a house which has to be requisitioned in the public interest is an executive order whereas an order laying down prices of commodities is a legislative order. There are also administrative directions, which are called 'administrative quasi-law' or 'administrative quasi-legislation'.[4] This includes promulgation of rules, announcement of statements of policy by the authority exercising power, and the issuance of directives for the guidance of the administrative authorities. These usually are used to control the exercise of wide discretion that is conferred on the executive authorities. Administrative directions are issued by a higher authority to subordinate authorities. They may apply to a specific case or may apply generally laying down principles of policy. They may be issued through a letter or a circular and they may even be oral in a very casual manner. They may be published in the form of pamphlets, press notes or public notices.

Why is administrative direction preferred to statutory rules? There are various reasons for this. Formal rule-making must be accompanied by formalities such as publication, laying before parliament or consultation with affected interests. No such formalities accompany the issuance of administrative directions. This gives the executive more freedom to experiment during the formative period of a policy. Thus, under Section 8 of the Income Tax Ordinance 1979 all officers and persons employed in the execution of the Act are required to observe and follow the orders, instructions and directions of the Central Board of Revenue. Under Clause (2) of the Section, every income tax officer is required to follow instructions issued to him by the commissioner or by the inspecting assistant commissioner. The issue of directions may be necessary either to co-ordinate the activities of the delegates or to enable them to follow a uniform policy. For example, under the Imports and Exports (Control) Act, 1947, the Government of India has been given power to control the import and export of commodities. The government has delegated its power to grant licences to various licensing authorities. To ensure that the various regional licensing authorities do not exceed the overall foreign exchange limit and that they observe the required priorities in granting licences, it is necessary to coordinate their activities by a central agency. Since the various factors would be in constant flux, this co-ordination may have to be achieved through the issuance of directions and not statutory rules. These administrative directions do not have force of law.[5]

Generally, the regulations or bye-laws made by statutory bodies or bodies such as co-operative societies which are registered under a statute are required to be confirmed by the government. It has been held that the power to confirm includes the power to rescind such confirmation just as the power to make bye-laws includes the power to cancel the bye-laws.[6]

3.2 THE NECESSITY OF DELEGATED LEGISLATION

The modern trend is that the parliament passes only a skeleton legislation, and leaves the details to the administrative agencies to provide through the rule-making power delegated to them under such legislation. This trend brings us to the need matrix of the phenomenon of delegated legislation or administrative rule-making.

The concept of "'delegated legislation" has gained momentum with the increase in population growth, the dire need for good governance' and the ultimate aim is to provide for the essential basic needs of every segment of the society to bolster and fulfil the attributes of a welfare State. Surely, the present day Parliament cannot possibly legislate on each and every detail of the vast legislative needs, hence the 'delegated legislation', whereby the legislature through legislation delegates to the government or any other specified authority to legislate through rules, regulations, orders, instructions or any other instrument in conformity with the dictates of the parent statute.[7]

The basis of need for administrative rule-making is that modern administration is so complex, detailed, and difficult, and requires such flexibility that it is not possible for the legislatures to directly and comprehensively handle legislative business in all their plenitude, proliferation, and particularisation. Therefore, the delegation of some part of legislative power becomes a compulsive necessity for viability. It is not possible for parliamentarians to focus on legislative detail, thereby leaving nothing to subordinate agencies. It is possible that in such a situation the annual output may be both unsatisfactory and negligible. Law-making is not a turn-key project readymade in all detail, and once this situation is grasped the dynamics of delegation easily follow.[8] From the above generalisation, the factors leading to the growth of delegated legislation may be summed up as follows:

(i) Legislation on the ever-broadening frontiers of a modern state is not possible without the technique of delegation. It may be correct to say that even if the parliament is convened all 365 days in a year and works 24 hours, it may not be able to give that quantity and quality of law that is required for the proper functioning of a modern government. Therefore, delegation of rule-making power is a necessity of modern times.

(ii) Legislation has become highly technical in the today's world because of the complexities of modern government. Therefore, it is convenient for the legislature to confine itself to policy statements only, as the legislators are sometimes not fully conversant with legal and technical skills, and leave the law-making sequence to the administrative agencies.

(iii) Ordinary legislative process suffers from lack of flexibility. A law passed by the parliament cannot be amended until its next session. Therefore, in situations which require frequent adjustments administrative rule-making may be the only answer.

(iv) In situations where crisis legislation is needed to meet emergent situations, administrative rule-making becomes a necessity because the ordinary law-making process is overburdened with constitutional and legal technicalities and formalities and would involve delay.

(v) Where government action involves discretion, i.e. expansion of public utility services, administrative rule-making is the only valid proposition.

(vi) There is a growing emergence of the idea of direct participation in the making of law by those who are supposed to be governed by it because indirect participation through their elected representatives has more often proved to be a myth. Therefore, administrative rule-making can be a more convenient and effective way to provide for this participation.

There are many other factors responsible for the growth of administrative rule-making. It will suffice to say that the technique of administrative rule-making is now regarded as useful, inevitable, and indispensable.

However, one must remember that though the technique of administrative rule-making is useful and inevitable, yet constitutional legitimation of unlimited power of delegation to the executive by legislature may, on occasion, be subversive of responsible government and erosive of democratic order.[9] At times, legislature passes only skeleton laws without laying down even a policy in clear terms, and leaves everything else to the discretion of the administrative agency. Therefore, the administration armed with the law-making power threatens to overwhelm the common man by trampling upon his liberty and property. The technocracy and the bureaucracy which draft subordinate legislation might perhaps be well-meaning and well-informed, but being insulated from parliamentary audit and isolated from popular pressure might make laws which are socially less communicable, acceptable, and effective.

Furthermore, if law-making is taken over by the government it may make it the administration by barrel of the secretariat pen.[10] Therefore, if the technique of administrative rule-making is to serve its laudable task, the norms of the jurisprudence of delegation of legislative power must be dutifully observed. These norms include a clear statement of policy, procedural safeguards, and control mechanisms.

The Supreme Court of Pakistan held[11] that rules and regulations being forms of subordinate legislation do not have substantial difference as power to frame them is rooted in the statute. Statutory bodies are invariably authorized under the Act to make or adopt rules and regulations not inconsistent with the Act, with respect to such matters which fall within their lawful domain to carry out the purposes of the Act. This rule making power of such bodies, called 'delegated legislation' has assumed importance in the contemporary age. 'The justification for delegated legislation is threefold. First, there is pressure on parliamentary time. Second; the technicality of subject matter necessitates prior consultation and expert advice on interests concerned. Third, the need for flexibility is established because it is not possible to foresee every administrative difficulty that may arise to make adjustment that may be called for after the statute has begun to operate. Delegated legislation fills those needs.'

3.3 DELEGATED LEGISLATION IN THE INDO-PAKISTAN SUBCONTINENT

Delegated legislation has a very long history in the Indo-Pakistan Subcontinent. The East India Company was granted powers, under the First Charter (1600) to make such reasonable laws as were necessary for the management of the Company. Similar provisions were made in the subsequent Charters, but for about hundred years the Company generally used these powers to make laws to its trade.[12]

The Charters of 1726 and 1753 enlarged the scope of this power by empowering the Company to make rules for the conduct of business in the Mayor's Courts. Thereafter the Regulating Act, 1773, further extended this power of the Company to make laws for the government of all the British possessions. However these laws were to be reasonable and required the approval of the Supreme Court at Calcutta. Hastings made extensive use of this power without following the prescribed conditions and procedures. He consolidated the regulations in a code which dealt with civil as well as criminal law. Chief Justice Impy's Civil Code (1781) provided the rules of procedure for the guidance of the civil courts. Thereafter, Cornwallis Code (1793) collected the existing regulation on the various subjects and ushered a Regulation Era (1793–1833). During this period the Company made full use of these powers and enacted hundreds of regulations in Bengal, Bombay, and Madras.[13]

Although it was a primary legislation from the Indian as well as Company's point of view, yet judged from the English constitutional theory and jurisprudence, it essentially belonged to the category of delegated legislation or subordinate legislation. The subordinate nature of these Regulations is established from the fact that during this period the Company did not delegate the legislative powers under these regulations to any another authority.

The Charter Act, 1833 granted vast legislative powers to the Governor General in Council to legislate for the whole of British India with the same effect as that of the British Parliament.[14] Thus, the Act brought a fundamental change in the legislative authority of the Company; the Indian Acts were bestowed with great authority, though they remained subordinate to the Acts of the British Parliament. Thus, the era of enacting laws through subordinate legislation came to an end, but the earlier Regulations remained in force side by side with new Acts.

The Indian Act which acquired the authority of the Acts of Parliament could now easily authorise the delegation of legislative powers to other organs of the government. This authority appears to have been rarely exercised by the Indian legislature before the Indian Councils Act, 1861 came into force. The Indian Councils Act, 1861 made the Indian legislature more respectable by increasing its powers and size. The restriction that the Indian legislature could not affect the prerogatives and the British Crown was also removed by this Act. The new council delegated the legislative authority in 1869 under the European Vagrancy Act, and rules were enacted for the first time in 1870 under this authority.[15] Other types of delegation, i.e. conditional legislation, authorising the bringing of law into force at a future date, or extending the laws etc., were somewhat common during this period and, except for these exemptions and declarations, the delegated power of legislation was not much exercised by the government.

The *Queen* v. *Burah*,[16] decided by the Privy Council in 1878, recognised the powers of the Indian legislature to delegate legislative functions to another authority organ of the state. In this case the power of the Lieutenant Governor of Bengal, granted under an Indian Act, to withdraw certain areas from the jurisdiction of ordinary courts and place them under designated officers came under discussion. The Calcutta High Court held that the Indian legislature was to be regarded as an agent or delegate of the Imperial Parliament which must, in all cases, execute the mandate, directly by itself, and therefore the provisions authorising the Lieutenant Governor to extend the Bengal Act to another area involved delegation of legislative power and were void and of no legal effect. On appeal the Judicial Committee of the Privy Council reversed the decision by holding that the decision of the High Court was erroneous and rested on a mistaken view, of the powers of the Indian legislature which, 'working within the limits laid down by the Imperial Parliament, had plenary powers of legislation, as large, and of the same nature, as those of the Parliament itself'.

The Privy Council decision strengthened the authority of Indian legislature which was hitherto being exercised with caution. Thereafter the legislature and executive made good use of this power in subsequent years. By the turn of the century, delegated legislation became very common and it rapidly increased in bulk. This process continued in the twentieth century and much more rapidly after Independence. Today, hardly any law is passed without containing a rule-making provision.

3.4 REASONS FOR GROWTH OF DELEGATED LEGISLATION

The traditional constitutional theory which postulates separation of powers was exposed to an enormous strain when legislatures started delegating legislative power to the executive in a big way. Irrespective of whether the constitutional purists approve of it or not, delegation of legislative power has become the need of the day. The main causes that led to the growth in volume of delegated legislation are as follows:[17]

(I) PRESSURES UPON PARLIAMENTARY TIME

The legislative activity of the State has increased manifold in response to the increase in its functions and responsibilities. The legislature is preoccupied with more important policy matters and rarely finds time to discuss matters in detail. It therefore formulates the legislative policy and delegates power to administration to make subordinate legislation for implementing the policy.

(II) TECHNICALITY OF THE SUBJECT MATTER

As the nature of many Acts is technical, it may be necessary to obtain the assistance of experts in providing for matters in detail.

Thus, for example, once legislature decides to restrict the use of dangerous drugs, it must be left to the medical experts to decide which drugs should be considered dangerous. It cannot be laid down by legislature itself because the subject is highly technical and the meaning may change when new aspects are discovered by medical research.

(III) THE NEED FOR FLEXIBILITY

A statutory provision cannot be amended except by an amendment passed in accordance with legislative procedure, which takes time. It may, however, be necessary to make changes in the application of a provision frequently in the light of experience. It is therefore convenient if the matter is left to be provided through subordinate legislation. Delegated legislation requires less formal procedure and can be a good device for flexibility.

(IV) STATE OF EMERGENCY

In times of emergency, the government may have to take swift action. All necessary future actions cannot be anticipated in advance and hence provisions cannot be made by legislature to meet all unforeseeable contingencies. It is safer to empower the executive to lay down rules in accordance with which it would use its emergency power. Thus, delegated legislation grew substantially during the times of wars and emergencies.

(V) NEED FOR REGULATION AND CONTROL OF ECONOMIC ENTERPRISE

A legislature is particularly inappropriate to perform the continuous tasks of regulation and guardianship which the state is required to perform with respect to private trade and business. An administrative agency must be free to formulate policy within the framework of a broad legislative policy embodied in the enabling Act. This is possible if the administrative agency can legislate. Situations that demand quick action may arise and the agency can meet them only if it has the power of subordinate legislation.

3.5 CLASSIFICATION OF DELEGATED LEGISLATION

Administrative rule-making or delegated legislation in Pakistan and India is commonly expressed by the expression 'statutory rules and orders'. However, this classification is not exhaustive, as it appears in other forms also, i.e. regulation, notification, bye-laws, schemes, and directions. These terminologies are confusing because different words are used for the same thing and the same words are used for different things.

3.5.1 TITLE-BASED CLASSIFICATION

(i)   *Rules*: The term 'rules' is defined in the General Clauses Act, 1897 as made in exercise of power conferred by any enactment and includes regulations made as 'rules' under any enactment. These rules may be made applicable to a particular individual or to the general public. It may include rules of procedure or the rules of substantive law. The term 'rule' was adopted and since then it is being used for delegated legislation, procedural as well as substantive.

(ii) *Regulations*: This term is not confined to delegated legislation. It means an instrument by which decisions, orders, and acts of the government are made known to public. But in the sphere of administrative rule-making, the term relates to the situation where power is given to fix a date for the enforcement of an Act or to grant exemptions from the Act or to fix prices, etc. The term 'regulation' is also used as a second tier of delegated legislation. Section 3(47) of the General Clauses Act, 1897 includes regulation in the category of rules. It reads: 'Rule shall mean a rule in exercise of power conferred by any enactment and shall include a regulation made as a rule under the enactment.'

(iii) *Orders*: This term is used to cover various forms of legislative and quasi-judicial decisions. Orders may be specific or general. The former refers to administrative action while the latter refers to administrative rule-making.

(iv) *Directions*: The term 'directions' or 'directives' are expressions of administrative rule-making under the authority of law or rules or orders made thereunder. These may be recommendatory or mandatory. If mandatory, these have the force of law.

(v) *Instructions*: Instructions are generally administrative directions issued for the guidance of subordinate officials. However, in some cases these instructions have been treated like statutory rules and considered binding on the government functionaries. In particular, such instructions have been given statutory sanctity in service matters provided they are made by the authority competent to make statutory rules.[18]

The Supreme Court has laid down the following principles under which instructions may be treated as rules:[19]

(a) Instructions should have been issued by an authority competent under the relevant law to make rules.

(b) They should have been expressed in precise terms and they could be applied with exactness.

(c) There should be nothing to indicate that such instructions were at any time subsequently superseded, or that they were not strictly applied in any case, or that they were departed from in relation to any considerable proportion of the cases; giving rise to an inference that 'they were not intended by the authority concerned to be of binding effect'.

Within this broad framework the courts have treated many departmental instructions binding like statutory rules.[20] For example, an office memorandum fixing seniority of government servant;[21] a circular letter issued by government determining the seniority of officers in the absence of rules;[22] instructions relating to service matters issued by provincial governor competent to amend the relevant rules;[23] the Railway Manual containing terms and conditions of railway employees;[24] a letter written to a government servant in pursuance of a government decision relating to the terms and conditions of his service;[25] directions to the Public Service Commission by the provincial government relating to the award of marks to the candidates;[26] a resolution of government establishing service cadres;[27] a statement of conditions issued by the provincial government relating to the tenancy of state lands;[28] and similar other instructions have been given statutory binding effect.[29]

However, departmental instructions cannot override the suits and regulations having statutory sanction. In such cases, instructions have no validity.[30]

(vi)   *Bye-laws*: This term has been confined to rules made by semi-governmental authorities established under the acts of legislatures.

(vii) *Schemes*: This term refers to a situation where the law authorises the administrative agency to lay down a framework within which the detailed administrative action is to proceed.

3.5.2 DISCRETION-BASED CLASSIFICATION

Another classification of administrative rule-making may be based on discretion vested in the rule-making authority. On the basis of 'discretion', administrative rule-making may be classified into subordinate and contingent or conditional legislation. This classification is linked up with the leading case *Field* v. *Clark*.[31] The impugned Act authorised the president by proclamation to suspend the operation of an Act permitting free introduction into USA of certain products upon his finding that the duties imposed upon US products were reciprocally unequal and unreasonable. The US Supreme Court upheld the validity of the Act on the grounds that the president is a mere agent of the Congress to ascertain and declare the contingency upon which the will of the Congress would prevail. The court further held that Congress cannot delegate its power to make a law, but it can make a law to delegate the power to determine some factors or state of things upon which the law intends to make its own action depend. Therefore, contingent or conditional legislation may be defined as a statute that provides control but specifies that they are to go into effect only when a given administrative authority finds the existence of conditions defined in the statute itself. In subordinate legislation the process consists of discretionary elaboration of rules and regulations. The distinction between the two is of 'discretion'. Contingent or conditional legislation is fact finding and subordinate legislation is discretionary. It may be noted that this distinction is hardly real. In contingent or conditional legislation also, a certain amount of discretion is always available. Contingent legislation formula is a fiction developed by the US Court to get away from the operation of the doctrine of separation of powers.

3.5.3 Purpose-based classification

Another classification of administrative rule-making would involve the consideration of delegated legislation in accordance with the different purposes which it is made to serve. On this basis the classification may be as follows:[32]

(i) *Enabling Acts*: Such Acts contain an 'appointed day' clause under which power is delegated to the executive to appoint a day for the Act to come into operation. In this category, legislature prescribes the gun and the target, and leaves it to the executive to press the trigger. It is aimed at giving the executive time to equip itself for the administration of the law. In this class of legislation, rule-making exercise is valid only to the extent it is preparatory to the Act coming into force.[33]

(ii) *Extension and Application Acts*: The technique of administrative rule-making may sometimes be used for extension and application of an Act in respect of a territory or for a specific duration of time or for any other such object. Power may be delegated to extend the operation of the Act to other territories. The extension procedure has been extensively employed in 'reciprocal legislation' and 'disability legislation'. Power may also be delegated to extend the duration of a temporary Act which is to come to an end at a given period. Sometimes power may be given to extend the operation of the Act to objects or persons other than those for which it was originally made.

(iii) *Dispensing and Suspending Acts*: Sometimes power may be delegated to the administrative authority to make exemptions from all or any provision of the Act in a particular case or class of cases or territory, when, in the discretion of the authority, circumstances warrant the same. The Registration Act, 1908 delegated power to a provincial government to exempt any district or tract of land from the operation of this Act. These exemption clauses are meant to enable administration to relieve hardship which may be occasioned as a result of uniform enforcement of the law. However, delegation of such power must satisfy the tests of validity under the constitution. Power may also be delegated to suspend the operation of any Act.

(iv) *Alteration Acts*: Though technically speaking any alteration amounts to amendment, yet alteration is a wider term and includes both modification and amendment. In legislative practice, the power to modify Acts has mostly been delegated as a sequel to the power of extension and application of laws. Power to modify has also been given to administrative authorities in cases which may be described as 'legislation by reference'. It is a device by which the power of modification is delegated to make the adopted Act fit into the adoptive Act. The power of modification is limited to consequential changes, but if overstepped, it suffers challenge on the grounds that it is not within the legislative intent of modification. Another type of alteration may be classified as 'amendment'. The most common example is the power to change the schedule of an Act. The courts have held the exercise of such power as valid provided that the changed items are *ejusdem generis* with the other items mentioned in the schedule to which the law clearly applies. Power to make alteration may sometimes include the power to 'remove difficulty' so that the various statutes may co-exist. This power may include the power to amend and repeal the enabling

Act as well as other Acts. This type of delegation may be classed as an exceptional type of delegation and, therefore, must not be used except for the purpose of bringing the Act into operation.

(v) *Taxing Acts*: Normally the purpose, incidence, and rate of tax must be determined by the legislature. However, the courts have upheld the delegation of taxing powers to the administrative authorities provided the policy of the taxing statute has been clearly laid down.

(vi) *Supplementary Acts*: Under this classification, power is given to the administrative agencies to make rules to elaborate, supplement or help to work out some principles laid down in the Act. In other words, power is delegated to the authority to make rules 'to carry out the purpose of the Act.'

(vii) *Approving and Sanctioning Acts*: In this type of legislation, power is delegated not to make rules but to approve the rules framed by other specified authority.

(viii) *Classifying and Fixing Standards Acts*: Under this type of delegation, power is given to the administrative authority to fix standard of purity, quality or fitness for human consumption. Courts have upheld the validity of this type of delegation on the grounds of necessity.

(ix) *'Penalty for Violation' Acts*: Sometimes power may be delegated to an administrative agency to prescribe punishment for the violation of rules. In the USA, the penalty for violation of administrative rules can be fixed by Congress. Making an act penal is a function of the Congress and cannot be delegated to the administrative agency. However, in England there are some instances where power to impose penalty has been delegated. London Traffic Act, 1924 provides that the administrative authority may provide, by regulation, the fines recoverable summarily for breaches thereof.

(x) *'Clarify the Provisions of the Statute' Acts*: In this case, power is delegated to the administrative authority to issue interpretations on various provisions of the enabling Act. United States Treasury

Department has been delegated the power to issue interpretations on various phases of taxation. However, usually these regulations are not binding. They are in the form of opinions for departmental guidance. But in some other cases they are regarded final and binding.

3.5.4 AUTHORITY-BASED CLASSIFICATION

Another classification of administrative rule-making is based on the position of the authority making the rules. Sometimes the rule-making authority delegates to itself or to some subordinate authority a further power to issue rules; such exercise of rule-making power is known as sub-delegated legislation.[34] Rule-making authority cannot delegate its power unless the power of delegation is contained in the enabling Act. Such authorisation may either be express or by necessary implication. If the authority further delegates its law-making power to some other authority and retains a general control of a substantial nature over it, there is no delegation as to attract the doctrine of '*delegatus non portest delegare*'. Sub-delegation makes the parliamentary control illusory and postpones the rule-making process. It must, therefore, be resorted to only in unavoidable circumstances.

3.5.5 NATURE-BASED CLASSIFICATION

Classification of administrative rule-making may also be based on the nature and extent of delegation. There are two types of parliamentary delegation:[35]

(I) NORMAL DELEGATION:
  (a) Positive: Where the limits of delegation are clearly defined in the enabling Act.
  (b) Negative: Where power delegated is expressed in negative terms and does not include power to do certain things, i.e. legislate on matter of policy or to impose taxation.

(II) EXCEPTIONAL DELEGATION:

    (a) Power to legislate on matters of principle.

    (b) Power to amend Acts of Parliament.

    (c) Power conferring such a wide discretion that it is almost impossible to know the limits.

    (d) Power to make rules without being challenged in a court of law.

Such exceptional delegation is also known as the Henry VIII clause. Under this clause, very wide powers are given to the administrative agencies to make rules including the power to amend and repeal. This type of delegation is delegation running riot. Even extraordinary conditions do not justify delegation outside the sphere of constitutional authority.

3.6 LIMITATION ON DELEGATED LEGISLATION

In Britain the doctrine of sovereignty of the parliament prevails, which implies that the parliament has unlimited power to make any law, and that the courts cannot question a parliamentary law on any ground. The result of this theory is that the parliament can delegate any amount of legislative power to an administrative agency. Therefore, in Britain, no restriction exists on the capacity of the parliament to confer its law-making powers on anybody it pleases and to any extent it deems fit. It is not necessary for the parliament to insert in a delegating statute any standard, policy or norm for guiding the delegate in exercising the power conferred on him. The delegate can be left free to draft delegated legislation in any way he likes and to evolve his own policy or standards in exercising the delegated power. However, the broader the delegation, the more difficult it becomes to control the delegate in exercising the power. It has often been emphasised that the parliament should not confer power in too broad or general terms, that it should define the limits of the power being delegated rather carefully so that the delegatee may be restrained from misapplying the power. However, the important point to note is that in Britain the remedy lies in the hands of the parliament itself; it can control the delegation of power by itself if it so pleases and there is no external agency to compel the parliament to define the norms or standards in the enabling statutes subject to which the delegated power may have to be exercised.

In the United States, on the other hand, the position is substantially different. The US Congress functions under a written constitution and the courts have power to interpret the constitution and declare a congressional statute unconstitutional if it does not conform to their views of the constitution. The US Supreme Court has invoked the doctrine of '*delegatus non portest delegare*' against the process of delegation. The doctrine means that a delegate cannot further delegate its powers. Thus the Congress, the courts argue, being a delegatee of the people, cannot further delegate its law-making functions to any other agency.[36] A significant objection against delegation also emanates from the doctrine of separation of powers which implies that the legislative and executive powers be kept distinct and separate from each other. In the USA, the question of delegation of legislative powers thus involves a conflict of values. On the one hand, the doctrine of separation insists that the legislative function be kept separate and distinct from the executive function. On the other hand, as already noted, the exigencies of modern government make it particularly impossible to concentrate all legislative power in the hands of the Congress which cannot possibly dispose of all legislative work itself in the sense of turning out comprehensive legislation complete in all details on every subject it undertakes to legislate upon. If the Congress were not willing to delegate law-making power to some agency then it may be impossible for it to enact the kind and quantity of legislation which the country may need. Thus, pragmatic considerations have prevailed over theoretical objections and, in course of time, the courts have relaxed the rigours of the doctrine of separation of powers and permitted broad delegation of power, subject to the rider that the Congress itself should lay down standards or policies for the guidance of the delegatee, that delegation should not be vagrant and uncontrolled, that the Congress should not give a blank cheque to the executive to make any rules it likes, for to do so would amount to an abdication of its functions by the Congress. If Congress transfers to others 'the essential legislative function with which it is vested', the statute doing so will be unconstitutional. Therefore, the courts insist that the Congress should itself declare the policy regarding the subject matter of legislation, and the power to lay down details to effectuate that policy may be delegated only to administration. The test, in the words of Justice Cardozo, is that 'to uphold delegation there is need to discover in the terms of the Act a standard reasonably clear whereby the discretion must be governed.'[37] This principle has been evolved to do service to the theory of separation. Prescribing legislative policy is regarded as an 'essential legislative function'; this function should be discharged by the Congress itself; it cannot be left to any delegatee. The Congress can thus leave 'non-essential legislative functions' to the executive. The working of the rule can be illustrated with reference to two cases. In *Panama Refining Co.* v. *Ryan*,[38] the Congress authorised the president to ban oil in interstate commerce when produced in excess of the quota fixed by each state. The majority of the judges of the US Supreme Court held the Act bad, for the Congress declared no policy, established no standards, and laid down no rule. There was no requirement, and no definition of circumstances and conditions in which transportation was to be allowed or prohibited. *Yakus* v. *US*[39] is a case on the other side. During World War II, the Office of the Price Administrator was set up to control prices. The relevant Act declared that the prices fixed ought to effectuate the declared policy of the Act to stabilise commodity prices with a view to prevent wartime inflation and its disruptive causes and effects. In addition, prices fixed had to be fair and equitable. In fixing prices, the administrator had to give due consideration to the prices prevailing within a designated base period. The delegation, though in effect extremely broad, was held valid for the Congress had stated the legislative objective and had prescribed the method of achieving that objective—maximum price fixing—and had laid down standards to guide the administrator's determination. The court found that the standards prescribed were sufficiently definite and precise to enable everyone to ascertain whether or not the administrator in fixing the designated prices had conformed to those standards.

It is very rare that the Supreme Court holds a congressional law bad on the grounds of excessive delegation. The Panama case is regarded as more of an aberration on the part of the judiciary rather than the precursor of a trend, for there are a few cases of significance where delegation has been held to be excessive and so unconstitutional.[40] The exigencies of modern government have let the courts to relent in their attitude towards delegation. The basic premise still remains that the Congress cannot delegate legislative power without prescribing standards, but whether this test is satisfied or not is a matter on which courts have adopted a liberal attitude. In a large number of cases, very vague phrases have been held to be adequate as laying down standards, so much so that one commentator has remarked that 'judicial language about standards is artificial.'[41] The fact remains that since 1937 no Act of the Congress has been struck down by the Supreme Court on the grounds of excessive delegation. Yet, still the courts reserve for themselves the power to declare delegation of legislative power as unconstitutional if they feel that in a given case the delegation is so broad and indefinite as to amount to an abdication by the Congress of its legislative function. Till such an extreme point is reached, courts permit delegation realising that the legislature today has to deal with complex socio-economic problems and if it is required to meticulously lay down standards for the delegate to follow then the whole legislative process would completely bog down. In spite of the dilution of the doctrine of non-delegation in the USA, the difference between Britain and the USA on the question of delegation is still somewhat real. Though, in both countries, delegation of legislative power has come to be established as a technique of legislative and administrative process, and broad delegations have come to be permitted, yet, while in the USA, the last word rests with the courts on the question as to how much delegation would be permitted in a given situation, in Britain it rests with the parliament as there is no constitutional limitation to restrain the parliament from assigning power where it likes.

In Pakistan and India, the question of permissible limits of delegation of legislative power has become important. Just on the eve of Independence, the Federal Court had held in *Jatindra Nath* v. *Province of Bihar*[42] that there could be no delegation of legislative power in India beyond 'conditional legislation'. It was a hangover of the colonial days. But then the question was whether the legislatures in independent Pakistan and India should be restricted to this limited form of delegation, or should it be given a greater freedom to resort to this technique? If the legislatures were to be permitted a greater freedom then the next question was, which of the two models—the British or the American, which differ from each other rather fundamentally—should be followed in Pakistan and India? The courts could hold either that a legislature could delegate as much power as it liked following the British model, or else that it, like the American Congress could not give to the delegate unlimited powers, and that it should state the policies subject to which the delegatee is to function in making legislation. Pakistan, India, and England have all parliamentary forms of government in which the executive is also a part of the legislature and can be closely supervised by it, but while Pakistan and India have written constitutions, Britain functions under an unwritten constitution. Also, while Pakistan and India, like the USA, have the system of judicial review of legislation, it does not prevail in Britain. But then, while in the USA, the presidential form of government is based on the principle of separation of powers, the system in Pakistan and India does not follow that principle in the area of executive–legislative relationship. The parliamentary form of government is based not on separation, but on co-operation, rather unison, of the two organs. Because of these similarities and dissimilarities between the Pakistani, Indian, British, and the American constitutions, it was open to the courts in independent Pakistan and India to follow either the British or the American model on the question of delegation of legislative power. Further, there is nothing in the Pakistani and Indian Constitutions either expressly prohibiting or permitting the legislature to delegate its legislative power to the administration. Therefore, if the courts had to find any restrictions on the legislature in the matter of delegation, it had to be on the basis of some general theories and principles of constitutional law, and not on the basis of a provision in the Constitution.

All delegated legislation has to be prospective in its effect and applicability, unless the same has been expressed to be otherwise and that too with the backing of the parent statute.[43]

The Supreme Court of India was faced in 1951 with all these questions in the famous case of *Re Delhi Laws Act*.[44] There were a few (Delhi being one of them) Part C States, under the direct administration of the central government, without having a legislature of their own. The parliament had to legislate for these states. As it was very difficult for the parliament to find the necessary time to do so in view of its other manifold engagements, Parliament passed a law, the Part C States (Laws) Act, 1950. It authorised the central government to extend to any Part C State, with such restrictions and modifications as it thought fit, any enactment in force in a Part A State, and while doing so it could repeal or amend any corresponding law (other than a central law) which might be operative at the time in the Part C State concerned. Undoubtedly, it was a very sweeping kind of delegation. The government could extend to a Part C State any law made by a state legislature (and not by the parliament), and even modify the law before extension. And if there was already a law in force in the Part C State on the point, it could either be repealed or modified when the law was being extended.[45]

The Supreme Court was called upon to adjudge the validity of this provision. Seven judges participated in the decision and seven opinions were delivered exhibiting a cleavage of judicial opinion on the question of limits to which the legislature in India should be permitted to delegate legislative power. Yet, on two points there was a unity of outlook amongst all these opinions. First, keeping the exigencies of the modern government in view, the parliament and state legislatures in India needed to delegate legislative power if they are to be able to face the multitudinous problems facing the country, for it is neither practicable nor feasible to expect that each of the legislative bodies could turn out a complete and comprehensive legislation on all subjects sought to be legislated upon. Second, since the legislatures derive their powers from the written constitution which creates them, they could not be allowed the same freedom as the British Parliament in the matter of delegation, and that some limits needed to be set on their capacity to delegate. But the judges differed on the question as to where to set the limit or draw the line: what were to be the permissible limits within which an Indian legislature could delegate its legislative power? One view propounded was that an Indian legislature could delegate its power to any extent subject to the limit that it did not efface itself or abdicate its powers, which meant that the legislature should never give up its control over the delegatee; that it must not destroy its own legislative power; it must retain in its hands the ultimate control over the authority so as to be able to withdraw the delegation whenever the delegatee did something wrong or foolish. The other view which approximated to the American approach, and which in theory at least is somewhat more restrictive than the first, was that the legislature should not delegate its essential legislative function which comprised the formulation of policy and enacting it into a binding rule of conduct. That meant that the legislature should lay down standards or policy in the delegating Act and the delegatee may be left with the power to execute the policy. By a majority, the specific provision in question was held valid subject to two riders: (a) that part of it was bad which authorised the government to repeal a law already in force in a Part C State; (b) the power to effect modifications in a state law in its application to a Part C State envisaged only such modifications as did not change the underlying policy of the law sought to be extended.

In the course of time, through a series of decisions, the Indian Supreme Court has confirmed the principle that legislature can delegate its legislative power subject to its laying down the policy.

Legislature must declare the policy of the law, lay down the legal principles and provide standards for the guidance of the delegatee to promulgate delegated legislation, otherwise the law will be bad on account of 'excessive delegation'. In applying the test of 'excessive delegation', apart from considering the breadth of the discretion conferred by an Act to promulgate delegated legislation, the courts also examine the procedural safeguards contained in the Act against misuse of power. A case in point is *H.R. Banthia* v. *India*.[46] S.5(2)(b) of the Gold Control Act, 1968 empowered the gold administrator, so far as it appeared to him to be necessary or expedient for carrying out the purposes of the Act, and to regulate the manufacture, distribution, use, disposal consumption, etc. of gold. The Supreme Court declared the provision invalid because it was very wide and suffered from the vice of 'excessive delegation'.

In a large number of cases the courts have considered the validity of various delegating provisions with reference to the doctrine of excessive delegation. The cases can be classified from the point of view of the nature of the power conferred under the following broad heads: (a) skeleton legislation; (b) power of inclusion and exclusion; (c) power of modification of the statute; and (d) power to impose tax. These categories are not mutually exclusive and have been adopted because of their most common occurrence. They are governed by the same overall principle of 'excessive delegation'. As a general proposition, it may be stated that judicial tendency is to uphold the power of delegated legislation, and it is only rare that it may be struck down on the grounds of 'excessive delegation'.

3.7 JUDICIAL CONTROL OF DELEGATED LEGISLATION

It has been discussed earlier that there are limits to the legislatures' competence to delegate legislative power. Where delegation goes beyond such limits, it is struck down by the courts. However, where delegation is within the constitutional limits, the courts exercise control over delegated legislation to see that it is *intra vires* the enabling Act and the constitution.

Delegated legislation may be assailed on any one of the following grounds: (i) that it is *ultra vires* the enabling Act; (ii) that it is *ultra vires* the constitution; (iii) that it is not made in accordance with the procedure prescribed by the enabling Act. The first two are the cases of substantive *ultra vires* and the third is the case of procedural *ultra vires*.

3.7.1 DELEGATED LEGISLATION ULTRA VIRES THE ENABLING ACT

The leading case on this point is *King Emperor* v. *Sibnath Bannerji*.[47] In this case, the Judicial Committee of the Privy Council held that a rule which was covered by the more general language used in Sub-section (1) of the enabling provision would not be invalid because it did not fall within the terms of Sub-section (2) of such provision which specifically enumerated the items of rule-making. Sub-clause (x) of Clause (2) of Section 2 of the Defence of India (Amendment) Act, 1940, authorised the making of rules for the detention of persons reasonably suspected of certain things such as being of hostile origin, or being about to act in a manner prejudicial to the public safety or interest or to the defence of British India. Under Rule 26 it was enough that the central government was satisfied with respect to any particular person that his detention was necessary with a view to preventing him from acting in any manner prejudicial to the defence of British India, the public safety, and the maintenance of public order. The Federal Court of India had held in *Keshav Talpade* v. *Emperor*[48] that Rule 26 was *ultra vires* the Defence of India Act as, according to Clause (x) of Section 2(2) a rule could confer a right to detain only such persons as were reasonably suspected of acting in any manner prejudicial to the defence of British India, the public safety or the maintenance of public order and did not confer power to detain a person because the government thought that he might do something thereafter or that he was a man likely to do it. The Privy Council reversed this decision and upheld the rule. It was pointed out that Clause (2) of Section 2 was merely illustrative. The impugned rule could be comprehended within the general power to make rules 'to carry out the purposes of the Act' which was given by Clause (1).

The Gujrat High Court in India reiterated the rule of Sibnath Bannerji's case that where general power of rule-making is in Clause (1) and specific power in Clause (2), Clause (2) merely illustrates but does not restrict the purposes mentioned in Clause (1)[49] In *Mohammad Hussain Gulam Mohammed* v. *State of Bombay*[50] the validity of Rules 53, 65, 66, and 67 made under the Bombay Agricultural Produce Market Act, 1939, was questioned before the Supreme Court on the grounds that they were in conflict with the enabling Act. Rule 53 provided that the market committee should levy and collect fees on agricultural produce bought and sold in the market area at such rates as might be specified in the bye-laws. The rule, however, failed to prescribe the maxima to which the bye-laws had to conform. Section 11 of the Act clearly stipulated that the maxima should be prescribed by the rules. The Supreme Court held that Rule 53 was *ultra vires* section 11. Rule 65 authorised the market committee to grant a licence for doing business in any market area. Section 5-A gave such power to a market committee only after a market was established under Section 5. Since no such market was established, the market committee could not grant licences. Insofar as the rule gave the power to issue licences to the market committee it was clearly *ultra vires* the Act. For similar reasons Rules 66 and 67 were held *ultra vires*.

No tax, fee or other pecuniary impositions may be levied by an instrument of subordinate legislation unless the enabling Act specifically authorises such imposition.[51] Where the statute authorises a local authority to levy tax on buildings on the basis of the 'annual rental which a hypothetical tenant may pay in respect of the building', the authority cannot make a rule authorising levy of tax at a uniform rate according to the floor area of the premises, irrespective of its letting value.[52] Similarly, where a statute empowers the levy of a rate on the annual value, the authority cannot fix it at a percentage of the capital value.[53] Similarly, it has been held that the rule-making authority cannot give retrospective effect to subordinate legislation unless the enabling Act expressly confers such power.[54] Usually, subordinate legislation is repealed when the parent law is repealed, unless there is an express provision in the repealing Act for saving the subordinate legislation.[55]

Subordinate legislation may be assailed as *ultra vires* if it encroaches upon the rights of private parties derived from the common law in the absence of an express authority under the enabling Act. In *Chester* v. *Bateson*,[56] a statute authorised the making of regulations for the public safety and successful prosecution of the war. One of the regulations made under the statute prohibited in certain cases, proceedings to recover possession of the dwellings of the workmen employed in the manufacture of war materials, and imposed penalty for taking such proceedings. It was observed that the regulation forbade the owner of the property access to all legal tribunals in regard to this matter and that there was no authority to do so given by the statute. It was held that the enabling Act could not have gone so far as to forbid access to courts in such a case and that so grave an invasion of the rights of the subjects was not intended by the legislature. The regulation was held invalid as being *ultra vires* the Act. Here the rule is that common law is to be presumed as subsisting unless it is changed by the parliament through legislation. If the enabling Act does not provide for change in the common law, the delegated legislation cannot effectuate it.

The Madhya Pradesh Excise Act, 1915, authorised the levy of excise duty on alcoholic liquors when they were either imported or exported or transported or manufactured within the state. A rule requiring the licensed vendors to pay excise duty on liquor remaining unsold by them below the ceiling limit was held to be *ultra vires* the Act.[57] Section 33 of the Bombay Police Act gave power to the commissioner and the deputy magistrate to make rules for 'regulating the conduct of and behaviour or action of persons constituting assemblies and processions on or along the streets'. Rule 7-A made under this power gave power to the commissioner or the district magistrate to refuse permission to hold a meeting. The rule was held *ultra vires* the Act since the Act authorised the making of rules for 'regulating' the meetings, not for totally banning them. The rule was also held to be an unreasonable restriction on fundamental right to assemble guaranteed by Article 19(1)(b).[58] The Madras Buildings (Lease and Rent Control) Act, 1960, authorised the controller to fix fair rents for the buildings according to certain principles laid down therein. One of the principles was that the cost of construction had to be determined on the basis of the cost incurred originally for construction. A rule made under the Act, however, provided that the value of the buildings reproduced on the date when the Act came into force should form the basis for such determination. The rule was held to be *ultra vires* the Act.[59]

It has been held that it is beyond the power of the rule-making authority to give retrospective effect to the rules.[60] A rule framed on 28 February 1955 but published in the gazette on 19 March 1955, was held to apply only after the later date. Where the difference in the date of publication and the date of its coming into force is very brief, the rules may be given retroactive effect provided that the date of coming into force is subsequent to the date of enactment.[61] Where a rule in question merely alters the procedure without altering its substantive provision, it may be given retrospective effect.[62]

The rules, being subordinate to the Acts, cannot govern or control the words of statute under which they are made,[63] and where the words of an Act are plain in their meaning it is not possible to rely upon the rules to defeat that intention.[64] Accordingly, in case of conflict between rules and the Act, the courts make an effort to resolve the conflict by adopting a reasonable interpretation, but here also the subordinate nature of rules is not forgotten and rules are interpreted in such a manner as not to become *ultra vires* of the Act.[65]

Rules may be *ultra vires* of the Act in a number of ways.[66] For example, when they are not made according to the laid down procedure, or they take away a right granted by the Act, or they enlarge or restrict the jurisdiction vested by the Act, or they authorise a course different from one authorised by the Act, or they inflict a penalty which is greater or different from the penalty provided by the Act, or they enlarge the provisions of the Act. But only a material inconsistency would make the rules invalid and inconsistency of words alone is not sufficient.[67]

It has been laid down by the Supreme Court of Pakistan that rules and regulations framed under a statute cannot transgress the limits set by the statute. The rule making body cannot frame rules which are in conflict with or in derogation of the substantive provisions of the statute under which the rules are framed and in case of any inconsistency with the parent statute the excessive rule will be considered illegal because it has gone beyond its delegated authority.[68] It must be kept in mind that when the legislature confers powers on a regulatory authority to frame rules it is expected that the rules will advance the purpose of the legislature and not run contrary to it. In case under section 23(2) of the Pakistan Electronic Media Regulatory Authority (PEMRA) Ordinance, PEMRA was provided with two regulatory objectives having separate regulatory tools yet at the same time aiming to achieve the same stated purpose of the Ordinance. The use of the word 'and' in Section 23(2) of the Ordinance separates the two distinct regulatory objectives, being fair competition and prevention of undue concentration. The regulatory objectives provide PEMRA with the scope of its regulatory duty which would enable it to achieve the stated purpose of the Ordinance at all times. The counsel for PEMRA on reading the and in Section 23(2) disjunctively, which as per his understanding means that PEMRA is authorized to prohibit broadcast media from operating distribution services and vice versa as the vertical integration of these two media enterprises will result in undue concentration of media ownership. However, the court found that the emphasis on a disjunctive reading is misplaced as the court was of the opinion that whether the 'and' is read conjunctively or disjunctively it would not change the intent of the law. The Ordinance requires the regulator to achieve diversity and plurality in content and the free flow of information by encouraging entities to operate media enterprises. Under Section 23(2) of the Ordinance the regulatory objecties of PEMRA are prescribed and in doing so the legislature did not impose any prohibition with respect to vertical integration of specific media enterprises in the electronic media. PEMRA has misunderstood its regulatory functions and the objectives of the law. The function of PEMRA is to carry out the stated purpose of the Ordinance and to ensure that it implements and enforces the objectives of Section 23(2) of the Ordinance. Hence PEMRA is required to regulate veritcal integration of all media enterprises so that they do not form concentrated ownership in a media market, which will give them a larger share of *that* market and enable them to prevent diversity and plurality in content In that market.[69]

By far, the most common instances of inconsistency between the Act and the rules occur when the rules adversely affect a right created by the Act. In *Dad Muhammad Khan* v. *Bassa*,[70] the suit of a money lender who had applied to the licensing authority for the renewal of his licence was dismissed on the grounds that his licence had expired under the rules. However, Section 3(5) of the Punjab Money Lenders Act provided that pending the disposal of application for renewal the licence was to remain effective. The High Court did not agree with the government decision and held that the rules being subordinate to the Act could not take away a right created by the statute under which they are framed. Similarly, in *Jaffar Khan* v. *Chief Election Commissioner*,[71] where Section 58(2) of the Electoral College Act, 1964, allowed any candidate to challenge the election by making an election petition but the rules framed under the Act provided for election petitions in respect of contested election and made no such provision for unopposed election return. Such a return was challenged before the Election Tribunal and the Tribunal ordered fresh election. This order was challenged in the High Court, but the Court dismissed the petition holding that the rules could not take away a right conferred by the Electoral College Act.

Moreover, the courts have also not allowed the rules to take away a right which is presumed to be part of the statute though not specifically provided by it. For example, in *Abdur Rehman* v. *Collector & DC Bahawalnagar*,[72] an elected member of union council who was removed from the office without an opportunity of being heard, challenged his removal and it was contended that the rules framed under the Basic Democracies Order, 1959, did not make any provision for the notice to the affected person or hearing him in his defence. The Supreme Court held that rules could not affect the right impliedly given by the statute.

The rules, being subordinate to the Act under which they are made, cannot enlarge its provisions. Otherwise they are inconsistent with the Act and therefore *ultra vires*. Where the definition of occupier under the Punjab Municipal Act, 1911, did not cover an owner who was not in actual possession and the rules made under the Act defined the occupier so as to include such as an owner, the Lahore High Court held[73] that the impugned rule was *ultra vires* the Act. Similarly the regulations having the effect on landlord–tenant relationship were held *ultra vires* the statute which related to controlling the construction of buildings.[74]

A similar inconsistency may arise between parent Act and the rules framed under it when a word not defined in the Act is defined by the rules and given an extended or restricted meaning. As words not defined in the Act are to be understood in their ordinary, dictionary meaning, the rule giving a special meaning to such words creates conflict between the two meanings. This question was discussed in *Hirjina Salt & Chemical Ltd* v. *Union Council Gharo*.[75] The salt works of petitioners were declared as 'market' by a notification issued under West Pakistan Union Councils Dharat (Market Fees) Rules, 1961. The parent statute, i.e. Basic Democracies Order, 1959, under which these rules were framed, had not defined the word 'market', which was defined by the Rules to mean the premises used for the sale of goods or for the manufacture of goods for sale and declared to be a market by the union council. Obviously, the second part of the definition was not covered by the ordinary meaning of the word 'market'. A demand for the payment of fee by the union council was challenged by the affected companies. But the Karachi High Court held that there was no inconsistency between the Basic Democracies Order and the Rules framed under it, as the definition of word 'market' did not conflict with any of the provisions of the Order. On appeal[76] the Supreme Court, though upheld the decision of the High Court on other grounds, held that words not defined in the main enactment should be understood in their ordinary, dictionary meaning.

As the rules cannot enlarge the provisions of an Act, they cannot also restrict the provisions of the Act. For example, the Displaced Persons (Compensation and Rehabilitation) Act, 1958, conferred appellate and revisional jurisdiction on various settlement authorities whereas the Permanent Transfer Rules, 1961, framed under the Act made a Permanent Transfer Order as final. Such an order was challenged in revision before the settlement commissioner who accepted the revision and this action of the settlement commissioner was challenged in a writ petition.[77] Justice Karam Elahi Chauhan dismissing the petition and holding that rules could not take away the jurisdiction given by the Act.

Another instance of such inconsistency occurred under the West Pakistan Family Court Act, 1964, and the rules framed under it. Section 9(6) of the Act provided that an application for setting aside an *ex parte* decree could be made within reasonable time to be determined by the Family Court after keeping in view the facts and circumstances of each case. On the other hand, Rule 13 of the WP Family Court Rules, 1965, prescribed a thirty-day period of limitation for such applications. An application for setting aside an *ex parte* decree made after the thirty-day period prescribed by the said rules was dismissed by the Family Court and a revised petition to challenge the order was also dismissed. Thereafter, the petitioner challenged the order in the Lahore High Court[78] in its constitutional jurisdiction. The High Court held that rule 13 was *ultra vires* the Family Court Act.

Similarly the rules cannot grant power not conferred by the statute. Where the rules framed under an Act to carry out the object or purposes of the Act gave extra powers to the provincial government, the rules were held *ultra vires*.[79] Again, local body if it was against law or public interest and the rules framed under the ordinance authorised the transfer of property with the approval of the commissioner, and the commissioner acting under these rules quashed a resolution for the transfer of property, it was held that the rules being subordinate to the Act could not grant powers in excess of the provisions of the Act.[80]

A penal statute is to be construed strictly. Therefore, the rules made under an enactment containing penal provisions must very squarely conform to such provisions.[81] Where an Act authorised the punishment of imprisonment up to six months or fine up to five hundred rupees or both but the rules framed under the Act provided for confiscation of the conveyance as well, it was held that rule authorising confiscation of conveyance was *ultra vires*.[82]

With regard to levying of duties through 'delegated legislation', it was held that the same was not *ultra vires*. What is to be considered is that the authority of delegating the said power to levy the duty has to be clear, unambiguous and precisely rendered to a particular authority. However, modern legislation saddles the said power to legislate with clear conditions or guidelines of rendering the same.[83]

Rules being subordinate to the parent Act cannot authorise a course of action different from the one provided by the Act. If the Act requires certain steps to be taken before exercising some powers, the rule cannot authorise the exercise of that power without taking those steps. For example, Rule 8 of West Pakistan Municipal Committee (Property) Rules, 1962, which authorised alienation of land by the chairman with the approval of the commissioner but did not provide for the conditions laid down in the Ordinance was held invalid.[84] In another case, the rules providing for the appointment of a committee to administer the affairs of a registered society was held beyond the Act as the Act had authorised the appointment of an administrator.[85] If the delegated legislation is within limits of the Act of legislature it has the force of law and is enforceable accordingly.[86] The Supreme Court has held that in such a case the courts do not go into the wisdom of delegated legislation.[87]

3.7.2 DELEGATED LEGISLATION *ULTRA VIRES* THE CONSTITUTION

Delegated legislation may be *ultra vires* the constitution if (a) the enabling Act itself is unconstitutional; (b) the enabling Act is constitutional but the delegated legislation is unconstitutional. In the first case, the delegated legislation may be *intra vires* the enabling Act but the enabling Act itself being *ultra vires* the constitution, the delegated legislation also becomes *ultra vires* the constitution. In the second case, the delegated legislation is *intra vires* the enabling Act but *ultra vires* the constitution. However, delegated legislation which is *ultra vires* the constitution also must be *ultra vires* the enabling Act because the legislature could not have given power to act *ultra vires* the constitution which is a valid argument.

(I) SUBORDINATE LEGISLATION IS INVALID BECAUSE THE ENABLING ACT IS UNCONSTITUTIONAL

A typical example where delegated legislation was held *ultra vires* the constitution because the enabling Act was *ultra vires* the constitution in *Tan Bug Taim* v. *Collector of Bombay*.[88] A rule made under the Defence of India Act providing for the requisition of immovable property was held invalid. The Act empowered the central government to make rules for the requisition of immovable property. The rule was held invalid because the subject of requisition of immovable property fell outside the legislative power of the federal legislature, it being on the State List. In *NMCS & WM Mills* v. *Ahmedabad Municipality*,[89] the Supreme Court held that since the state legislature had power to levy a tax only on land and buildings, the same could not be levied on machinery contained in or situated on the building even though the machinery was there for the use of the building. In *Chintaman Rao* v. *State of MP*[90] the enabling Act empowered the collector to make regulations for regulating or prohibiting the manufacture of *bidis* during the agricultural season with a view to improving agriculture. The collector prohibited the manufacture of *bidis* during the agricultural season with a view to diverting labour into agriculture. The Supreme Court held that the regulation went beyond what was required to improve agriculture. The total prohibition prevented even those persons who were incapable of working in agriculture due to age or infirmity from working in the *bidi* industry. Such persons were denied their means of livelihood. As this had no relation to the purpose of the Act, it was an unreasonable restriction upon the fundamental right to carry on an occupation guaranteed by the constitution. The Act gave power of total prohibition to the collector. Such power could be used within and without the constitution. As the two were not severable, the Supreme Court held that the entire provision was unconstitutional. Subordinate legislation of the collector was also held invalid because the enabling Act itself was unconstitutional.

(II) Enabling Act is constitutional but subordinate legislation is unconstitutional

In *Narendra Kumar* v. *Union of India*,[91] it was argued that if the enabling Act was valid, rules made under it could not be assailed as being unconstitutional. This argument was rejected. In *Messrs Dwarka Prasad* v. *State of UP*,[92] Clause 3(1) of the UP Coal Control Order, 1953, issued under Section 3 of the Essential Supplies (Temporary Powers) Act, 1946, provided that 'no person shall stock, sell, store for sale or utilise coal for burning bricks or shall otherwise dispose of coal in this State except under a licence in Form A or B granted under this Order or in accordance with the provisions of this Order.' Clause 3(2)(b) laid down that nothing contained in Sub-clause (i) 'shall apply to any person or class of persons exempted from any provision of the above sub-clause by the State Coal Controller.' The Supreme Court held that Clause 3(2)(b) was *ultra vires* because it gave unrestricted power to the state controller to make exemptions, and even if he acted arbitrarily, from improper motives, there was no check over him and no way of obtaining redress. It was held that such a power was an unreasonable restriction upon the fundamental right of freedom to carry on trade or business guaranteed by Article 19(1)(g).

Where a bye-law provided that no person should establish a market for wholesale trade in vegetables except with the permission of the board, but there was no provision authorising the municipal board to issue licences, such bye-law was held to be an unreasonable restriction upon the fundamental right to occupation.[93] Regulation 236(b) of the UP Police Regulations which authorised the policeman to pay domiciliary visits at night to the house of the person who was under police surveillance as being of suspicious character was held unconstitutional as being contrary to Article 21. It may be noted that in this case although the Supreme Court observed that these regulations were mere administrative directions and, therefore, had no force of law it examined the question of their consistency with the Constitution.[94] Rule 4-B of the Central Civil Services (Conduct) Rules, 1955, was held unconstitutional as it unreasonably restricted the fundamental right to freedom of assembly, freedom of association and freedom of speech of forbidding government employees from staging demonstration.[95]

In *NMCS & W. Mills* v. *Ahmedabad Municipality*,[96] Rule 7(3) of the Bombay Provincial Municipal Corporation Act (59 of 1949) was held invalid on account of excessive delegation of power by the legislature, Rule 7(2) provided that all parts and machinery contained or situated in or upon any building or land and belonging to any classes specified from time to time by public notices by the commissioner, with the approval of the Corporation, shall be deemed to form part of such building or land for the purpose of fixing the rateable value thereof. It depended on the arbitrary will of the commissioner as to what machinery he would specify and what he would not. There was no right of appeal. The Supreme Court held that this rule vested arbitrary and uncanalised power in the commissioner and such power could not be delegated by the legislature.

Subordinate legislation may be held unconstitutional if it is discriminatory. Thus a provision of the rules providing for the management of the Jain temples, which restricted voting right to persons above the age of 21 who had donated not less than Rs 500 to the temples during the previous ten years and who were residing within the state was held to be discriminatory.[97] A rule reserving seats in medical college for the sons and daughters of government officers[98] or a rule treating B.Sc. (Hon.) students preferentially for admission to a medical college[99] was held to be discriminatory.

3.7.3 REASONABLENESS OF DELEGATED LEGISLATION

Another aspect of substantive *ultra vires* of delegated legislation is the question of its reasonableness. In Britain, the rule is that while delegated legislation enacted by government departments is not subject to the test of reasonableness,[100] other delegated legislation may be assailed as being unreasonable.[101] In the USA, unreasonableness of a statutory regulation would render it invalid as it would be hit by the 'due process of law' clause of the fifth and fourteenth amendments.[102] No distinction is made between delegated legislation enacted by government departments and other delegated legislation for that purpose in the USA. In India, if delegated legislation imposes restriction upon any of the fundamental rights guaranteed by Article 19, reasonableness of such restriction is justiciable. Apart from this, whether the courts will declare delegated legislation invalid on the grounds of unreasonableness is not settled. One view is that the subordinate legislation would be invalid if unreasonable.[103] Another view is that the validity of statutory rules cannot be questioned on the grounds of unreasonableness because the rules made under a statutory authority become part and parcel of the statute and, therefore, stand on a different footing from the bye-laws with the result that though the latter can be challenged on the grounds of unreasonableness, the former cannot be so challenged.[104] The scope for judicial review of reasonableness of subordinate legislation is greater in Pakistan and India than in England because of the inclusion of the guarantees of fundamental rights in the Pakistani and Indian constitutions. Where, however, subordinate legislation does not invade any of the fundamental rights and is otherwise valid, the courts do not go into the question of its reasonableness.

In the case of bye-laws and other subordinate legislations made by bodies other than the governments, the courts go into the question of their reasonableness. The test for holding a bye-law unreasonable was given by Lord Russell in *Kruse* v. *Johnson* as follows:[105]

> If, for instance, they were found to be partial and unequal in their operation as between different classes; if they were manifestly unjust; if they disclosed bad faith; if they involved such oppressive or gratuitous interference with the rights of those subject to them as could find no justification in the minds of reasonable men, the court might well say, 'Parliament never intended to give authority to make such rules; they are unreasonable and *ultra vires*.'

Closely allied to the grounds of unreasonableness is the ground of *mala fide* or bad faith on the part of administration. In Britain, the courts have long exercised the right to declare invalid administrative actions which, while *prima facie* authorised by statute, are proved to have been taken for ulterior motives.[106]

3.7.4 EXCESSIVE DELEGATION

What are the permissible limits of delegation of legislative powers is a question of great constitutional importance but one which is extremely difficult to answer.

The modern welfare state cannot meet the expectations of people without having sufficient powers, and for this reason the device of delegated legislation which was criticised in the past has become acceptable today. Nonetheless, the representative legislature enjoys more confidence than the executive officials. Therefore, it is expected to perform itself the essential legislative functions and entrust only the filling in of details to other agencies. This statement may appear to be simple in theory but not in practice, as Justice Hamoodur Rehman observed in the *Sirajul Haq Patwari* case:[107]

> The line of separation between the powers that have to be exercised directly by the legislature itself and those that may be delegated is incapable of clear definition. Difficulties, therefore, often arise not in

determining the governing principles but in the application of those principles to concrete cases.

In the United Kingdom the parliament is supreme. Therefore, it can delegate its functions to any extent to an administrative authority. As there are no constitutional safeguards like those available in the USA, the courts are to a great extent helpless in the face of clear statutory provisions. Even a decision of the highest court, i.e. the House of Lords can be made ineffective by retrospective legislation. This was actually done through War Damages Act, 1965, which was enacted in order to counter the decision of the House of Lords in *Burmah Oil Co.* v. *Lord Advocate*.[108] Wade has rightly stated: 'Faced with an Act of Parliament, the court can do no more than make certain presumptions for example that property will not be taken without compensation and that European Convention on Human Rights will be respected.'[109] However, the absence of legal control does not mean that there is no control at all. Thus, for example, political limitations will often make it difficult for the parliament to make unreasonable laws.

In USA, on the other hand, constitutional limitations of the Congress are well established. As already noted the theory of separation of powers contains a prohibition against delegated legislation, and although the compulsions of modern welfare states have made substantial inroads on this theory, yet the courts are not willing to abandon them altogether. Thus, Professor Cushman correctly asserts that courts have been forced to recognise that some legislative powers must be delegated if government is to function, and doctrines have been devised which, while paying lip service to the non-delegation doctrine, permit important and necessary exception to it.[110] A brief discussion of some important American cases dealing with delegated legislation will be instructive in this regard.

From early constitutional times, the American Supreme Court has expressed the difficulty of providing a guiding formula, and no less a person than Chief Justice Marshall said, 'A line has not been exactly drawn which separates those important subjects which must be entirely regulated by the legislature itself from those of less interest, in which general provisions may be made . . . to fill up the details.'[111] Nonetheless, for a long time the delegation of legislative powers did not pose much doctrinal problem because of its small magnitude. But the twentieth century has seen great expansion in legislative activity and legislature, which is unable to cope with the problem which has surrendered vast legislative powers to the executive.

The case of *Schechter Poultry Farm* v. *United States* is probably the most important on the subject of delegated legislation. A congressional Act authorised the president to approve 'codes of fair competition', for the regulation of particular trade or industry and the violation of such codes was made punishable. No specific policies or standards were prescribed by the Act and the Supreme Court condemned the provision as 'delegation running riot'[112] for it gave the president unfettered discretion to enact laws for the control of trade and industry throughout the country. Similarly, another provision of the Act was held invalid for unconstitutional delegation in *Panama Refining Co.* v. *Ryan*.[113] In another case of that period the Supreme Court held that the Congress could not 'delegate any of its legislative powers except under a prescribed standard.'

The underlying reason of these cases is the extent of delegation.[114] The Congress had made the most sweeping delegation of all times without caring for what the Supreme Court had said three years back: 'Congress may declare its will, and after fixing a primary standard, devolve upon administrative officer the power to fill up the details by prescribing the administrative rules and regulations.'[115]

World War II brought a great change in the attitude of the Supreme Courts towards delegated legislation. *Yakus* v. *United States*,[116] upheld the wide delegation of powers[117] under emergency Price Control Act, 1942, which authorised the price administrator to fix the maximum prices for various commodities. Again, in *Lichter* v.

United States,[118] the Supreme Court upheld wide delegation under War Contracts Renegotiation Act, 1942, which authorised the heads of services to renegotiate military supply contract to prevent excessive profits. The term 'excessive profit' was not clearly defined by the Act but the Supreme Court sustained it by holding that providing a specific guiding formula to the administration was not necessary where the legislative policy required flexibility.

The court in *Yakus* and *Lichter* cases was definitely influenced by the fact that impugned legislation related to emergency. Nonetheless, its decision on a peacetime legislation was not much different in *National Broadcasting Co.* v. *United States*,[119] where very broad standards like public interest or necessity were considered sufficient for the subject matter of legislation.

In two comparatively recent cases the Supreme Court has maintained this lenient attitude. Thus, for example, in *United States* v. *Mazuire*[120] the authorisation to the Red Indian tribes to regulate the introduction of liquor in their territories was upheld. Similarly, in *Federal Energy Administration* v. *Algonguin*[121], the President's powers under an Act to adjust imports of an article if it threatened to impair the national security was held valid.

No doubt, for the last some decades, the American Supreme Court has been upholding laws having very broad standards, and no doubt the traditional theory of non-delegation has been enfeebled. Nonetheless, the classic Schechter doctrine has never been overruled; in fact it has been reasserted.[122] Admittedly, it is true that since the Schechter case, the US Supreme Court has not declared invalid any delegation by Congress, but it is equally true that since then Congress has also not delegated the legislative powers at that scale.

Moreover, the courts have been influenced by the safeguards that have been evolved to control the delegated legislation, the most important being public participation in making such legislation. The mandates of Administrative Procedure Act, 1946, coupled with some administrative practices have democratised the process of making delegated legislation. Such legislation has people's sanction at its back and deserves lenient treatment from the courts. It has been rightly observed that 'the emphasis has now shifted from the constitutionality of delegated legislation to the procedure for making it.'[123]

Since the Privy Council decision in *R. v. Burah,* it became a well settled rule that although the Indian legislature was a non-sovereign body having powers expressly limited by the Acts of the parliament which created it, yet acting within those limits it was not in any way an agent of the parliament and it had plenary powers of legislation at large and of the same nature as those of the parliament itself. Thus, the Indian legislature could delegate its powers to another agency without much restriction.

This traditional theory was modified to some extent with the change of political conditions. Thus, towards the end of the British rule, Justice Munir held in a full bench case[124] of the Lahore High Court that while delegating its powers the legislature must lay down the principle or policy of legislation. He observed:

> The question of the constitutionality or unconstitutionality of a law was to be determined not by the principle of maxim *delegatus non portest delegare,* but by the consideration whether legislature, in performing its functions of law-making, has laid down the principle of legislation and left merely the filling up of details to the executive or whether by empowering the executive to make the rules, legislature has delegated to the executive the power to lay down the principles of legislation itself. If in the statute the legislature has laid down a principle or a policy but left it to the executive to carry out that principle or policy subject to well-defined restrictions, the enactment would be constitutional but if the legislature has left it to the executive to lay down the principle or policy and thus given to it absolute and unrestricted discretion to legislate in the form of the power to make rules, the enactment would be unconstitutional.

The first case on delegated legislation in post-Independence period was *Sobho Gyanichandani* v. *Crown,*[125] decided by the Federal Court in 1952. The Public Safety Ordinance, 1949, a temporary statute having life of one year, authorised the central government to extend the life of the ordinance. When such an extension made by the central government was challenged, the Federal Court held this delegation invalid. Chief Justice Abdul Rashid observed that the legislature cannot delegate its power of making, modifying or repealing any law to an external authority, and that the power to extend the life of an enactment is in the nature of legislative power which cannot be delegated. Similarly, Justice Akram held that ancillary powers can be delegated but matters of fundamental nature or general policy cannot be delegated. Justice Cornelius also took the view that essential legislative functions could not be delegated whereas ancillary powers may validly be delegated to the executive. However, he indicated two cases where legislative functions could be validly delegated without following this rule; firstly, where it is not possible to lay down any definite comprehensive rules, and secondly, where the policy of the legislature is implicit in the statute. Thus, the court evolved the theory that essential legislative powers cannot be delegated, and this theory was in great contrast to the rule laid down by the Privy Council in the case of *R. v. Burah.*

In *East & West Shipping Co. v. Pakistan*,[126] Chief Justice Munir again emphasised the theory that delegated legislation is not prohibited if the policy of the law is discoverable from the statute. While he recognised the exception that vesting of discretion is allowed when it is impracticable to lay down a definite comprehensive rule, he introduced another exception that wide powers may be given for the administration of licensing system which is meant to protect the general welfare of the society.

The rule of legislative policy was also followed by the Supreme Court in *District Magistrate v. Kazim Raza.*[127] In this case, the petitioner had challenged the rule-making power of the Government under Section 17 of the Arms Act, 1878, on the grounds that legislature had not laid down any policy or criterion for the grant or refusal of such licences. But the court upheld the delegation. Justice Hamoodur Raman observed that by making this delegation legislature had not effaced itself or created a new legislative body, and that it was impossible in this case to provide for every detail and the machinery to carry it into effect. He recognised the theory of 'legislative policy' and observed:[128]

> It is clear from the examination of the provisions of Arms Acts that the policy of legislation clearly discernible therein is that no one should have any right to possess or carry any kind of arms or ammunition except when permitted to do so by the appropriate authority and even then upon such terms and conditions as the authority might consider it necessary to prescribe by rules having regard to the conditions prevailing in a given area where the arm in question was to be possessed or carried.

He further observed that 'manifestly the firearm being a subject about which legislature may legitimately think it fit to give a wide discretion to those entrusted with the administration of its licensing particularly having regard to the fact that it is impracticable in such a case to lay down a definite comprehensive rule'.

Justice Kaikaus, while concurring in the result, declared the impugned rules *ultra vires* and expressed the opinion that, 'delegated legislation will be valid only if the policy and the framework are provided by legislature and the government is only to fill in the details'. It will be noted that this policy–detail dichotomy was also substantially accepted by the majority. But the majority was content with the very thin policy given by legislature because a definite comprehensive rule was impracticable.

In *Muhammad Ismail & Co.* v. *Chief Cotton Inspector*,[129] the validity of some provisions of the West Punjab Cotton Control Act, 1949, was challenged on the grounds that it amounted to excessive arid unconstitutional delegation of powers to the executive because it vested unguided discretion in the government for the imposition of fee under the Act. The court held that the impugned clause contained sufficient indication of policy to be followed by the executive authorities and that the field of choice had been limited by legislature itself which provided the framework within which the executive authority was to function.

The high water mark of the application of the doctrine of 'legislative policy' came in the decision of Dacca High Court in *Ghulam Zamin* v. *A.B. Khondker*.[130] The president had enacted Inter Provincial Trade Ordinance, 1964, which empowered the central government to regulate the movement or transportation of any commodity between the two provinces. A full bench of the court held the ordinance unconstitutional on the grounds that legislature did not lay down the policy of legislation and had in fact effaced itself. The court recognised the rule of legislative policy and held that legislature after enunciating the essential legislative principles or standard was entitled to delegate to outside agencies such functions which were essential to an effective exercise of the legislative power with which it had been endowed by the constitution, and that legislature could not abdicate its legislative functions or efface itself by delegating all its functions. In fact, the ordinance had not laid down any policy or standard and it had given unlimited legislative powers to the central government. Thus, it was a skeleton law and was rightly declared invalid.

A full bench of the Dacca High Court in another case[131] applied these principles to a somewhat different type of delegation under Section 57, Electoral College Act, 1964. The petitioner had challenged the delegated power of the provincial government with relation to the demarcation of constituencies. The case was originally decided by a full bench of three judges which opined that Section 57 did not amount to excessive delegation. But thereafter a larger bench of five judges was constituted to consider the law points involved in the decision and this bench reversed the earlier decision and held that the powers given under Section 57 amounted to excessive delegation of legislative powers. But on appeal the Supreme Court reversed this decision.[132] The question of delegated legislation attracted some attention of the Judges. Chief Justice Cornelius and Justice S.A. Rehman held the delegated power of demarcation of local units as administrative functions. Chief Justice Cornelius even expressed his doubts about challenging the legislation except under Article 6 of the Constitution. Justice Fazal-e-Akbar considered the provisions as conditional legislation and relying on the law laid down in *R. v. Burah* and *King Emperor v. Binori Lal Sharma*, he upheld the law. Justice Hamood-ur-Rehman termed the functions as administrative and went on to say that the theory of excessive delegation was not much applicable to our constitutional system. However, he recognised that legislature cannot totally efface itself or abdicate its legislative functions and that where legislature has sufficiently expressed its will and exercised its judgment as to the territorial extent, scope and subject matter of the legislation, the provisions of details may be left to be done by another agency. Justice Yaqub Ali devoted considerable attention to this aspect of the case. He held that if the law promulgated on the subject is known to have a certain policy and the outside body to which its execution is entrusted has framed regulations which provide uniformity and ensure against arbitrariness, then the law will not be struck down for excessive delegation. According to him, 'The Court's opinion with regard to excessive delegation should be formed not on the mere absence of standards, but on factual lack of procedural safeguards.'

In *Ghulam Jilani* v. *Government of West Pakistan*,[133] the arrest of three opposition political leaders made under Rule 32 of Defence of Pakistan Rules, 1965 was challenged on the grounds *inter alia* that uncontrolled legislative functions had been conferred on the central government to make rules for the detention of any person. Section 32(2)(x) of the Ordinance,[134] which authorises the government to make such rules had in fact clearly enumerated the grounds of such detention and therefore the Supreme Court felt no hesitation in upholding it. Chief Justice Cornelius held that section 32(2)(x) was not an excessive delegation of legislative power. He said:[135]

> The detailed provisions contained in this clause are worded with precision to meet particular needs, and sufficiently support the view of the High Court, that there are ample guidelines contained in this clause to meet fully the criticism that this clause constitutes excessive delegation of legislative power. Any rules made under this clause must be adapted to one or other of the numerous cases that are provided for.

Similarly, in *Zahur Elahi* v. *State*[136] the Supreme Court dealt with the detention of an opposition political leader under Defence of Pakistan Rules, 1971. The majority held that the detention was not validly made under the Defence of Pakistan Rules. Therefore, they did not touch the larger question of the validity of delegation. Chief Justice Muhammad Yaqub Ali, however, held in his dissenting opinion that the detention was validly made and relying on the above dictum of Chief Justice Cornelius in *Ghulam Jilani* v. *Province of W. Pakistan*, also held the delegation valid because according to him the legislative policy had been provided in the statute in the statute.

Zaibtun Textile Mills v. *CBR*[137] is an important case where the problem of delegated legislation was discussed at great length. By an amendment in the Central Excise and Salt Act, 1944, it was provided that the Central Board of Revenue, instead of levying the excise duty on textile mills according to their production, might levy the duty on the production capacity of such mills. It was also provided that the Board shall specify the guiding principles for the determination of production capacity. The Government of Pakistan appointed a committee of experts to determine the production capacity of cotton textile factories. The excise duty which was determined according to the formula recommended by the committee became the subject of challenge in this case. The judges of the Division Bench were equally divided. Justice A.K. Sheikh held that it was the duty of the legislature to record its own judgment that the excise duty was to be levied on the basis of production capacity. According to him, the variation in the levy and collection of taxes is as much an essential legislative function as the levy and collection of taxes is in the first instance. Accordingly, he condemned the delegation of legislative powers under the Act as invalid.

On the other hand, Justice Ghulam Safdar Shah held the delegation valid. He asserted that the legislative policy or guideline and standard were not indispensable if the statute did not grant uncontrolled arbitrary powers without any procedural safeguards.

Thus, he appeared to have abandoned the theory of legislative policy and standards which was being followed by the courts for about the last two decades.

Justice Noorul Arifin, to whom the case was sent to resolve the difference, took a view similar to that of Justice Ghulam Safdar Shah. However, he did not go to the extent of abandoning the well established theory of legislative policy or standards. According to him the impugned amendment did not suffer from the vice of excessive delegation as the legislature did not efface itself or abdicate its essential legislative functions. He observed:

> Considering the nature of the subject with which the legislature had to deal, sufficient legislative guidance, by way of declaring the legislative policy and primary legislative standards and also secondary legislative principles according to which the delegatee is required to act have been fully set out in the amendment which also contains both substantive as well as procedural safeguards.[138]

On appeal, the Supreme Court upheld this decision.[139] While dealing with the delegation of power to the Central Board of Revenue to levy excise duty on production capacity in lieu of actual production, Justice Zafar Hassan Mirza held:[140]

> No serious exception can be taken in conferment of discretionary power upon officers or functionaries for the exercise of alternate power according to exigencies of the situation prevailing at a particular time or place. Invariably the choice between the two courses of action would seem to fall in the field of implementation of the law made by legislature.

Although this was enough to dispose of the issue of delegation, yet he considered it necessary to lay down some rule for the guidance of the courts. He observed that our constitution does not envisage a rigid separation of powers so as to prohibit the delegation of legislative powers to the executive, that 'no specific test can be formulated and laid down for general application in every case', and that 'each case has to be determined in the context of its particular circumstances in the background of broad principles. . . .'

The question of excessive delegation once again came before the Supreme Court in a recent case[141] where it was held:

> The crux of the matter is that in determining whether there has been an unconstitutional delegation of legislative powers in which powers are granted is an important element of consideration, and in the final analysis the question is one of a kind and degree and each case of questioned delegation of authority must depend upon the facts of that particular case.

3.8 Legislative Control of Delegated Legislation

Every delegate is subject to the authority and control of the principal and the exercise of delegated power can always be directed, corrected or cancelled by the principal. Hence parliamentary control over delegated legislation should be a living continuity as a constitutional necessity.[142] The fact is that due to the broad delegation of legislative powers and the generalised standard of control also being broad, the judicial control has shrunk, raising the desirability and the necessity of parliamentary control.

In the USA, the control of Congress over delegated legislation is limited because neither is the technique of 'laying' before the Congress extensively used nor is there any congressional committee to scrutinise it. This is due to the constitutional structurisation in that country in which it is considered only the duty of the courts to review the legality of administrative rule-making. There is even authority that the negative resolution technique so widely used in Britain would be unconstitutional in an American legislature.[143]

In Britain, due to the concept of parliamentary sovereignty, the control exercised by the parliament over administrative rule-making is very broad and effective. Parliamentary control mechanism operates through 'laying' techniques because under the provisions of Statutory Instruments Act, 1946, all administrative rule-making is subject to the control of the parliament through the Select Committee on Statutory Instruments. Parliamentary control in England is most effective because it is done in a non-political atmosphere.

In Pakistan and India, parliamentary control of administrative rule-making is implicit as a normal constitutional function because the executive is responsible to the parliament.

3.8.1 DIRECT GENERAL CONTROL

Direct but general control over delegated legislation is exercised through:

(i) *Debate on the Act which contains delegation*: Members may discuss anything about delegation including necessity, extent, type of delegation, and the authority to whom power is delegated.

(ii) *Questions and notices*: Any member may ask questions on any aspect of delegation of legislative powers and if dissatisfied can give notice for discussion.

(iii) *Moving resolutions and notices in the House*: Any member may move a resolution on motion, if the matter regarding delegation of power is urgent and immediate, and reply of the government is unsatisfactory.

(iv) *Vote on grant*: Whenever the budget demands of a ministry are presented any member may propose a cut and thereby bring the exercise of rule-making power by that ministry under discussion.

(v) *A private member's bill seeking modifications in the parent Act or through a debate*: At the time of discussion on the address by the President to the joint session of Parliament, members may discuss delegation. However, these methods are rarely used.

3.8.2 DIRECT SPECIAL CONTROL

This control mechanism is exercised through the technique of 'laying' on the table of the House rules and regulations framed by the administrative authority.

As mentioned earlier, in the USA the control of the Congress over the exercise of delegated legislation is limited; however, it does not mean that the technique of 'laying' is non-existent. The notable use of this technique was made in the Reorganisation Acts of 1939 to 1969, which authorised the president to reorganise the executive government by administrative rule-making. The Acts of 1939 and 1945 provided that the presidential organisation plans were not to have any effect for a specified period during which they could be annulled by Congress through a concurrent resolution of both Houses. The classic annulment through this process has been the rejection by the Senate of President Truman's plan to abrogate the provisions of the Taft-Hartley Act, 1947 providing for a separation of functions between National Labour Relations Board and the independent Office of General Council.[144]

In Britain, the technique of laying is very extensively used because all the administrative rule-making is subject to the supervision of the parliament under the Statutory Instruments Act, 1946 which prescribes a timetable.[145] In a majority of cases, the administrative rules and regulations are made subject to annulment by either House of Parliament within forty days from the date of laying. A less common technique is the deferring of the effectivity of the administrative rules unless positively approved by the Parliament.

In Pakistan and India, there is no special law like the Statutory Instruments Act, 1946 to regulate the technique of 'laying'. Here, the use of this technique is made by making a stipulation in the enabling Act providing that the rules and regulations made thereunder shall be laid on the table of the House. 'Laying' in Pakistan and India may take various forms:

(I) LAYING WITH NO FURTHER DIRECTION: In this type of laying, the rules and regulations come into effect as soon as they are laid. It is simply to inform the House about the rules and regulations.

(II) LAYING SUBJECT TO ANNULMENT OR LAYING SUBJECT TO NEGATIVE RESOLUTION: In this process, the rules come into effect as soon as they are placed on the table of the House but shall cease to have effect if annulled by a resolution of the House.

(III) LAYING SUBJECT TO AFFIRMATIVE RESOLUTION: This technique may take two shapes:

(a) that the rules shall have no effect or force unless approved by a resolution of each House of Parliament; or

(b) that the rules shall cease to have effect unless approved by an affirmative resolution.

In both these processes, it is the duty of the government to move a resolution.

(IV) LAYING IN DRAFT SUBJECT TO NEGATIVE RESOLUTION: Such a principle is based on Section 6 of the Statutory Instruments Act, 1946 in Britain which provides that when any Act contains provision for this type of laying the draft rules shall be placed on the table of the House and shall come into force after forty days from the date of laying unless disapproved before that period.

(V) LAYING IN DRAFT SUBJECT TO AN AFFIRMATIVE RESOLUTION: In this type of laying the instruments or draft rules shall have no effect unless approved by the House.

In Britain, Section 4 of the Statutory Instruments Act, 1946 provides that the instruments must be laid on the table of each House before they come into operation. If, for any reason, the rules are to come into force before laying, a notice to this effect must be sent to the Lord Chancellor and the Speaker.

The earliest instance of the laying provision found in India is in the Immigration Act, 1922. Between 1929 and 1939 only three Acts made provisions for laying, namely Insurance Act, 1938, Agriculture Products Act, 1938, and Motor Vehicles Act, 1939.

After a gap of five years, the Central Excise Act and Salt Act, 1944 and the India Air Craft Act, 1944 made provisions that the rules framed thereunder must be laid on the table of the House. Only in a few Acts, i.e. Insurance Act, 1938 and Air Craft Act, 1944 provision was made for laying subject to a negative resolution. The negative resolution procedure differs from its counterpart in Britain, as in Pakistan and India it includes the power of modification also. Three other Indian Acts, namely Representation of the People Act, 1951, Indian Services Act, 1951, and Indian Development and Regulation Act, 1951 contain only the right of modification of the rules and not annulment. The period during which the rules could be modified varies from seven days to one month. It may be noted that in England there is a uniform period of 40 days.

(VI) LEGAL CONSEQUENCES OF NON-COMPLIANCE WITH THE LAYING PROVISIONS: In England, the provisions of Section 4(2) of the Statutory Instruments Act, 1946 makes the laying provision mandatory for the validation of statutory instruments. In Australia also, the provisions of Interpretation Act provide that the failure to comply with the laying provision would render the rules void.

In India, however, the consequences of non-compliance with the laying provisions depend on whether the provisions in the enabling Act are mandatory or directory. In *Narendra Kumar* v. *Union of India*,[146] the Supreme Court of India held that the provisions of Section 3(5) of the Essential Commodities Act, 1955 which provided that the rules framed under the Act must be laid before both Houses of Parliament, are mandatory, and therefore Clause 4 of the Non-Ferrous Metal Control Order, 1958 has no effect unless laid before the parliament. However, in *Jan Mohd.* v. *State of Gujrat*[147], the court deviated from its previous stand point. Section 26(5) of the Bombay Agricultural Produce Markets Act, 1939 contained a laying provision but the rules framed under the Act could not be laid before the provincial legislature in its first session as there was then no functioning legislature because of emergency during World War II. Nevertheless, the rules were placed on the table of the House in its second session. Court held that the rules remained valid because the legislature did not provide that non-laying at its first session would make the rules invalid.

This decision may not be considered as a deviation from the normal rule because of the very special circumstances attending the case. This becomes clear from the decision of the Supreme Court in *Hukam Chand* v. *Union of India*.[148] In this case, Section 40 of the Displaced Persons (Compensation) Act, 1954 empowered the central government to make rules and required them to be placed before the parliament subject to a negative resolution. The government added an explanation to Rule 49 and gave it a retrospective operation under which non-urban land could be allotted to displaced persons. The Supreme Court of India held that out of three recognised types of laying, it comes in the second category which is a mandatory provision of the law. Therefore, the rules were struck down as *ultra vires* of the powers of the administrative agency. In *Atlas Cycle Industries Ltd* v. *State of Haryana*[149], the Supreme Court, however, held the impugned provision of law which provided that every order by the central government or its officer or authority 'shall be laid before both Houses of Parliament as soon as may be after it is made' as merely directory and did not make 'laying' a condition precedent to the making of the order.

Even if the requirement of laying is only directory and not mandatory, the rules framed by the administrative authority without conforming to the requirement of laying would not be permissible if the mode of rule-making has been consciously violated. However, laying would not cure any invalidity of the rules.

3.8.3 INDIRECT CONTROL

This control is exercised by the parliament through its Committees. In India, a Committee known as the Committee on Subordinate Legislation of Lok Sabha was appointed on 1 December 1953. It consisted of 15 members nominated by the speaker for a period of one year. The chairman was appointed by the speaker from amongst the members. The committee had the power to appoint sub-committees and could refer any matter for its consideration. The committee had also the power to compel the attendance of any person and to compel the production of documents and records. This committee has been constituted in every Lok Sabha and its main functions are to examine:

   (i) Whether the rules are in accordance with the general object of the Act.

  (ii) Whether the rules contain any matter which could more properly be dealt within the Act.

 (iii) Whether it contains imposition of tax.

 (iv) Whether it directly or indirectly bars the jurisdiction of the court.

  (v) Whether it is retrospective.

 (vi) Whether it involves expenditure from the consolidated fund.

 (vii) Whether there has been unjustified delay in its publication or laying.

(viii) Whether, for any reason, it requires further elucidation.

However, if the role of this committee of parliament has to be strengthened then a separate law like the Statutory Instruments Act in Britain providing for uniform rules of laying and publication must be passed. The Committee may be supplemented by a specialised official body to make the vigilance of administrative rule-making more effective.[150]

3.9 Procedural Control of Delegated Legislation

Parliamentary control over administrative rule-making is admittedly weak because the legislators are sometimes unaware of legal skills. A constant search, therefore, is on for an alternative mechanism which, besides providing effective vigil over administrative rule-making, can guarantee effective participation of the people for better social communication, acceptance, and effectivity of the rules.

Procedural control mechanism has the potential to meet the above-noted requirements by allowing specific audit of rules by those for whose consumption they are made. Procedural control mechanism operates in three components: (i) antenatal publicity, (ii) consultation, and (iii) post-natal publicity.

3.9.1 ANTENATAL PUBLICITY

In Pakistan and India, there is no separate law governing the procedure of administrative rule-making, and the parent Act may or may not provide for procedural requirement. However, in some cases the parent Acts have provided for antenatal publicity. Section 30(3) of Chartered Accountants Act, 1949 and Section 43 of Co-operative Societies Act, 1912 may be cited as examples where it was provided that the rules must first be published in draft form to give an opportunity to the people to have their say in the rule-making.

Antenatal publicity required by the enabling Act attracts the application of Section 23 of the General Clauses Act, 1897 which requires that:

  (i) the rules be published in draft form in the gazette.
 (ii) objections and suggestions be invited by a specific date mentioned therein.
(iii) those objections and suggestions be considered by the rule-making authority.

It may, however, be noted that the procedure prescribed in the General Clauses Act, 1897 applies only to rules, regulations and bye-laws and the administrative rule-making appearing under any other name is not governed by it.

American experience shows that antenatal publicity is most beneficial in practice, because those subject to administrative regulations tend to be members of trade or business organisations which perform the routine task of scanning the Federal Register and alert their members about the proposed rule-making. It may be noted that in America, 'lobbying' is an institution, and vigorous efforts are made to support the organisation's viewpoint before the administrative agency. Keeping in view the utility of antenatal publicity, Section 4 of the Federal Administrative Procedure Act, 1946 provides for the publication of proposed rules in the Federal Register. The Agency concerned must then afford an opportunity to the interested persons to participate in the administrative rule-making through submission of written data, views or arguments, with or without opportunity of being heard orally. The Act also provides an escape clause where this procedure can be dispensed with in cases of its impracticability, or it being unnecessary or contrary to public interest. It may be noted that the requirements of Section 4 apply only to substantive rules and, therefore, has no application to interpretative rules, general statements of policy, rules of agency organisation, procedure, and practice. American experience shows that the escape clause has been used in very few cases and it has not been abused.

In Britain, unlike the USA, the emphasis is on informal procedural requirements. The original rules of antenatal publicity and prior consultation laid down in Rules Publication Act, 1893 have been repealed by the Statutory Instruments Act, 1946 which now provides for publication of rules. In Britain, the law contains no general requirement for antecedent publicity or any right to hearing. However, in individual cases, the parliament may provide for antenatal publicity and prior consultation. Factories Act, 1961 may be cited as an illustration where antenatal publicity of rules, people's participation through consideration of their objections by individual or public hearing were provided by the parliament. It does not mean that antenatal publicity and people's participation are absent in Britain. These are provided as a matter of unavoidable administrative necessity. It is correct to say that today it is almost unthinkable that the Minister of Health can run the National Health Service through his rule-making power without consulting the medical profession. Britain, therefore, abandoned its attempt to judicialise rule-making the same year as the USA enacted the Administrative Procedure Act, 1946 which laid down an ambitious programme of public participation.

3.9.2 CONSULTATION WITH AFFECTED PERSONS

This control mechanism makes administrative rule-making a democratic process and, therefore, increases its acceptability and effectivity. In Pakistan and India there is no general law which provides for prior consultation with affected persons before rules and regulations are framed by the administrative authorities. Therefore, the provision of prior consultation is sometimes provided in the enabling Act itself. Such a provision if contained in the enabling Act is considered as mandatory and its violation is visited with the invalidity of rules.[151] In India, the provisions for prior consultation made in the enabling Act may be grouped into five possible headings:

(I) OFFICIAL CONSULTATION WITH A NAMED BODY: Banking Companies Act in India provides for prior consultation with the Reserve Bank of India before making rules under the Act.

(II) CONSULTATION WITH ADMINISTRATIVE BOARDS: Mines Act, 1901 sets up administrative boards to advise the government and makes obligatory prior consultation with the board before the central government can make rules under the Act.

(III) CONSULTATION WITH A STATUTORY BOARD IN CHARGE OF A PARTICULAR SUBJECT: Under the Tea Board Act, the tea board has been constituted as a statutory body in charge of the whole subject of tea cultivation, development, and marketing, etc. The Act makes it obligatory to consult this Board before the government can frame rules under the Act.

(IV) CONSULTATION WITH THE INTERESTED PERSONS: Local Bodies Laws in Pakistan and India authorise the municipalities to frame rules for the imposition of tax but made it obligatory to publish draft rules through public notice in a newspaper or otherwise and to consult the inhabitants of the area likely to be affected by such a tax.

(V) PREPARATION OF RULES BY THE AFFECTED INTERESTS: In order to guarantee complete efficacy and acceptability, Mines Act empowers the owners of mines to draft rules themselves for the safety and prevention of accidents in mines and submit the draft rules to the inspector of mines. Such rules become operative on being approved by the government. In the same manner, Forward Contract (Regulation) Act, 1952 gave power to a recognised association to make draft rules and submit them to the government. The rules become effective on approval by the central government with such modifications as it may deem fit.

As mentioned earlier, in Britain the Statutory Instruments Act, 1946 does not mandate prior consultation. However, there is no less public participation in the rule-making process in England. It is provided by the administrative authority as the only workable proposition. In England public participation is provided by another technique of consulting statutory advisory agencies which are supposed to reflect public opinion and to express independent views. Therefore, Tribunals and Inquiries Act, 1958 requires prior consultation with the Council on Tribunals before procedural laws are made for tribunals and inquiries.

In the USA, Section 4 of the Administrative Procedure Act, 1946 provides only for opportunity to submit data, views or arguments. It does not provide for any oral hearing, adversary or auditive. However, it is not uncommon that in the USA, the statutes themselves provide for hearing over and above the minimum laid down in the Administrative Procedure Act, 1946. Unless the statute provides otherwise, the hearing is always informal resembling hearing before a legislative committee rather than before a court. The consultative practices include correspondence, consultations, conferences, Gallup poll techniques and public hearings auditive or adversary type. Besides these, the practice of consulting advisory committees is also widely followed. For example, under the Fair Labour Standards Act, 1938, the wage orders had to originate from the Industry Advisory Committee consisting of the employer, employees and public representatives.

3.9.3 POST-NATAL PUBLICITY

Post-natal publicity is a necessary element in the rule-making process because the dictum that ignorance of law is no excuse is based on the justification that laws are accessible to the public.

In Pakistan and India, there is no general law prescribing the mode of publication of rules; therefore, the practice of publication differs from statute to statute. In some cases, the statute lays down that the rules must be published in the official gazette but in other cases the administrative authority is left free to choose its own mode of publication. In such cases publication is necessary in any 'recognisable' or 'customary' manner.

The Supreme Court of India held in *Harla* v. *State of Rajasthan*[152] that a law cannot be enforced unless published. In this case, during the minority of the then Maharaja of Jaipur, the Council of Ministers was appointed by the Crown representative to look after the administration. The council by a resolution enacted the Jaipur Opium Act which was never published in any form. One Harla was prosecuted for the contravention of this law because he was in possession of opium in a more than permissible quantity. The court held that the rules of natural justice demand that the laws be published before they are enforced. The same position was maintained by the Supreme Court in *State of Kerala* v. *P.J. Joseph*.[153] In this case, the government of Cochin authorised the Board of Revenue to sanction extra quota of foreign liquor on payment of 2 per cent commission. The court was of the view that this authorisation does not have the force of law because the rule was never published.

Unless the rule-making authority has laid down a date on which the rules shall come into force, the rules generally come into force on the date of publication.[154] However, because of the special nature of service rules, Allahabad High Court has held in *Banarasi Das* v. *UP Government*[155] that the service rules come into operation from the date they are made. Administrative agency can give retrospectivity to their rules provided the rules are not invalid on the grounds of their retrospective operation.

In Britain, Section 3 of the Statutory Instruments Act, 1946 provides that rules should not come into force unless published. Sub-clause (2) of Section 3 further provides that in case of a prosecution for the breach of any rule, it would be a good defence to plead that the rules were not made known. Section 2(1) of the Act provides the mode of publication. It lays down that unless otherwise provided, the copies of statutory instruments of general nature must be sent to the Queen's printer to be printed, numbered, and sold to the public.

In the USA, before the passage of the Federal Register Act, 1935 there was no provision for the publication of administrative rules and regulations. However, Section 5(1) of the Federal Register Act provides that all the rules which are required to be published must be published in the Federal Register. Unless it is so published it cannot be enforced against any person except one who has actual notice of it. These provisions have been further reinforced by the Administrative Procedure Act, 1946. Section 4(c) defers effectivity of the rules by 30 days from the date of publication so that everyone has an opportunity of knowing them, unless the agency decides otherwise in public interest. After the publication of rules in the Federal Register, the rules are classified, indexed, and codified under the provisions of Section 31(a) of the Federal Register Act. In Pakistan and India there is no law providing for codification and indexing of administrative rules.

3.10 RETROSPECTIVITY

Under English law, the parliament is supreme and it can legislate on any subject to any extent. It can also make laws having retrospective effect. However, such laws are generally considered repugnant to rule of law and the parliament does not exercise this power unless there are exceptional circumstances and extreme necessity for such laws.[156] To what extent the power to make retrospective legislation is available to the executive while performing legislative function under an Act of Parliament is not very clear. There is very little authority on this issue,[157] but it is generally believed that power to make retrospective delegated legislation should not be resorted to by the executive.

In Pakistan, however, there is a constitutional prohibition against retrospective penal laws. But there is no such prohibition against other laws and subject to the constitution, legislature has plenary powers to legislate including the power to legislate with retrospective effect. Moreover, it is presumed that the procedural laws are retrospective. Similarly the curative and beneficial laws are also retrospective in their operation.

At the same time it is also well established that delegated legislation cannot operate retrospectively. The case law on the subject is quite clear and the following cases will illustrate this assertion.

In *Rehmatullah* v. *Deputy Settlement Commissioner*,[158] the Supreme Court held that a government notification under the Displaced Persons Compensation and Rehabilitation) Act could not have retrospective effect. Chief Justice Cornelius observed:[159]

> It is of course settled law that power given by a statute to act by notification . . . cannot be effectively exercised with retrospective effect, whatever the language that may be employed, and consequently the Central Government's notification of 12 September 1959, must supposed to have effect from that date and no earlier date, notwithstanding the use of words calculated to give it effect as from 8 August 1959.

Similarly, in *Sheikh Fazal Ahmad* v. *Ziaullah Khan*,[160] the Supreme Court condemned retrospective operation of rules. Registration of Claims Act, 1956, empowered the government to frame rules. Rule 6 of these rules allowed review within 90 days, but a subsequent amendment allowed review beyond 90 days, and the old orders were reviewed under the amended rule. Justice Kaikaus, relying on the *Rehmatullah* case, held that the delegated power of legislation, being a limited one, could not include retrospective law-making. He said:[161]

An obvious objection to this amendment is that it is a notification by the government in exercise of the power of subordinate legislation and such power does not include a power to give retrospective effect. The power of subordinate legislation which is exercised by the executive is a very limited power . . . the subordinate legislative power is to be permitted only to the extent to which it is necessary for the proper exercise of its function by the legislature and a power to legislate with retrospective effect has never been accepted as included in a power of subordinate legislation.

These two cases laid the foundation of the rule prohibiting retrospective delegated legislation in Pakistan. In subsequent cases, courts felt no hesitation in striking down such legislation; for example in *Mardan Industries Ltd* v. *Government of Pakistan*,[162] where the petitioners were granted a four-year complete exemption from excise duty as an incentive for setting up industry in special areas, but when the industry went into production the government withdrew the exemption by a subsequent notification. The Peshawar High Court accepted the constitutional petition challenging the legality of the action by holding that the subordinate delegated legislation was under a constitutional disability to make notification which was retrospective in operation so as to take away or impair vested rights. In a similar case before the Supreme Court, Justice Yaqub Ali cited the *Mardan Industries* case with approval and held invalid a notification having retrospective effect.[163]

Section 19(1) of Business Profit Tax Act, 1947, authorised the application of provisions of Section 34 of the Income Tax Act and under this authority the Central Board of Revenue by a notification of 4 July 1958, adopted Section 34 with effect from 1 April 1957. On these facts the Karachi High Court,[164] on a reference from Income Tax Appellate Tribunal, held that the subordinate delegated authority could not give retrospective effect to a notification. Similarly, the Lahore High Court in *Abdul Majid* v. *Chief Administrator Auqaf*[165] declared a notification having retrospective effect as invalid. The court held that retrospectivity is the work of legislature and an administrator has no legislative powers to give retrospective effect to the notification.

Thus, the doctrine of prohibition against retrospective delegated legislation has become well established in the legal system of Pakistan. In 1974, for example, the Supreme Court decided three cases on the basis of prohibition against retrospective delegated legislation.[166] And to the same effect are some other cases decided thereafter.[167]

However, legislature is competent to make retrospective laws and can also delegate the power to legislate with retrospective effect. For example, in *Corning Glass (Pakistan) Ltd* v. *Karachi Gas Supply Co.*,[168] the Karachi High Court observed that unless authorised by statute, the delegated legislation cannot take effect retrospectively. Similarly, Justice Zafar Hussain Mirza, in another case, at the Sindh High Court,[169] held that 'in the absence of some power in the statute' an authority exercising delegated power to legislate cannot effect rights or create liabilities retrospectively. In *Muhammad Ismail* v. *Province of Punjab*,[170] the Lahore High Court expressly declared that delegated power of legislation can be used retrospectively if the parent Act authorises such legislation. This was a case under Canal and Drainage Act, 1873.[171] Section 75 of the Act which was amended in 1965 provided that the government could make rules charging water rates with retrospective effect. Under this authority the government issued a notification on 1 December 1966 and declared the enhanced water charges to be leviable from Kharif 1962, and Justice Dr Nasim Hasan Shah felt no hesitation in upholding the impugned notification.

Apart from express authority to make retrospective delegated legislation, there were a few pre-Independence cases in which retrospective operation of exemptions under pre-emption law had been held valid on implied authority of the Act. The Supreme Court[172] has also held such exemptions valid for similar reasons. Apart from the implied authority of the Act, such cases can be justified on the grounds that as pre-emption law places restrictions on the valuable rights of property, the exemption clauses be given liberal interpretation. Also, the Privy Council ruling in the *Barran* case held the exemption as conditional legislation to which the restriction of delegated legislation would not be applicable.

To sum up, delegated legislation cannot have retrospective effect unless authorised by the parent Act.

3.11 SUB-DELEGATION

Under English law there is presumption of statutory interpretation, based on the principle *delegatus non portest delegare*, that when a statute delegates the legislative function to a particular authority, that function should be exercised by the authority itself and should not be further delegated. This rule appears to be based on public policy, otherwise there will be no end to further delegation, i.e. sub-delegation, further sub-delegation, and so on. Since it is simply a presumption, it operates subject to the statutory provisions and if the statute authorises the sub-delegation in that case it will not be invalid.[173] During World War I, the power to make defence regulations was freely sub-delegated without express authority of the Defence Act, but surprisingly the validity of such delegation was never challenged. However, during World War II the Emergency Powers (Defence) Act, 1939, expressly gave such powers to the executive, which extensively used it during the war.

The Pakistani courts have generally followed these principles of English law. The maxim *'delegatus non protest delegare'* has been applied by the courts in the field of delegated legislation. In *Anwar Ali* v. *Fayaz Ali*,[174] a division bench of the Lahore High Court dealt with the question of sub-delegation of legislative authority. The Road Transport Board Rules, 1957, without express sanction of the parent Act, authorised the board to frame certain regulations. The action taken under these regulations was challenged on the grounds that the rules could not authorise the board to make the regulations. Justice Faizullah who delivered the judgment of the bench accepted the dictum of Justice B.Z. Kaikaus in an unreported case of 1957 in which it was observed:[175]

> It is an accepted principle that there can be no further delegation of the legislative power which is granted to executive authorities. It is legitimate for legislature, after providing the framework, to leave details

to be filled in by executive, but of this power which is confined within well known limits there can be no further delegation.

Similarly, in the case of *Muhammad Sharif* v. *Secretary to the Government of Punjab*,[176] the Supreme Court refused to recognize the statutory status of regulation made by the college governing council created by administrator of a municipal committee who delegated to the council certain powers relating to appointment, promotion, and removal etc. of the college employees. Justice Anwarul Haq expressed in these words:[177]

> The power to frame rules under the Act, is vested by Section 240, in the Provincial Government. Clause (n) of sub-section (I) of this section deals with the subject of employment, punishment, suspension or removal of officers and servants of the committee. It is clear that this rule-making power cannot be delegated to any sub-committee or the College Governing Council. . . .

As discussed above the prohibition against sub-delegation is based on the rule of statutory construction. Therefore, legislature is competent to provide for sub-delegation and, in cases where it is done so, the validity of such delegation cannot be successfully challenged in the courts. The Defence of India Act, 1939, provided a classic example of sub-delegation. The Act empowered the central government to make Defence of India rules. The Act further provided that the rules could empower the central government and the provincial governments to make orders, which could further confer the rule-making powers on the administrative agencies.[178]

The Defence of Pakistan Ordinance, 1965, also provides a clear example. Section 3(1) of the Ordinance empowered the central government to make rules under the ordinance. Section 3(4) authorised the central government to delegate its powers to its subordinate officers, a provincial government or their subordinate officers and Section 3(5) authorised a provincial government to sub-delegate the powers delegated to it by the central government. Under this ordinance, the central government framed Defence of Pakistan Rules, 1965. Under Rule 131 of these Rules, the Essential

Commodities Control Order, 1965, was issued and Section 24 of the Order provided for making of further rules.[179]

Apart from the emergency laws, sub-delegation has not been resorted to in any statute though some statutes authorise different categories of delegation of legislative powers at different administrative levels. For example, the Punjab University Act, 1973, provides for statutes to be made by the University Senate (Section 31), the regulations to be made by the syndicate on the recommendation of the Academic Council (Section 32), and rules to be framed by various authorities.

3.12 PUBLICATION OF DELEGATED LEGISLATION

In Britain, the Statutory Instruments Act of 1946 provides for publication, printing, and sale of copies of statutory instruments. Until 1890, delegated legislation was almost undiscoverable. It was partly buried in the London Gazette and partly scattered over the parliamentary papers and other departmental documents and files without any system whatsoever. The Rules Publication Act, 1893, established a system of registration and publication of statutory rules and orders. Section 2 of the Statutory Instruments Act, 1946, retaining Section 3 of the Rules Publication Act, 1893, which provides that immediately after a statutory rule has been made it should be sent to the Queen's printer to be numbered in accordance with the regulations made under the Act and except for the causes provided in such regulation, copies of it are to be printed and sold by the Queen's printer. The regulations require the government department which sends an instrument to certify that such instrument is general or local according to its subject matter. The stationery office is required to publish from time to time a 'Statutory Instruments Issue List' showing the serial number and short title of each statutory instrument and the date of the first issue by that office. At the end of each calendar year, the stationery office publishes an annual volume containing the text of the general regulations. The contents of the annual volume are arranged subject-wise in alphabetical sequence with an index and a classified list of local instruments. An index called 'Guide to Government Orders' is published at the end of every third year. According to Section 3(2) of the Statutory Instruments Act, in any proceedings against any person for an offence under a statutory instrument, it will be a good defence that the instrument had not been issued by the stationery office at the date of the alleged offence unless it is proved that on that date reasonable steps had been taken for the purpose of bringing the purport of the statutory instrument to the notice of the persons likely to be affected by it.

In the USA, provisions for publication of rules have been made in the Federal Register Act, 1935. It establishes the Federal Register and provides for daily publication of all documents having general applicability and legal effect and prescribes a penalty. It expressly provides that no document required to be published under the Act shall be valid as against any person who has not had actual knowledge thereof 'until it has actually been filed for publication'.

In Pakistan and India, there is no general statutory provision requiring publication of delegated legislation. The Indian Supreme Court, however, held that the enforcement of the rules which had not been published was against the rules of natural justice.[180] A statute delegating legislative power usually requires that the rules be made by notification in the official gazette.

Although in practice the publication of delegated legislation in Pakistan and India is secured through provisions in the enabling Acts requiring such publication. There is no system of bringing out annual compilations of general rules or orders. The public has no easy means of knowing whether a statutory power of making rules and orders under a particular Act has been exercised, and if so, when such rules were made and where they can be found. The absence of a proper index or guide adds to the existing difficulties. The Committee on Subordinate Legislation, appointed by the Lok Sabha made the following suggestions: (a) that the government should ensure that their notifications containing particular constitutional and statutory rules and orders were published in proper parts and sections of the gazette; (b) that a yearly consolidated index be issued; (c) that a monthly index be prepared covering all notifications published in any part and section of the gazette; (d) that notifications regarding rules in each part and section of the gazette be centrally numbered from year to year with a distinctive prefix; and (e) a notification regarding rules should be referred to by the central number and year of its publication.

As a consequence of these suggestions, the Government of India has evolved the following scheme of publication of rules with effect from 1 March 1958.[181] Statutory rules and orders are serially numbered into their separate groups each with a distinctive prefix. Statutory rules and orders of a general character issued by the ministries of the central government (other than the Ministry of Defence) and by central authorities (other than the Union Territories Administration) are prefixed as GSR, are numbered serially and are published in Part II, Section 3, Sub-section (i) of the Gazette of India. Ordinary issues of this part of the gazette are published every Saturday; extraordinary parts are published as and when the need arises. Those which are not of a general character are published in Part II, Section 3, Sub-section (ii), are prefixed as SO, and are numbered centrally and separately. Statutory rules and orders issued by the Ministry of Defence are prefixed as SROs, and numbered separately, serially and centrally and are contained in Part II, Section 4 of the Gazette of India. Rules and orders made by other officers or authorities are contained in other parts of the gazette. Each of them is an annual series.

3.13 SUB-DELEGATION AND ITS PUBLICATION

Although the maxim '*delegata portestas non portest delegari*' does not apply to delegation of legislative power by the legislature, it does apply to the subordinate law-making authorities. Thus in *Ganpati Singhji* v. *State of Ajmer*,[182] certain statutory rules were held invalid because they sought to sub-delegate legislative power. Such sub-delegation was not expressly authorised by the enabling Acts and hence these rules were held *ultra vires* the enabling Act.

This is, therefore, an additional ground for questioning the validity of subordinate legislation.

A problem has arisen regarding the publication of sub-delegated legislation such as orders, directions, etc. to be issued by administrative officers. Non-compliance with such orders or directions sometimes is punishable. The statutes, however, provide no procedure for the publication of such legislation. In Britain, it was held in *Blackpool Corporation* v. *Locker*[183] that the provision requiring publication is not applicable to sub-delegated legislation and that there is no statutory or common law duty on the minister to publish the same. This is a great lacuna. The Indian Committee on Subordinate Legislation has suggested that the rules should specifically lay down a procedure for bringing such sub-delegated legislation to the notice of the persons concerned. In *Narendra Kumar* v. *Union of India*,[184] the Supreme Court observed that the publication of sub-delegated legislation is necessary to give it legal force when the parent statute contains a provision requiring a notification of the rules in the official gazette.

Notes

1. M.P. Jain and S.N. Jain, *Principles of Administrative Law* (3rd edn., 1979) 22–23.
2. Salmond, *Jurisprudence* (9th edn.) 210.
3. The Indian Mines and Minerals Act, 1957. Section 13 gives rule-making power to the central government and Section 15 gives a similar power to the state government.
4. Allen, *Law and Order* (3rd edn., 1965) 192.
5. *Raman and Raman* v. *State of Madras*, AIR 1959 SC 694.
6. *Muhammad Faruk* v. *State of UP*, AIR 1970 SC 93.
7. *Khalid Mahmood* v. *NWFP*, PLD 2011 Peshawar 120.
8. From the judgment of Krishna Iyer, J, in *Avinder Singh* v. *State of Punjab* [1979] 1 SCC 137, 147.
9. *Avinder Singh* v. *State of Punjab* [1979] 1 SCC 137.
10. Ibid., p. 147.
11. *Zarai Taraqiati Bank* v. *Said Rehman*, 2013 SCMR 642.
12. Dr Dil Muhammad, 'Delegated Legislation', PLJ 1993 Magazine 151, 154.
13. Ibid.

14. A.B. Keith, *A Constitutional History of India, 1600–1935* (Allahabad: Central Book Depot, 1937) 133–5.
15. Supra Note 10, pp. 154–5.
16. *Queen* v. *Burah* [1878] 5IA 178.
17. S.P. Sathe, *Administrative Law* (2nd edn., Bombay: N.M. Tripathi Pvt Ltd, 1974) 62–63.
18. Supra Note 10, p. 157.
19. *Pakistan* v. *Sh. Abdul Hamid*, PLD 1961 SC 105.
20. A few cases have given contrary decisions primarily on peculiar circumstances of these cases, e.g. *Government of West Pakistan* v. *Nasor M. Khan*, PLD 1965 SC 106; *Mohammad Amin Durrani* v. *Government of West Pakistan*, PLD 1966 SC 99; and *Wali Mohammad* v. *Secretary, Home Department*, PLD 1972 Quetta 33.
21. *Pakistan* v. *Sh. Abdul Hamid*, PLD 1961 SC 105. See also *Faizullah Khan* v. *Pakistan*, PLD 1974 SC 291.
22. *Musud Alunad* v. *Pakistan*, PLD 1976 SC 1951.
23. *Province of West Pakistan* v. *Din Mohammad*, PLD 1964 SC 21. See also *Mukhrar Ahmed* v. *Government of West Pakistan*, PLD 1971 SC 846 and *Muhammad Yusaf Chauhan* v. *Salim Khan*, PLJ 1991 SC 350.
24. *Pakistan* v. *Abdul Ghani*, PLD 1964 SC 68.
25. *Government of West Pakistan* v. *A.A. Aziz*, PLD 1966 SC 188.
26. *Habib ur Rahman* v. *West Public Service Commission*, PLD 1973 SC 144.
27. *Faizullah* v. *Government of Pakistan*, PLD 1974 SC 291.
28. *Abdul Rab* v. *Wall Muhammad* [1980] SCMR 139 and *Muhammad Asghar* v. *Sofia Begum*, PLD 1976 SC 480.
29. See *Muhammad Ashraf* v. *Board of Revenue, West Pakistan*, PLD 1968 Lah. 1155; *Ali Muhammad* v. *Province of West Pakistan*, PLD 1969 Lah. 951; *Mehrab Khan* v. *Taj Muhammad*, PLD 1961 Quetta 1; and *Ali Jan* v. *Commissioner FCR*, PLD 1970 Quetta 93.
30. *Ardeshar Cowasjee* v. *Multiple Associates*, PLD 1993 Kar. 237.
31. [1892] 143 US 649.
32. I.P. Massey, *Administrative Law* (Lucknow: Eastern Book Company, 1980) 70–73.
33. *Venkateswaraloo* v. *Superintendent of Central Jail*, AIR 1953 SC 49.
34. Massy, Supra Note 30, pp. 73–4.
35. Ibid., pp. 74–5.
36. Horst P. Ehmke, '*Delegata Potestas Nor Potest Delegari*: A maxim of American Constitutional Law' [1961] 47 Cornell LQ 50; Jaffe, 'An Essay on Delegation of Legislative Power' [1947] 47 Col. LR 359.
37. *Panama Refining Co.* v. *Ryan* [1935] 293 US 388, 434. It is known popularly as the Hot Oil case.
38. Ibid.
39. [1944] 321 US 414.

40. Besides Panama, two other cases are *Schechter* v. *US* [1935] 295 US 495 and *Carter* v. *Carter Coal Co.* [1936] 298 US 238.

41. Davis, *Administrative Law* (1951) 54. Also Jaffe, 'An Essay on Delegation of Legislative Power' [1947] 47 Col. LR 359; *Lichter* v. *US* [1948] 334 US 742.

42. AIR 1949 FC 175.

43. *Khalid Mahmood v. NWFP*, PLD 2011 Peshawar 120.

44. AIR 1951 SC 332.

45. Jain and Jain, Supra Note 1.

46. AIR 1970 SC 1453.

47. AIR 1945 PC 1.

48. AIR 1943 FC 1.

49. *Jayantilal* v. *Union of India*, AIR 1970 Gujrat 108.

50. AIR 1962 SC 97.

51. *Yasin* v. *Town Area Committee* [1952] SCR 572.

52. *Lokmanya Mills* v. *Barsi Borough Municipality*, AIR 1961 SC 1358.

53. *Gordhandas* v. *Municipal Commissioner*, AIR 1963 SC 1742.

54. *M.L. Bagga* v. *Murhar Rao*, AIR 1956, Hyd. 35; *Shivdeo Singh* v. *State of Punjab*, AIR 1959 Punjab 453.

55. *Harichandra* v. *State of MP*, AIR 1965 SC 932.

56. [1920] 1 KB 829.

57. *Bimal Chandra Banerjee* v. *State of MP*, AIR 1971 SC 517.

58. *Himmatlal* v. *Police Commissioner, Ahmedabad*, AIR 1973 SC 87.

59. *K.C. Nambiar* v. *IV Judge of the High Court of Small Causes, Madras* [1970] 2 SCJ 23.

60. *Income Tax Officer, Alleppey* v. *M.C. Ponnoose*, AIR 1970 SC 385; *The Cannanore Spg. & Wvg. Mills* v. *Custom Collector*, AIR 1970 SC 1950.

61. *T.K. Musaliar* v. *Venkatachalam*, AIR 1956 SC 246.

62. *Mohd. Ghouse* v. *Andhra State*, AIR 1957 SC 246.

63. *Re New Sind*, AIR 1942 Sind 65.

64. *United Industries Bank Ltd* v. *Mohan Bashi Shaha*, PLD 1959 SCX 296.

65. *KBCA* v. *Hashwani Sales & Services Ltd*, PLD 1993 SC 210 and *Nek Muhammad* v. *Government of Punjab*, PLD 1990 SC 672.

66. *Government of Pakistan* v. *Sajjad Haider Syed*, PLJ 1990 SC 331.

67. *Saphira Textile Mills Ltd* v. *Government of Sind*, PLD 1990 Kar. 402; PLD 1965 Lah. 77.

68. *Ahmad Hassan* v. *Government Punjab*, 2005 SCMR 186.

69. *Independent Newspapers Corporation (Pvt.) Ltd.* v. *Federation of Pakistan*, PLD 2017 Lahore 289.

70. PLD 1965 Lah. 77.

71. PLD 1965 Pesh. 245.

72. PLD 1964 SC 461.

73. 245 *Joti Parshad* v. *Emperor*, AIR 1924 Lah. 134.

74. *Hashwani Sales & Services Ltd* v. *Karachi Building Control Authority*, PLD 1986 Kar. 393.

75. PLD 1972 Kar. 145.

76. PLJ 1982 SC 295.

77. *Ahmad Abbas Zaidi* v. *Settlement Commissioner*, PLD 1968 Lah. 166.

78. *Chairman Railway Board* v. *Wahabuddin & Sons*, PLD 1990 SC 1034; *Meharban Khan* v. *Fayyaz Begum*, PLJ 1984 Lah. 227.

79. *Abdul Kafil* v. *Faqir*, PLD 1962 Pesh. 51.

80. *Hashmatullah* v. *K.M. Corporation*, PLD 1971, Kar. 514.

81. See *Nizam Impex* v. *Govt. of Pakistan*, PLD 1990 Kar. 208 (Even a subsequent amendment in the Act could not cure the inconsistency.)

82. *Bashir Ahmad* v. *State*, PLD 1971 Pesh. 226.

83. *Khalid Mahmood v. NWFP*, PLD 2011 Peshawar 120.

84. *Municipal Committee Bannu* v. *Muhammad Khan*, PLJ 1982 Pesh. 7.

85. *A. Moghni* v. *Registrar Cooperatie Society*, PLD 1957 Kar. 184.

86. *Ghulam Sarwar* v. *M.C. Sukkur*, PLD 1993 Kar. 415 and *Ardeshar Cowasjee* v. *Multiline Associates*, PLD 1993 Kar. 237.

87. *Karachi Building Control Authority* v. *Hashwani Sales & Services Ltd*, PLD 1993 SC 210.

88. AIR 1946 Bom. 266.

89. AIR 1967 SC 1801.

90. AIR 1951 SC 118.

91. AIR 1960 SC 430.

92. AIR 1954 SC 224.

93. *Rashid Ahmed* v. *Municipal Board, Kairana*, AIR 1950 SC 163.

94. *Kharak Singh* v. *State of UP*, AIR 1963 SC 1295.

95. *O.K. Ghosh* v. *E.X. Joseph*, AIR 1963 SC 812.

96. AIR 1967 SC 1801.

97. *Labh Chandra* v. *State*, AIR 1969 Pat. 209.

98. *G. Venkataratnam* v. *Principal, Osmania M.C.*, AIR 1969 AP 35.

99. *R.S. Singh* v. *Darbhanga Medical College*, AIR 1969 Pat. 11.

100. *Sparks* v. *Edward Ash. Ltd* [1943] KB 223; *Taylor* v. *Brighton Borough Council* [1947] KB 736; [1947] 1 All ER 864.

101. *Kruse* v. *Johnson* [1898] 2 QB 91 at 99–100.

102. Schwartz, *Introduction to American Administrative Law* (1958) 73–74.

103. *Bhushanlal* v. *State*, AIR 1952 All 866, 870–71; *IE Newspapers (Bombay) P. Ltd India*, AIR 1986 SC 540.

104. *Mulchand* v. *Mukund*, AIR 1952 Bom. 296; *Subbarao* v. *IT Commr*, AIR 1952 Mad. 127; *Sophy Kelly* v. *State of Maharashtra* [1967] LR 186, Bom. 69.

105. [1898] 2 QB 91, 99–100.

106. *Sydney Municipal Council* v. *Campbell* [1925] AC 338.

107. *Province of East Pakistan* v. *Sirajul Haq Patwari*, PLD 1966 SC 854, 952.

108. [1965] AC 75.

109. H.W.R. Wade, *Administrative Law* (5th edn.) 750.
110. Cushman, *Cases in Constitutional Law*, 62.
111. *Wayman* v. *Southard* [1825] 10 Wheat 1, 43.
112. [1935] 295 US 495.
113. [1935] 293 US 388.
114. *United States* v. *Chicago* [1935] 282 US 311, 324.
115. *United States* v. *Shrevport Grain & Elevator Co.* [1932] 287 US 77, 85.
116. [1944] 321 US 414.
117. See Davis, *Treatise on Administrative Law* (1958) 100.
118. [1948] 334 US 742.
119. [1943] 319 US 190.
120. [1975] 419 US 544.
121. [1976] 426 US 548.
122. See *National Cable Television Assn.* v. *US*, 415 US 415.
123. Schwartz and Wade, *Legal Control of Government*, 87.
124. AIR 1944 Lah. 33 (FB).
125. PLD 1952 PC 29.
126. PLD 1958 SC (Pak) 41.
127. PLD 1961 SC 178.
128. On p. 185.
129. PLD 1966 SC 388
130. PLD 1965 Dacca 156.
131. *Sirajul Haq Patwari* v. *Sub-Divisional Magistrate*, PLD 1966 SC 854.
132. *Province of East Pakistan* v. *Sirajul Haq Patwari*, PLD 1966 SC 854.
133. PLD 1967 SC 373.
134. Ordinance XXIII of 1965.
135. At p. 387.
136. PLJ 1977 SC 147.
137. PLD 1971 Kar. 333.
138. At p. 459.
139. *Zaibtun Textile Mills* v. *CBR*, PLD 1983 SC 358.
140. At p. 379.
141. *Federation of Pakistan*, PLJ 1988 SC 493 at p. 500, per Muhammad Haleem, CJ.
142. *Avinder Singh* v. *State of Punjab* [1979] 1 SCC 137.
143. Schwartz, 'Legislative Control of Administrative Rules and Regulations: The American Experience', 30 New York University Law Review, 1031.
144. Ibid., p. 1036.
145. Sections 5–7.
146. AIR 1960 SC 430.
147. AIR 1966 SC 385.
148. [1972] 2 SCC 601.
149. [1979] 2 SCC 196.
150. I.P. Massey, Supra Note 30, pp. 96–7.

151. *Banwarilal Agarwalla* v. *State of Bihar*, AIR 1961 SC 849.
152. AIR 1951 SC 467.
153. AIR 1958 SC 296. See also *Narendra Kumar* v. *Union of India*, AIR 1960 SC 430.
154. *State of Maharashtra* v. *George*, AIR 1965 SC 722; *Bakul Cashen Co.* v. *S.T. Officer Quilon*, AIR 1987 SC 2243.
155. AIR 1959 All. 393.
156. War Damages Act, 1965, is the only recent example of retrospective law made by the British Parliament.
157. H.W.R. Wade, *Administrative Law* (5th edn.) 751.
158. PLD 1963 SC 633.
159. At p. 644.
160. PLD 1964 SC 494. See also *Muhammad Ismail* v. *Chief Cotton Inspector*, PLD 1968 SC 388 and *Government of West Pakistan* v. *Nasir M. Khan*, PLD 1965 SC 106.
161. At p. 501.
162. PLD 1965 Pesh. 47.
163. *Collector of Central Excise & Land Customs* v. *Azizuddin Industries Ltd*, PLD 1970 SC 439.
164. *Commissioner of Income Tax* v. *Adamjee*, PLD 1967 Kar. 194.
165. PLD 1972 Lah. 66.
166. *Faizullah Khan* v. *Government of Pakistan*, PLD 1974 SC 291; *Kohinoor Textile Mills Ltd* v. *Commissioner of Income Tax*, PLD 1974 SC 284 and *Commissioner of Income Tax* v. *Kruddsons Ltd*, PLD 1974 SC 180.
167. *Nizamuddin Yahya* v. *Addl. Chief Land Commissioner*, PLD 1987 SC 260; *Shahnaz Maqbool* v. *Province of Sind*, PLD 1979 SC 32; *Dawood Yamaha* v. *Government of Pakistan*, PLD 1986 Quetta 148; and *Faisal Spinning Mills* v. *State Bank of Pakistan*, PLD 1993 Kar. 360.
168. PLD 1977 Kar. 1068.
169. *Muhammad Bashir Butt* v. *Taheri*, PLD 1980 Kar. 458.
170. PLD 1977 Lah. 226.
171. Act VIII of 1873.
172. *Bibi Jan* v. *R.A. Monny*, PLD 1961 SC 69.
173. *Vine* v. *National Dock Labour Board* [1957] AC 488.
174. PLD 1962 Lah. 483.
175. Cited in PLD 1962 Lah. 493 at 489.
176. PLJ 1973 SC 132.
177. At p. 138.
178. See Ramachandran, *Administrative Law* (2nd edn.) 74.
179. Similar legislative measures were also taken during the 1971 war.
180. *Harla* v. *Rajasthan*, AIR 1951 SC 467.
181. S.P. Sathe, *Administrative Law*, Supra Note 15, pp. 99–100.
182. AIR 1955 SC 188.
183. [1948] KB 349.
184. AIR 1960 SC 430.

CHAPTER IV

Administrative Adjudication and Discretion

4.1 REASONS FOR GROWTH OF ADMINISTRATIVE ADJUDICATION

A significant aspect of the expansion of functions of administration in the modern era is the power of adjudication by administrative authorities. Normally, the function of adjudicating upon disputes between two individuals or between the state and an individual is vested in the court, but it would be wrong to suppose that the courts enjoy a monopoly of the entire business of adjudication. Side by side with the courts, innumerable administrative bodies have sprung up to carry on the function of adjudication in a variety of situations, claims, and controversies. Sometimes the task of adjudication is merely incidental to administration; at other times it is more than incidental and it begins to assume a very close resemblance with the work usually assigned to the judiciary. This tendency or practice of vesting adjudicatory functions in persons, bodies or institutions outside the ordinary hierarchy of regular law courts is becoming increasingly pronounced with the passage of time. This development has not yet exhausted its momentum; every day some new adjudicatory body is created for one purpose or the other, and therefore the system of adjudication by-bodies outside the system of courts is becoming more and more important and pervasive with the lapse of time. The trend has been manifesting itself in Britain, the United States, and practically in every democratic country.

The main causes of evolution of the system of adjudication outside the courts are practically the same as have led to the emergence of delegated legislation, i.e. extension in governmental operations, activities, and responsibilities because of the socio-economic changes which are taking place in the country. For example, the government is engaging itself progressively more and more in planning, in providing social services to the people, in controlling the conditions of employment, and in providing and promoting health, safety and general welfare of the community. Along with the expansion in governmental operations, the tax base has also been broadened resulting in the levy of new taxes and, consequently, leading to a vast proliferation of tax assessing authorities. The modern government has come to undertake many functions and regulate many matters which generate a number of occasions when an individual may be at issue with the administration, or with another citizen or body as to his rights, and this creates the need to adjudicate on disputes sometimes between citizens and the government, and sometimes between one citizen and another. This, in turn, has necessitated the development of the techniques of administrative adjudication which may better respond to social needs and requirements than the elaborate and costly system of decisions through court litigation. If all the cases generated by the operations of the newly enacted socio-economic legislation of today were to be left to the courts for adjudication, then not only will it place a huge burden on the judicial machinery clogging it beyond redemption, but it will also slow down the administrative process because of long delays which usually occur in the court proceedings. The courts are already faced with a huge backlog of cases, and further entrusting to them the task of adjudicating upon the many newly arising controversies as a result of the expansion of the operations of the state would make matters worse. It is proverbial that an ordinary judicial proceeding is tardy, dilatory as well as expensive and, consequently, in most of the cases arising in the course of administrative functioning such a procedure would be completely inadequate. The formality of atmosphere in a court is not always conducive to the quick disposal of the innumerable problems which modern administration generates. In many cases, what is needed is an informality of atmosphere untrammelled by too elaborate and technical rules of procedure or evidence. Effective implementation of new policies often demands speedy, cheap, and decentralised determination of a large number of cases—advantages which are offered by administrative adjudication.

Another important reason for the new development is that while the courts are accustomed to deal with cases primarily according to law, the exigencies of modern administration often make it incumbent that some types of controversies be disposed of by applying not the law, pure and simple. But by applying considerations of policy as well; for example, what may be in the 'public interest', 'expedient', or 'reasonable'. Such questions often arise and these have to be answered not only on the basis of law and fact but also by applying policy considerations—factors such as position of finance, position of foreign exchange, priorities and allocations between competing claims, and the like. It is only adjudication outside the ordinary judicial system which can take care of such matters.[1] An ordinary court is hardly a fit instrument for such an exercise. The judges often tend to be too literal or technical in their interpretation of legislation and such an approach may not be suitable to most of the modern socio-economic legislation which is of an experimental nature. All this leads to entrusting the task of determining disputes under such legislation to bodies (other than the ordinary courts) which can have flexibility of approach.

Then, there is also the question of expertise. A judge is a generalist, while many cases arising out of the modern administrative process need an expert knowledge of particular subjects to which these cases relate. An expert may be in a better position to adjudicate upon such matters than a generalist lawyer or judge in a regular court. Thus, technical problems or questions involving complicated accountancy or economic factors may have to be better left to be determined by specialised adjudicatory bodies than the judges of the courts who, by their training and approach, may not have enough expertise to deal with them. Perhaps because of the lack of such expert knowledge, the Indian Supreme Court in *Collector of Customs* v. *Ganga Setty*[2] was prompted to give due deference to the executive determination holding that it would interfere only where the executive adopted an interpretation which no reasonable person could adopt or which was clearly perverse.

Some of the reasons, therefore, for entrusting adjudication of certain administrative matters by the legislature to bodies other than the courts are less expensive, have greater accessibility, are more expeditious, providing expertise, freedom from technicalities, flexibility of approach, etc. These adjudicatory bodies have grown not to satisfy any political dogma or philosophy, but out of practical necessity to cope with certain problems of public concern. For example, the Income Tax Appellate Tribunal provides expeditious and, relatively at a lesser cost, justice to the income taxpayers as compared with the dilatory and expensive relief obtainable through a regular court system. The tribunal works in an informal atmosphere, is not bound by technical rules of evidence and is free from procedural rigidities. Because of its composition and specialisation in income tax cases, it possesses the necessary expertise to deal with complicated questions of tax laws and accountancy. Administrative adjudication is mostly done by informal process. In a case, written representations by the parties to administrative adjudication were considered sufficient compliance with the principles of natural justice.[3]

On the other hand, too much emphasis on administrative justice has its own dangers. There is a great value in an independent judiciary administering law in an open court. There cannot be the same degree of independence in the case of a member of an administrative body. The judge has a legal training, decides cases according to accepted tenets of law, gives reasons for his decisions, follows precedents and publishes his decisions. There is a cross-examination of witnesses and legal representation of the litigants in a court of law. These important features of the legal system are not all to be found in the system of administrative adjudication.

4.2 Problems of Administrative Adjudication

Administrative justice has given rise to controversies in Pakistan and India. While people are not alarmed when the administration is given law-making powers, certainly many people feel disturbed when it is given adjudicatory powers. People doubt the independence of administrators as judges and also fear their anti-legal approach. However, a few common problems with which the whole administrative adjudicatory process suffers may be discussed as under.

i) Number of administrative agencies and their complexities

Administrative agencies with adjudicatory powers have mushroomed. Since 1947, these agencies have proliferated so much that an attempt even to prepare a comprehensive list seems impossible. Every statutory scheme contains its own machinery for decision-making. A large number of parallel bodies adjudicating on the same kind of disputes and giving diverse decisions are no exceptions. This complicates the task of administrative law in drawing uniform principles for uniform application. Therefore, the need to reorganise this formidable number into a system with fewer units cannot be overemphasised.

ii) Variety of procedures adopted

As the administrative agencies are proliferating, so is their procedure. Even the best of the lawyers cannot say with certainty how he would proceed before a particular agency. Sometimes the procedure is laid down in the Act under which the agency is constituted. Sometimes the agency is left free to develop its own procedure. Sometimes the agency is invested with the powers of a civil court in matters of compelling attendance and production of documents. But in a great number of cases the agency is required to follow only the minimum procedure of the principles of natural justice. Since such principles are not rigid and do not apply uniformly in all situations; the consequent uncertainty results at times in arbitrary actions. In the interests of justice and liberty, insistence on procedural regularity is essential. In the USA and Britain, a fair amount of certainty, though limited, has been achieved by the Administrative Procedure Act, 1946 and Tribunals and Enquiries Act, 1958 respectively. In Pakistan and India, no such attempt has been made so far though it is overdue. However, the Supreme Court of Pakistan held that statutory functionary exercising administrative powers must conform to the steps and methods prescribed in the Act.[4]

iii) Unsystematic appeal system

An appeal is a definite safeguard against an unfair decision in the administration of justice. However, no uniform system of appeals has been followed in administrative adjudications. Sometimes administrative decisions are made appealable before an independent tribunal as in tax cases and sometimes appeal is provided before higher administrative agency.

iv) Defective decision-making process

A few statutes allow appeals on questions of law only. The period for allowing appeals also differs from agency to agency. Some Acts do not provide for any appeal and make the decision of the administrative agency final. Section 6 of the Land Acquisition Act, 1894 makes the decision of the collector regarding public purpose final. To eliminate this ad hocism in appeals from the decisions of the administrative agencies, it is necessary that at least one appeal on questions of fact be allowed before higher administrative authority and another appeal on questions of law to a court of law.

Unlike American law, English law provides the right to appeal to a law court from administrative decisions. This is done not only in the interest of justice, but also with a desire to keep the judicial system unitary. On questions of fact, as a general rule, there is no appeal, but since the courts recognise 'no evidence' and 'jurisdictional facts' as questions of law, the deficiency to a large extent is mitigated. In the USA, the decision of the hearing examiner is appealable before the agency and the decision of the agency is subject to the ordinary review powers of courts under the constitution and the Administrative Procedure Act. Some of the defects and shortcomings of the administrative decision-making process are discussed as under:

(a) Lack of publication: Unlike courts, not all the administrative agencies exercising judicial power publish their decisions. Their decisions, therefore, escape the pale of public criticism. The absence of this necessary safeguard can cause the quality of administrative justice to suffer. In some cases, even no record is prepared and justice is administered in an informal manner. It is because of this reason that in the USA the Administrative Procedure Act, 1946 insists on formal record in all administrative adjudications. In Britain, the procedure is so informal that no transcript is insisted upon to save time and expense.

(B) UNPREDICTABILITY OF DECISIONS: Judicial decisions are required to have a certain degree of predictability. On similar facts, decisions are expected to be the same because of the doctrine of precedent. Predictability of decision is an essential ingredient of the doctrine of the rule of law which insists that justice must be done through known principles. In administrative adjudication, this essential element of predictability is frequently absent. Administrative agencies exercising adjudicatory powers do not follow the doctrine of precedent; hence they are not bound to follow their own previous decisions. This ad hocism not only makes the development of law incoherent but also violates the principles of the rule of law.

(C) ANONYMITY OF DECISIONS: In administrative adjudication, though not always, decisions are made in a 'hole and the corner' fashion. No one knows from where the decision comes. One fine morning a person receives a communication that the president or a governor, as the case may be, is pleased to take such and such decision in his case. This divided responsibility wherein one person hears and another person decides the case is against the concept of fair hearing.[5]

Anonymity in decision-making or institutionalisation of decisions remains an intricate problem of administrative law. In the USA, the problem has been solved through the agency of 'hearing officers'. Under the provisions of the Administrative Procedure Act, 1946 a group of semi-independent hearing officers is maintained. They preside over cases not heard by agency's heads themselves. The appointment, tenure, and promotion of these officers are in the hands of the Civil Service Commission to make them independent from the control of any agency. At the hearing, these hearing officers exercise all the powers of a trial judge. They are required to make initial decisions after the hearing which becomes the decision of the agency unless appealed from. The entire record of the hearing is certified by the hearing officer.

In Britain, the system developed after the Tribunals and Enquiries Act, 1958 does not go to the extent of the American law. There the inspectors who are the counterparts of the American hearing officers hold enquiry and hear, but do not decide. They can only make recommendation to the minister who can either accept or reject the inspectors' recommendations. In Pakistan and India, if administrative justice is to command respectability and public confidence, some such system as has been developed in the USA and Britain is inevitable.

v) COMBINATION OF EXECUTIVE AND JUDICIAL FUNCTIONS

In India, except in the case of civil servants, in all disciplinary proceedings the functions of a prosecutor and the judge are either combined in one person or in the same department. In such a situation bias is generally inevitable.[6] In the USA and Britain the problem has been solved though not entirely by internal separation through the agency of hearing officers and Inspectors. The Administrative Procedure Act, 1946 further provides that no official with an investigative or prosecuting function can participate in the decision-making.[7]

VI) RELAXATION OF EVIDENCE REQUIREMENT

In Pakistan and India, the technical rules of the Evidence Act do not apply to administrative adjudications. The gap is filled, though inadequately, by the judge-made rule of 'no evidence'. The Indian Supreme Court explained the substance of this rule in *State of Haryana* v. *Rattan Singh*.[8] In this case, a bus of the Haryana Road Transport with Rattan Singh as conductor was taken over by the flying squad. The inspector found eleven passengers without tickets though they had paid the money for it. However, the inspector did not record the statement of those persons as required under the rules. After the formality of enquiry, the services of the conductor were terminated. All the courts up to the High Court quashed the decision on the grounds of insufficiency of evidence and violation of rule as none of the eleven witnesses was examined and the Inspector did not record the statement of witness as required by law. On appeal by the state, the Supreme Court reversed the decision and held that the simple point in the case was whether there was some evidence or not—not in the technical sense governing the regular court proceedings but in a common sense way as a man of understanding and worldly wisdom would accept. Viewed from this angle, sufficiency of evidence in proof of findings of a domestic tribunal is beyond scrutiny. The evidence of the Inspector was held to be some evidence and the decisions of the courts below were reversed.

The end result of the decision is that in an administrative adjudication if there is some evidence in some corner of the record, the decision is valid no matter it may not be any evidence at all in accordance with the accepted norms of a judicial decision. *Nand Kishore Prasad* v. *State of Bihar*[9] highlights the problem. In this case, the appellant was a clerk in the district magistrate's office. He was prosecuted before a criminal court for embezzling a certain amount, but was acquitted. Thereafter, disciplinary administrative proceedings were initiated against him and the appellant was found guilty, and hence removed from service. Upholding the decision of the administrative authority in a writ proceeding, the Supreme Court held that this was not a case of 'no evidence' but of evidence which was inadequate to carry a conviction in a criminal court. In disciplinary proceedings, however, the order passed cannot be interfered with on the grounds that the evidence would be insufficient in a criminal trial. It is true that this 'no evidence' rule result in inadequate basis for action has not earned any credibility for administrative justice. The Supreme Court of Pakistan took the view in *Maudoodi's* case[10], that in a matter of administrative nature, the courts would be entitled to intervene only when the case happens to be one of 'no evidence'. However, if the conclusions of the administration are based on some evidence, the courts would respect them.

In Britain, the courts do not disturb the findings of fact by an administrative authority unless it is based on no evidence. *Coleen Properties Ltd* v. *Minister of Housing and Local Government*[11] is an illustrative case on the point. In this case a first class building was included in a clearance order for undertaking a housing project. The Housing Act, 1957 provided that a first class building cannot be so included unless it is 'reasonably necessary' for the whole scheme. The inspector who gave the hearing recommended the exclusion of this building. The minister overruled the inspector's findings and confirmed the clearance order. The court quashed the minister's order on the grounds that there was no evidence of 'necessity' before the minister. This may prove the beginning of a shift in the approach of English Court from a literal 'no evidence' rule to more substantial 'probative evidence' rule, thus bringing the law close to the American 'substantial evidence rule'.

The American law allows wide judicial review of finding of facts by administrative authorities. Courts can re-examine the facts to find out whether there is substantial evidence to support the administrative action. But how much evidence is substantial has been a complex question of American administrative law.

Before the Administrative Procedure Act, 1946 the approach of the courts was that so much evidence as, standing alone would be sufficient to support administrative action, would be substantial.[12]

After the passing of the Administrative Procedure Act, which requires in Section 10(e) that the determination of 'substantial evidence' must be based on the whole record, two significant changes have been brought in judicial behaviour: (a) the determination of 'substantial evidence' must be made not by weighing evidence supporting the administrative action alone but after taking into consideration the evidence of the other side also; (b) the quantum of evidence necessary to constitute 'substantial' must be such that it can be accepted by any reasonable man as 'substantial'. Therefore, in *NLRB* v. *Universal Camera Corpn.*,[13] the court struck down the action of the Board on the grounds that though the action of the Board is based on some evidence, but after considering the evidence of the opposite side, no reasonable mind can accept such evidence as 'substantial'.

Beyond the above area, the evidence projections of the administrative authorities are also uncertain. However, the Indian Supreme Court, while deciding a bonus dispute in *Bareilly Electricity Supply Co.* v. *Workmen*,[14] laid down the broad evidence projections of administrative authorities exercising adjudicatory powers. The Supreme Court observed that administrative tribunals are not bound by the strict rules of evidence and procedure. They follow the principles of natural justice. But this does not mean that they can act on something which is not evidence at all. On the other hand, what it means is that no material can be relied upon to establish contested facts which are not spoken to by persons who are competent to speak about them and are not subjected to cross-examination by the party against whom they are sought to be used. If a balance sheet is produced, it does not itself become the proof of the entries therein. If the entries are challenged, then every entry must be proved by producing books. If a letter or other document is produced to establish a fact, then either the writer must appear or an affidavit must be filed. Even if all the technicalities of the Evidence Act are not applicable it is inconceivable that the tribunal can act on what is not evidence but hearsay, nor is it conceivable that the tribunal can base its awards on copies of documents the originals of which, though in existence, are not produced and proved either by affidavits or by witnesses who have executed them, if they are alive and can be produced. Again, if the party wants an inspection it is incumbent on the tribunal to permit inspection so far as it is relevant to the enquiry. The applicability of these principles is well-recognised and admits no doubt.[15] However, the remarks of the Supreme Court relate to an independent tribunal, therefore, no other administrative authority exercising adjudicatory power is bound by it.

In Britain, generally, the legal rules of evidence are not followed by tribunals. Therefore, a tribunal may take into consideration an unauthenticated document without calling the author to prove it. In the USA also in cases of non-regulatory agencies the same informality in matters of evidence persists.[16]

In order to create confidence among the people in administrative justice, a code prescribing a minimum procedure for administrative agencies exercising adjudicatory powers must be adopted; till this is done, judicial review must be enlarged by using the test of reasonableness of administrative findings of fact and law.

VII) OFFICIAL BIAS

In administrative justice, official perspective is inherent and can be presumed. In any disciplinary proceeding, the presumption is of guilt rather than innocence. The actions are taken on the basis of expediency and various other extralegal considerations. This projection of official perspective does more damage where the administrative agency is not required to follow the standard rules of evidence and procedure. It is certain that official perspective and bias do infest administrative adjudication.

Official or departmental bias is one of the most baffling problems of administrative law. At times, bias arising from strong and sincere conviction as to public policy may operate as a more serious disqualification than even the pecuniary interest. Therefore, in cases where a minister would approach an issue with a desire that the decision should go one way rather than another, the parliament should provide that the matter should be judged by an independent tribunal. However, the problem of departmental bias is something which is inherent in the administrative process itself. Realising this, the Appeal Court in *Franklin* v. *Minister of Town and Country Planning*[17] held that the mere desire of the minister that the issue be decided in a particular way would not vitiate administrative action unless bad faith or improper purpose is proved. In India, the Supreme Court quashed the decision of the Andhra Pradesh Government nationalising road transport, among other grounds, on the grounds of departmental bias because the secretary of transport who had initiated the scheme also heard the objections.[18] Realising the inevitability of departmental bias in the administrative process, the Supreme Court however quickly added a caveat to its approach and held in the second case[19] that if the minister hears the objections the decision would be valid because he is a formal head of the department. In the USA and Britain the problem has been minimised to a great measure by internal separation wherein hearing officers are inducted to give hearing.

VIII) BARGAINING FOR LESSER PUNISHMENT

Plea bargaining means the bargaining of a 'plea of guilty' with lesser charges and punishment. It is very common that a poor employee is bullied by an over-bearing superior to accept the charge against him on the promise that a lesser punishment will be awarded. Plea bargaining, besides being immoral, violates the accepted canons of justice. It does more damage where the people are poor and the unemployment rate is very high.

IX) POLITICAL INTERFERENCE

Instrumentalities of administrative justice are, by their very nature, subject to some manner of political interference, though this cannot be said with certainty about every tribunal. No statistics are available to prove the quantum of political interference, but a strong conviction persists among the people that administrative justice is polluted by political interference. Some system must therefore be devised to invest administrative agencies exercising adjudicatory powers with a reasonable degree of freedom, responsibility, and security of tenure.

X) CONSULTATION OFF-THE-RECORD

Section 5(c) of the Administrative Procedure Act, 1946 provides that no administrative authority exercising adjudicatory powers is to consult any person or party upon any fact in issue except upon notice and opportunity for all parties to participate. This is done to avoid off the record consultations by the authority in a manner that may prejudice the case of the other party. In Britain, a standard rule has developed which applies to all enquiries. If a minister differs from the findings of fact by an inspector, or receives any new evidence, or takes into consideration any new issue after the close of the hearing, he must bring it to the notice of the other party and must reopen the enquiry if so demanded by the other party. This limitation on off-the-record consultation has avoided such problem as was involved in *Errington* v. *Minister of Health*.[20]

In Pakistan and India, there is no law to eliminate the dangers inherent in off-the-record consultation by an administrative authority. The principles of natural justice only demand that the authority must not base its decision on any evidence which is not brought to the notice of the other party. Since there is no legal requirement for the preparation of a 'record' in the sense in which it is insisted upon in the USA, off-the-record consultation which may prejudice the mind of the authority is endemic.

XI) REASONED DECISIONS

In the USA, the right to reasoned decision arises from the provisions of the Administrative Procedure Act and also from the due process clause of the constitution. In Britain, the provisions of the Tribunals and Enquiries Act, 1958 require an agency to give reasons only when demanded.

In Pakistan and India, apart from the requirement (if any) of the statute establishing the administrative agency, there is no requirement for the administrative authority to give reasons. The Supreme Court in *Tara Chand* v. *Municipal Corpn. Delhi*[21] also held that there is no principle of natural justice requiring a statutory tribunal to give reasons in every case. In order to develop faith in administrative justice, it is essential as a general requirement that every administrative agency must give reasons at least when demanded. In Pakistan, Section 24-A of the General Clause Act, 1897 requires every administrative authority to give reasons for its orders.

XII) LEGAL REPRESENTATION

Apart from the requirement of a specific statute there is no general requirement of the principle of natural justice that the administrative agency should always allow legal representation and cross-examination in every case. In the USA, the requirement of legal representation and cross-examination is insisted upon by the due process clause and the Administrative Procedure Act. In Britain, the administrative procedure being more informal, this requirement is not insisted upon in every case.

From the above discussion, it appears that the one problem with which administrative justice in Pakistan and India is confronted is the problem of organisation and procedure of the administrative agencies exercising adjudicatory powers. If there is merit in a flexible procedure there is also the danger that informality may not develop an anti-legal posture. Therefore, the need for a minimum procedure code cannot be overemphasised. This will combine the elements of flexibility and certainty in the realm of administrative justice.

4.3 ADMINISTRATIVE POWER AND DISCRETION

The residue of administrative function which is left after distinguishing legislative and quasi-judicial functions is known as purely administrative function. An administrative function understood in this sense is either ministerial or discretionary in nature. A ministerial function of administration is one which involves no amount of discretion. According to Griffith and Street,[22] 'a ministerial act is to be distinguished from other official acts in that the law prescribes the duty to be performed with such certainty as to leave nothing to the exercise of discretion or judgment.' The execution of warrants may be cited as the most familiar example. A discretionary power on the other hand grants to the administrative authority freedom to act in any manner it thinks fit. Discretionary powers of the administrative authorities have enormously increased since the functions of the State have increased and become complex. The administrative authorities have to face a variety of situations whose course cannot be predicted with any amount of certainty. To meet such situations they must possess capacity to take decisions on the spot or on the occasion. As legislature cannot definitely anticipate such situations, it has to confer discretion on the executive. Discretion is not the distinguishing feature of the purely administrative function. Even bodies performing legislative and quasi-judicial functions have discretionary power. In case of a quasi-judicial body, while the authority may be required to act according to the principles of natural justice, its ultimate decision is non-reviewable on the merits.[23]

The statutes, conferring power or discretion on public officers and not expressly coupled with a duty to exercise the power or discretion, have often been construed as imposing a duty to exercise that power, particularly where the power given is to be exercised in the interest of the public or a specified section of the public. In such cases, there may be something in the nature of the thing empowered to be done, something in the object for which it is to be done, something in the conditions under which it is to be done, something in the title of the person or persons for whose benefit the power is to be exercised, which may couple the power with a duty and make it the duty of the person in whom the power is reposed to exercise that power when called upon to do so.[24]

Administrative discretion is one which is to be exercised in accordance with policy or expediency. It does not involve any judicial element. Grant of a licence to import under the Import and Export (Control) Act, 1947, is a good instance of administrative discretion. Discretion is also exercised by the administrative authorities under various regulatory enactments such as the Foreign Exchange Regulation Act, 1947; and the Capital Issues (Control) Act, 1947. Economic controls and regulations necessarily imply a large amount of administrative discretion. Similarly discretion is conferred by the law of preventive detention.

Because of the complexity of socio-economic conditions which administration in modern times has to contend with, the range of ministerial functions is very small and that of discretionary functions is much larger. It is realised that a government having only ministerial duties with no discretionary functions would be extremely rigid and unworkable and that, to some extent, officials must be allowed a choice as to when, how, and whether they would act. The reason for this attitude is that more often than not, administration is required to handle intricate problems which involve investigation of facts, making of choices and exercise of discretion before deciding upon what action to take. Thus, modern tendency is to leave a lot of discretion with various authorities. Discretion implies power to make a choice between alternate courses of action. Legislation is often very broadly worded; it does not specify clearly, definitely or articulately the conditions and circumstances subject to which, and the norms with reference to which, administration is to exercise powers conferred on it. Discretion is the all-pervading phenomenon of modern age. Discretion is conferred in the area of rule-making or delegated legislation; for example, when the statutory formula says that government may make rules which it thinks expedient to carry out the purposes of the Act, in effect a broad discretion and choice are being conferred on the government to make rules. Legislature hardly gives any guidance as to what rules are to be made. Similarly, discretion is conferred on adjudicatory and administrative authorities on a liberal basis, that is, the power is given to apply a vague statutory standard on a case to case basis.

Rarely does legislature enact a comprehensive legislation complete in all details. More often, the legislation is sketchy or skeletal, leaving many gaps and conferring powers on administration to act in a way it deems 'necessary' or 'reasonable', or if it 'is satisfied' or 'is of opinion'. Rarely does legislature clearly enunciate a policy or a principle subject to which the executive may have to exercise its discretionary powers. Quite often, legislature bestows more or less an unqualified or uncontrolled discretion on the executive. Administrative discretion may be denoted by such words or phrases as 'public interest', 'public purpose', 'prejudicial to public safety or security', 'satisfaction', 'belief', 'efficient', 'reasonable', etc. An American scholar says in this regard:

> When we speak of administrative discretion, we mean that a determination may be reached, in part at least, upon the basis of considerations not entirely susceptible of proof or disproof. A statute confers discretion when it refers an official for the use of his power to beliefs, expectations, or tendencies instead of facts, or to such terms as 'adequate', 'advisable', 'expedient', 'equitable', 'fair', 'fit', 'necessary', 'wholesome', or their opposites. These lack the degree of certainty. . . . They involve matter of degree or an appeal to judgment. The discretion enlarges as the element of future probability preponderates over that of present conditions; it contracts where in certain types of cases quality tends to become standardised, as in matters of safety; on the other hand, certain applications of the concepts of immorality, fraud,

restraint of trade, discrimination or monopoly are so controversial as to operate practically like matter of discretion.[25]

The need for 'discretion' arises because of the necessity to individualise the exercise of power by the administration, i.e. the administration has to apply a vague or indefinite statutory provision from case to case. There are at least three good reasons for conferring discretion on administrative authorities: (a) The present day problems which administration is called upon to deal with are of complex and varying nature and it is difficult to comprehend them all within the scope of general rules. (b) Most of the problems are new, practically of the first impression. Lack of any previous experience to deal with them does not warrant the adoption of general rules. (c) It is not always possible to foresee each and every problem, but when a problem arises it must, in any case, be solved by the administration in spite of the absence of specific rules applicable to that situation. From the point of view of the individual, however, there are several disadvantages in the administration following the case-to-case approach as compared with the adoption of a general rule applicable to all similar cases. In the first place, case-to-case decisions operate on the past facts. A general rule usually avoids retroactivity and operates prospectively that one has prior notice of the rules and thus may regulate his conduct accordingly. In a case-to-case approach, the individual may be caught by surprise and may not be able to adjust his affairs in the absence of his ability to foresee future administrative action. Secondly, the case-to-case approach involves the danger of discrimination amongst various individuals. There always exists a possibility of not receiving like treatment under like circumstances. Thirdly, the process is time-consuming and involves decision in a multiplicity of cases.

In view of these manifold disadvantages, as discussed above, a general rule is preferable to the case-to-case approach, and ought to be adopted wherever possible.[26] It is desirable to have administrative uniformity to the extent possible, because, as a matter of general principle, substantial lack of uniformity would lead not only to administrative chaos but also to collapse of public confidence in administrative fairness. In any individual case, it is highly relevant to take into account what has been done in other cases of a similar nature, otherwise a decision may result which could be regarded as being improper or discriminatory.

There are three possible ways in which exercise of discretion can be made objective. First, the laws conferring discretion may itself seek to lay down the elements and standards which the authority has to apply in exercising its discretion and selecting a course of action. This means that the degree of discretion should be restricted by law itself as far as possible. Secondly, when legislature fails to lay down standards, administration can itself lay down standards by using its powers of delegated legislation. The power of delegated legislation can be used by administration to lay down rules of conduct observable not only by the people, but also by administration itself, in given situations. If a statute leaves a lot of discretion in the hands of administration the technique of delegated legislation can be used by it to lay down criteria with respect to which the discretion is to be exercised. Thus, rules can be promulgated by administration to channelize the broad stream of statutory discretion into narrow streams, by limiting its own freedom of action by laying down the norms according to which, the grounds on which, and the procedures according to which the administrative discretion conferred by a statute is to be exercised in individual cases. If that is done, proper application of power can be ensured. It also would help in anticipating administrative decision in individual cases, thus, making individual's right somewhat certain and reducing the chances of abuse of administrative discretion. Rules would also help in uniform application of the law in a large number of cases which may have to be handled, especially when a number of parallel and co-equal administrative authorities have to cope with cases arising under a particular scheme. Thirdly, on a lower plane and to some extent, administrative directions and norms of practice can be used, instead of the rules, for the purpose of achieving uniformity in discretionary decisions, but these should be resorted to only when the scheme is too much in an experimental stage and constant adjustments may have to be made for sometime to come. Otherwise, rules are preferable to directions as they can be enforced judicially. But it needs to be emphasised that no amount of rules or directions can really eliminate the need of discretion because individual cases and situations are bound to arise which may fall outside the guiding norms and administration will have to take some decision therein. Not all acts of the administration can be bound by fixed rules. Many times, it might not be possible to prescribe intelligible standards for administration to follow. All these considerations, however, make it inevitable that discretion be vested in administration to take care of individual cases.

The broader the discretion, the greater the chance of its abuse. In the words of Justice Douglas of the US Supreme Court: 'Where discretion is absolute, man has always suffered. . . . Absolute discretion . . . is more destructive of freedom than any of man's other inventions.'[27] And also: 'Absolute discretion, like corruption, marks the beginning of the end of liberty.'[28] It thus becomes necessary to devise ways and means to minimise the danger of absolute discretion. To achieve such an objective, a multipronged strategy has to be adopted. Laying down standards, as discussed above, is one strategy for the purpose because it makes discretion less than absolute. In Pakistan and India, the courts have also sought to spell out some limits on conferment of broad discretionary powers by invoking the fundamental rights guaranteed by the constitution. Besides, there are three more techniques which may be or are adopted for the purpose in view: (a) Certain pre-decisional procedures may have to be followed by the concerned authority before exercising its discretionary powers. An adjudicatory body is required to follow principles of natural justice or fairness. For other bodies, the relevant law may prescribe some procedural norms. (b) There is control by the courts, and they have evolved several norms to control the exercise of discretion by administration. (c) There ought to be some post-decisional review mechanism such as tribunals, ombudsman, etc. apart from courts. It may be emphasised that control of discretionary powers is perhaps the most critical problem of modern administrative law.[29]

4.4 JUDICIAL CONTROL OF ADMINISTRATIVE DISCRETION

While no one will dispute that modern government cannot function without administrative discretion, the problem for the administrative lawyer is to ensure its exercise in accordance with the rule of law. The courts exercise control over the acts of executive to see that no action except that which is permitted under law is taken by the administrative authorities. In Britain, the principle of judicial review was stated by Lord Atkins as follows:[30]

> In accordance with British jurisprudence no member of the executive can interfere with the liberty or property of a British subject except on the condition that he can support the legality of his action before a court of justice.

An administrative body is under a duty to act justly, fairly, and reasonably,[31] and where it acts unreasonably, capriciously or arbitrarily, the court will interfere with its judgment.[32] For instance, in nominating candidates for admission to a medical college, the government cannot act despotically and throw rules of equity, justice, and good conscience to winds. Government, even in administrative acts, is bound in duty to act justly, fairly, and reasonably. A failure in such direction tenders an act invalid in law.[33] It is equally clear that where a statute confers on a functionary absolute discretion to take or not to take a step and he exercises his discretion one way or the other, the court will not compel him to do what in the exercise of his discretion he has decided to do or not to do.[34] Moreover, it is well established that where he is required to act in his discretion and he has so acted, his discretion will not be interfered with.[35]

If the administrative action in question is ministerial, the executive can be compelled to perform it by a writ of *mandamus*. Thus the constitutions of Pakistan and India require that the authority putting a person to preventive detention must communicate to such person, as soon as may be, the grounds that led to his detention so as to enable him to make a representation.[36] Detentions have been held invalid where there was inordinate delay in the communication of the grounds or where the grounds that were communicated were vague[37] or irrelevant.[38] When an administrative authority acts beyond its power or does a thing which it is not competent to do, the courts prevent it from acting so. Thus where a detinue under Rule 30(1)(b) of the Defence of India Rules, 1962, sought permission from the Government of Maharashtra to send the manuscript of his book which was purely of scientific interest, out of jail to his wife for its publication, and the state government refused the permission, it was held that the state government acted contrary to law in refusing to send the manuscript.[39]

Article 199 of Pakistan Constitution empowers the high courts to exercise powers of review on the grounds that the proceedings taken by the relevant authority are 'without lawful authority', i.e. without jurisdiction. The high courts' jurisdiction to issue writs is founded exclusively on the doctrine of *ultra vires*.[40] The ground of error of law apparent on the face of the record was no longer available.[41] On the other hand, the courts have asserted their authority to intervene 'when the case proves to be one of no evidence'.[42] In English law 'no evidence' constitutes an error of law apparent on the face of the record,[43] but not a jurisdictional error, since a right to quash for excess of jurisdiction does not extend to circumstances where the decision is against the weight of the evidence. As a result, in Pakistan the notion of 'want of jurisdiction' has been stretched to the point of the rightness test.[44] The expression 'without lawful authority' has been loosely used to justify the granting or withdrawal of review in identical cases. Sometimes, the courts have expressed their inability to intervene, saying that the impugned action was not 'without lawful authority'. But they have shown their readiness to set aside a wrong decision in a similar situation, holding that the decision was 'without lawful authority'. Thus, in *Jamal Shah* v. *Election Commission*,[45] involving the rejection of certain ballot papers at an election by the Election Commission, the court declined review, saying that rejection or acceptance of ballot papers in an election on the merits of the dispute within the jurisdiction of such authority, and the decision, though erroneous, was 'with lawful authority'.

In a subsequent case,[46] involving the same issue, i.e. rejection of certain ballot papers by the election tribunal, the Supreme Court held that the ballot papers in question were free from any defect and the tribunal had acted wantonly in cancelling them. This time the rejection of ballot papers was held to be 'without lawful authority'. In strict logic, according to the decision in *Jamal Shah*'s case, rejection or acceptance of ballot papers was within the discretion of the election authority, and therefore the determination of the question whether certain ballot papers were free from any defect belonged properly to its discretionary sphere of jurisdiction. In reality, the Supreme Court acted on the rightness test by determining the question for itself and finding that the tribunal's decision was wrong, although, the interference was formally grounded on the rule 'without lawful authority', i.e. without jurisdiction.

After *Jamal Shah*'s case, the Supreme Court of Pakistan pursued the position that errors of law *intra vires* were not reviewable in the writ jurisdiction of the high courts.[47] However, recently, the Supreme Court has re-established the jurisdiction of the high courts to review all errors of law:[48]

a)   When a tribunal commits an error of law that error affects its jurisdiction, i.e. it acts *ultra vires*. In this way the court has adopted the reasoning of the House of Lords in the *Anisminic* case,[49] i.e. that all errors of law go to jurisdiction;

b)   Under Article 4 of the Constitution of Pakistan, every individual has a right to be dealt with in accordance with law. Therefore where the law has not been correctly applied it is a proper case of interference by the high court in the exercise of the writ jurisdiction.

The outcome of all these is that any error of law on the part of a tribunal or a public authority in understanding the law, in applying it or in laying down the law can and must be corrected in the constitutional jurisdiction, because if it is left uncorrected it will result in subverting the rule of law.[50] But, this is a departure from the orthodox theory of jurisdiction that power to decide carries with it the authority to decide wrongly as well as rightly both on point of fact and law.[51]

4.4.1 ABUSE OF DISCRETION

Under this general heading of judicial control, there may fall a number of specified and separate grounds that are discussed below:

i) MALA FIDES

Mala fides or bad faith means dishonest intention or corrupt motive. Even though it may be difficult to determine whether or not the authority has exceeded its powers in a particular case because of the broad terms in which the statute in question may have conferred power on it, the administrative action may, nevertheless, be declared to be bad if the motivation behind the action is not honest. At times, the courts use the phrase '*mala fides*' in the broad sense of any improper exercise or abuse of power. In one case, the Supreme Court of India has observed: '. . . *mala fides* exercise of power does not necessarily imply any moral turpitude as a matter of law. It only means that the statutory power is exercised for purposes foreign to those for which it is in law intended.'[52]

In this sense, *mala fides* is equated with any *ultra vires* exercise of administrative power. Here, however, the term '*mala fides*' is not being used in the broad sense, but in the narrow sense of exercise of power out of dishonest intent or corrupt motive. *Mala fides*, in this narrow sense, would include those cases where the motive behind an administrative action is personal animosity, spite, vengeance, or personal benefit to the authority itself or its relations or friends. In *Partap Singh* v. *Punjab*[53], the Supreme Court used the phrase '*mala fides*' for initiating administrative action against an individual 'for satisfying a private or personal grudge of the authority'. In this case, the appellant, a civil surgeon in the employment of the state government, was initially granted leave preparatory to retirement, but subsequently it was revoked, and he was placed under suspension and disciplinary action was started against him on the charge that he had accepted a bribe of Rs 16/- from some patient prior to going on leave. The appellant alleged that the disciplinary action against him had been initiated at the instance of the chief minister to wreak personal vengeance on him as he had refused to yield to the illegal demands of the chief minister and members of his family. From the sequence of events, certain tape recordings which had been made by him of his talks with the chief minister, and the absence of an affidavit by the chief minister denying the allegations against him or documents containing evidence contradicting those allegations, the court concluded that the charge of *mala fide* was proved and, accordingly, quashed the governmental action. The case shows that even if the government acts within its legal authority, and has legal power to take disciplinary action for misconduct against a civil servant, it could not so act if the action was motivated out of malice. In one sense—and this was pointed out by the court itself—it was a case of *ultra vires* since the purpose of the power vested in the government to take disciplinary action was to ensure probity and purity in the public service, and not to wreak personal vengeance. In another sense, it was not a case of *ultra vires* for the order was regular on its face; the government had a clear authority to take disciplinary action for the alleged misconduct of its employees and, accordingly, the government action was literally *intra vires*. In this sense, *mala fides* is a distinct ground for quashing administrative action apart from *ultra vires*.[54]

In *Rowjee* v. *Andhra Pradesh*,[55] under the schemes prepared by the State Road Transport Corporation, certain transport routes were proposed to be nationalised. The schemes owed their origin to the directions by the chief minister. It was alleged that the chief minister had acted *mala fide* in giving the directions. The charge against him was that the particular routes had been selected because he sought to take vengeance on the private operators on those routes, as they were his political opponents. From the course of events, and the absence of an affidavit from the chief minister denying the charge against him, the court concluded that *mala fide* on the part of the chief minister was established.

In another case,[56] the petitioner, a kerosene dealer, was detained under the Defence of India Rules with a view to prevent him from acting in a manner prejudicial to the maintenance of supplies and services essential to the life of the community. The petitioner alleged that his detention was unjustified as the moving spirit behind his detention was the deputy superintendent of police (Civil Supplies Cell) and that he had made false reports against the petitioner so that he could be eliminated as a wholesale kerosene dealer, and the relatives of the concerned officer might benefit by obtaining the distributorship for kerosene. The DSP filed no affidavit to controvert the allegations made against him, and the affidavit filed on behalf of the government by the home secretary was very defective in many material respects. After considering all the material and relevant facts, the Supreme Court declared the order of detention to be 'clearly and plainly *mala fide*'.

The burden of proving *mala fides* is on the individual making the allegation, as the order is regular on its face and there is a presumption in favour of administration that it exercises its power in good faith and for public benefit. The burden on the individual is not easy to discharge as it requires going into the motives or the state of mind of an authority, and it is hardly possible for an individual to know the same and it is all the more difficult to establish it before a court.[57] The difficulties inherent in proving *mala fides* are brought out by the Supreme Court in *E.P. Royappa v. State of Tamil Nadu*.[58] Although three out of the five judges on the bench felt that there were circumstances to create suspicion about the *bona fides* yet the burden is very heavy on the person who alleges it. The very seriousness of allegation of *mala fides* demands proof of a high degree of credibility. The motive of an authority can, however, be inferred from the course of events and other material which the individual may lay his hands upon. The Supreme Court has emphasised that *mala fides* should be established only by direct evidence, that is, that must be discernable from the order impugned or must be shown from the notings in the file which preceded the order. 'If bad faith would vitiate the order, the same can, in our opinion, be deduced as a reasonable and inescapable inference from the proved facts.'[59] It is difficult for the individual to collect sufficient evidence as he does not have access to the government record. However, as mentioned above, the course of events, public utterances of the authority, statements in the pleadings or affidavits filed by the authority, or failure to file the affidavits denying the allegation, etc. may lead to the establishment of the charge of *mala fides*. Where malice was imputed for procuring order which from circumstances seemed to be possible, the Supreme Court of Pakistan held, that unless the same was explained by the concerned administrative authority, it would be difficult to justify it.[60] The authority while passing orders in administrative matters must follow rules and principles of justice and equity so that even a person upon whom such order has been passed should not stamp such order as *mala fide* and result of bias or malice.[61] *Mala fides* may also be inferred from the authority ignoring apparent facts either deliberately or by sheer avoidance. It is not necessary for the individual to prove what particular official of the government acted *mala fide*—there is no such burden on the individual as facts lie within the knowledge of the government.[62] Because of the difficulty of proving *mala fides*, only a few cases have occurred so far in which administrative orders may have been quashed on this ground.[63]

II) IMPROPER PURPOSE

If a statute confers power for one purpose, its use for a different purpose would not be regarded as a valid exercise of the power and the same could be quashed. In this era of conferment of broad discretionary powers on administrative authorities, 'improper purpose' has become an important ground to control the exercise of administrative powers and, thus, to control administrative action. Because of the broad phraseology used in a statute to confer discretion on the authority concerned, an order passed by it may look, on its face, to be proper and within the ambit and scope of its statutory power. But nevertheless, the real purpose for which the power has been exercised may be contrary to the purposes and objectives of the statute in question. To determine 'improper purpose' in a particular case, it is necessary to go into the motives or the real reasons for which the administrative action has been taken.

'Improper purpose' is broader than 'mala fides', for whereas the latter denotes a personal spite or malice, the former may have no such element. The action of an authority may be motivated by some public interest (as distinguished from private interest) but it may be different from what is contemplated by the statute under which the action has been taken. Here it is not so much relevant to assess whether the authority is acting in good faith or bad faith. What is relevant is to determine whether the purpose in view is one sanctioned by the statute which confers power on the authority concerned. For instance, the government may be empowered to acquire property if it is 'satisfied' of the existence of a public purpose for such acquisition. If the government validly reaches a conclusion as to the existence of a public purpose, its order would be legal, provided of course that the circumstances which it has found to exist do in law constitute a public purpose.[64]

A few examples of the power exercised for improper purpose are: property acquired ostensibly for a public purpose by a municipal corporation at its expense, but really for the improvement trust at the latter's expense;[65] a house requisitioned ostensibly to provide accommodation to the officer of the state, but really as a means to eject the petitioner because of the religious susceptibilities of the landlord;[66] or refusal to give permission to construct building with a view to bring pressure on the owner to provide drainage for the adjoining building. In a case of requisitioning of some property, the order mentioned the purpose of requisition as office or residence of a government officer, it being a purpose of the state. Instead, the property was left in the possession of a co-operative society for running a fair price shop. The requisition order was quashed as under the relevant law no order of requisition could be passed for a co-operative society.[67] In all these cases, the authority had power to do what it ostensibly did, but since it really exercised the power to achieve an objective other than the one authorised by the law, the action was held bad and struck down.

In the area of preventive detention, it has been held in a few cases that the power of preventive detention cannot be used as a convenient substitute for prosecuting a person in a criminal court. Thus, in *Srilal Shaw* v. *State of West Bengal*,[68] a preventive detention order was issued against a person mainly on the grounds that he had stolen some railway property. He had documents to show that he had purchased the goods in question in the open market. A criminal case filed against him was dropped and was detention order passed instead. The order was declared to be bad. The court thought that it was a typical case where, for no apparent reason, a person who could easily be prosecuted under the punitive law was being preventively detained. Again, in *L.K. Das* v. *State of West Bengal*,[69] it was held that the power of detention could not be used on 'simple, solitary incident' of theft of railway property, and the proper course to prosecute the person was in a criminal court. In some of the cases the court has used the phrase 'colourable exercise of power',[70] a term which does not differ substantially from 'improper purpose'. It has, however, been ruled in some cases that a prior court case, or lack of it, would not make the detention order invalid.[71] It is only after the court has reached the conclusion that on the facts a criminal trial would suffice, that the detention order would be held invalid. But where the court is satisfied that the facts warrant preventive detention, then a criminal trial on the same facts would be regarded as immaterial. This involves passing of value judgment or going into the merits of the detention order, or to say that the detaining authority should act reasonably.

iii) Irrelevant considerations

A power conferred by a statute must be exercised on the considerations mentioned in the statute or relevant to the purpose for which it is conferred. If the authority concerned pays attention to, or takes into account, circumstances, events or matters wholly irrelevant or extraneous to those mentioned in the statute, then the administrative action would be *ultra vires* and should be quashed. Whenever any administrative authority is given power to pass some order, it should exercise its authority independently by taking into consideration all relevant circumstances. Where such an authority had made a decision and issued order thereunder, under extraneous influence, such order should be quashed as invalid.[72]

The ground of 'irrelevant considerations' gives an additional dimension to the judicial review because courts assess the relevancy of considerations on which power is exercised with reference to the purpose and tenor of the Act. If the Act itself spells out the relevant criteria which have to be taken into consideration in exercising the given power, then the task of the courts is somewhat easy, as they can see whether a consideration not mentioned in the Act has affected the exercise of discretion of the authority concerned. If the courts confine themselves only to determine whether a consideration not mentioned in the Act formed basis of the discretion, then the judicial review would be extremely limited as the statutes do not usually spell out detailed considerations. But, the courts do not generally view their role in such mechanical or restrictive terms. Even when a statute does not fully spell out the relevant criterion or consideration, and may appear to confer power in almost unlimited terms, the court may, by looking into the purpose, tenor and provisions of the Act, assess whether extraneous or irrelevant considerations have been applied by the administration in arriving at its decision. As has been emphasised by the House of Lords in the Padfield case,[73] legislature confers discretion on administrative authorities with the intention that it should be used to promote the policy and objects of the Act, and the policy and objects of the Act must be determined by construing the Act as a whole. The construction of a statute is always a matter of law for the court. The court can quash an exercise of discretionary power if it has been exercised for reasons which, in the opinion of the court, are not good reasons or are bad reasons. This gives scope to judicial creativity through the interpretative process, for the courts can control, to some extent, a statutory power conferred even in very broad terms. But this also creates some uncertainty as no one can be sure, until the highest court has pronounced its decision, whether a consideration is relevant or not to the power conferred by a statute.

A simple situation of quashing administrative action is presented where the order mentions formal grounds or considerations which are irrelevant. Thus, by way of illustration, in *Ram Manohar Lohia* v. *Bihar*,[74] the petitioner was detained under the Defence of India Rules, 1962 to prevent him from acting in a manner prejudicial to the maintenance of 'law and order', whereas the rules permitted detention to prevent subversion of 'public order'. The court struck down the order as, in its opinion, the two concepts were not the same, 'law and order' being wider than 'public order'. Again, in *R.L. Arora* v. *State of UP*,[75] under the Land Acquisition Act, 1894 a piece of land was acquired by the government for a private company for the construction of a textile machinery parts factory. The administrative machinery contained in Sections 6 to 37 of the Act for acquisition of land for a company can be put into force only after necessary consent of the appropriate government has been obtained. Under Section 40 of the Act, the government could not give its consent for the acquisition unless it was satisfied that 'such acquisition is needed for the construction of a work, and that such work is likely to prove useful to the public.' The question arose whether the consent given in the instant case by the government was valid. The court conceded that it was a matter of subjective satisfaction for the government as to which piece of land it should acquire, and for what specific purpose, so long as it was within the broad purpose mentioned in the statute. It was also a matter within the satisfaction of the government that the work to be constructed would be useful to the public and that satisfaction would not be open to challenge, but would be based on the meaning given to the relevant words in the Act. It was for the court to interpret the words in the statute and to say what those words meant and to see whether the government was satisfied according to the meaning given to those words by the court. 'The government cannot both give meaning to the words and also say that they are satisfied on the meaning given by them.'[76] The court found that the purpose for which the consent was given by the government was not the one authorised by the Act. In the view of the court, the work to be constructed on the land should be directly useful to the public and not the product of the company which was going to construct the work.

The General Manager, Telephones, Delhi, disconnected the petitioner's telephone under the Telegraph Rules. The ground was that the telephone was being used for illegal *satta* purposes. The relevant rule empowered the divisional engineer, in the event of any emergency, to disconnect any subscriber. The court emphasised that the existence of an emergency was a prerequisite to the exercise of power and the satisfaction as to emergency had to be that of the divisional engineer. He had to arrive at such satisfaction rationally based on relevant material. The order of disconnection was therefore quashed because it was made on a ground not germane to the relevant rule.[77] The Supreme Court of Pakistan held that autonomous administrative bodies like Regional Transport Authorities have to function as such under the provisions of the Act. They cannot act merely as agents to government and import considerations extraneous to the Act in deciding applications. It is under legal obligation to deal with all applicants before it fairly, justly, equitably and in accordance with the law.[78]

In the above cases, the statute involved had mentioned the considerations and the court considered the validity of administrative action by interpreting those considerations. Even where the statute is silent as to the considerations, and the statutory power is expressed in almost unlimited terms, the court may read some limitations with reference to the purpose and object of the statute, and quash an order if it goes beyond such limitations.[79] To illustrate, under Section 12(5) of the Industrial Disputes Act 1947, read with Section 10, the government has prima facie an unlimited power to refuse to make a reference of an industrial dispute to a tribunal for adjudication except that it has to record its reasons for refusing to make a reference. In *State of Bombay v. K.P. Krishnan*,[80] the government refused to refer an industrial dispute with regard to the payment of bonus for a certain year to a tribunal for adjudication for the reason that the 'workmen resorted to a go-slow during the year.' The court held that the reason given by the government was extraneous and not germane to the dispute. The government had acted in a punitive spirit and this was contrary to the objective of the statute which was designed to investigate and settle disputes.

In another case, the petitioner, was granted an export licence under the Imports and Exports (Control) Act, 1947 for exporting certain quantity of cast iron bearings and turnings subject to the condition that the licensee 'shall have to supply 10 tons of heavy melting scrap for export of every 100 tons of turnings and bearings (both steel and cast iron) to the furnace owner nominated by the Iron and Steel Controller.' The statute was silent as to the imposition of such a condition. In fact it conferred an unqualified power on the government to control the import and export of commodities. Since the objective of the statute was to control exports and not the internal distribution of a commodity, therefore, the condition imposed in the licence was held to be outside the objectives of the statute.[81] Thus, public functionary vested with power in respect of determination of rights of a citizen *qua* the state resources is required to exercise the same fairly and properly on sound judicial principles, and keeping in view relevant considerations having logical nexus with the object of law and not arbitrarily and whimsically.[82]

IV) RELATIONSHIP OF FACTS TO CONSIDERATIONS

If the courts were to confine themselves to the grounds (or considerations) mentioned in the order without going into the facts, they would not prove very effective in controlling administrative discretion because the official taking a particular action could simply state his order in terms of the statutory language. But the courts have expanded their review power by examining the facts to find out whether those facts are relevant to the grounds (considerations) or not, or whether there was rational or causal connection between the facts and the grounds, or whether it was possible to draw reasonable inference as to the grounds mentioned in the order from the facts, or whether a reasonable person properly trained in law could have reached the decision which the administration reached.

Under the Preventive Detention Act, 1950 a person could be detained on several grounds mentioned therein. The authority detaining a person was required to communicate the grounds for detention to the detinue. If a person is detained on any ground which is not germane or relevant to the grounds mentioned in the Act for ordering detention, then the order of detention can be quashed.[83] Some cases in which reasons (or facts), on which detention of a person was ordered and which were not found to have relevance to the grounds mentioned in the Act were: when a person is detained in the interest of law and order, because he published pamphlets containing scurrilous attacks on the judiciary which might have undermined the confidence of the people in the proper administration of justice but did not endanger law and order as such;[84] and detention of a person in the interest of maintenance of public order, because he committed a theft of overhead traction wire disrupting rail service for several hours which might interfere with the maintenance of supplies essential to the community but did not threaten maintenance of public order.[85] However, cases often do not arise in such simple settings and they present fact situations which call for some degree of exercise of value judgment by the courts. Generally, the law regarding preventive detention is intended to prevent or preclude activities prejudicial to the maintenance of 'public order', which is one of the leading grounds for preventive detention. 'Public order' is usually regarded as a narrow concept compared with the expression 'law and order'. It is not every contravention of law that can be said to affect the 'public order'. It has been held by the Supreme Court of India that a line of demarcation has to be drawn 'between serious and aggravated forms of disorder which directly affect the community or injure the public interest and the relatively minor breaches of peace of a purely local significance which primarily injure specific "individuals" and only in a secondary sense of public interest.'[86] Only the former comes within the category of 'public order'. What is serious and aggravated may not be easy to articulate and in determining this some degree of discretion is always involved. One or two instances of breaking the law or indulging in offences by a person, it has been held, do not amount to a threat to public order. However, a number of such instances of a serious nature by a person do so.[87] Thus, an order of preventive detention on the grounds that the detinue committed a murderous attack on a person causing his death was quashed by the court because the facts raised only a 'law and order' problem whereas under the law preventive detention was authorised on the grounds of 'public order'.[88] From a review of detention cases during the last few years, it may be said that the courts are now more prone to intervene with the executive determination of the necessity to detain a person on the grounds of irrelevant considerations than it was so earlier.[89]

In *Barium Chemicals Ltd* v. *Company Law Board,*[90] the board ordered an investigation into the affairs of the company of the Companies Act, 1956. Under the section, the board can order investigation into the affairs of a company, if, in the opinion of the board there are circumstances suggesting that (a) the business of the company was being conducted with intent to defraud its creditors, or members, etc.; (b) the persons concerned in the formation of the company or its management have been guilty of fraud, misfeasance or other misconduct towards the company or any of its members; (c) the members of the company have not given full information about the affairs of the company. The basis of the order of investigation in the Barium case was that there had been delay and faulty planning of the project resulting in double expenditure and continuous losses to the company, that the value of its shares had gone down considerably and that some eminent persons had resigned from the board of directors. The court, by a majority,[91] quashed the order of the government as these facts had no relevance to the question of fraud by the company. The two dissenting judges, however, thought that the circumstances were not extraneous to the grounds mentioned in the order. They raised the query whether it would be farfetched to say that these circumstances could reasonably suggest to the board that these happenings were not just pieces of careless conduct but were deliberate acts of omissions of the managing director of the company with the ulterior motive of earning profit for himself.

Judicial intervention on the grounds that facts and circumstances are irrelevant (or extraneous) to the conclusion drawn by the authority for taking action certainly falls short of judicial intervention on the grounds of insufficiency or unsatisfactory character of the reasons. How much short it falls is a matter which it may not be easy to articulate. Judicial intervention on this basis would depend on the subject matter involved and the feelings of a judge about the injustice of the case. The ground seems to be flexible enough to be stretched one way or the other—sometimes even the line between the limited ground of irrelevant circumstances and that of inadequacy of facts may just become blurred.

The point is further illustrated by the following two cases. *Rohtas Industries* v. *S.D. Agarwal*[92] also involved investigation of a company under the Companies Act. The investigation was ordered on the grounds that there were several complaints of misconduct against one of the leading directors of the appellant company in relation to other companies under his control for which he was being prosecuted, and that the company had arranged to sell preference shares of another company held by it for inadequate consideration. About the former, the court (majority) was of the opinion that it was not a relevant circumstance. About the other ground, the court found no evidence of the shares having been sold for inadequate consideration. The case of *P.J. Irani* v. *Madras*[93] concerned administrative action taken under the Madras Buildings (Lease and Rent Control) Act, 1949 which was enacted to regulate the letting of the residential and non-residential buildings, to control the rents of such buildings and to prevent unreasonable eviction of tenants therefrom. A provision in the Act authorised the state government to exempt any building or class of buildings from the provisions of the Act. It transpired that the government had exercised this power to exempt a building with a view to evict a tenant in the building who had continued in possession after the termination of his tenancy. The Supreme Court held by majority that the reasons for which the government had granted the exemption were not those which were countenanced by the policy or purpose of the Act which was to prevent unreasonable eviction of tenants and the power of exemption was to be applied where the statutory protection caused great hardship to the landlord or was the subject of abuse by the tenant himself. Therefore, the exemption was held to be invalid.

(v) Difference between improper purpose and irrelevant considerations

The difference between a power exercised for an improper purpose and on irrelevant considerations is often imperceptible.[94] For instance, where land is acquired by an authority ostensibly for itself but really for another authority, the power may be said to be exercised, in one sense, for an improper purpose, but in another sense, after the authority took into consideration an irrelevant factor, namely, acquisition of land for another authority, the consideration for the administrative action being acquisition for itself. A point to note is that the purposes for which an administrative power is being conferred on an authority under a statute, or the considerations on which the same is to be exercised, are not normally mentioned in the statute; the courts have to spell out the same from the tenor of the Act in question. Therefore, the courts could either say that the power has been exercised for an improper purpose or on irrelevant considerations. In either case, the authority is acting *ultra vires*, i.e. exceeding its authority. However, the ground of improper purpose is applied to cases where the irregularity is not apparent on the face of the order or from the reasons mentioned therein. Even then the line of distinction between the two is not easy to draw at times. It may be hard to distinguish between an irregularity on the face of it and a latent irregularity. The crux of the matter is that the motives of an authority for the exercise of power are important for determination by the courts. If improper motive is established, and particularly when the improper motive is the dominant motive for administrative action, the order should be quashed. It would be immaterial whether it is said to be quashed on the grounds of improper purpose or irrelevant considerations.

(VI) MIXED CONSIDERATIONS

The courts are frequently called upon to determine the question as to what would be the legal status of an order which might be based partly on relevant and partly on irrelevant (or non-existent) considerations? Would such an order be deemed to be bad? However, the attitude of the courts on this question does not depict a uniform approach in all types of cases. In preventive detention cases, courts have taken strict view of the matter and have held such an order invalid if based on any irrelevant ground mixed with relevant grounds, reasoning that it would be difficult to say as to what extent the irrelevant grounds weighed in the mind of the administrative authority and whether it could have passed the order only on the basis of the relevant and valid grounds. In *Shibbanlal* v. *Uttar Pradesh*,[95] the petitioner was detained on two grounds: first, that his activities were prejudicial to the maintenance of supplies essential to the community, and second, that his activities were injurious to the maintenance of public order. Later the government revoked his detention on the first ground as either it was insubstantial or non-existent but continued it on the second. The court quashed the original detention order. The principle has been stated by the Supreme Court of India in the following words:[96]

> Where power is vested in a statutory authority to deprive the liberty of a subject on its subjective satisfaction with reference to specified matters, if that satisfaction is stated to be based on a number of grounds or for a variety of reasons, all taken together, and if some of them are found to be non-existent or irrelevant, the very exercise of that power is bad. This is so because the matter being one for

subjective satisfaction, it must be properly based on all the reasons on which it purports to be based. If some of them are found to be non-existent or irrelevant, the Court cannot predicate what the subjective satisfaction of the said authority would have been on the exclusion of those grounds or reasons. To uphold the validity of such an order in spite of the invalidity of some of the reasons or grounds would be to substitute the objective standards of the Court for the subjective satisfaction of the statutory authority.

But then the court also added a rider: 'In applying those principles, however, the court must be satisfied that the vague or irrelevant grounds are such as, if excluded, might reasonably have affected the subjective satisfaction of the appropriate authority.'[97] Thus if some ground of comparatively unessential character is defective then the order based on subjective satisfaction would not be invalid. The detention order would be quashed if the bad ground was not inconsequential in nature. There, however, does not seem to be any case on preventive detention where the detention order, which was based both on relevant and irrelevant grounds, was upheld on the basis of this rider. In a number of subsequent cases the court has quashed the detention order if it was based on good and bad grounds.[98]

But the court does not seem to take the same strict view in other cases not involving personal liberty. Whether mixed considerations would lead to quashing of an administrative action or not in other situations depends on the court's judgment whether or not 'the exclusion of the irrelevant or non-existent grounds would have affected the ultimate decision.' In *Maharashtar* v. *Babulal Kirparam*, the state government superseded a municipal corporation because it was 'not competent to perform the duties imposed on it' by the relevant Act. This opinion of the government was formed on two grounds: deterioration of the financial position of the corporation because of over-spending, and its neglect to undertake improvement of water supply. The Supreme Court of India came to the conclusion that the first ground could not be sustained as no reasonable person, on the materials before the government, could possibly form the opinion that the charge was proved. The court, however, found that the state government could have formed its opinion, as it did, on the second ground. Nevertheless, the court did not quash the governmental action as it felt 'reasonably certain that the state government would have passed the order on the basis of the second ground alone.' In another case[99] involving dismissal of a civil servant, the court found that only some of the findings and not all adopted by the disciplinary administrative tribunal, on which the order to dismiss the government servant was based, could be sustained. Nevertheless, the dismissal order was upheld. The court explained that the power of the government to impose appropriate punishment was final. If the order could be supported on any finding as to the civil servant being guilty of grave delinquency for which the punishment could lawfully be imposed, it was not for 'the court to consider whether that ground alone would have weighed with the authority in dismissing the public servant.'

The principle emerging from the above cases appears to be that an administrative order based on both relevant and irrelevant (or non-existent) considerations is not invalid if the court is satisfied that the authority would have passed the order even on the basis of the relevant and existing ground, and that the exclusion of the irrelevant or non-existent ground would not have affected its ultimate decision.

When an order contains some valid and some invalid portions, and these are severable, and if after exclusion of the invalid part, the rest of the order remains viable and self-contained, the court is not bound to quash the entire order. It can quash the invalid portion of the order and allow the rest of the order to stand if the invalid portion is not an integral part of the order and its deletion does not render the valid portion as truncated and ineffective. For example, in *State of Mysore* v. *K.C. Adiga*,[100] land was validly assigned to the respondent but an illegal condition was attached thereto. The court quashed the condition but not the assignment declaring, 'the fall of illegal condition does not lead to the fall of the assignment sans that condition.'

(VII) IGNORING RELEVANT CONSIDERATIONS

If in exercising its discretionary power an administrative authority ignores relevant considerations, its action will be invalid. It may, however, be difficult to establish in a case that the authority has left out relevant considerations and the difficulty in this regard seems to be far greater than in a situation where irrelevant considerations have been taken into account. Unless detailed reasons are given by the authority from which it can be inferred that it took action after ignoring material considerations, it is hard to have the action quashed on this basis. Because of the difficulty of proof, not many cases have occurred in this area. The position may, however, be illustrated by referring to *Shanmugam* v. *SKVS (P) Ltd*[101] A regional transport authority called for applications for grant of stage carriage permit for a certain route. Under the statute, the authority had broad powers to grant the permits in public interest. But the government attempted to control the discretion of the authority by prescribing a marking system under which marks were to be allotted to different applicants on the basis of viable unit, workshop, residence (branch office) on the route, experience and special circumstances. What is of relevance here is that under the marking system residence or place of business on the route was considered to be in the interest of the public, but the respondent was not given any marks for having a branch on the route on the grounds that he had branches elsewhere. Quashing the refusal of permit to the respondent, the Indian Supreme Court ruled:

> Whatever conflict there may be, on which we do not express any opinion, in a tax law or the company law, in the context of the marking system and the evaluation of an amenity in the interest of the public, it is obviously an untenable position to hold that even if a company has a well equipped branch on a route in respect of which a permit is applied for, it shall be ignored if the company has some other branch somewhere unconnected with that route.

Similarly, in *Rampur Distillery Co.* v. *Company Law Board*,[102] the Company Law Board acting under the Companies Act, 1956 refused to give its approval for renewing the managing agency of the company concerned which had been the managing agents of the Rampur Distillery since 1943. The law conferred practically an unlimited discretion on the board to accord approval. The reason given by the board for not giving its approval was that a commission of enquiry headed by Justice Vivian Bose had severely criticised the dealings of the managing director of the managing agents in relation to various other companies of which he was the director. In the view of the commission, the said director was guilty of grossly improper conduct in relation to those companies in the year 1946–47. The court did not dispute that the past conduct of the director was a relevant circumstance in considering the question of fitness of the managing agents for the purpose of giving its approval for renewing the same, but it insisted that the board should also take into account the present acts and activities of the directors of the managing agents. Since the board did not take into account this aspect, it left out a relevant consideration and the action of the board was, therefore, held to be bad.

(VIII) COLOURABLE EXERCISE OF POWER

At times, the courts use the idiom 'colourable exercise of power' to denounce an abuse of discretion. Colourable exercise means that under the 'colour' or 'guise' of power conferred for one purpose, the authority is seeking to achieve something else which it is not authorised to do under the law in question. Viewed in this light, 'colourable exercise of power' would not appear to be a distinct ground of judicial review of administrative action but would be covered by the grounds already noticed, i.e. improper purpose or irrelevant considerations. The same appears to be the conclusion when reference is made to cases where the ground of 'colourable exercise of power' has been invoked. In the *Somawanti* case,[103] the Supreme Court stated as follows with reference to acquisition of land under the Land Acquisition Act:

Now whether in a particular case the purpose for which land is needed is for public purpose or not is for the State Government to be satisfied about . . . subject to one exception. The exception is that if there is a colourable exercise of power the declaration will be open to challenge at the instance of the aggrieved party. . . . If it appears that what the Government is satisfied about is not a public but a private purpose or no purpose at all the action of the Government would be colourable as not being relatable to the power conferred upon it by the Act and its declaration will be a nullity.

The above quotation would show that the term 'colourable exercise of power' is used in the sense of using a power for a purpose not authorised by the Act conferring the power on the authority concerned. The term 'colourable' has also been used at times in the sense of *mala fide* action.[104] Colourable means that the power is exercised ostensibly for the authorised end but really to achieve some other purpose; in other words, the exercise of power is illegal but it has been given the guise of legality.[105] Colourable exercise and improper purpose, as discussed earlier, appear to converge and the two phrases can be used interchangeably.

However, only because a wide power has been conferred, the same by itself would not lead to a presumption that the same is capable of misuse or on that count alone the provisions of Article 14 (Equality before law) of the Constitution would be attracted. But, when a statute confers a wide power upon a statutory authority, a closer scrutiny would be required.[106]

4.4.2 REASONABLE EXERCISE OF POWER

While reviewing exercise of administrative powers, courts have also used such language as that the authority should consider the question fairly and reasonably before taking action.[107] The term 'unreasonable' means more than one thing. It may embody a host of grounds mentioned already, such as the authority acting on irrelevant or extraneous considerations or for an improper purpose or *mala fide*, etc. Viewed thus, 'unreasonableness' does not furnish an independent ground of judicial control of administrative powers apart from the grounds already mentioned. Thus in *Sheo Nath* v. *Appellate Assistant Commissioner*,[108] the Supreme Court of India stated that the words 'reason to believe' (for initiating reassessment proceedings) used in the Income Tax Act 'suggest that the belief must be that of an honest and reasonable person based upon reasonable grounds and that the Income Tax Officer may act on direct or circumstantial evidence but not on mere suspicion.' However, it is obvious that the court was using the term 'reasonable' in the narrow sense as stated above. It went on to say:

> The Income Tax Officer would be acting without jurisdiction if the reason for his belief that the conditions are satisfied does not exist or is not material or relevant to the belief required by the section. The Court can always examine this aspect, though sufficiency of the reasons for the belief cannot be investigated by the Court.

'Unreasonableness' may also mean that even though the authority has acted according to law in the sense that it has not acted on irrelevant grounds or exercised power for an improper purpose, yet it has given more weight to some factors than they deserved as compared with other factors. Interference on this ground requires going into the relative importance of different factors and their balancing which amounts to substituting the discretion of the judiciary for that of the executive. Courts do not normally exercise such wide powers to interfere in the exercise of administrative discretion, except that the Supreme Court has shown some liberality of approach in a few preventive detention cases where the power was used to evade the normal criminal justice process. In these cases the court taking its own view of the facts quashed or upheld the administrative action. In some of these cases the court specifically mentioned reasonableness of administrative action. Thus in *Ram Bali* v. *State of West Bengal*,[109] the court stated that 'in some cases, the facts may so clearly indicate that an ordinary criminal prosecution would suffice and that the necessity to order the detention of an offender for one of the objects of the Act could not be said to be reasonably made out.'

Unreasonableness may furnish an independent ground for interference by the courts when the Constitution of India so requires. For example, Article 25 of the Pakistan Constitution 1973 and Article 14 of the Constitution of India guarantee equality before law but the courts have permitted reasonable classification to be made. However, discriminatory administrative action taken under an otherwise valid law could still be violative of the equality clause. In *Mannalal Jain* v. *Assam*,[110] the Supreme Court struck down discriminatory administrative action even though the law was valid.

At times, the law may require reasonable administrative behaviour; for example, reasonable grounds to believe by an authority to take action. What power of judicial review do the courts get under such a formula? In a case under the Sea Customs Act, 1878 which required that the burden of proving that the goods were not smuggled would be on the person from whom goods were seized in the 'reasonable belief' that they were smuggled goods. An officer had seized gold from the appellant. The seizure of the gold was challenged on the grounds that there was nothing on record to show that the officer concerned acted on 'reasonable belief' that the gold had been smuggled. The argument raised was that the question as to whether there was reasonable belief or not was a justiciable one and that there should be material on record to show that the belief could have been reasonably entertained. The court found enough basis in the facts of the case for a reasonable belief, i.e. that the appellant was carrying large quantity of gold and that the circumstances of his journey were suspicious.[111] The court pointed out that it was dealing with a question as to whether the belief in the mind of the officer who effected the seizure was reasonable or not, it was 'not sitting in appeal over the decision of the said officer'. All that it could consider was whether there was ground in existence which *prima facie* justified the said reasonable belief.

'Reasonableness', however, provides quite a flexible basis for the courts to interfere, and in other factual situations requiring reasonable administrative action, the scope of judicial review may be much wider. As has been stated, in such situations, 'The scope of review is determined by practical realities, and it would be absurd to suppose that the attitude of the courts towards such words as "reasonable grounds" in one legislative context must necessarily be repr   iced in every other.'[112] This can be illustrated by reference to t o English cases. In Britain, the implications of the word 'reasonable' used in a statute to qualify discretion have been the subject matter of discussion for long. *Liversidge* v. *Anderson*,[113] a war-time case, involved a Regulation of the Defence (General) Regulations which ran as follows:

> If the Secretary of State has reasonable cause to believe any person to be of hostile origin . . . and that by reason thereof it is necessary to exercise control over him, he may make an order against that person directing that he be detained.

The House of Lords was faced with the question whether the words 'reasonable cause to believe' should be given an objective or subjective meaning. In the former case, it would be for the courts to determine whether the secretary of state had reasonable cause to believe; in the latter case, the secretary of state could himself decide without any control by the courts as to whether he had reasonable cause. The House of Lords, by a majority, interpreted the words subjectively and held that parliament had conferred an absolute discretion on the secretary of state, that he must satisfy himself that he had reasonable cause and that he need not satisfy anyone else. This ruling was widely criticised by the academic writers as it disclosed a definite bias in the courts towards subjective interpretation. But then it was a war-time case. In *Nakkuda Ali* v. *Jayaratne*,[114] the Privy Council stated that it would be very unfortunate if the decision in the *Liversidge* case came to be regarded as laying down any general rule as to the construction of such phrase. The case is merely an authority for the proposition that the words 'if AB has reasonable cause to believe' were capable of meaning 'AB honestly thinks that he has reasonable cause to believe' in the context of the case. In *Nakkuda Ali*, the Privy Council held that when the legislature used the word 'reasonable', it must have been intended to serve in some sense as a condition limiting the exercise of an otherwise arbitrary power. But if the question whether the condition has been satisfied is to be conclusively decided by the man who wields the power, the value of the intended restraint would in effect be nothing. In the instant case, it was held that the words 'where the controller has reasonable grounds to believe that any dealer is unfit to be allowed to continue as a dealer' would impose a condition that there must exist in fact reasonable grounds, known to the controller, before he could validly exercise the power of cancellation of the licence. Therefore, though the belief of the controller that the dealer was unfit was subjective, existence of reasonable grounds on which the belief could be founded was objective and constituted a limitation on his power.

The courts have, on the whole, been extremely reluctant to import the requirement of reasonableness (at least in the broad sense of going into the merits) into a statute by implication. In *S. Narayan* v. *Union of India*,[115] the Supreme Court held that the court has no jurisdiction to go into the reasonableness of telephone rates fixed by the government. However, in one case[116] the statutory language 'if he is satisfied' has been held to mean 'if he is reasonably satisfied' which, according to the court, meant that the satisfaction cannot be arbitrary or capricious and that it must be objective and based on the materials placed before the decision-maker by the parties concerned. But this approach appears to be an exception rather than the rule.

In this connection, reference may be made to the case law in Britain. In *Associated Provincial Picture Houses* v. *Wednesbury Corp.*[117] the principle has been asserted that unreasonableness may be a ground for attacking an administrative decision. Of course, the test for unreasonableness was very stringent. The decision could be attacked on this ground only if it was 'so unreasonable that no reasonable authority could ever have come to it', and to prove a case of that kind would require something 'overwhelming'. There are not many cases in which administrative decisions may have been challenged on this ground. In *Roberts* v. *Hopwood*,[118] it was held that a local authority having power to pay 'such wages as it may think fit' was bound to exercise its discretion reasonably and that a payment of £4 per week in 1921–22 to the lowest grade worker was so unreasonable as to be *ultra vires* in spite of the generality of the discretion. Lord Wrenbury interpreted the words 'may think fit' as 'may reasonably think fit'. In his view, it made no difference in the meaning whether the word 'reasonably' or 'reasonable' was in or out, because 'a person in whom is vested a discretion must exercise his discretion upon reasonable grounds. Discretion does not empower a man to do what he likes merely because he is minded to do so—but what he ought. . . . He must act reasonably.' In *Hall & Co.* v. *Shoreham UDC*[119] the defendant granted the plaintiff planning permission on the condition that he would construct a road on his land and dedicate its use to the public. No compensation was payable to the plaintiff for the loss of the land to be used for the road. The court held the condition void for unreasonableness. The court found no clear authority in the Act for imposing such a condition. The course adopted by the defendant was characterised as 'utterly unreasonable'.

Sometimes, the courts have stated that they would quash an administrative action if no reasonable body would have reached such a decision.[120] Thus, while quashing an administrative action under the Companies Act, 1956 the Supreme Court stated in *Rohtas Industries* v. *S.D. Agarwal*:[121]

> We do not think that any reasonable person much less any expert body like the Government on the material before it, could have jumped to the conclusion that there was any fraud involved in the sale of the shares in question.

Where under a statute, the state government could supersede the corporation if it appeared to the government that the corporation was not competent or it persistently defaulted in performing its duties. Explaining the provision, the Supreme Court held that it would not review the facts as an appellate body, but could set aside the order of supersession 'if no reasonable person on a proper consideration of the materials before the State Government could form the opinion that the corporation is not competent to perform, or persistently makes default' in performing its duties.[122] In such cases, the test of intervention by a court is not what it considers as unreasonable but whether, in its opinion, a reasonable body would have come to such a decision, or when the action is 'oppressive or palpably absurd'.[123] To this extent, no new principle appears to emerge as the same result could possibly be achieved by pressing into service the ground of 'irrelevant or extraneous' considerations as the basis of reviewing the action rather than invoking the test of a reasonable man.[124] Judicial review of administrative action on this account, therefore, appears to be more restrictive than when the authority is required to act reasonably under the statute. Of course, because of the fine distinctions between the two it is not clear whether the test of 'unreasonable action pure and simple' is in any way different from the test of 'a decision which no reasonable body would reach'.

In France, the procedure followed for annulling administrative action is known as *'recours en annulation pour exces de pouvoir'*. The object of this procedure is to quash an administrative act or decision which is improper. The test of reasonableness is much broader in France than what it has been possible to achieve in the common law system. It is an overriding principle of the French administrative law that an administrative act is proper and, therefore, lawful only if it is reasonable, the opposite of capricious or arbitrary, and, further, the administrator must produce the reason before the tribunal (Conseil d'État [Council of State]) whenever it thinks that there is sufficient ground for producing the reason.[125] Thus an administrative action can be examined under the test of reason. Whatever grounds of quashing an administrative action are available in Britain are also available in France but superadded to those is the test of reasonableness. In France, the ground of *'l' detournement de pouvoir'* means that though the public authority has presented the external legal formalities, yet it has used the power granted to it to secure a purpose outside the intended scope of the power. Further, in France, beyond this there is the much developed ground of '*la violation de la loi*' which goes much further and is vastly multifarious. The implications are that the Conseil d'État can quash an administrative action which appears to it not to be in accord with the French legal system though it does not infringe any positive enactment. Thus, the Conseil imposes on the administration conformity to a standard of conduct not enacted as obligatory by any statute.

4.4.3 AUTHORITY NOT EXERCISING DISCRETION

Where discretion has been conferred on an authority, it is expected to exercise it by applying its mind to the facts and circumstances of the case in hand. If the authority takes action without applying its mind to the case before it, the action would be bad. In such a situation, the authority is deemed to have failed to exercise the discretion. There are many situations in which such a flaw can arise.

(I) NON-CONSIDERATION OF THE MATTER BY THE AUTHORITY

An administrative order is bad if it is issued without the authority considering the matter and forming an opinion thereon. The Motor Vehicles Act, 1939 says: 'Where any State transport undertaking is of opinion . . .', it would mean that the transport corporation should consider the scheme of nationalisation of certain bus routes and form its own opinion as regards the matter. Where a scheme was published by the manager without the corporation applying its mind thereto and the scheme was approved by the governor, the court held it invalid because the corporation had not applied its mind.[126] The Court ordinarily would not substitute its own finding over the finding of the executive authority unless the latter's opinion is unreasonable or is based on irrelevant or extraneous considerations or is against the law declared.[127]

(II) ACTING UNDER DICTATION

A situation of non-application of its mind by the authority concerned arises when it does not consider the matter itself but exercises its discretion under the dictation of a superior authority. This, in law, would amount to abdication of power by the authority concerned and would be bad. Although the authority purports to act itself, yet, in effect, it is not so as it does not take the action in question in its own judgment which obviously is intended by the statute. *Commissioner of Police* v. *Gordhandas Bhanji*[128] illustrates the point. The Bombay Police Act, 1902 granted authority to the Commissioner of Police to grant licences for the construction of cinema theatres. The commissioner granted a licence to the respondent on the recommendation of an advisory committee but later cancelled it at the direction of the state government. The court held the cancellation order bad as it had come from the government and the commissioner merely acted as a transmitting agent. In *Punjab* v. *Suraj Parkash*,[129] the Supreme Court of India held that the state government could not give any instruction to the consolidation officer functioning under the East Punjab Holdings (Consolidation and Prevention of Fragmentation) Act, 1948, as there was no provision in the Act empowering the state government to give any such instructions to the consolidation officer. Where the director of industries was empowered to grant a licence, but the state government constituted a committee consisting of a deputy minister as the chairman, the director of industries, and two other officers as members for the purpose. When the committee rejected the petitioner's application for such a certificate, the Mysore High Court quashed its decision because the director had not exercised his own judgment but merely acted as the conduit pipe of the committee. To the contention of the director that the committee was only an advisory committee, the court replied that since a deputy minister was the chairman of the committee it was not possible for the director to disregard its decision.[130]

Similarly, the Supreme Court quashed an order of the Cane Commissioner, Bihar, by which he had excluded ninety-nine villages from the area reserved by him in favour of the appellant sugar company under the Sugarcane Control Order. The reason was that the cane commissioner had been dictated by the chief minister who had imposed his opinion on the cane commissioner. The court observed that under the sugarcane law, the power was exercisable by the cane commissioner. Therefore, he alone should have exercised the power and could not abdicate his responsibility in favour of the state government or the chief minister. It was not proper for the chief minister to have interfered with the commissioner's functions.[131] The Lahore High Court quashed an administrative decision when it was found to be taken on dictation of another which was required to be taken by the authorised administrative authority on its independent judgment.[132] The administrative functionary while exercising its powers must conform to steps and methods prescribed in the Act. When a statute limits things to be done in a particular form, it necessarily includes in itself the negative, that is, it should not be done in any other manner.

(III) IMPOSING FETTERS ON THE EXERCISE OF DISCRETION

A case of non-application of mind also arises when the authority having discretion chooses to impose fetters on its own discretion by announcing rules of policy to be applied by it rigidly to all cases coming before it for decision. When a statute confers power on an authority to apply a standard (as is the case in administrative discretion), it is expected of it to apply it from case to case, and not to fetter its discretion by declaration of rules or policy to be followed by it uniformly in all cases. What is expected of the authority is that it should consider each case on its merits and then decide it one way or the other. If, instead, it lays down a general rule to be applicable to each and every case, then it is preventing itself from exercising its mind according to the circumstances of each case and this amounts to going against what the statute had intended the authority to do. An old Bombay High Court case, *Gell* v. *Teja Noora*,[133] may be cited in support of the proposition. Under the Bombay Police Act, 1863, the commissioner of police had discretion to refuse licence for any land conveyance which he might consider to be insufficiently sound or otherwise unfit for the conveyance of the public. Instead of applying his discretion to grant the licence or not after examining each carriage, he issued a general order setting forth the details of construction which he required to be adopted in each victoria presented to him for a licence. He also announced that he had a sample victoria prepared, and that all new victorias must conform to the pattern. The court held the order to be illegal because the discretion had to be exercised 'after the commissioner had made himself in some way acquainted with the character of the carriage to be licensed, and had considered whether it, as an individual carriage, is fit for the conveyance of the public. In the exercise of this discretion he is not to fetter himself with rules which would prevent him in each case being quite free to consider the merits of each particular carriage.'

As stated earlier, one of the reasons for conferring administrative discretion through a statute is that there are cases where it is not possible to reduce it within the four corners of a rule. If the administrative authority attempts to lay down a rule, it violates that principle and acts illegally. However, it does not mean that an administrative authority should not at all be encouraged to lay down some general policy norms even though the statute has failed to do so. Wherever possible, it should lay down the principles for the exercise of its discretion. In fact, in some situations this may even be inevitable if the authority is to discharge its functions effectively and uniformly particularly when the cases to be dealt with are very large in number. Therefore, the desirability of laying down general principles of policy has to be reconciled with the duty of the authority not to fetter its own discretion.[134] Such a balance would be achieved if the authority lays down a general rule or policy, but, at the same time, keeps an open mind to consider whether in a particular case before it that policy or rule is applicable or not. The authority should also keep an open mind to consider such cases on merits as do not fall within this general rule.[135] In fact, in the *Gell* case itself, there was a suggestion that if the order of the commissioner would have been in a slightly different form, and had stated that the particular form of victoria would satisfy his requirement, there would have been no harm in it. Two Calcutta High Court cases very well illustrate the legal position in this regard. In one case, where the administrative authority was empowered to acquire from a producer 'available surplus' of food grains which was to be determined by taking into account the estimated yield of the producer and his family consumption etc., the court recognised that the 'available surplus' of a producer could be determined on the basis of the average expected yield of the locality; otherwise, the 'administrative machinery required to investigate the case of about four million cultivators would be so stupendous and costly that the very object of the . . . [law] would be frustrated.'[136] In the second case,[137] the court insisted that if a producer wants, he should be given an opportunity to explain his peculiar circumstances by reason of which his 'available surplus' is less than the average. The Supreme Court of Pakistan held that while deciding an administrative matter, the administrative authority can obtain the material on which he is to act in such manner as may be feasible and convenient provided that the affected party had fair opportunity of correcting or contradicting any relevant statement prejudicial to it.[138]

A number of decisions by the English courts also lay down a similar principle. It is well settled there that adopting a rigid policy and exercising discretion accordingly is wrong. A general policy may, however, be adopted but each case should be decided on its merits; each case is to be considered to see whether the general policy is applicable to it. The question will have to be considered whether, based on the facts of a particular case, there is enough to take it out of the general rule which the authority concerned might have laid down.[139] The court observed in a case:

> . . . [a] Minister charged with the duty of making individual administrative decisions in a fair and impartial manner may nevertheless have a general policy in regard to matters which are relevant to those decisions, provided that the existence of that general policy does not preclude him from fairly judging all the issues which are relevant to each individual case as it comes up for decision.[140]

The principle has been reiterated by the House of Lords in *British Oxygen Co. Ltd* v. *Minister of Technology*.[141] Lord Reid stated that a minister having a discretion may formulate a policy or make a limiting rule as to the future exercise of his discretion, if he thinks that good administration requires it, provided that he listens to any applicant who has something new to say. The general rule is that anyone who has to exercise a statutory discretion must not 'shut his ears to an application'.

The position is thus well established that the exercise of statutory discretion cannot be fettered by adopting a rigid policy or a mechanical rule.[142]

(IV) ACTING MECHANICALLY AND WITHOUT DUE CARE

Another example of an authority having statutory discretion not exercising its discretion arises when the authority passes the order mechanically and without applying its mind to the facts and circumstances of the case before it. This situation is typified by *Emperor* v. *Sibnath Banerji*[143] where a preventive detention order was quashed because it had been issued in a routine manner on the advice of the police, without the home secretary himself applying his mind to the materials before him and satisfying himself, independently of the police recommendation, that an order of preventive detention was called for. It transpired at the hearing of the case before the court that the home department followed the practice of issuing a detention order automatically whenever the police recommended it, and the home secretary did not personally satisfy himself on the materials placed before him whether the issuance of the order of preventive detention in a particular case was justified or not. It was held that the home secretary's personal satisfaction in each case of detention was a condition precedent to the issuance of the order, otherwise it would be quashed.

Under the Prevention of Corruption Act, 1947, the sanction of the government is necessary for prosecuting a public servant for certain offences. It has been held that the sanction under the Act is not intended to be an automatic formality. The authority giving the sanction should consider for itself the evidence before it comes to a conclusion whether the prosecution in the circumstances be sanctioned or forbidden. The facts constituting the offence charged should be placed before the sanctioning authority which should decide the matter after applying its mind to them. The sanctioning authority should consider the evidence before it and after consideration of all the circumstances of the case sanction the prosecution. It is necessary that the fact of the application of the mind of the sanctioning authority should either appear from the sanction itself or should be proved by some other evidence.[144] Where while issuing a search warrant, the authority did not strike out the irrelevant columns in the printed form which ought to have been done and the blanks in the form had not been filled in, it was held that this indicated that the authority had issued the warrant without applying its mind as to the necessity of search.[145]

A case of non-application of the mind may arise when the authority concerned acts in a casual manner without due care and caution in exercising its discretion. In a preventive detention case, *Jagannath v. State of Orissa*,[146] six grounds were mentioned in the order of detention on the basis on which the subjective satisfaction of the government was formed. These grounds were verbatim reproduced from the relevant provision in the Act. In between the various grounds mentioned in the order, instead of using the conjunctive 'and', the disjunctive 'or' had been used. In the affidavit filed before the court by the Home Minister on behalf of the government, he mentioned only two grounds on which his personal satisfaction to detain the petitioner was based. The court ruled that the order was bad as the minister had not applied his mind to all the grounds mentioned therein. When several grounds were mentioned for detaining a person, it was necessary that the detaining authority should be satisfied about each one of the grounds.[147]

In *G. Sadanandan v. State of Kerala*,[148] the court commented adversely on the casual manner in which the detaining authority had acted in passing the order. The order was quashed with a strong reminder to the administration that it should be more careful in exercising its powers. The court thus pointed out that the tendency of the authorities to treat these matters in a somewhat 'casual and cavalier manner' which conceivably results from the continuous use of unfettered powers by them may ultimately pose a serious threat to the basic values of the democratic way of life.

The ground of non-application of mind is a new and developing ground to challenge the exercise of administrative discretion. In this regard, the Supreme Court judgment in *Barium Chemicals Ltd* v. *Rana*[149] is worthy of notice. Under the Foreign Exchange Regulation Act, 1947, the central government, if it considered necessary or expedient to obtain and examine for the purpose of the Act, any information, book or other document in the possession of any person, it may by order in writing require any such person to furnish the same to it. The words 'considers it necessary or expedient' seem to indicate that an unqualified discretion was given to the government to obtain such information, but the Supreme Court interpreted the words as postulating 'that the authority concerned has thought over the matter deliberately and with care and it has been found necessary as a result of such thinking to pass the order'. The court would quash the order if the order were to show that there was no careful thinking or proper application of the mind as to necessity of obtaining and examining the documents, etc.[150]

In some statutory provisions, exercise of a power is made conditional on the officer concerned having 'reason to believe' in something. Under the Aluminium (Control) Order, 1970, issued under the Essential Commodities Act, 1955, the controller was authorized to 'seize any aluminium in respect of which he has reason to believe that a contravention of this order has been, is being, or is about to be committed'. The Delhi High Court in *Hindustan Aluminium* v. *Controller of Aluminium*[151] quashed an order seizing aluminium in the possession of the petitioner. The court emphasized that any exercise of a statutory power interfering with the property rights of the citizens is possible only after strictly complying with the pre-conditions for the exercise of such a power. 'The reason to believe that any contravention of the Control Order has taken place' is a pre-condition to the seizure of goods. The 'reason to believe' must relate to the period of time when the impugned seizure was made; any subsequent acquisition of belief in this regard would not be of any avail.

Usually, the statute would say that the government may pass an order if it is of the opinion that it is 'necessary or expedient to do so'. Can an order be challenged on the ground that it has no recital saying that the government has formed the requisite opinion before issuing the order? Can the absence of such a recital be treated ipso facto as an evidence of non-application of mind by the decision-maker? The judicial view regarding such an argument is that the validity of the order does not depend upon such a recital, if the requisite opinion was formed before the order was made. The formation of the requisite opinion is the condition precedent to making of the order and the government can establish this fact by other means.[152]

4.4.4 NON-COMPLIANCE WITH PROCEDURAL REQUIREMENTS

Exercise of discretionary power can be held to be bad because the authority concerned did not comply with the procedural requirements laid down in the statute, provided that the court holds the compliance with the procedure to be mandatory. It is for the court to decide whether a procedural requirement is mandatory or directory. For example, a provision requiring the decision-making body to consult another authority before arriving at a decision is usually considered mandatory. In *Narayana* v. *State of Kerala*,[153] the provision in question authorised the state government to revoke the licence of a licensee for supply of electric energy in public interest but only after consulting the state electricity board. The court ruled that consultation with the board was a condition precedent for exercising the power of revocation of licence and was thus mandatory. Although the board's opinion was not binding on the government, nevertheless, consultation with it was an imperative condition for revoking the licence. Another case on a similar point is *Naraindas* v. *State of Madhya Pradesh*.[154] The government was authorised to prescribe textbooks for various courses in schools in consultation with the Board of Higher Education. The government consulted the chairman but not the entire board. The government's notification prescribing textbooks was accordingly held void. Under the Land Acquisition Act the collector is required to give an opportunity of being heard to a person filing objections against the proposed land acquisition. This duty to afford the opportunity of hearing has been held to be mandatory in *Mandir Sita Ramji* v. *Lt. Governor of Delhi*.[155] If property is acquired without complying with this procedure, it would be quashed.

4.4.5 ADMINISTRATIVE DISCRIMINATION

In addition to the above grounds of review of administrative action by the courts, another ground available in Pakistan and India is that of administrative discrimination under Articles 25 and 14 of their respective constitutions. Previously, it has been considered that where a statute is discriminatory either because it does not make a reasonable classification or confers an unregulated discretion on the executive, the statute itself would be void as unconstitutional. There may, however, be a situation where the statute itself does not suffer from any such vice, but the administrative authority entrusted with the duty of carrying the statute into operation may act in a discriminatory manner, or may not follow the policy or principle laid down in the Act to regulate its discretion. In such a case, the charge of violation of equal protection might be upheld against the administration and its action quashed. The classic case on the point is an American case, *Yick Wo* v. *Hopkins*.[156] By an ordinance, the city of San Francisco made it unlawful to carry on a laundry, without the consent of the board of supervisors, except in a brick or stone building. In administering it, 200 Chinese launderers were denied permission, even though they complied with every requisite, while 80 non-Chinese under similar circumstances were permitted. Two Chinese brought the matter before the US Supreme Court which held that the ordinance had been administered with 'a mind so unequal and oppressive as to amount to a practical denial by the State' of equal protection of laws. The court went on to state: 'Though the law itself be fair on its face and impartial in appearance, yet, if it is applied and administered by public authority with an evil eye and an unequal hand, so as practically to make unjust and illegal discriminations between persons in similar circumstances, material to their rights, the denial of equal justice is still within the prohibition of the Constitution.'

This principle has been applied in Pakistan and India as well. The equality clause secures 'every person against arbitrary discrimination whether occasioned by the express terms of the statute or by their improper application through duly constituted agents.'[157] 'Equal protection clause can be invoked not merely where discrimination appears on the express terms of the statute itself but also when it is the result of improper or prejudiced execution of the law.'[158] When administrative discretion is conferred subject to a standard or policy declared in the Act, then discretion exercised in disregard of the standard or policy can be challenged.[159] Public functionaries are not supposed to fix a different standard and criteria for different persons in similar situation without change of circumstances.[160]

Though the principle is established that discriminatory administrative action can be challenged on the ground of discrimination, yet, in practice, it is not easy to succeed in having an action quashed, and it is only in a few cases that the challenge to administrative action has actually succeeded. The attitude of the courts generally is to sustain administrative action against attacks of discrimination. The courts start with a presumption that the administration of a particular law has not been discriminatory. Furthermore, abuse of power is not easily assumed where discretion is vested in high officials. It is for the complainant to prove that there has been an abuse of power, and this is a heavy burden to discharge though the courts have said that the onus is not to prove to the hilt but such as will render the absence of bona fides reasonably probable. If in a particular case the order is impeached as discriminatory, and the petitioner points out the circumstances which *prima facie* and without anything more would make out the exercise of the power discriminatory *qua* him, it would be incumbent on the authority to explain the circumstances under which the order has been made and the court would then scrutinise the circumstances of the case with regard to the object sought to be achieved by the enactment and come to its own conclusion with respect to the bona fides of the order.[161] The administrative authority concerned has a good defence if it can prove its bona fides.

Where auction of government property was scrapped and the government decided to dispose of its property through negotiations wherein only the lowest bidder was invited and all others were ignored, it was held that the authorities had not adhered to rule of equality and had acted arbitrarily and discriminately.[162] Even in disposal of the property through negotiations, the procedure should have been such as was reasonable, fair and transparent, in public interest and inspired public confidence being above board. The procedure should have been non-discriminatory and aimed at, on the one hand, to provide equal opportunity to eligible persons and on the other hand to avoid loss to the exchequer.

It may be easier to convince the court of discrimination when a large number of people are involved (as in *Yick Wo* v. *Hopkins*) than when discrimination is alleged by one person only. The leading case in this area is *Ram Krishna Dalmia* v. *Justice Tendolkar*.[163] A commission of inquiry was appointed into Dalmia affairs under the Commissions of Inquiry Act, 1952. Section 3 of the Act as well as the notification appointing the commission were challenged as discriminatory. However, Section 3 was held valid because the discretion conferred thereunder was not unguided as it was to be exercised subject to the policy and conditions laid down in the Act, i.e. a commission could only be appointed to inquire into a definite matter of public importance. Against the notification, it was contended that the petitioner and his companies had been arbitrarily singled out for the purpose of hostile and discriminatory treatment and subjected to a harassing and oppressive inquiry. The court held that the parliament having left the selective application of the Commissions of Inquiry Act to the discretion of the government, the latter must act on the information available to it and the opinion it formed thereon. It is to be presumed, until the contrary is proved, that the government would act honestly, properly and in conformity with the policy and the principles laid down by the parliament. The court further held that the quality and characteristics said to exist in the petitioners' companies were so peculiar or unique as to constitute a good or valid basis on which the petitioners and their companies could be regarded as a class by themselves. The facts disclosed 'afford sufficient support to the presumption of constitutionality of the notification' and 'it is for the petitioners to allege and prove beyond doubt that other parsons or companies similarly situate have been left out and the petitioners and their companies have been singled out for discriminatory and hostile treatment.' The petitioners failed, in the opinion of the court, to discharge this onus.

The Assam Food Grains (Licensing and Control) Order, 1961 enumerated five matters which the licensing authority was to keep in view in granting or refusing a licence. One of these matters was that a co-operative society was to be preferred to anyone else in certain circumstances in granting a licence. This clause, it was held, was not invalid for it was not completely unrelated to the objects of the Essential Commodities Act, 1955, under which the order in question was issued. But when the government directed the licensing authority to grant licences under the order only to a specified co-operative society, in order to create a monopoly in its favour, and the licensing officer acted accordingly, then a discrimination arose against others and this was held invalid.[164]

In *Satwant Singh* v. *Assistant Passport Officer*, an order refusing to issue a passport to the petitioner was held to be violative of Article 14 as there was no law governing the issue of a passport by the executive and it was entirely a matter of discretion for the executive to issue it or not. The Supreme Court observed: '. . . in the case of unchannelled arbitrary discretion, discrimination is writ large on the face of it. Such a discretion patently violates the doctrine of equality, for the difference in the treatment of persons rests solely on the arbitrary selection of the executive.'[165]

The Government of India issued a memorandum raising the age of retirement from 55 to 58 years subject to certain conditions. The respondent was not given the benefit of this memorandum. The court quashed the order holding it to be a violation of Article 14.[166] Before the government places the name of a person on the blacklist debarring him from government contracts, he should be given an opportunity being heard as blacklisting creates a disability and prevents the concerned persons from entering into lawful relationship with the government for purposes of gain.[167] The wage board for working journalists divided the newspapers and news agencies into seven classes on the basis of gross revenues. According to this test, an agency should have come within the third category, but the wage board placed it in a higher category. This was held to be discriminatory.[168]

4.4.6 DOCTRINE OF PROMISSORY ESTOPPEL

Where contracts have been *bona fide* and legally entered upon and had given rise to rights and liabilities enforceable at law then certainly vested rights had come into existence which could not be overridden except by express words of an authority competent to legislate retrospectively, competent to override or impair such vested rights. An agency or authority not empowered to override or impair vested rights cannot achieve that end simply by giving its dispensation in the form of a declaration.[169] This is what is known as the doctrine of promissory estoppel. It is meant to protect innocent citizens who enter into contract under the declared rules or policies of the government from arbitrary withdrawal of such rules or policies retrospectively. The doctrine saves the contracts made and acts performed under such rules or policies before their withdrawal because of the vested rights that have arisen from such contracts or acts.

Such a vested right was protected and preserved in the case of *Union of India and others* v. *Anglo-Afghan Agencies*[170] by invoking aid the principle of promissory estoppel in the following words:

> We hold that the claim of the respondents is appropriately founded upon the equity which arises in their favour as a result of the representation made on behalf of the Union of India in the Export Promotion Scheme, and the action taken by the respondents acting upon that representation undertaken by the respondents acting upon that representation under the belief that the government would carry out the representation made by it. On the facts proved in this case, no ground has been suggested before the Court for exempting the government from the equity arising out of the acts done by the exporters to their prejudice relying upon the representation. This principle has been recognised by the Courts in India and the Judicial Committee of the Privy Council in several cases.

The doctrine of promissory estoppel is subject to the following limitations:[171]

(i) The doctrine of promissory estoppel cannot be invoked against the legislature or the laws framed by it because the legislature cannot make a representation;

(ii) Promissory estoppel cannot be invoked for directing the doing of the thing which was against law when the representation was made or the promise held out;

(iii) No agency or authority can be held bound by a promise or representation not lawfully extended or given;

(iv) The doctrine of promissory estoppel will not apply where no steps have been taken consequent to the representation or inducement so as to irrevocably commit the property or the reputation of the party invoking it; and

(v) The party which has indulged in fraud or collusion for obtaining some benefits under the representation cannot be rewarded by the enforcement of the promise.

Thus, the doctrine of promissory estoppel does not extend to legislative and sovereign functions, but executive functions are not excluded from the operation of the doctrine. In India, an earlier view that the doctrine did not extend to the executive functions was subsequently overruled by the Indian Supreme Court in *Union of India* v. *Godfrey Philips*[172] in the following words:

> There can therefore be no doubt that the doctrine of promissory estoppel is applicable against the government in the exercise of the governmental, public or executive functions and the doctrine of executive necessity or freedom of future executive action cannot be invoked to defeat the applicability of the doctrine of promissory estoppel. We must concede that the subsequent decision of this Court in *Jeet Ram* v. *State of Haryana* (1980) 3 SCR 689; AIR 1980 SC 1285 takes a slightly different view and holds that the doctrine of promissory estoppel is not available against the exercise of executive functions of the State and the State cannot be prevented from exercising its functions under the law. This decision also expresses its disagreement with the observations made in the *Motilal Sugar Mills* case AIR 1979 SC 621 that the doctrine of promissory estoppel cannot be defeated by invoking the defence of executive necessity, suggesting by necessary implication that the doctrine of executive necessity is available to the Government to escape its obligation under the doctrine of promissory estoppel. We find it difficult to understand how a Bench of two Judges in the *Jeet Ram* case could possibly overturn or disagree with what was said by another Bench of two Judges in the *Motilal Sugar Mills* case. If the Bench of two Judges in the *Jeet Ram* case found themselves unable to agree with law laid down in the *Motilal Sugar Mills* case, they could have referred the *Jeet Ram* case to a larger Bench, but we do not think it was right on their part to express their disagreement with the enunciation of the law by a co-ordinate Bench of the same Court in the *Motilal Sugar Mills*.

4.4.7 ONUS OF PROOF

In *Narayan* v. *State of Maharashtra*,[173] the Supreme Court of India has discussed, somewhat elaborately, the question of onus of proof in cases in which an exercise of discretionary power is challenged on any of the grounds mentioned above. The commissioner, Bombay Division, issued a notification under the Land Acquisition Act notifying his intention to acquire certain lands for developing and utilising them into a 'residential and industrial area'. The notification also stated that the said lands being 'waste or arable' and their acquisition being 'urgently necessary' the commissioner was pleased to direct under Section 17(4) that the provisions of Section 5-A 'shall not apply in respect of the said lands'. Section 5-A provides for filing of objections against the proposed acquisition of land and a collector's enquiry into the said objections. The Bombay High Court quashed the notification under Section 17(4) on the ground that the government had not discharged its burden of showing facts constituting the urgency which impelled it to give directions under Section 17(4) dispensing with the enquiries under Section 5-A. The court pointed out that while the petitioner had repeatedly asserted in the petition that the urgency clause had been applied without any valid reason, the government in its affidavit never stated any facts whatsoever and brought no material on record whatever on which the commissioner formed his opinion. The court insisted that the burden of proving such circumstances at least prima facie was on the commissioner which he had failed to discharge. The government appealed to the Supreme Court. It claimed that the question whether any urgency existed or not for exercising the power under Section 17 was 'a matter solely for the determination of the commissioner' and it was not a justiciable matter.

The court first clarified the scope of judicial review in this area. Even when the formation of an opinion by an administrative authority in a subjective matter, that opinion has to be based upon some relevant materials in order to pass the test which the courts impose. That test basically is: Was the authority concerned acting within the scope of its power or in the sphere where its opinion and discretion must be permitted to have full play? The court would not interfere if it came to the conclusion that the authority concerned was acting within the scope of its powers and had some material, however meagre, on which it could reasonably base its opinion. The court would, however, interfere in cases in which the power was exercised in such an obviously arbitrary or perverse fashion, without regard to the actual and undeniable facts, or, in other words so unreasonably as to leave no doubt whatsoever in the mind of the court that there had been an excess of power. There may also be cases where the mind of the authority had not been applied at all to what was legally imperative for it to consider.

In the instant case, the main dispute was whether the petitioner was required to bring the material before the court to support his contention that no urgency existed, or whether, once the petitioner denied that any urgency existed, it was incumbent on the government to satisfy the court that there was material upon which the respondents could reach the opinion as mentioned in Section 17(4). The main question to be decided, therefore, was that of burden of proof. It ruled that it was for the petitioner to substantiate the grounds of his challenge either by leading the evidence or showing that some evidence had come from the respondent's side indicating that his challenge to an order was made good. If he failed to discharge that onus, his petition would fail.

The issue in the instant case was whether the conditions precedent to the exercise of power under Section 17(4) had been fulfilled or not. Reading Section 17(4), not in isolation, but along with Section 5-A, the mind of the concerned officer was to be applied not only to the question whether the land in question was waste or arable, but also to the question whether there was an urgency of such a nature that even the summary proceedings under Section 5-A should be eliminated. The public purpose indicated in the instant case was development of land for industrial and residential purposes. Prima facie, this did not call for any such action as to make immediate possession, without even a summary enquiry being held, imperative. Such schemes usually take quite long to fructify and the summary enquiry under Section 5-A could be completed without any impediment to such schemes. On the basis of the apparent facts, therefore, there was an apparent absence of such an urgency so as to eliminate Section 5-A enquiry. The recital indicated that the commissioner applied his mind only to the question whether the land was waste or arable and whether its acquisition was urgently needed. The commissioner did not apply his mind at all to the question whether there was such an urgency as to require elimination of the Section 5-A enquiry. Thus the recital held defective and the burden rested on the state to remove this defect, if possible, by evidence to show that there were some exceptional circumstances which necessitated elimination of Section 5-A enquiry and that the commissioner had applied his mind to this essential question. Therefore, the burden could correctly be placed on the state in this case. The failure of the state to produce the evidence of facts especially within its knowledge, which rested on it under Section 106, taken together with attendant facts and circumstances including the recitals, had enabled the petitioner to discharge his burden.

4.4.8 CONCLUDING REMARKS

Although the courts have developed a number of grounds to attack an administrative discretionary action, the fact, however, remains that the judicial review in the area is still only peripheral and, by and large, it does not comprehend or extend to the merits of the administrative action: This by itself is a limitation of consequence. But even in the area of available judicial review, it is not easy to get the relief sought, and have the administrative action quashed. The major difficulty is one of proof of such grounds as *mala fides*, improper purpose, irrelevant considerations, etc. The courts are extremely reluctant to order the administrative authority concerned to produce the relevant files so that they may look into them to satisfy themselves that the action taken was not in any way vitiated, and that no ground existed on which the courts could quash it. The courts have repeatedly refused to examine the government record to find out the real reasons underlying an administrative action. Even if the court directs the government to produce its records, the government enjoys certain privileges in the matter and can at times get away without producing the record. In most of the cases involving challenge to administrative action, the courts have nothing more to go by than the order in question and the affidavits.

It may be that a statute under which an action is being taken may obligate the administrative authority concerned to give reasons for its action. In such cases, the courts have been in a somewhat better position to scrutinise the validity of the administrative action in question. Also, in the area of preventive detention, as stated earlier, it is obligatory on the detaining authority to give the grounds of detention to a detinue, and in a number of cases, the courts have scrutinised the grounds and quashed the orders of preventive detention. Generally, if the obligation to give reasons was not imposed under the statute, the courts did not impose the obligation to give reasons unless there was a provision for an administrative appeal. Even when the statute prescribed the purposes for which, and the grounds on which, the power could be exercised, the authority concerned was under no obligation to reveal the reasons or the facts which in its view warrant the action in question. It is only rarely that the party challenging the administrative action succeeds in presenting some evidence in support of his contentions against the validity of the administrative action in question and gets relief from the court on that basis. In most of the cases, the person challenging an action would have to depend upon the circumstances of deficiencies and lacunae in the affidavits filed by the authority in support of its action to obtain any relief. Certain decisions of the Supreme Court indicate that the courts are now ready to probe into the exercise of the administrative discretion somewhat more deeply. Still the courts are reluctant to go into the question whether a fact revealed by the administration in the affidavit or the order was in existence or not. The court's reluctance to look into the departmental files remains a major hindrance in the way of challenging an administrative action and this saps the efficacy of the judicial review to a considerable extent.

It will be a great advantage to the individual affected by an administrative action if the administration were to disclose to him the reasons and the relevant facts for acting in the way it is. He can then decide whether he should challenge the action or not in a court of law. Many challenges to administrative action are made at present because the individual affected, being ignorant of the reasons and other circumstances, does not know whether the action suffers from any flaw or not. In the area of quasi-judicial adjudication, an obligation to make speaking orders has come to be imposed on the concerned bodies. A similar development is imperative in the area of exercise of administrative powers. The Conseil d'État in France has gone far in the direction of requiring administrative decisions to contain reasons. In Britain, the Tribunals and Inquiries Act, 1958 imposes a statutory duty to give reasons, if requested, for decisions by most tribunals and by ministers required to hold statutory inquiries.[174] In Pakistan an amendment has been made in 1997 in General Clauses Act, 1897 introducing therein Section 24A which requires that the authority officer or person making any order or issuing any direction under the powers conferred by or under any enactment should, so far as necessary or appropriate, give reason for making the order or issuing the direction.[175] Thus the requirement to give reason has been made statutory in Pakistan.

Notes

1. In the words of Wade and Phillips, '. . . modern government gives rise to many disputes which cannot appropriately be solved by applying objective legal principles or standards and depend ultimately on what is desirable in the public interest as a matter of social policy.' *Constitutional Law* (1965) 699. See also Report of the Franks Committee 8, 9 (1957).
2. AIR 1963 SC 1319.
3. *Port Services (Private) Ltd* v. *Pakistan*, PLD 1995 Karachi 374.
4. *Faridsons Ltd* v. *Government of Pakistan*, PLD 1961 SC 537.
5. *G. Nageswara Rao* v. *APSRTC*, AIR 1959 SC 308.
6. In *Hari K. Gawali* v. *Dy. Commr. of Police*, AIR 1957 SC 559, Supreme Court held that where the functions of a prosecutor and the judge are exercised by two persons no matter of the same department, there is no violation of principles of natural justice.
7. Section 8(b).
8. [1977] 2 SCC 491.
9. [1978] 3 SCC 366.

10. *Syed Abul Ala Maudoodi* v. *Government of West Pakistan*, PLD 1964 SC 673.
11. [1971] 1 WLR 433.
12. *Interstate Commerce Commission* v. *Union Pacific Rly. Co.*, 222 US 541 [1912].
13. 190 F 2d 429 [1951].
14. [1971] 2 SCC 617, 629.
15. Ibid., p. 629.
16. *Richardson* v. *Perales*, 402 US 389 [1971].
17. [1948] AC 8; [1947] 1 All ER 612. In 1957, the Frank Committee also made a similar recommendation, p. 5.
18. *Gullapalli Nageswara Rao* v. *APSRTC*, AIR 1959 SC 308.
19. *Nageswara Rao* v. *State of AP*, AIR 1959 SC 1376.
20. [1935] 1 KB 179.
21. [1977] 1 SCC 472.
22. Griffith & Street, *Principles of Administrative Law* (4th edn., London: Sir Issac Pitman & Sons Ltd, 1967] 147.
23. *Nagendra Nath Bora* v. *Commissioner of Hills Division*, AIR 1958 SC 398; *Gullapalli Nageswara Rao* v. *AP State Road Transport Corporation*, AIR 1959 SC 308.
24. *Julius* v. *Bishop of Oxford* [1880] 5 AC 214.
25. Freund, *Administrative Powers over Persons and Property* (1928) 71.
26. See Baker, 'Policy by Rule or Ad Hoc Approach: Which should it be?', 22 Law and Contempt. Prob. 657 (1957); Friendly, *Federal Administrative Agencies: The Need for Better Definition of Standards* (1962), Chapters I and VII; Davis, *Discretionary Justice* (1969).
27. *US* v. *Wunderlich*, 342 US 98, 101 [1951].
28. *New York* v. *United States*, 342 US 882, 884 [1951].
29. In Australia, a full-fledged enquiry was conducted on the review of administrative discretions; see Final Report of the Bland Committee on Administrative Discretions (1973). The report has led to the creation of an ombudsman and a general administrative tribunal to review discretionary decisions in many cases.
30. *Eshugbayi* v. *Government of Nigeria* [1931] LR 670 (CA).
31. *Hadi Ali* v. *Government of West Pakistan*, PLD 1956 Lah. 824.
32. *Abdul Majid* v. *Province of West Pakistan*, PLD 1956 Lah. 615; *Robert* v. *Hopwood* [1925] AC 578; *Mayor and Councillors of East Iremantle Corporation* v. *Anwois* [1902] AC 213; *R.* v. *Bishop of London* [1889] 24 QBD 213.
33. *Khola Jabeen* v. *Government of the North-West Frontier Province*, PLD 1976 Pesh. 97; *Presiding Officer* v. *Sadruddin Ansari*, PLD 1967 SC 569; *Abdul Aziz* v. *Mohammad Ali*, PLD 1967 Lah. 762; *Syed Hadi Ali* v. *Government of West Pakistan*, PLD 1956 Lah. 824; cf. *Nasim Mehmood* v. *King Edward Medical College*, PLD 1965 Lah. 272.

34. *Mir Zaman* v. *Government of West Pakistan*, PLD 1969 Lah. 71; *Mayor of Westminster* v. *London & North-Western Railway Co. Ltd* [1905] AC 426; *Alcroft* v. *Bishop of London* [1891] AC 675; *R.* v. *Boteler*, 122 ER 718.

35. *Farid Sons Ltd* v. *Government of Pakistan*, PLD 1961 SC 537; *Adams* v. *Nagle* [1938] 303 US 532; *Geirad Trust Co.* v. *Helbering*, 301 US 540; *Mayor of Westminster* v. *London & North-Western Railway Co. Ltd* [1905] AC 426; *Walter* v. *Mellon*, 281 US 766.

36. Article 10 of the Pakistan Constitution, 1973; Article 22(5) of the Indian Constitution.

37. *State of Bombay* v. *Atmaram Shridhar Vaidya*, AIR 1951 SC 157; *Ram Krishan* v. *State of Delhi*, AIR 1953 SC 318; *Hari Kishan* v. *State of Maharashtra*, AIR 1962 SC 911.

38. *Shibbanlal Saksena* v. *State of UP*, AIR 1954 SC 179; *Dwarka Das Bhatia* v. *State of Jammu & Kashmir*, AIR 1957 SC 164.

39. *State of Maharashtra* v. *Prabhakar*, AIR 1966 SC 424.

40. *Badrul Huque Khan* v. *Election Tribunal*, PLD 1963 SC 704; *Jamal Shah* v. *Election Comm*, PLD 1966 SC 1.

41. *Jamal Shah* v. *Election Commission*, PLD 1966 SC 1.

42. *Abul Alla Maudoodi* v. *Government of West Pakistan*, PLD 1964 SC 673 at 709.

43. *R.* v. *Birmingham Compensation Appeal Tribunal, exp Road Haulage Executive* [1952] 2 All ER 100 n.

44. As Lord Summer said in *R.* v. *Nat Bell Liquors Ltd* [1922] 2 AC 128, 152: 'To say that there is no jurisdiction to convict without evidence is the same thing as saying that there is jurisdiction if the decision is right, and none if it is wrong.'

45. PLD 1966 SC 1.

46. *Akbar Ali* v. *Razi-ur-Rahman*, PLD 1966 SC 492.

47. In the cases of *Muhammad Hussain Munir*, PLD 1974 SC 139 and *Zulfiqar Khan Awan* [1974] MR 530.

48. *US Corpn. of Pakistan Ltd* v. *Punjab Labour Appellate Tribunal*, PLD 1987 SC 447.

49. [1969] AC 147.

50. *Noorwar Jan* v. *Senior Member BRNWFP*, PLD 1991 SC 531.

51. *R.* v. *Nat Bell Liquors Ltd* [1922] 2 AC 128 at 152.

52. *Jaichand* v. *West Bengal*, AIR 1967 SC 483, 485.

53. AIR 1964 SC 72.

54. See de Smith, *Judicial Review of Administrative Action* (3rd edn., London: Stevens and Sons Limited, 1973) 282, 293.

55. AIR 1964 SC 962.

56. *G. Sadanandan* v. *State of Kerala*, AIR 1966 SC 1925. For a few other cases on *mala fides*, see *S.S. Sen* v. *State of Bihar*, AIR 1972 Pat. 441; *Vincent Ferrer* v. *District Revenue Officer*, AIR 1974 AP 313.

57. *Haryana* v. *Rajendra*, AIR 1972 SC 1004; *N.P. Mathur* v. *State of Bihar*, AIR 1972 Pat. 93; *Hukam Singh* v. *State of Punjab*, AIR 1975 P. & H. 148.
58. AIR 1974 SC 555.
59. *Partap Singh* v. *State of Punjab*, AIR 1964 SC 72 at 83.
60. *University of Punjab* v. *Ruhi Farzana* [1996] SCMR 263.
61. Ibid.
62. *Punjab* v. *Ramjilal*, AIR 1971 SC 1228.
63. *Re Manick Chand Mahata* v. *Corporation of Calcutta* [1921] ILR Cal. 916.
64. *Muhammad Jamil Asghar* v. *The Improvement Trust*, PLD 1965 SC 698.
65. *Ahmed Hossain* v. *State*, AIR 1951 Nag. 138.
66. *Re Manick Chand Mahata* v. *Corporation of Calcutta*, ILR 1921 Cal. 916.
67. *ACC Store* v. *R.K. Mehra*, AIR 1973 P. & H. 342.
68. AIR 1975 SC 393. Also *Noor Chand* v. *State of West Bengal*, AIR 1974 SC 2120.
69. AIR 1975 SC 753. Also *Debu* v. *State of West Bengal*, AIR 1974 SC 816, but see *Anil Dey* v. *State of West Bengal*, AIR 1974 SC 832.
70. For instance, the *L.K. Das*, the *Noor Chand* and the *Dabu* cases. See also *Zafar-ul-Ahsan* v. *The Republic of Pakistan*, PLD 1960 SC 113.
71. For instance, *Ashni Kumar* v. *State of West Bengal*, AIR 1972 SC 2561; *Haradhana Saha* v. *State of West Bengal*, AIR 1974 SC 2154; *Samir Chatterjee* v. *State of West Bengal*, AIR 1975 C 1165.
72. *A.W. Malik* v. *The Authorised Officer*, PLD 1970 Dacca 178; *Muhammad Yousaf* v. *Province of Sindh*, PLD 1976 Kar. 1219; *Riaz Ahmad* v. *Secretary*, PLD 1977 Lah. 307; *Aziz Ahmad* v. *Secretary*, PLD 1984 Quetta 106; *Muhammad Jafar Tarar* v. *District Magistrate* [1990] CLC 281; *Tariq Transport Company* v. *Sargodha-Bhera Bus Service*, PLD 1958 SC 437; *Imtiaz Ahmad* v. *Ghulam Ali*, PLD 1963 SC 382; *Muhammad Naseem Khan* v. *Government of NWFP* [1990] CLC 1693; *Pakistan* v. *The Punjab Labour Court No. 2* [1982] CLC 711; *Masood Khan* v. *Settlement Commissioner* [1986] CLC 515; *Ameer* v. *Sikandar* [1986] CLC 2046; *Khalid Mahmud Khuhro* v. *Federation of Pakistan* [1986] CLC 2320; *Mir Sultan* v. *The Punjab Labour Appellate Tribunal* [1989] CLC 1495; *Murree Brewery Company Ltd* v. *Director-General* [1991] MLD 267; *Director of Rationing* v. *The Corporation of Calcutta*, AIR 1960 SC 1355; *District Magistrate* v. *Faqir Sayed Fayyaz ud Din*, PLD 1965 SC 371; *Syed Ali Abbas* v. *Vishan Singh*, PLD 1967 SC 294; *Abdul Qadir* v. *Government of West Pakistan*, PLD 1967 SC 506, *Chohan Flying Coach Service, Sahiwal* v. *Regional Transport Authority* [1993] CLC 1853, and *Dadabhoy Investment (Pvt) Ltd* v. *Federation of Pakistan*, PLD 1995 Kar. 33; *Jawed Hotel* v. *CDA*, PLD 1994 Lahore 315; and *Arif Builders* v. *Government of Pakistan*, PLD 1997 Karachi 627.
73. *Padfield* v. *Minister of Agriculture* [1968] AC 997.
74. AIR 1966 SC 740.
75. AIR 1962 SC 764 (the first *Arora* case).

76. Ibid., p. 722.

77. *Hukam Chand* v. *Union of India*, AIR 1976 SC 789.

78. *Ikram Bus Service* v. *Board of Revenue*, PLD 1963 SC 564.

79. See *Laker Airways Ltd* v. *Dept. of Trade* [1977] 2 WLR 234.

80. AIR 1960 SC 1223.

81. *PS Traders and Exporters* v. *Eapen*, AIR 1963 Bom. 50. Also see *Gujrat* v. *Krishna Cinema*, AIR 1971 SC 1650.

82. *M. Zahoor-ul-Haq* v. *Quarter Master General* [1994] CLC 2449.

83. *Krishna Murari* v. *Union of India*, AIR 1975 SC 1877.

84. *Sodhi Shamsher Singh* v. *State of Pepsu*, AIR 1954 SC 276.

85. *Sushanta Goswami* v. *State of West Bengal*, AIR 1969 SC 1004.

86. *Pushkar Mukherjee* v. *State of West Bengal*, AIR 1970 SC 852.

87. *Shyamal Chakraverty* v. *Commissioner of Police, Calcutta*, AIR 1970 SC 169. Similarly, *Re Chitranjan Dutta and others*, decided on 5 September 1969 (SC), several cases of theft of railway copper wire by the detinue were held to justify his detention on the ground of his activities being prejudicial to the maintenance of supplies essential to the community.

88. *Manu Bhushan* v. *West Bengal*, AIR 1973 SC 295.

89. A detention order can also be quashed if it is based on vague grounds; *Prabhu Dayal Deorah* v. *D.M. Kamrup*, AIR 1974 SC 183.

90. AIR 1967 SC 295.

91. There were four separate opinions in the case. The dissenting opinion was delivered by Mudholkar, J, with whom Sarkar, CJ, agreed. Hidayatullah, Bachawat, and Shelat, J delivered separate but concurring opinions. Hidayatullah, J, stated that from the circumstances mentioned by the government no inference as to fraud could be drawn and the action of the government was in the nature of a fishing expedition. Bachawat, J was of the opinion that the circumstances suggested by the government could not reasonably suggest that the business of the company was being conducted to defraud persons. Shelat, J, reached the conclusion that the circumstances were not relevant to the grounds mentioned in the Act.

92. AIR 1969 SC 707.

93. AIR 1961 SC 1731.

94. Taylor, 'Judicial Review of Improper Purposes and Irrelevant Considerations' [1976] 36 Camb. LJ 272.

95. AIR 1954 SC 179.

96. *Dwarka Das* v. *Jammu and Kashmir*, AIR 1957 SC 164.

97. *Bhushan* v. *State of West Bengal*, AIR 1973 SC 295; *Kuso Sah* v. *State of Bihar*, AIR 1974 SC 156; *Prabhu Dayal* v. *Dist. Magistrate*, AIR 1974 SC 183; *Bhupal Chandra* v. *Arif Ali*, 1974 SC 255: *Biram Chand* v. *State of UP*, AIR 1974 SC 1161; *Dwarika Prasad* v. *State of Bihar*, AIR 1975 SC 134.

98. AIR 1967 SC 1353. Also *Swarn Singh* v. *State of Punjab*, AIR 1876 SC 232.

97. *State of Orissa* v. *Bidyabhushan Mohapatra*, AIR 1963 SC 779. Also *State of Uttar Pradesh* v. *Chandra Mohan*, AIR 1977 SC 2411.

98. AIR 1976 SC 853. Also see *Mahboob Shariff* v. *Mysore State Tr. Authority*, AIR 1960 SC 321.

99. AIR 1963 SC 1626.

100. AIR 1970 SC 1789.

101. *Somawanti* v. *State of Punjab*, AIR 1963 SC 151. Also *Arnold Rodricks* v. *State of Maharashtra*, AIR 1966 SC 1788.

102. *Valjibhai* v. *State of Bombay*, AIR 1963 SC 1890, 1892.

103. *Zafar ul Hassan* v. *Republic of Pakistan*, PLD 1960 SC 113.

104. *Kishan Chand Arora* v. *Commr. of Police*, AIR 1961 SC 705 ('If [the applicant] thinks . . . the Commissioner has acted unreasonably in rejecting his application he is not without remedy.'); *State of Bombay* v. *K.P. Krishnan*, AIR 1960 SC 1223 ('The government must consider the question fairly and reasonably.'); *Jyoti Sarup* v. *Board of Revenue*, AIR 1953 All. 25, 29 ('*Mandamus* will not lie where the duty is clearly discretionary and the party upon whom the duty rests has to exercise his discretion reasonably and within his jurisdiction.'). But see *KD Co.* v. *K.N. Singh*, AIR 1956 SC 446.

105. AIR 1971 SC 2451.

106. *Hardev Motor Transport* v. *State of M.P*, (2006) 8 SCC 613.

107. AIR 1975 SC 623.

108. AIR 1962 SC 386.

109. *Pukhraj* v. *Kohli*, AIR 1962 SC 1559.

110. de Smith, *Judicial Review of Administrative Action* (3rd edn., London: Stevens and Sons Limited, 1973) 306.

111. [1942] AC 206.

112. [1951] AC 66.

113. AIR 1976 SC 1986.

114. *Chandreshwari Pd.* v. *State of Bihar*, AIR 1956 Pat. 104.

115. [1947] 2 All ER 680.

116. [1925] AC 578.

117. [1964] 1 All ER 1.

118. Kapur, J, in *Mahboob Sheriff* v. *Mysore ST Authority*, AIR 1960 SC 321. Also *Rampur Distillery Co.* v. *Company Law Board*, AIR 1970 SC 1789; *M.A. Rasheed* v. *State of Kerala*, AIR 1974 SC 2249.

119. AIR 1969 SC 707.

120. *Maharashtra* v. *Babulal*, AIR 1967 SC 1353, 1355.

121. de Smith, *Judicial Review of Administrative Action*, Supra Note 111, 310.

122. See *Associated Provincial Picture Houses Ltd* v. *Wednesbury Corp.* [1947] 2 All ER 680.

123. Hamson, *Executive Discretion and Judicial Control* (1954); Schwartz, *French Administrative Law and the Common Law World* (1954); Rene David, '*Droit Administratif* in France' in Dicey, *Law of the Constitution* (9th edn., 1939) 495.

124. *Manikchandra* v. *State*, AIR 1973 Gau.1.

125. AIR 1952 SC 16. An English case on the point is *Simms Motor Units Ltd* v. *Minister of Labour* [1946] 2 All ER 201.

126. AIR 1963 SC 507.

127. *Secretary, Government of Punjab v. Khalid Hussain Hamdani*, 2013 SCMR 817.

128. *Mount Corp. v. Director of Industries*, AIR 1965 Mys. 143. See also *Sri Ram Vilas Service* v. *Road Traffic Board*, AIR 1948 Mad. 400; *Rambharosa* v. *Bihar*, AIR 1953 Pat. 370.

129. *Purtabpore Company Ltd* v. *Cane Commissioner of Bihar* [1969] 1 SCC 308. Also see *PF Co-op. Society* v. *Collector, Thanjavur*, AIR 1975 Mad. 81; *Orin Moyong* v. *Government of Assam*, AIR 1974 Gau. 27. See also *Punjab* v. *Hari Kishan*, AIR 1966 SC 1081 and *Ruttonjee* v. *West Bengal*, AIR 1967 Calcutta 450.

130. *Ahmad Zaman Khan* v. *Government of Pakistan*, PLD 1977 Lahore 735.

131. [1903] 27 ILR Bom. 307.

132. Franks Committee Report [1957] 63.

133. *Rex* v. *Torquay Licencing Justices ex parte Brockman* [1951] 2 KB 784.

134. *Atulya Kumar* v. *Director of Procurement and Supply*, AIR 1953 Cal. 548, 556.

135. *Girita Mohan* v. *Addl. District Magistrate*, AIR 1954 Cal. 97.

136. *Faridsons Ltd* v. *Government of Pakistan*, PLD 1961 SC 537.

137. *H. Lavender and Son* v. *Minister of Housing* [1970] 3 All ER 871.

138. *Siringer* v. *Minister of Housing* [1970] 1 WLR 1281, 1298.

139. [1970] 3 WLR 488.

140. A few cases other than those cited before on this proposition are: *Kesavan Bhaskaran* v. *State of Kerala*, AIR 1961 Ker. 23; *Coal Mines P.F. Commissioner* v. *J.P. Lalla*, AIR 1976 SC 676; *Kumkum* v. *Principal, Jesus and Mary College*, AIR 1976 Del. 35.

141. AIR 1945 PC 156.

142. *Juswant Singh* v. *Punjab*, AIR 1958 SC 124. The sanction was quashed in *State* v. *Bansilal Luhadia*, AIR 1962 Raj. 250, as it could not be established that all the material facts of the case had been brought to the notice of the sanctioning authority.

143. *Board of Revenue* v. *R.S. Jhaver*, AIR 1968 SC 59, 67.

144. AIR 1966 SC 1140.

145. Also see *Kishori Mohan* v. *West Bengal*, AIR 1972 SC 1749; *Anant Mukhi* v. *West Bengal*, AIR 1972 SC 1256.

146. AIR 1966 SC 1925.

147. AIR 1972 SC 591.

148. AIR 1976 SC 203.

149. AIR 1976 Del. 225.

150. *Y. Eswariah Choudry* v. *Government of AP*, AIR 1974 AP 96.

151. AIR 1974 SC 175.

152. AIR 1974 SC 1232.

153. AIR 1974 SC 1868.
154. 118 US 356 [1885].
155. *West Bengal* v. *Anwar Ali*, AIR 1952 SC 75.
156. *Kathi Raning* v. *Saurashtra*, AIR 1952 SC 123, 131.
157. See *Bidi Supply Co.* v. *India*, AIR 1956 SC 479; *Kedar Nath* v. *West Bengal*, AIR 1953 SC 404; *Pannalal Binjraj* v. *India*, AIR 1957 SC 397; *Dalmia* v. *Justice Tendolkar*, AIR 1958 SC 538.
158. *Ghulam Mohayyuddin* v. *Government of Punjab* [1995] PLC (CS)188.
159. *Pannalal Binjraj* v. *India*, AIR 1957 SC 397, 409.
160. *Arif Builders* v. *Government of Pakistan*, PLD 1997 Karachi 627.
161. AIR 1958 SC 538.
162. *Mannalal Jain* v. *Assam*, AIR 1962 SC 386.
163. AIR 1967 SC 1836.
164. *India* v. *Moolchand*, AIR 1971 SC 2369.
165. *EE & C Ltd* v. *State of West Bengal*, AIR 1975 SC 266.
166. *The PTI* v. *Union of India*, AIR 1974 SC 1044.
167. *Federation of Pakistan* v. *Muhammad Aslam* [1986] SCMR 916.
168. AIR 1968 SC 718.
169. *Pakistan* v. *Salahuddin*, PLD 1991 SC 546.
170. AIR 1986 SC 806.
171. AIR 1977 SC 183.
172. H.W.R. Wade, *Administrative Law* (4th edn., Oxford: Clarendon Press, 1977) 464.
173. General Clauses (Amendment) Act, 1997 (Act XI of 1997).
174. H.W.R. Wade, *Administrative Law* (4th edn., Oxford: Clarendon Press, 1977) 464.
175. General Clauses (Amendment) Act, 1997 (Act XI of 1997).

CHAPTER V

Judicial Review of Administrative Action

5.1 NEED FOR JUDICIAL CONTROL OF THE ADMINISTRATIVE PROCESS

General principles of law are applicable to judicial review in respect of executive acts. Judicial review has developed principles like the common law itself, gradually from case to case, due to pressures of particular situations, the lessons from experience, the guidance of ideal and general principles, and the influence of legislation. It has developed by the courts, which have the power of final interpretation of statutory laws, and a concomitant power to provide judge-made remedies where the statutes are silent. The function of judicial review is to act as 'a check against excess of power in derogation of private right', yet judicial review cannot supervise all administrative adjudications, for it exists to check, not to supplant them.[1]

The scope of judicial review has often depended on whether a given function is classified as judicial or administrative in nature. The administrative finding of facts are not generally reviewed unless the administrative finding goes to the very jurisdiction or the findings are manifestly wrong in which case they are likely to be characterised as erroneous in point of law.[2] Nevertheless there has been a significant increase both in the frequency with which judicial review has been invoked and the readiness of the courts to intervene.

The functionaries of state derive their powers from the constitution or laws and are required to act clearly within the defined parameters of law. Their exercise of governmental power is a sacred trust and they are required to perform their duties as trustees. Whenever dealing with public at large, whether by way of giving jobs or entering into contracts or issuing quotas or licences or granting state largesse, they are required to act reasonably, impartially, without any arbitrariness and within the defined sphere of their powers.[3]

The administrative process has many advantages. The advantages of administrative tribunals are that their process is speedy and inexpensive; they make available technical knowledge and experience for the discharge of quasi-judicial functions in specialised fields; the assistance which they lend to the efficient conduct of public administration; and the ability they possess to lay down the standards and to promote a policy of social improvement.[4] Nevertheless, in its efforts to enact social legislation, labour laws, and tax measures; in its policy of trade control and regulation of industrial planning; and in its eagerness to provide the benefits of health insurance, unemployment benefits, and minimum wages; the state raises issues which may not be purely legal and yet it is necessary that they should not be determined in an arbitrary and autocratic manner.[5] There are issues at times raised before administrative tribunals that are concerned with policy rather than law and call for expert knowledge in the matters concerned. It is also undesirable that flexibility and informality of the administrative bodies contribute towards the resolution of problems that dominate contemporary industrial and urban societies. All this made the emergence of administrative bodies inevitable as a response to various challenges of the modern era. Nevertheless, with the present workload, the administrative bodies have ceased to be cheap or even speedy. Their main *raison d'etre* is specialisation and expertise.

The development of the administrative process poses many serious problems of our time. It affects the relationship between public power and personal rights. It magnifies the problem of reconciling freedom and justice for the private citizen with the necessities of a modern government demands regarding the promotion of far-reaching social or economic policies. The extended powers and functions of the modern state hold potential threats to justice and freedom. 'Properly exercised, the new powers of the executive lead to the welfare state but abused they lead to the totalitarian state.'[6] Even in matters relating to social legislations, knowledge of law and legal procedure, a judicial mind or a judicial approach may at times be necessary to determine the questions involved.[7] The proceedings before administrative tribunals are not always inexpensive and speedy, and flexibility and informality in the conduct of proceedings before administrative tribunals, at times, raise the possibility for arbitrary exercise of authority. Human frailties may further demean such arbitrariness into corruption, nepotism, partiality, tyranny etc.

It has been established through experience that if the administrative authorities are allowed to function unfettered of judicial control, then exercise of authority is likely to become colourable through arbitrariness, capriciousness, political influence, policy considerations and other such expediencies. This is the historical rationale for the introduction of judicial review of the administrative actions of authorities. However, even this solution is not without its problems and several serious questions arise from time to time before the superior courts while exercising judicial review of the actions and orders of the administrative bodies. The crucial questions, generally, are: how and to what extent is the administrative process to be subjected to judicial control? How are reasonable standards of justice to be imparted to administrative determinations? To what extent judicial restraint is to be exercised in the review of administrative actions? These and various other aspects will be considered in the course of discussion over the various modes and measures of exercise of judicial control of administrative actions.

5.2 PRACTICE AND CONCEPT OF JUDICIAL REVIEW OF ADMINISTRATIVE ACTION

5.2.1 BRITAIN

The concept of judicial review of administration action has developed in common law countries like England, the USA, India, and Pakistan. Administrative Law was not studied as a separate or developed branch of law because of the opposition it met from influential writers like A.V. Dicey. The very idea of an administrative adjudicatory authority entrusted with power to determine private rights and obligations by decisions in individual cases was anathema to English lawyers. Administrative law was thought to be inconsistent with the maintenance of the rule of law.

Professor Dicey wrote: 'In England and in countries which, like the United States, derive their civilisation from English sources, the system of administrative law and the principles upon which it rests are in truth unknown.'[8] The 'Diceian analysis' of administrative law left a lasting impression on English legal thought though it was untrue even in Dicey's time. For example, factory laws and other legislation relatable to industrial relations had come into being even in his times. It is becoming increasingly untrue, since the modern state claims to care for the individual from cradle to grave. Dicey's analysis was far from accurate, completely prejudicial, without any effort to understand the obvious benefits of French administrative system.

Old beliefs die hard, but today there is plenty of evidence that the study of administrative law in Britain has fully recovered from Dicey's denial of its existence.[9] The post-war period in Britain was a steady rise in the number of tribunals and administrative bodies to deal with the problems following the war. Despite early protestation from influential authors like Lord Hewart in *The New Despotism* published in 1931 and Hayek in *The Road to Serfdom* published in 1944, which called attention to the dangers of expanding state apparatus, the administrative bodies and tribunals have come to stay in Britain. Attempt has been made to regulate the working of such tribunals by the creation of the office of Parliamentary Commissioner under the Parliamentary Commissioner Act, 1967, to investigate complaints of maladministration. To facilitate the judicial review of administrative actions, the Administration of Justice (Miscellaneous Provisions) Act, was passed in 1938 abolishing prerogative writs of *mandamus*, prohibition and *certiorari* in order to meet the demands of the modern era, replacing them by orders of the same names. This gave an easier and speedier procedure and ensured the twin objectives of Dicey's Rule of Law, namely, the observance of law by public authorities and the preservation of individual liberties.[10]

5.2.2 The United States of America

Creation of administrative bodies was also met with initial resistance in the United States of America from the legal profession as well as writers of influence.[11] But the growth of administrative agencies has been accepted as inevitable. The legislative measures of the 'New Deal' were mainly implemented through the medium of the administrative agencies.[12] At the same time, it has been recognised that in a government of limited powers, these agencies of regulations must themselves be regulated. Judicial review has been found as an effective manner of regulating administrative agencies. The controversies about the powers of administrative agencies and the scope of judicial review have clarified the issues and paved the way for a reasonable amount of judicial control over the agency actions.

5.2.3 Pakistan and India

In Pakistan and India, development of judicial review of administrative action has closely followed the pattern of Britain and the USA. There has not been marked opposition to the administrative process but it has been accepted as an inevitable consequence of national planning and growth of the welfare state. The focus of inquiry has, therefore, shifted from the question of desirability of the administrative process to that of control. The problem has finally been recognised as one of safeguards.[13] Judicial review of administrative action is commonly exercised through writ jurisdiction of the superior courts. It has been deemed necessary that the rule of law and conformity to the provisions of the constitution are maintained and the multitudinous administrative authorities are brought under the control of the courts of law.

In Pakistan, there is no procedure similar to that of French administrative law which, with variations, appears to be in operation over the whole of Europe with the exception of the United Kingdom, or to a system of administrative courts which prevails in the United States. Under each of these systems, there is quasi-judicial tribunal provided, to which a person injured by any action of public servant performed in the exercise of public powers may have instant recourse, and these Tribunals are invested with powers to bring all the underlying processes into the light of day, and apply necessary correction to the respective action by issuing appropriate directions to the respective authorities.[14] An administrative order is subject to judicial control where, firstly, it suffers from illegality which means the decision maker must understand correctly the law that regulate his decision making power and must give effect to it. Secondly, where the order is irrational or unreasonable or the order suffers from procedural impropriety. Judicial review would also apply to prevent arbitrariness and favourtism by government bodies.[15] The Supreme Court could exercise the power of judicial review to adjudge any administrative action on the touchstone of fundamental rights in order to protect such rights and enunciating the law in respect thereof.[16]

5.2.4 FRANCE

The doctrine of review of order of administrative bodies by the ordinary courts is foreign to civil law countries like France and West Germany. Administrative law had been regarded as a concept belonging to continental Europe, particularly France. Dicey is said to have told a French lawyer: 'In England we know nothing of administrative law and we wish to know nothing about it.'[17] The Lord Chief Justice of England stigmatised the term 'administrative law' as 'continental jargon'.[18]

Court structure in France is strictly separated into distinct jurisdictions: judicial courts and administrative courts. The two sets of courts exercise their jurisdictions independently of one another and orders passed by courts on the one side cannot be reviewed by the courts on the other side. The Conseil d'État (Council of State) has the highest administrative jurisdiction and also acts as an advisory body to the government on matters of legislation.[19] It hears appeals from the administrative tribunals and is also a court of original jurisdiction in several administrative actions. Due to administrative reforms, carried out by the Decree of 30 September

1953 (modified by the Decree of 11 June 1954), a number of administrative tribunals were created with original jurisdiction in most administrative matters.[20] The Conseil d'État still acts as an administrative court of first instance in a limited number of cases. A court of conflicts has been constituted, composed of judges from both jurisdictions, which settles questions of conflict of jurisdiction between judicial and administrative courts.

5.3 THE JURISDICTIONAL PRINCIPLE OR DOCTRINE OF ULTRA VIRES

5.3.1 SCOPE

Study of judicial control revolves around the question of how far the courts can go in examining the decisions of administrative tribunals in proceedings of review. The limits of judicial control are, however, set by the distinction between review and appeal, i.e. between reviewable jurisdictional matters and unreviewable errors committed within jurisdiction. Where a court has jurisdiction to entertain an application, it does not lose its jurisdiction by coming to a wrong conclusion. It has been repeatedly held by the superior courts in the common law countries that a court or tribunal having jurisdiction to decide a matter has jurisdiction to decide it rightly or wrongly and that the superior courts have no jurisdiction to interfere with its decision merely on the ground that the decision was wrong in law.[21] This jurisdictional principle or the *ultra vires* doctrine was denoted in England as excess of legal authority by independent statutory bodies and railway companies in the middle years of the nineteenth century. It was later extended to common law corporations, municipal corporations, all types of local government authorities and finally to the Crown and its servants and even to inferior judicial bodies.[22] In Pakistan and India, this doctrine has been extended to nearly all government, semi-government, autonomous and statutory functionaries or departments of central and provincial governments, administrative authorities and tribunals, criminal courts, licensing authorities, boards of education and examiners, boards of revenue, co-operative societies, court of wards, custodian of evacuee property, claims commissioner, settlement and rehabilitation authorities, border area committees, district boards, election tribunals, excise authorities, taxing authorities, industrial and labour tribunals, land acquisition authorities, medical council, municipalities, rent controllers, central bank, universities, sea customs authorities etc., if they exceed their jurisdiction.

5.3.2 REVIEW UNDER THE JURISDICTIONAL PRINCIPLE

The jurisdictional principle which determines the reviewability of an administrative action is often expressed as 'want or excess of jurisdiction'.[23]

In theory, the jurisdictional principle enables the courts merely to prevent the inferior courts, tribunals or authorities from acting in excess of their powers but in reality, they have increasingly entered into the heart of the subject matter by interfering on grounds of reasonableness, bad faith, extraneous considerations, unfairness, manifest injustice, arbitrariness etc. Procedural errors are also held jurisdictional defects if the procedural requirement is mandatory.[24] However, on a point of law, if administration has adopted a construction or interpretation which is a possible one, the courts would support the administrative action based on such construction or interpretation.[25] On a point of procedure, the essential duty is to secure fairness under the principles of natural justice. The most important aspect of the question is: to what extent does the jurisdictional principle enable the reviewing courts to control the exercise of power by the administrative authorities? Various principles applied in Pakistan and India, are examined below.

(1) REASONABLENESS

In Britain, it was held that, if an action is so unreasonable that no reasonable authority could do it, the court might well say: The parliament never intended to give the authority such power; the actions are unreasonable and *ultra vires*.[26] In Pakistan and India, the English doctrine of reasonableness has been adopted in the rule that powers, particularly discretionary ones, have to be exercised judiciously and not 'arbitrarily or capriciously'.[27] Arbitrary exercise of jurisdiction has been called abuse of jurisdiction.[28] Where land could be auctioned for 'public purpose', if the 'immediate need' for possessing it was established, the order of requisition was held arbitrary, since the requirement of 'public purpose' and 'immediate need' were not provided.[29] Where an election tribunal cancelled certain ballot papers which were proved to be free from defect, the Supreme Court of Pakistan held that the tribunal had acted wantonly in excluding from count those ballot papers as spoilt and it struck down such order.[30] However, the term 'reasonable' is not susceptible of a precise definition. It implies a comparative and not an absolute standard, since what is reasonable can only mean what a person, required to act reasonably and honestly, thinks to be reasonable in the circumstances of a particular case. Similarly, the sense of right and wrong or, what is the same thing; the sense of natural justice is not the natural reaction of a savage in a state of nature to external human action, but the reaction intuitively felt by an educated person living in a civilised society to another person's act.[31]

(II) IMPROPER MOTIVE OR MALA FIDE

The courts have claimed their power to inquire into the 'state of mind of an administrator who will . . . after due consideration, come to an honest decision as to whether to exercise the power or not, for the purpose authorised by Parliament' and to intervene in cases of bad faith, unfair dealings,[32] and improper considerations.[33] Thus, a local authority with power of compulsory acquisition of land for coast protection cannot acquire land for a promenade,[34] with power to effect civic extension or improvement cannot acquire land compulsorily merely to reap the benefit of enhanced values,[35] nor can an education authority use its power to dismiss teachers on educational grounds to effect economy.[36] It is for the reviewing court to say whether in any given case the purpose is genuine and *bona fide.* Thus, in *Westminster Corporation* v. *London and North Western Railway Co.*[37] the corporation, having power to construct underground public conveniences, built conveniences and also provided a subway. This was held to be a reasonable and bona fide exercise of power.

The courts can also inquire into the motives of the authorities passing orders when such orders are under review. Where the government issued notifications for acquisition of land, declaring that the land was needed for a 'public purpose' while in fact it was required for a commercial company, the acquisition was held invalid.[38] Proceedings have been held *mala fide* when a statute is used merely as a cloak to cover an act which in fact is not taken though it purports to have been taken, under the statute.[39] A *mala fide* order means that which is passed not for the purpose contemplated by the enactment granting the power to pass the order, but for some other collateral or ulterior motive. A *mala fide* act or order is a fraud on the statute and by its nature without jurisdiction.[40] However, actions and orders of tribunals or authorities are not lightly struck down by the superior courts as *mala fide. Mala fide* is one of the most difficult things to prove and the onus is entirely upon the person alleging *mala fides* to establish it. This is because, to start with, there is a presumption of regularity with regard to all official acts and until that presumption is rebutted, the action cannot be challenged merely upon a vague allegation of *mala fide.*[41]

The jurisdiction of civil courts can never be taken away with respect to *mala fides* because a *mala fide* act is in its very nature an illegal and void act and the court can always pronounce such act to be *mala fide* and therefore, void.[42] However, no *mala fide* can be pleaded against a statute and for that reason, it cannot be regarded as being void.[43] The plea of *mala fide* must be specifically raised and where one kind of *mala fide* is pleaded, the petitioner cannot change the allegation into one alleging different kind of *mala fide.*[44]

(III) IRRELEVANT CONSIDERATIONS

It is an established principle that in exercising discretion, the authorities must have regard for all relevant considerations and disregard all irrelevant considerations.[45] Where a settlement officer rejected an application for permission to effect an exchange of holdings on the grounds that (a) the granting of permission would entail considerable work on the part of officers of the department, and (b) the applicants were big land-holders, the Indian Supreme Court held that these reasons were not germane or pertinent for the rejection of the petition.[46] The grant of a stage carriage permit on the grounds that the applicant was granted permits on other routes was held to be based on irrelevant consideration.[47]

(IV) ACTING UNDER DICTATION

Discretionary powers must be exercised only by the persons authorised by the statute. One of the rules to ensure this policy is that the persons so authorised must not act under dictation. Where a licensing tribunal acted under directions issued by the government which were not authorised by the statute, its decision was set aside on judicial review.[48] Even where the government delegates certain authority to one of its officers, such officer is required to act on his own satisfaction and not under dictation from his delegator. A district magistrate, empowered by the government to order arrest and detention, could only do so on his own satisfaction and should not refer the matter to government for according its satisfaction.[49] Where a commissioner, delegated with the powers by the government to requisition immovable properties under a statute, acted on the directive of the government, his orders were set aside for having acted under dictation. It was held that it was not a reasonable exercise of his discretion.[50]

(V) ABDICATION OF AUTHORITY OR DISCRETION

Persons invested with a discretion must exercise it properly and are not allowed to surrender their power to any other authority.

Thus, where the chief settlement commissioner did not apply his independent mind to the question (of divisibility of a house and the entitlement of one of the parties to the dispute) raised in the petition for revision but merely countersigned the note put up by the settlement commissioner, it was held that he had not exercised the jurisdiction vested in him.[51] Similarly, expulsion from a scholarship scheme by a government department did not render a student liable to be expelled from the university. Expulsion from the university had to be ordered by the proper authority in accordance with the relevant statutes and regulations.[52] When a commissioner, delegated with the powers by the government to requisition immovable properties under a statute, acts on the directive of the government, his orders were struck down as being abdication of his own authority by him.[53]

(VI) SUBJECTIVE DISCRETION

The decision in Liversidge v. Anderson[54] gave rise to the policy of inferring absolute discretionary power granted in subjective terms in Britain. In this case the detention of a person was left to the subjective satisfaction of detaining authority. This decision had repercussions in various countries which were formerly British colonies. However, subsequently exercise of subjective discretion by a tribunal or authority allowed under an enactment has been brought under judicial review. Expressions such as 'shall make such orders as it may think fit' do not allow a tribunal to make a fanciful or capricious order unrelated to the case before it. The order should be in accordance with the rule of reason and justice and in accordance with law.[55] Exercise of judicial control over the subjective discretion of administrative bodies is not without its difficulties. Where an authority could detain persons when it 'suspects on grounds appearing to such authority to be reasonable', it was held that the reasonableness of the grounds is personal to the authority and is not objective so that the courts can examine their reasonableness.[56]

(VII) DISCRETION NOT TO BE FETTERED BY POLICY

Another rule is that discretion must not be fettered by self-created rules of policy. In English law, this has led to the rule against estoppel, as regards the statutory authorities.[57] In *Province of East Pakistan* v. *M. Yaseen*,[58] the government, in order to encourage construction of houses by private enterprise, announced a policy that no house built after 1950 would be requisitioned. The petitioner's house was erected in 1952, but it was, nevertheless, requisitioned by the government. It was held that a mere statement of policy could not fetter the statutory authority of requisition of properties.

In *Indian Metals & Ferro Alloys Ltd* v. *Union of India*,[59] the Supreme Court of India held that a state government was not bound to dispose of applications for a mining lease on a 'first come, first served' basis. A mining lease should be granted to an applicant who can exploit the mineral most effectively.

(VIII) RULE AGAINST DELEGATION

Another rule is the rule against delegation, i.e. an exercise of discretionary powers cannot be delegated to a separate body unless such delegation is authorised by the statute.[60]

(IX) DOCTRINE OF LEGITIMATE EXPECTATION

The Supreme Court of India discussed the 'Doctrine of Legitimate Expection' and its impact in the following words: [61]

> The doctrine of legitimate expectation has its genesis in the field of administrative law. The Government and its departments in administering the affairs of the country are expected to honour their statements of policy or intention and treat the citizens with full personal consideration without any iota of abuse of discretion. The policy statements cannot be disregarded unfairly or applied selectively. Unfairness in the form of unreasonableness is akin to violation of natural justice. It was in this context that the doctrine of legitimate expectation was evolved which has today, become a source of

substantive as well as procedural rights. But claims based on legitimate expectations have been held to require reliance on representations and resulting detriment to the claimant in the same way as claims based on promissory estoppel. Unfairness in the purported exercise of power can amount to an abuse or excess of power. Thus the doctrine of "legitimate expectation" has been developed, both in the context of reasonableness and in. the context of natural justice. The State actions have to be in conformity with Article 14 of the Constitution, of which non-arbitrariness is a significant fact. There is no unfettered discretion in public law. A public authority possesses powers only to use them for public good. Although the doctrine of legitimate expectation is essentially procedural in character and assures fair play in administrative action, but it may, in a given situation, be enforced as a substantive right.

The doctrine of legitimate expectation can be invoked if the decision which is challenged in the court has some person aggrieved either (a) by altering rights or obligations of that person which are enforceable by or against him in private law; or (b) by depriving him of some benefit or advantage which after (i) he had in the past been permitted by the decision maker to enjoy and which he can legitimately expect to be permitted to continue to do until there has been communicated to him some rational grounds for withdrawing it on which he has been given an opportunity to comment; or (ii) he has received assurance from the decision-maker that it will not be withdrawn without giving him first an opportunity of advancing reasons for contending that it should not be withdrawn. Indian scenario in the field of legitimate expectation is not different.

On the basis of the above findings, the Lahore High Court held that it is now well established proposition of law that he, who basis his claim on the concept of legitimate expectation, has to rely on the representation of public authority, and that their denial is the infringement of his right. The Court will intervene only, if the decision of denial is arbitrary, unreasonable, abuse of powers and is against the principle of natural justice and that the decision is not taken in public interest.[62]

The rule of legitimate expectation is not a part of any codified law, rather it's doctrine has been coined and designed by the Courts primarily for the exercising of their power of judicial review of the administrative actions. As per Halsbury's Laws of England,[63] it is prescribed:-

> A person may have a legitimate expectation of being treated in certain way by an administrative authority even though he has no legal right in private law to receive such treatment. The expectation may arise from a representation or promise made by the authority including an implied representation or from consistent past practice.

In *R. v. Secretary of State of Transport ex parte Greater London Council*,[64] it is propounded that:-

> Legitimate, or reasonable, expectation may arise from any express promise given on behalf of a public authority or from the existence of a regular practice which the claimant can reasonably expect to continue. The expectation may be based on some statement or undertaking by or on behalf of the public authority which has the duty of taking decision.

In the judgment reported as *Union of India v. Hindustan Development Corporation*.[65] it has been held:-

> The legitimacy of an expectation can be inferred only if it is founded on the sanction of law or custom or established procedure followed in regular and natural sequence. It is also distinguishable from a genuine expectation. Such expectation should be justifiably legitimate and protectable. Every such legitimate expectation does not by itself fructify into a right and therefore it does not amount to a right in the conventional sense.

It is thus clear from the above that the doctrine only has nexus to administrative decisions and actions, and no one can have resort to it, for the purposes of claiming any right found upon any decision of the Court, which decision and the law laid down therein is found by the Court to be *per incuriam*.[66]

5.4 REVIEW OF FINDINGS OF LAW AND FINDINGS OF FACT

5.4.1 SCOPE

The distinction between questions of law and questions of fact is important not only in the proceedings of judicial review but also in those involving the rights of appeal to the high court on points of law arising under statutes and constitutional provisions. The distinction is also material where the court is empowered to act on its own initiative to deal with cases involving questions of law. The English courts' view of what is a question of law and what is a question of fact has been far from being unanimous. In *Edwards* v. *Bairstow*,[67] where the question was whether a certain transaction (purchase and sale of machinery as an isolated transaction) amounted to a 'trade' for tax purposes, the House of Lords treated the issue as one of law. The test of an error of law was stated to be one where the tribunal had made a decision which could not have been reasonably made.

The most important limitation on judicial review of administrative tribunals and quasi-judicial bodies is that the courts do not interfere with an administrative body's determination of facts except when its conclusion is not supported by any evidence at all.[68] A distinction between a question of law and a question of fact has to be drawn in this context. There is often no difficulty in making such distinction. The erroneous refusal or admission of evidence by a tribunal obliged to observe the rules of evidence is an error of law. The meaning that a lawyer should attribute to the terms of a policy of insurance is a question of law. The question whether the holder of a policy has renewed the policy before its expiry is one of fact. A finding of fact may be defined as an assertion that a phenomenon exists, has existed or will exist, independently, of any assertion as to its legal effect.[69] Perplexing problems may, however, arise in analysing the nature of the process by which a tribunal determines whether a factual situation falls within or without the limits of a category or standard prescribed by a statute or other legal instrument. Despite the controversy regarding the real nature of the difference between questions of law and fact, the scope of judicial review of administrative action is dominated by the distinction between the two. The separation of functions is founded on the principle that the administrative tribunal would find the facts and the courts would not interfere unless the absence of evidence or the perversity of the finding required them to intervene.[70] As a result of this rigid dichotomy of law and fact, the courts have refrained from deciding disputed questions of fact.[71] The courts have, similarly refused to correct orders in the application of documentary evidence or affidavits, or errors in drawing inferences or omissions to draw inferences.[72] The courts have also refused to review findings of fact for insufficiency of evidence.[73] At the same time, courts have reviewed findings of fact of tribunals where such findings go to the very root of the jurisdiction of a tribunal or are based upon no evidence or inadmissible evidence. Thus, the important question is: to what extent do the courts have jurisdiction to review questions of fact and questions of law? This is the question examined in the following paragraphs.

In Pakistan, the power of judicial review available to high courts does not extend to investigation into questions of fact or appraisal of evidence touching issues falling within the authority of administrative tribunals or executive functionaries where finding of fact is based on evidence.[74] The only exception is where finding is *ex facie perverse* and not supported by any evidence.[75] Where finding of facts is based on no evidence, or is arbitrary, fanciful, based upon misreading of evidence or is in disregard of material evidence or material available on record or taking into consideration irrelevant or inadmissible evidence or in violation of any rule of law or statute, then the same can be set aside in exercise of judicial review.[76]

5.4.2 REVIEW OF 'JURISDICTIONAL FACTS'

The British courts have refused to review decisions of inferior tribunals if based on evidence. This led to a tendency towards review of facts even if they went to the jurisdiction. They have, however, extricated themselves from such tendency by establishing their authority to review facts if they are collateral.[77] This has become an exception to the general unreviewability of questions of fact. This is known in American law as Jurisdictional Fact' and in English law as the 'Collateral Fact'. This doctrine is based on the general rule that no court or tribunal of limited jurisdiction can give itself jurisdiction by a wrong decision on a point collateral to the merits of the case upon which the limits to its jurisdiction depends. This principle applies regardless that its decision may be final on all particulars making up together that subject which, if true, is within its jurisdiction and notwithstanding the necessity in many cases to make a preliminary inquiry as to whether some collateral matter be or be not within its jurisdiction limits. Yet upon this preliminary question, its decision must always be open to inquiry in a superior court.[78] In dealing with an award made by the Compensation Commission, the US Supreme Court held that the question whether there existed the relationship of master and servant was one of those where the determinations of fact are fundamental or 'jurisdictional' in the sense that there is a condition precedent to the operation of the statutory scheme.[79] Review of such fundamental or jurisdictional fact is necessary to avoid establishment of a government of bureaucratic character.

The courts in Pakistan and India have followed the doctrine of 'jurisdictional fact', in review of facts. It was held that a notice under Section 248 of the Civil Procedure Code[80] was necessary in order for the court to give jurisdiction to sell property by way of execution as against the legal representative of a deceased judgment debtor, and that it was by service of such notice that court acquires jurisdiction to sell the property in question.[81] The Indian Supreme Court held that the jurisdiction of an Industrial Tribunal under the Industrial Disputes Act, 1947, is dependent upon the dispute being an 'industrial dispute' as defined in the Act. The tribunal has to determine, before exercising jurisdiction, whether or not the dispute is an industrial dispute and this finding is liable to be challenged and set aside in judicial review by the superior courts.[82] Where the relationship of landlord and tenant is denied, and an objection is taken to the jurisdiction of the rent controller, it was held that such objection must be treated as a preliminary objection and must be resolved before taking any further action.[83] Such a finding of the controller on the jurisdictional fact was liable to be set aside in judicial review.

A purely administrative officer who is empowered to pass an order if certain circumstances exist has no jurisdiction to determine those circumstances and the objective existence of those circumstances is an essential condition of the validity of his order. In respect of every order passed by him, the court can make enquiry and if it finds that all the circumstances needed for passing the order were not present, it will declare the order to be void. Of course, although the officer has been granted no jurisdiction to determine any facts, he will have to ascertain whether the requisite circumstances exist for otherwise he cannot pass the order; but his conclusion as to the existence of these circumstances binds nobody and it is open to any person affected to challenge his act on the ground that those circumstances do not in fact exist. An administrative officer or authority may be given jurisdiction to determine some facts on proof of which he can pass an order and in that case, he will act in a quasi-judicial manner for the determination of those facts. So far as special judicial tribunals are concerned, they are given jurisdiction to determine certain facts but they are not judges of the facts which are the foundation of their jurisdiction nor can they define the limits of their own jurisdiction. It is possible, of course, that a special tribunal may be made judge of its own jurisdiction, but this would be a very exceptional provision and one which should be made by altogether clear words.[84] Where the jurisdiction of the lower tribunal depends on the existence of a fact, the absence of that fact must be specifically pleaded before the tribunal; otherwise the question would not be permitted to be raised before the high court in exercise of judicial review.[85] Similarly, if jurisdiction depends on the evidence of a fact, a wrong decision as to that fact to assume jurisdiction will amount to usurpation of jurisdiction warranting the setting aside of such finding as to that fact.[86]

5.4.3 Review of 'other facts'

The difficult, yet important task is to distinguish 'jurisdictional facts' from 'other facts'—a distinction that would determine the reviewability of a question.[87]

The idea of review of facts other than jurisdictional facts has not been acceptable to the courts in Britain, Pakistan, and India. They refuse to exercise judicial control where it involves reviewing sufficiency of evidence.[88] Similarly, a right to quash for excess of jurisdiction does not extend to circumstances where the decision is against the weight of evidence. In the sphere of questions of law the courts have shown very little hesitation to review orders of inferior courts and tribunals, but they have demonstrated a consistent reluctance rather opposition to do the same in the matter of questions of fact. The courts have refused to review decisions in 'appreciation' of documentary evidence, and conflicting evidence, and have consistently refused to re-evaluate or 'weigh the evidence' that was available before the inferior courts and tribunals.[89] Despite the refusal of the courts to review facts other than collateral ones, absence of evidence has always been recognised as a sufficient justification for interfering with the finding of facts even when they are within the jurisdiction of the tribunals. The courts have also reviewed findings of fact based not only on grounds of no evidence but also on those of wrong evidence or inadmissible evidence. These cases are discussed below.

(i) Cases of 'no evidence'

Where the record shows that there was no evidence, there may be review of order so based. Where a person was convicted under an enactment under which it was an offence to sell bread wholesale before it had been baked for twenty-four hours and it was found that there was no evidence that the bread had been so sold, the conviction was quashed.[90] Lord Denning has observed that if a minister acted on no evidence the court would be entitled to interfere with his order.[91] A person was suspended from service for alleged misconduct, one of the charges being that he was 'seen moving about with women of ill-fame and questionable character, keeping company with bad elements and thus leading a life unbecoming of a government servant'. The only evidence in support of this allegation was that 'he drinks and did so in a hotel where drinks were supposed to be surreptitiously served' and that 'he was found in a hotel with two girls who were receptionists and who also used to drink and some time accept 'offers of drinks from customers'. The order of suspension was quashed as being based on no evidence.[92] It was observed in this case that, in order to hold a person guilty on circumstantial evidence, the circumstances or the circumstance must be such as would irresistibly lead to an inference of guilt of the person charged with the offence.

Where a public servant was dismissed for having allegedly attempted to offer a bribe to a deputy director so that latter might support his representation regarding his seniority to the union public service commission, the Supreme Court upheld the order of the high court quashing the order on the grounds that it was not supported by any evidence at all.[93] Where the petitioner was convicted under Section 6 of Act I of 1956 for contravening clause 3 of the Bengal Rice Mills Control Order, 1943, by keeping a certain quantity of sugar without the necessary permit, the conviction was set aside by the High Court as having been based on no evidence at all.[94] The Supreme Court of Pakistan has held that on a point of evidence it is only when the case proves to be one of no evidence, that the courts will be entitled to intervene.[95]

'No evidence' does not mean only a total dearth of evidence. It extends to any case where the evidence, taken as a whole, is not reasonably capable of supporting the findings, or where, in other words, no tribunal could reasonably reach that conclusion on that evidence.[96] Where the election authority made an order as a result of the evaluation of the corroborative documentary evidence of the contesting parties, it was held that the order could not be said to have been based on no evidence.[97]

(II) WRONG OR INSUFFICIENT GROUNDS

The courts in Pakistan and India are prepared to review not only on grounds of no evidence, but also on those of wrong evidence. The superior courts intervene where a tribunal has acted on no evidence or has refused to admit admissible evidence or has admitted inadmissible evidence.[98] The superior courts can interfere with and review findings of fact of subordinate courts, tribunals or other authorities if the finding is based on no evidence, complete misreading of evidence, inadmissible evidence or an exclusion of valid or material piece of evidence.[99] But at the same time, orders of inferior courts, tribunals and other authorities have not been interfered with or reviewed on the grounds of insufficiency of evidence adduced to sustain the finding.[100] The superior courts are not to act as appellate courts in exercise of their power of review under constitutional jurisdiction.[101] It has been held on the contrary by the House of Lords that insufficiency of evidence to sustain a finding raises an error of law which the reviewing court would correct, if it can find the error.[102]

In Pakistan, it was held that the court could interfere with the finding that an evacuee property was an evacuee trust property if authority in recording the finding had acted on evidence which was legally inadmissible or had refused to admit admissible evidence or if the finding was not supported by any evidence at all. In such cases, the error would be an error of law.[103]

(III) NON-TRANSPARENCY

Non-transparancy in public contracts particularly involving public money attracts the doctrine of judicial review of administrative acts. Judicial quest in administrative matters is meant for finding the right balance between the administrative discretion to decide matters whether contractual or political in nature or issues of social policy. Thus, they are not essentially justifiable and there has to be need to remedy any unfairness. Such unfairness is set right by judicial review, which is concerned with reviewing not only the merits of the decision in support of which the application for judicial review is made, but the decision-making process itself.[104] If the contract has been entered into without ignoring the procedure which can be said to be basic in nature and after an objective consideration of different options available taking into account the interest of the state and the public, then the court cannot act as an appellate authority by substituting its opinion in respect of decision made for entering into such a contract. But, once the procedure adopted by an authority for the purpose of entering into a contract is held to be against the mandate of the Constitution, the courts cannot ignore such action saying that the authorities concerned must have some latitude or liberty in contractual matters and any interference by the court amounts to encroachment on the exclusive right of the executive to take such decision.[105]

There is no cavil with the proposition that as far as transparency in the implementation of the policy, if available, in the process of awarding a contract is concerned, it squarely falls within the jurisdiction of the court available to it under the Constitution and the power of judicial review.[106] It is duty of the court to ensure that the relevant laws are adhered to strictly to exhibit transparency. It is universally recognized principle that transactions involving public money must be made in transparent manner for the satisfaction of the people, who are the virtual owners of the national exchequer, which is being invested in this project.[107]

5.4.4 ERROR OF LAW APPARENT ON THE FACE OF THE RECORD

The courts in Britain have established their power to quash the decisions of inferior tribunals and administrative agencies for error on the face of the record. What must be emphasised is that the high court's power to quash a decision merely because it displays some mistake in the record of its proceedings is an altogether exceptional power. It is exceptional because it is not a form of 'jurisdictional' control, i.e. it is not a branch of the doctrine of *ultra vires*.[108] The court review actions on the principle of error of law apparent on the face of the record. Lord Denning, while upholding the principle of exercise of review on the basis of error on the face of the record, wrote that it would be quite intolerable if in a case of error of law, there was no means of correcting the error.[109] The Indian Supreme Court set aside an assessment order on the principle of error of law apparent on the face of the record.[110] The Supreme Court of Pakistan has held that the high courts are competent to interfere with the orders of tribunals if such orders were based on misreading of evidence or suffered from error apparent on the face of the record.[111] In this case, Chief Land Commissioner had not dealt with the matter of the genuineness of the gift but proceeded on the sanction or rejection of mutation. It was held that the view that without settling the question of mutation, the authorities were not justified in or authorised to validate gift was well founded and was thus an error apparent on the face of record.

Since the decision of the House of Lords in *Anisminic Ltd* v. *Foreign Compensation Commission*,[112] where the error of law committed by the tribunal (in construing a statutory order requiring that the claimant's successor in title should have been of British nationality) was held to have destroyed its jurisdiction, the distinction between errors *ultra vires* and errors *intro vires* is said to have declined. It is said that since *Anisminic*, the requirement that an error of law within the jurisdiction must appear on the face of the record is now obsolete.[113] By contrast, the Indian courts still insist that only patent errors of law are reviewable.[114]

The error of law apparent on the face of the record as a principle of judicial control is not without its problems as a line has to be drawn between ordinary error of law and error of law apparent on the face of the record. One of the safeguards provided is that if on a question of law two opinions are possible and the inferior tribunal has adopted one of the two possible views, then its decision does not disclose an error of law apparent on the face of the record.[115] In English law, if the reviewing court can find from the record that (1) a tribunal has determined a point of law, and (2) the determination is mistaken, the principle of error of law is involved.[116] In American law, the function of review placed on the courts is fully performed when they determine that there has been a fair hearing, with notice and an opportunity to present the circumstances and arguments to the decisive body, and application of the statute was made in a just and reasonable manner. Where decision of an administrative agency that certain 'producers of coal' were not 'producers within the meaning of the Act in question' was at issue, it was held that the decision of the agency was final.[117] The law in Pakistan and India is more akin to the American law than the English law on the principle of error of law. In Pakistan and India, the principle of error of law apparent on the face of the record has been, to a large extent, denuded of its utility by review of tribunals' decisions 'on a true, interpretation of the statute'. By granting review on a true interpretation of the statute the courts, in effect, exercise a power of statutory appeal on points of law which is not necessarily confined to error of law apparent on the face of the record. In spite of this development, the rule of error of law apparent on the face of the record is likely to retain its utility, as it provides the basis for review of no evidence, wrong evidence, and wrong conclusion from evidence.

5.4.5 PROPORTIONALITY AND SUITABILITY

The courts can examine and judicially review the executive discretion exercised on the ground of *proportionality*. Alongwith reasonableness, proportionality is now a central standard directing the action of the executive branch. The point of departure is that a disproportionate act that infringes upon a human right is an illegal act. The court, which guards the legality of the acts of the executive branch, performs judicial review over these acts and examines whether they fulfill the tests of proportionality. Proportionality is a standard that examines the relationship between the objectives the executive branch wishes to achieve, which has the potential of infringing upon human rights, and the means it has chosen in order to achieve that infringing objective. The fiduciary duty, from which the administrative duty of fairness and administrative reasonableness are derived, demands administrative proportionality as well. "The courts will quash exercises of discretionary powers in which there is not a reasonable relationship between the objective which is sought to be achieved and the means used to that end, or where punishments imposed by administrative' bodies or inferior courts are wholly out of proportion to the relevant misconduct.[118] An administrative measure must not be more drastic than necessary[119] or to sum up in a phrase-not taking a sledgehammer to crack a nut. According to De Smith's *Judicial Review of Administrative Actions*[120] the standards of proportionality and unreasonableness are inextricably intertwined. Unreasonableness contains two elements of proportionality when it requires the weight of relevant considerations to be fairly balanced and when it forbids unduly oppressive decisions. Under the first element, proportionality is a test requiring the decision-maker to maintain a *fair balance*. Under this category the courts evaluate whether manifestly disproportionate weight has been attached to one or other considerations relevant to the decision. The second element is that the courts consider whether there has been a disproportionate interference with the claimants rights or interests. A more sophisticated version of proportionality provides for a *structured test*. Here the courts ask first whether the measure, which is being challenged, is suitable to attaining the identified ends (the test of *suitability*). Suitability here includes the notion of "rational connection" between the means and ends. The next step asks whether the measure is necessary and whether a less restrictive or onerous method could have been adopted (the test of *necessity* - requiring minimum impairment of the rights or interest in question). Applying the test of proportionality to the executive discretion the Supreme Court of Pakistan held that the order of the authorized officer fails to maintain fair balance by removing a person from service because he absented himself from duty for a day. The executive discretion also fails the *structured* test of proportionality including the test of suitability and test of necessary requiring minimum impairment of the right of the petitioner[121]

An assault on a superior at a workplace amounts to an act of gross indiscipline. The respondent was a teacher. Even under grave provocation a teacher was not expected to abuse the head of the institution in a filthy language and assault him with a *chappal*. Punishment of dismissal from service, therefore, cannot be said to be wholly disproportionate so as to shock one's conscience.[122]

5.5 PRINCIPLES OF NATURAL JUSTICE

5.5.1 SCOPE

The principles of natural justice occupy a unique place in administrative law. They provide the standards of administrative justice; they focus attention on the important question: how far is it right for the courts of law to try to impart their own standards of justice to the administration?[123] In English law, the rules of natural justice perform a function, within a limited field, similar to the concept of procedural due process as it exists in the United States.[124] The 'due process' clause is, however, enshrined in the United States' Constitution. Consequently, the rules of natural justice enjoy constitutional sanctity and even the legislature does not possess the authority to relieve administration from their demands. In Britain, on the other hand, the theory of parliamentary sovereignty precludes any such notion and can include provisions in a statute that can dispense with the requirement of natural justice in any given case. The English judges base the principles of natural justice on moral and ethical foundations as embodied in the justice of common law, which they assert, 'will supply the omission of the legislature'. In Pakistan and India, the principles of natural justice stand somewhere in between the English law and US Constitution because the due process clause has not been stated in the constitution in so many words but similar principles have been laid down in the constitution though couched in different words.[125] In India, the principles of natural justice stand on the same footing as the English law. As a result, express words in the statute can exclude their application in particular cases but otherwise the principles of natural justice are to be read into the relevant law.[126]

The law in Pakistan is that principles of natural justice are applicable to proceedings of all authorities, judicial, quasi-judicial or administrative, unless their application is excluded by the statute under which the authority acts.[127] Hence, the principles of natural justice, unless they are expressly excluded by the law under which a tribunal is acting, are applicable to tribunals which are called upon to adjudicate on private rights.[128] Some of the important principles of natural justice, disregard of which has been considered by courts to be a sufficient ground for quashing decisions of inferior tribunals, are that a man cannot be a judge in his own case;[129] that no party is to be condemned unheard;[130] that a party must in good time know the precise case he is to meet; and that a party is entitled to know why a matter has been decided against him.[131]

However, the principles of natural justice can be ignored under extreme administrative exigencies. The Supreme Court of India observed that:-

> The principles of natural justice are not rigid or immutable and hence they cannot be imprisoned in a straitjacket. They must yield to and change with exigencies of situations. They must be confined within their limits and cannot be allowed to run wild. While interpreting legal provisions, a court of law cannot be unmindful of the hard realities of life. The approach of the Court in dealing with such cases should be pragmatic rather than pedantic, realistic rather than doctrinaire, functional rather than formal and practical rather than 'precedential'. In certain circumstances, application of the principles of natural justice can be modified and even excluded. Both in England and in India, it is well established that where a right to a prior notice and an opportunity to be heard before an order is passed would obstruct in the taking of prompt action, such a right can be excluded. It can also be excluded where the nature of the action to be taken, its object and purpose and the scheme of the relevant statutory provisions warrant its exclusion. The maxim *audi alteram partem* cannot be invoked if import of such maxim would have the effect of paralyzing the administrative process or where the need for promptitude or the urgency so demands. The principles of natural justice have no application when the authority is of the opinion that it would be inexpedient to hold an enquiry and it would be against the interest of security of the Corporation to continue in employment the offender workman when serious acts were likely to affect the foundation of the institution.[132]

Nevertheless the principles of natural justice should only be ignored in exceptional cases otherwise the result would be gross injustice.

5.5.2 BIAS

The maxim of *nemo ju dex in causa sua*, i.e. a judge should not adjudicate upon a cause in which he is interested, was recognised in English law even in the formative stage of common law, and now constitutes a very important principle of judicial control of administrative action. A decision made by Lord Chancellor in a Chancery suit in favour of a canal company was set aside on the grounds that the Lord Chancellor was a shareholder in that company.[133] Thus, a biased judge is disqualified from adjudicating upon the subject matter of the case litigated before him.

House of Lords in *Franklin* v. *Minister of Town and Country Planning*[134] adopted flexible approach on bias. However, in that case the Minister of Town and Country Planning selected Stevenage as the first site under the New Towns Act 1946—a selection which the minister affirmed as final in the course of a public speech before he considered the inspector's report. It was alleged that the minister had prejudged the issue by publicly declaring the policy and had, therefore, precluded himself from giving fair and unbiased consideration to the report of the Inspector. The question was whether the law required the minister to give the matter impartial consideration. The House of Lords held that there was no law requiring the minister to be unbiased. He was free to be biased provided he followed the procedure laid down in the Act.

Bias, which can vitiate proceedings before a tribunal, is generally divided into three types. These types are described as official bias, personal bias and pecuniary interest. Where the mind of a judge is not free to decide on purely judicial grounds and is directly or indirectly influenced by, or exposed to the influences of either motives of self-interest or opinion about policy or any other consideration not relevant to the issue, then the decision of such a judge is said to be suffering from bias. For the convenience of classification, bias resulting from prejudgment on issues of law and policy is called an 'official bias'. Where the mind of the judge is influenced in favour of one party or against another party, it is described as personal bias. Where the judge has some pecuniary interest in the subject matter before him for adjudication, his decision is also said to suffer from bias.

(i) OFFICIAL BIAS

In the case of official bias, there may be no personal ill will, but there may be evidence of an abnormal desire to uphold a particular departmental policy which would prevent an impartial adjudication of the dispute.[135] Where the Secretary of the Transport Department heard objections to a scheme of nationalisation of transport and one of the parties to the dispute was the Transport Department, it was held that the hearing given by the Secretary of the Transport Department offended against the principles of natural justice and that functions of the State in hearing the objections were quasi-judicial.[136] This position has been considerably modified in subsequent cases.[137]

Thus in Indo-Pakistan law, although in earlier decisions the courts used to apply the rule against bias to the adjudication by administrative bodies which were entrusted with the formulation of the policies, they seem to be slowly coming to the position that prevails in Anglo-American law, i.e. that bias in the sense of preconceived view on issues of policy is no ground for disqualification.

(ii) PERSONAL BIAS

The second type of bias is personal bias. A judge may be actuated by an attitude of hostility or favouritism towards one party or the other. The likelihood of bias because of personal attitudes and relationship, is inferred from personal animosity, personal friendship, family relationship, personal and vocational relationship, or employer and employee relationship.[138] Courts rely upon the dictum that justice should not only be done, but should manifestly and undoubtedly be seen to be done.[139] It means that even an appearance of bias is likely to disqualify a judge. The trend in English law is, however, towards the 'real likelihood' test which connotes a narrower application of the rule.[140]

In *Asma & Jilani* v. *Government of Punjab*,[141] the Supreme Court of Pakistan held that mere association with the drafting of a law did not necessarily disqualify a judge from interpreting that law. In *M. Gangappa* v. *Government of Andhra Pradesh*[142] Ekbote, J, said:

> A bias, if it is to be a disqualification, must mean something more than an ideological bent of mind or the policy bias of a government department'. The Ministers and their departments are committed to their own policies which inevitably they tend to favour. In English law the debate has continued as to the choice between the 'reasonable suspicion' test and 'real likelihood' test. In *Metropolitan Properties Ltd* v. *Lannon*,[143] which concerned allegations of bias on the part of a rent assessment committee Lord Denning, MR[144] applied:—the 'real likelihood' test while Edmund Davies, LJ, and Danckwerts, LJ, preferred the 'reasonable suspicion' test. In *R.* v. *Colchester–Stipendian Magistrate, Ex p. Beck*,[145] Lord Widgery in rejecting any breach of the bias rule applied the 'real likelihood' test to the case of a magistrate who had allegedly been supplied by the prosecution with documents containing matter prejudicial to the accused prior to the committal proceedings. In UK, APE ACAS[146] applied the 'real likelihood' test concerning the allegations of an association between a party and the decision-making body. However, in *R.* v. *Liverpool City II Ex p. Topping*,[146] the court applied the 'reasonable suspicion' in condemning the practice of making available to the justices prior to the hearing other unrelated charges against the accused.

In English law, 'personal bias' has been established from a variety of circumstances: (a) personable relationship where the son was the chairman of a rent tribunal while the father was the tenant of the same landlord;[147] (b) the presence of the accuser in course of deliberations of the deciding body;[148] (c) common membership between the deciding body and its enquiry committee or the prosecuting body;[149] (d) an overlap in the membership or even informal contact (e.g. by the presence of a member of one at the meeting of the other) between a trial body and its appellate counterpart;[150] (v) consultation between the trial body and a party whose mind is closed on the matter e.g. a referee who has already expressed an opinion.[151]

The rule of personal bias in American law, though recognised as a ground for disqualification, is less rigidly applied than in English law. The personal bias has to be proved as substantial. When an examiner had found, without exception, that the witnesses of the company were untrustworthy and those of union were reliable, the Supreme Court rejected the plea of personal bias and held that 'total rejection of an opposed view cannot itself impugn the integrity or competence of the trier of fact'.[152]

In Pakistan and India, the courts have applied the rule against bias strictly wherever personal prejudice or ill-will could be proved from the proceedings or from the conduct of the parties. Thus where a government servant was dismissed for misconduct due to insulting behaviour towards his superior officer and the dismissal was based on findings of an inquiry held, and charges framed, by the officer himself, relating to acts of discourtesy towards himself, the entire proceedings were quashed.[153] Where the appellant was dismissed from railway service by the deputy chief commercial superintendent, most of the charges levied against the said employee related to his conduct qua the deputy chief commercial superintendent himself who himself considered the employee's representation and passed the dismissal order. This order was quashed by the Supreme Court, as the said deputy chief commercial superintendent sat as a judge in his own case. The Supreme Court emphasized, 'anyone who has a personal stake in any inquiry must keep himself aloof from the conduct of the inquiry'.[154] When a selection committee is constituted for the purpose of selecting candidates on merits, and one of its members happens to be closely related to a candidate appearing for selection, such member should withdraw not only from participation in the interview of the candidate related to him but altogether from the entire selection process, otherwise all selections would be vitiated on account of reasonable likelihood of bias affecting the selection process.[155] Similarly, where a government servant was suspended, his leave preparatory to retirement revoked, and a departmental inquiry ordered against him, the order was set aside on the grounds of personal animosity of the ministry in charge.[156] Schemes of nationalisation of motor transport have been invalidated on the grounds of personal bias of the minister.[157] Personal bias is a question of fact to be decided in each case. Where bias is suggested free from pecuniary interest, it often becomes necessary to consider whether there is reasonable ground for assuming the possibility of a bias and whether it is likely to produce in the mind of the litigant or the public at large a reasonable doubt about the fairness of the administration of justice. The decision of the bar council tribunal, which was appointed to make an enquiry into the alleged misconduct of a lawyer, was set aside on the grounds of bias because the chairman of the tribunal had acted for the opposite side in a previous case of the misconduct of the petitioner lawyer.[158] It was held by a high court in India that a lawyer for one of the parties to a case cannot sit on the appellate tribunal to hear the appeal in the same case.[159]

(iii) Pecuniary interest

In English law, pecuniary interest, however slight, disqualifies an adjudicator. The test is not whether a decision has been actually affected by such interest but whether a litigant could apprehend that a bias attributable to a judge might have operated against him.[160] Recent tendency, however, points to a somewhat narrower application of the rule. Thus, where six out of seven justices were members of a co-operative society and derived small dividends from it, that did not disqualify them from granting a spirits licence to the society.[161] In the American law also, a judge is disqualified from adjudicating upon an issue if he stands to gain or lose by the decision.[162] The American courts, however, put a restricted interpretation on the rule. However, a judge is disqualified from adjudicating upon an issue if he stands to gain or lose by the decision.[163] In the 'tripartite tribunals' which include representatives of groups who are openly partisan, the members are not disqualified.

The rule of pecuniary bias disqualifying a judge also operates in the Indo-Pakistan sub-continent. Where an accused was tried and convicted by the Presidency Magistrate of criminal breach of trust as a servant in respect of certain goods belonging to the company and the Magistrate was shareholder in the company which prosecuted the accused, it was held that the magistrate was disqualified from trying the case and conviction was set aside.[164] The courts, however, make a distinction between pecuniary interest and personal bias. It has been held that in the case of pecuniary interest, the smallest interest in the subject matter of the inquiry would result in disqualification of the judges as a matter of course.[165] But, if the interest alleged is some other kind of interest, it becomes necessary to consider whether there is reasonable ground for assuming the possibility of bias.[166]

5.5.3 Rule against bias

(i) Acquiescence and waiver: It has been held that a party may be deemed to have waived his objection to the exercise of jurisdiction on the grounds of bias if he has not taken this objection at the earliest opportunity after having acquired clear and full knowledge as to the facts constituting such disqualification.[167] While some defect of jurisdiction, of which the case of bias is one, may be waived by submission to the jurisdiction, certain types of *ultra vires* would still be entitled to relief in spite of the failure to raise objection at the proper time. Thus the courts have distinguished between what is called (a) latent and patent defects and (b) total and contingent want of jurisdiction. Where there is a patent want of jurisdiction, i.e. want of jurisdiction is apparent on the face of the proceedings, it cannot be cured or waived by submission to jurisdiction.[168]

In Pakistan, *Ghulam Rasul* v. *Crown*[169] was the first case on the issue. Here, the Legal Remembrancer, having advised the Crown to file an appeal from an acquittal in a murder case, was subsequently appointed a judge of the high court and was a member of the bench which heard the appeal. Although counsel agreed to hearing by the bench, yet the judgment was held to be affected by bias and hence illegal. It was held that aggrieved party is not deemed to waive his right to object even if it was agreed to by his counsel on his behalf.

In a suit for specific performance of an alleged contract, the sale of a piece of land was decreed by the trial court and the decree confirmed by the appellate subordinate judge. On the defendant's appeal to the high court, the plaintiff's suit was dismissed. By special leave the plaintiff went up to the Supreme Court. It was proved on record that the trial court was biased in favour of the plaintiff. It was held by the Supreme Court that the trial of the case had been 'vitiated by bias in the mind of the trial judge, and, therefore, his entire proceedings and all subsequent proceedings in appeal should be set aside, and the case should be remitted for trial by a competent court'.[170]

(II) PATENT AND LATENT WANT OF JURISDICTION: The defect of bias, it is obvious, does not belong to the category of patent want of jurisdiction. It is presumably a case of latent want of jurisdiction. A plausible explanation is that the defect of bias does not often appear on the face of the proceedings; it depends in most cases on the personal knowledge of the parties, and if a person has knowledge of the facts constituting bias, then the same would give rise to his right to object to jurisdiction of the tribunal before he participates in the proceedings. The court assumes that party has waived or abandoned its right to object.[171]

On the same issue, the courts have also distinguished between what is known as 'total' want of jurisdiction and 'contingent' want of jurisdiction. In the former case, the tribunal has no jurisdiction to entertain the cause by reason of the status of the parties, nature of the subject matter, or defective composition of the tribunal itself. In such a case, the tribunal has no jurisdiction from the very beginning and, therefore, a party, by taking a step in the cause before it, and does not waive his right to object to the want of jurisdiction.[172] A contingent want of jurisdiction arises where the tribunal having jurisdiction over the subject matter of the dispute or cause omits to comply with some procedural requirements upon which its jurisdiction depends. Where the jurisdiction of the tribunal thus rests upon the fulfilment of a condition, and a party, instead of objecting that such a condition has not been fulfilled, takes a step in the proceeding, he cannot raise objection afterwards.[173] Bias is considered to be a case of contingent want of jurisdiction.

5.5.4 THE RIGHT TO A HEARING

(i) PRINCIPLE OF AUDI ALTERAM PARTEM

The principle of *audi alteram partem*, i.e. hearing both sides of the question, goes back several centuries and has been applied in a variety of circumstances; it may be regarded as one of the foundations of English justice. Fortescue, J, said of this principle in *R. v. Chancellor of Cambridge*:[174]

> The laws of God and man both give the party an opportunity to make his defence, if he has any. I remember to have heard it observed by a very learned man upon such an occasion, that even God himself did not pass sentence upon Adam, before he was called upon to make his defence. Adam (says God), where art thou? Hast thou not eaten of the tree, whereof I commanded thee that thou should not eat? And the same question was put to Eve also.

It is said that the principle of *audi alteram partem* was upheld in Magna Carta and Lord Coke subscribed to that view.[175] The right of hearing was insisted upon in cases involving the removal of an incumbent from property purchased within a definite period, deprivation of the privilege of being a burgess of a city, and removal of a person from his position for his neglect to sit in the court.[176] The principle is rooted in the precedents and affirmed by recent authority may be safely taken as too deeply entrenched in English common law to be shaken. In the English law, the notion developed that unless a proceeding is judicial or quasi-judicial as distinguished from administrative, the principles of natural justice have no application to it. This notion has undergone remarkable change in the case of *Ridge* v. *Baldwyn*.[177] In that case, the watch committee dismissed a police constable without telling him the grounds or inviting any submission. It was held by the House of Lords that the dismissal was in breach of the principle of *audi alteram partem* and was thus void. The distinction between administrative and judicial functions was brushed aside and it was maintained that the exercise of powers which affects the right and property of the private individual is necessarily judicial and cannot be administrative or ministerial.

In *Durayappah* v. *Fernando*,[178] the judicial committee of the Privy Council sought to make a fresh attempt to analyse the judicial element in the exercise of power in order to ascertain the applicability of the rule of *audi alteram partem*. It was held that 'three matters' ought to be considered in this connection. Firstly, what is the nature of the property, the office held, status enjoyed or services to be performed by the complainant? Applying this test to the facts of the case, the court said that the municipal council was invested by statute with the administration of a large area and the discharge of important duties. Where the Legislature has enacted a statute, setting up municipal authorities with considerable measure of independence from the central government within defined local areas and fields of government, no minister should have the right to dissolve such an authority without allowing the right to be heard on that matter unless the statute, in express words, excludes such a right. In other words a right of considerable importance could not be infringed without allowing the right of a hearing. Secondly, in what circumstances, or on what occasions is the administrative authority entitled to intervene? In the instant case, the statute empowered the Minister to dissolve the council on one of the three grounds: (a) incompetence; (b) permanent default in the performance of duties imposed on it; (c) persistent refusal or neglect to comply with any provision of law. It was held that, in such a case, the minister can act only after observing the principle of *audi alteram partem*. It was, however, suggested that, had the minister been empowered to dissolve the council only for incompetence and on no other ground, it might have been argued that, as 'incompetence' is very vague and difficult to define, the parliament did not intend the principle to apply.

In Pakistan, the application of the principle of *audi alteram partem* has closely followed the precedents in the English law. Where compensation for acquisition of property was determined without notice to the party affected, it was set aside on the basis of breach of the principle of *audi alteram partem*.[179] Where an order is made to the prejudice of a party without hearing him as, for instance, where arrears recoverable as land revenue have been determined against a person,[180] or a person's sentence has been enhanced or other adverse order made without hearing him,[181] or where a trade licence has been cancelled for misconduct without hearing the party,[182] the order is liable to be set aside in judicial review.

The principle has been made applicable to administrative tribunals as well.[183] The theoretical distinction between administrative and judicial acts has been disregarded in the decisions of the Supreme Court. The tribunals, especially in cases where they are required to adjudicate upon the civil rights of the parties, are under an obligation to act judicially and are bound to follow the fundamental rules of evidence and fair play which are embodied in the principles of natural justice. They are required to give an opportunity to the party affected, make some kind of enquiry, give a hearing and to collate evidence, if any, considering all the facts and circumstances bearing on the merits of the controversy before any decision is given by them. These are the essential elements of a judicial approach to the dispute. Prescribed forms of procedure are not necessary to be followed provided in coming to the conclusion these well-recognised norms and principles of judicial approach are observed by the tribunal.[184] Where a person aggrieved by an order of requisition appealed to Chief Commissioner, Karachi, who dismissed it without giving her an opportunity of being heard, the high court set aside the order of dismissal and ordered that the appeal be reheard. The chief commissioner appealed to the Supreme Court, where it was contended that (a) the common law doctrine applied to judicial proceedings and not to proceedings before the chief commissioner, which were administrative in character, and (b) that the right of hearing was not provided by the statute and, therefore, could not be invoked by the respondent. It was held that it was a principle of natural justice that no one should be dealt with to his material disadvantage or be deprived of his liberty or property without having an opportunity of being heard and making his defence. Accordingly, when a statute gave a right of appeal, it was to be understood as silently implying, when it did not expressly provide, that the appellant had the right of being heard. As regards the right of hearing, there is no difference between proceedings which are strictly judicial and those which are in the nature of judicial proceedings though administrative in form.[185] Where it was contended that since no order could be passed against the assessee in a proceeding under section 33-A of the Income Tax Act, 1922, it was not necessary to give an opportunity of hearing to the party who has filed the application. It was held that the mere fact that a tribunal cannot pass an order of a particular kind does not necessarily involve the proceedings which would otherwise be judicial, ceases to be so. If no opportunity of hearing is given to the applicant, then the order of the Commissioner of Income Tax passed in such proceedings would be void and of no legal effect.[186]

The rule of *audi altrem partem* is not confined to proceedings before courts, but extends to all proceedings, including the administrative proceedings which affect the person or property or other right of the parties concerned in the dispute.[187] This rule applies even though there may be no positive words in the statute or subordinate legislation whereby the power is vested to take such proceedings, for in such cases, the requirement is to be implied as the minimum requirement of fairness.[188] Therefore, where an order is made to the prejudice of a party without hearing him, as, for instance where arrears recoverable as land revenue have been determined against a person,[189] or a person's sentence has been enhanced, or other adverse order has been made without hearing him,[190] or where a trade licence has been cancelled for misconduct without hearing the party,[191] the order may be vacated in *certiorari*.[192] Similarly, if a benefit under law is granted to someone, then withdrawal of that benefit behind his back on a subsequent change in law is an action without lawful authority.[193] For instance, in case of expulsion of university students, expulsion order being impugned on grounds that there was no fair opportunity of showing cause and that act of students did not fall within mischief of the General Discipline Rules of the University,[194] the court has dismissed the petition against order after incorporating willingness of university to reconsider students' cases.[195]

The law in India restricted the operation of the principle to judicial proceedings only. The term 'judicial' could be extended by statutory construction to many administrative actions as well.[196] But the basic element in theory remained that the principle of natural justice is relevant only in judicial proceedings. The earliest case dealing with this question was the *Province of Bombay* v. *Khushaldas Advani*.[197] In that case, a flat in Bombay, in the occupation of one Khushaldas Advani, was requisitioned by the government under a certain Ordinance 31. Khushaldas Advani was not allowed any opportunity of being heard against the order. He, thereupon, filed a writ petition in the high court, which quashed the requisition order. On appeal, the Supreme Court reversed the decision, holding that the order of the state government was an administrative order and not a judicial or quasi-judicial one. However, later in India the courts have laid down a new test, i.e. the nature of the rights affected, for the purpose of drawing a distinction between judicial and administrative acts. Thus in *Board of High School* v. *Ghanshyam*,[198] it was held as under:

'Now it may be mentioned that the statute is not likely to provide in so many words that the authority in passing the order is required to act judicially: that can only be inferred from the express provisions of the statute in the first instance in each case and no one circumstance along will be determinative of the question whether the authority set up by the statute has the duty to act judicially or not. The inference whether the authority, acting under a statute where it is silent, has the duty to act judicially will depend on the express provisions of the statute read along with the nature of the right affected, the manner of the disposal provided, the objective criterion if any to be adopted, the effect of the decision on the person affected and other indicia afforded by the statute. A duty to act judicially may arise in widely different circumstances which it will be impossible and indeed inadvisable to attempt to define exhaustively.'

Later in India, principles of natural justice of right of hearing have been extended to administrative decisions as well. The Indian Supreme Court held that before a government contractor is blacklisted, he should be given a hearing because it is an implied principle of the rule of law that any order having civil consequences should be passed only after following the principles of natural justice.[199] In a matter of cancellation of permission to construct a building, the Supreme Court insisted that a personal hearing be given to the lessees by the concerned authority. The court said, 'On a matter of such importance where the stakes are heavy for the lessees who claim to have made large investments on the project and where a number of grounds require the determination of factual matters of some complexity, the statutory authority should, in the facts of the cases, have afforded a personal hearing to the lessees.' Quashing the order of the concerned authority, the court suggested that the authority should 'afford a reasonable opportunity including an opportunity of personal hearing and of adducing evidence wherever necessary to the respondent lessees'.[200]

(II) BREACH OF THE AUDI ALTERAM PARTEM RULE: A JURISDICTIONAL DEFECT

In the case of right of hearing, there is controversy about whether the breach of the rule can be treated as want or excess of jurisdiction which renders a proceeding void. It is argued that since jurisdiction exists when there is power to enter on an enquiry, breach of procedural rules does not go to jurisdiction. Consequently, the exercise of an undoubted jurisdiction in breach of *audi alteram partem* does not constitute a jurisdictional defect. The effect of failure to give hearing is merely to render a decision voidable and the defect cannot be equated with want or excess of jurisdiction.[201] In spite of such seeming uncertainty, the case law tilts heavily in favour of the view that a failure to give hearing renders a decision without jurisdiction and a nullity.[202]

(III) EXCEPTIONS TO THE PRINCIPLE OF AUDI ALTERAM PARTEM

Although the importance of the principle of natural justice has been recognised in the administrative process of various systems, there are certain areas in which their applicability remains somewhat indeterminable. Thus, it is said that the rule of *audi alteram partem* cannot be invoked in the spheres of 'policy', and 'private law principles'.

(a) *Policy*: The issue as to whether a decision of policy operates as an exception to reviewability by the courts and applicability of the rule of hearing was clearly raised and decided in *Darlassis v. Minister of Education*.[203] In that case, the order of the minister was challenged on the ground that the minister had received and acted on information regarding the subject matter of the public inquiry without affording the objector any right of hearing. It was held that the decision of the Minister of Housing not to release the alternative site from housing purposes was a decision of policy which the objector could not question with the result that the decision of the minister was no longer a quasi-judicial matter but an administrative decision on a matter of policy. The courts have no authority to interfere with the way in which the minister carries out his national policy.[204] In India, in the matters involving policy, the courts can withhold review if they are of the opinion that the government was acting administratively. But where the fundamental rights of citizens come in conflict with the enforcement of policy, the courts have reviewed administrative decisions. Thus, where the government adopted the policy of cancelling the grants made by the former rulers of the native states without giving hearing, the holders of the grant successfully challenged the policy.[205] Similarly, in Pakistan, it has been held that it is not for the court to examine the soundness of policy behind legislation. The court should, however, see that powers given to a tribunal are exercised in a manner laid down in law and in consonance with well known principles and procedures.[206] Thus, in Pakistan and India, the courts have wider powers to demand observance of the principles of natural justice with regard to policy matters.

(b) *Private Law Principles*: The essence of administrative law, as evolved in Britain and in the countries which have inherited English legal traditions, is the supervisory functions of the superior courts over administrative actions. The proper discharge of that duty demands an effective system of public law. However, these supervisory functions do not generally extend to private law principles (e.g. the law of master and servant). The rule of *audi alteram partem* is ousted in the law of master and servant. The question in a pure case of master and servant does not depend at all on whether or not the master has heard the servant in his own defence.[207] The Supreme Court of Pakistan held in a case involving dismissal of an employee of a statutory corporation that the case is governed by the ordinary law of master and servant and the master is entitled to terminate the service of a servant without notice.[208]

In addition to the principles of natural justice discussed above, the courts have also applied other principles of natural justice while exercising judicial review of administrative actions and orders.

(iv) Reasonable opportunity of defence

It has been held by the courts that giving notice to the party concerned is not adequate in all cases. The party should also be afforded reasonable opportunity of producing his defence. The affected party should, in good time, know the precise case he is to meet.[209] In *Muhammad Murtaza* v. *University of Sind*,[210] the University Syndicate decided to give the petitioner 15 days' time for submitting his explanation against the proposed action. The petitioner, who was ill at the time, requested for extension of time by 6 weeks which was refused by the university authorities. It was held that such refusal amounts to denial of reasonable opportunity to the petitioner and for that reason alone, the order passed against him stands vitiated and is liable to be set aside.

(v) Reasoned decisions

It has been a recognised principle of natural justice that a party is entitled to know why a matter has been decided against him.[211]

The principle has been described in the expression 'speaking orders' by the courts in Pakistan and India. The requirement of reasoned decisions helps to widen the scope of judicial review. All decisions of administrative authorities are expected to include a statement of findings and conclusions as well as the reason or basis therefore upon all the material issues of fact, law or discretion presented on the record.[212] In the absence of any reasons, it is difficult to define what considerations, if any, prevailed with the administrative body concerned in arriving at its decision on the various points involved therein.[213] In another case, it was held that the administrative authorities should give reason for all quasi-judicial decisions.[214] The Supreme Court of India quashed an order cancelling a licence under UP Sugarcane Dealers Licensing Order 1962, since no reasons had been given.[215] The Supreme Court of Pakistan has held that orders passed judicially should be speaking orders.[216] It has been held that Central Board of Revenue exercises quasi-judicial functions and is required to state reasons for passing adverse orders.[217] In Pakistan, Section 24A of the General Clauses Act, 1897 (introduced in 1997 through an amendment) requires all executive authorities to give reasons for their orders wherever necessary or appropriate.

The Supreme Court of India has engrafted an exception on the rule of reasoned decisions. While hearing an appeal under Section 60 of the Bombay Police Act from an externment order passed under Section 56, the state government need not give reasons for rejecting the appeal; the reason being that if the authorities were to discuss the evidence in such a case, it would be easy to fix the identity of the witnesses who can then be harassed by the externee or his friends.[218]

5.6 REMEDIES

The remedies provided for redressing the wrong done to citizens by the actions of administrators can be divided into two categories: private law remedies, i.e. actions for damages, injunctions, and declarations; and public law remedies, i.e. prerogative or constitutional writs of prohibition, *certiorari*, and *mandamus*.

5.6.1 PRIVATE LAW REMEDIES

Private law remedies include actions for damages, injunctions, and declarations.

(I) ACTION FOR DAMAGES

In English law, an action for damages used to lie against the local authority or public corporations[219] but not against the Crown. The English doctrine of sovereign immunity is based upon the maxim: 'The King can do no wrong'. The English doctrine of sovereign immunity found its way into American law but it has been vigorously attacked by American commentators and thus the doctrine has suffered rapid decline. In the USA, payment of tort claims by various governmental units is governed in part by general statutes such as Federal Tort Claims Act, 1957.

In English law, the scope of this remedy has lately been widened. The contention that an applicant for a statutory licence could never have a right to damages for malicious use of licensing power was rejected.[220] In *Rookes* v. *Barnard*,[221] Lord Devlin suggested that exemplary damages are an appropriate remedy for oppressive, arbitrary or unconstitutional actions by the servants of the government.

In Pakistan and India, a distinction is made as a result of historical developments between the local authorities and the statutory corporations, on the one hand, and the state, on the other for purposes of an action for damages. Thus a corporation, which has the same liability as any individual in all civil matters, can be liable for damages in all cases where a master would be liable for the acts of his servant acting within the scope of his employment.[222] If the servant of a statutory body like a municipality led to a prosecution in circumstances whereunder he would be liable for damages and had acted in excess of the powers conferred on him by the statute, then the employer, namely the statutory body, would be equally liable.[223] Negligence or nuisance caused by failure to perform a statutory duty has been held to render a corporation liable in damages. Thus, where the failure of the municipal corporation to maintain and repair drainage resulted in nuisance, the corporation was held liable for damages.[224] Again, where owing to the negligence of a municipal board in maintaining pipelines in a proper state of repair, damage was caused to a private house, the municipal board was held liable.[225] Where a shipping authority acted under orders of the government which resulted in the delayed mailing of the plaintiff's ship and thereby caused loss to him, the government was held liable for damages.[226] In a case of false imprisonment by government servants, the government was held liable for damages,[227] whereon the plea of 'sovereign act', it was sought to resist an action for damages for illegal detention and disposal of some movable property belonging to the plaintiff by the District Magistrate, the Supreme Court rejected the contention.[228] Where the plaintiff suffered injuries in a road accident owing to the negligence of the employees of the government in stacking *bajri*, it was held that the stacking of *bajri* in a negligent manner for repairs to a highway cannot be said to be a sovereign act and cannot be protected as such.[229]

The Indian Supreme Court held that exemplary damages can be awarded against public servants whose actions are arbitrary, discriminatory, *mala fide* and illegal. In *Common Cause Regd. Society v. Union of India*,[230] such an award was made in judicial review proceedings. In that case, the allotment of petrol pumps from the discretionary quota by a minister was found to be arbitrary, discriminatory, *mala fide*, and illegal. His action was quashed and exemplary damages of Rs 50 lakh (five million) were awarded against a minister.

(II) INJUNCTIONS

Historically, the injunction has been as wide as prohibition in its functions in English law. The Court of Chancery used injunctions in much the same manner as prohibition to restrain proceedings in common law courts. In modern English law, however, it is a relatively unimportant method of reviewing administrative action.[231] It has never been available against the Crown. The Crown Proceedings Act, 1947, reaffirms this position under Section 21(1). Under recent rulings of the British Courts, the scope of injunctions has become wider in English law. It is now available against the Crown[232] and to prevent the enforcement of the statutes that are incompatible with directly applicable European Community law.[233]

Injunction is a judicial process by which one who has invaded or is threatening to invade the rights, legal or equitable of another, is restrained from continuing or commencing such wrongful act. In Pakistan and India, remedies of injunctions have been regulated by the Specific Relief Act, 1877. In India, this Act has been repealed by the Specific Relief Act, 1963 but in Pakistan, it continues to apply. The law of injunctions under the new Indian Act is the same as under the repealed Act. These Acts provide for perpetual injunction, mandatory injunction, and temporary injunction.

A perpetual injunction may be granted to prevent the breach of an obligation existing in favour of the applicant, whether expressly or by implication.[234] A perpetual injunction usually takes long time and the interest of justice may require that the order must issue soon. In such a case, the plaintiff can file an application for temporary injunction which, if issued by the court, is to continue until time specified by the court or until further order of the court.[235] Temporary injunctions can be granted at any stage of the suit and are regulated by Order XXXIX of the Code of Civil Procedure, 1908. In order to obtain temporary injunction, a plaintiff has to establish that:

(a) he has a *prima facie* case,

(b) balance of convenience is in his favour, that is, he is in possession of the property in dispute or exercising the right claimed,

(c) irreparable loss and injury will be caused to him if temporary injunction is not granted to him, that is, his relief is not capable of pecuniary evaluation, and

(d) he binds himself to pay damages to the defendant in case his claim is not established in the final adjudication.

If the plaintiff succeeds in his suit, such temporary injunction is converted into perpetual injunction, and if the plaintiff fails, it is cancelled.

A mandatory injunction can be issued to prevent the breach of an obligation and to compel the performance of certain acts which the court is capable of enforcing.[236] It is an order of the court not only restraining a person from future wrongful acts but directing him further to restore, so far as possible, the former state of things. A mandatory injunction thus provides not only prohibition but also imposes a positive duty on the defendant to do some thing.

The plaintiff in a suit for injunction, whether perpetual or mandatory, can also claim damages either in addition to, or in substitution of, such injunction. The court may, in its discretion, award damages.

The following are the general principles that regulate the relief of injunction:

(a) It is pre-eminently a discretionary remedy.[237] The plaintiff cannot claim it as a matter of right. It is more in the nature of an equitable relief than a legal remedy.

(b) The exercise of this discretion is not arbitrary but is regulated by settled principles.

(c) It may be refused when the conduct of the plaintiff is such as to disentitle him from the assistance of the court, or where equally efficacious relief can be obtained by any other usual mode of proceeding or when award of damages can be an adequate remedy to the aggrieved party.[238] A plaintiff who seeks injunction must be able to satisfy the court that his own acts and dealings in the matter have been fair and honest and free from any taint of fraud or illegality, otherwise he is not entitled to the relief.[239]

(d) Where the plaintiff establishes his right and there is actual or threatening violation thereof, injunction would be granted more or less as a matter of course, unless it is found, in the circumstances of the case, inexpedient and unjust.

(e) The court in determining the fact whether injunctions should be granted or not is generally guided by the consideration of the balance of convenience in each case.

(f) It cannot be granted to interfere with the public duties of any department of the central government or any provincial government, or with the sovereign acts of a foreign government.[240] The expression 'public duty' does not include tortious act of an officer of government. Permanent injunction was granted restraining the defendant government from assessing compensation in accordance with inapplicable enactments and a mandatory injunction was granted directing the defendant to award compensation in accordance with the applicable law.[241]

In *Raja Ram* v. *State of Uttar Pradesh*,[242] it was held that if a notice issued by a Magistrate under Section 18(3) of the Electricity Act, requiring the plaintiff to demolish a portion of his building is invalid, the plaintiff would be entitled to the injunction restraining the defendant, on whose application the notice as issued, from demolishing it. Section 56(d) of the Specific Relief Act[243] cannot bar the suit because it cannot be said to be a public duty of any department of the government to demolish the construction of a citizen except as provided under the law. Even granting, for the sake of argument, that the constructions were unauthorised and were liable to be demolished under the provisions of law, they could be demolished only after the issue of a valid notice. Without a valid notice, the demolition of constructions could not be said to be a public duty. The injunction as a remedy would enjoy many advantages over the prerogative remedies as they are understood in English law. Firstly, an injunction lies against administrative as well as judicial and quasi-judicial proceedings, while *certiorari* and prohibition lie only in respect of the latter class of proceedings. The court can grant a mandatory injunction, i.e. a positive order to do something as well as a negative order to refrain from doing something,[244] while *certiorari* and prohibition are confined to negative acts, i.e. either the quashing of a decision or the prohibiting of proceeding further. An injunction can be granted in lieu of or in addition to damages. Indeed, it is now accepted that once the statutory notice of a suit against the state has been given, an action is maintainable.[245] A further advantage is that in common law a public authority can use injunctions against a private party to prevent breaches of law, e.g. prevent persistent violations of planning law despite the availability of alternative statutory enforcement machinery under the planning law.[246]

(III) DECLARATIONS

The origin of declaratory action in English law is said to be equitable. It was originally available in the Court of Chancery only where the plaintiff sought in addition to the declaration of some consequential relief.[247] A declaratory action signifies a judicial remedy, which conclusively determines the rights of the parties. Any person entitled to any legal character, or to any property, may institute a suit against any person denying or interested to deny him title to such character or right, and the court may, in its discretion, make therein a declaration that he is so entitled, and the plaintiff need not in such suit ask for any further relief. Sections 1 and 14 of the Court of Chancery England instrument state a special case for the opinion of the court which could consider the matter without administering consequential relief. Section 50 of the Court of Chancery Procedure Act 1852 provided that no suit should be open to objection on the grounds that merely a declaratory decree was asked for. Still, the court hesitated to grant a declaration without giving the reliefs incidental to the declaration.[248] In India and Pakistan, no court can make any such declaration where the plaintiff, being able to seek further relief than mere declaration of title, omits to do so.[249] In a purely declaratory judgment, there is no direct order against any one or in favour of any one but only the mere definition of the rights and obligations of the parties.

Declaratory suits can also be filed against government bodies, local authorities, and statutory authorities. Declarations can be issued by the courts in the matters dealt with by the administrative authorities, where entitlement to any legal character or right is involved. Mutations passed by revenue authorities can be set aside by declaratory decrees. Suits can be filed seeking declaration that acts or orders of municipal or local authorities are *ultra vires*.[250] It has been held that Civil Court, being a court of ultimate jurisdiction and even if jurisdiction is barred, it is competent to consider any illagality and *malafide* committed by any forum, tribunal or authority. Where administrative act/order of the authority is found to be without jurisdiction and illegal, such matter can be decided after framing of issues and recording the evidence.[251]

Grant of declaratory decree is a matter of discretion with a court. A party who comes to court with unclean hands is not entitled to declaratory decree. Acquiescence or laches disentitles a party from obtaining declaratory relief.[252] Declaratory relief can be refused where the declaration sought appears to be either useless or an infructuous one.[253] The relief may also be refused where other appropriate or alternative legal remedy is available. Courts do not grant a declaration when it has no utility.[254]

The declaratory actions are more popular a remedy in England and the USA than in Pakistan and India, as a means of challenging decisions of administrative tribunals. The difficulties pointed out in the way of declaratory actions in Pakistan and India are:

(a) that it is not a speedy and efficacious remedy,

(b) that it is a statutory remedy and can be excluded by a statute, and

(c) that two months' notice is required to be given under Section 80 of the Code of Civil Procedure before filing suit for declaration against the government or public officer. The effect of this restriction has been much too diluted by the amendment in Section 80 of the Code of Civil Procedure in 1962 which provides that the default in giving such statutory notice would disentitle the plaintiff to any costs of the suit if settlement as regards the subject matter of the suit is reached or the government/public officer concedes the plaintiff's claim.[255]

The Madras High Court repeatedly held that the courts have the jurisdiction to make declaratory decrees apart from Section 2 of the Act.[256] The Allahabad High Court took the same view.[257] Uncertainty was introduced by certain observations in a subsequent Privy Council case. That was the case of *Sheoparsan Sing* v. *Ramnandan Prasad*.[258] In the course of the judgment, Sir Lawrence Jenkins, who was formerly the Chief Justice of the Calcutta High Court, said: 'The Court's power to make a declaration without more is derived from Section 42, Specific Relief Act, and regard must therefore be had to its precise terms'. These observations led other high courts in India to the conclusion that power to make a declaration is confined to the provisions of Section 42, Specific Relief Act, while the Madras High Court maintained that *Sheoparsan Singh* v. *Ramnandan Prasad* was a case of special circumstances.[259] On the other hand, the high courts of Calcutta,[260] Patna,[261] Bombay,[262] and Punjab[263] held that Section 42-D of the Specific Relief Act is exhaustive on the subject of declarations. The Indian Supreme Court has, however, resolved the conflict in a recent case in favour of the view that Section 42 of the Specific Relief Act is not exhaustive of the circumstances in which a declaratory decree may be made and the courts have power to grant such a decree independently of the requirements of the Section.[264]

In Pakistan also, there is a difference of opinion on this question. In *Shafaquatullah Quadi* v. *University of Karachi*,[265] the Sind Chief Court held that Section 42 of the Specific Relief Act is exhaustive and no declaration can be allowed unless it can be brought within the four corners of this section. The West Pakistan High Court at

Lahore, on the other hand, took the view in *Salim Ullah* v. *Mst Motia Begum*[266] that Section 42 of the Specific Relief Act is not exhaustive with regard to the suits in which declaratory *decrees* can be granted in proper cases. The question whether a declaratory suit can be maintained outside Section 42 of the Act came before the East Pakistan High Court in *Kumudini Welfare Trust of Bengal Ltd* v. *Pakistan.*[267] The High Court, relying on the Privy Council cases of *Robert Fischer* v. *Secretary of State for India in Council*[268] and *Pratab Singh* v. *Bhabuti Singh,*[269] decided the question in the affirmative. The latter case came before the judicial committee in 1913. There, the suit was brought by the minor appellants for a declaration that a certain compromise deed and a decree passed in two pre-emption suits were not binding on them. It was held in that case that, although the suit was not brought under Section 42 of the Specific Relief Act, the declaration prayed for should be made. In Pakistan, the predominant view seems to be that a declaration can issue outside Section 42 of the Specific Relief Act 1877.

5.6.2 Prerogative writs and constitutional remedies

(I) General

In English law, the expression 'prerogative remedies' refers to the writs of *habeas corpus*, *certiorari*, prohibition, *mandamus*, and *quo warranto*. The writ of *quo warranto* has been abolished and injunctions may now issue from the Queen's Bench Division in similar circumstances. All other writs, except *habeas corpus*, have been displaced by a modified procedure of orders of the same name after promulgation of Administrative Justice (Miscellaneous Provisions) Act, 1938.

In Pakistan and India, such writs derive their authority from the constitutional provisions. Articles 32 and 226 of the Indian Constitution have empowered the Supreme Court and the high courts respectively to issue directions, orders or writs in the nature of *habeas corpus*, *mandamus*, prohibition, *quo warranto*, and *certiorari*. In Pakistan, Article 199 of the Constitution of

1973 empowers the high courts to issue similar orders though the names traditionally given to them have not been mentioned. In the constitutions of Pakistan and India, writs or orders can also be issued for the enforcement of fundamental rights conferred by these constitutions. Of these, the writ of *habeas* plays a part, though not a large one, in administrative law, since some administrative authorities and tribunals have powers of detention.[270] Writ of *quo warranto* is used mostly to examine the legality of claim which a party asserts to an office or to franchise.[271] Writs of *certiorari*, prohibition and *mandamus* have been established as the most important remedies in administrative law.[272]

In Pakistani law, apart from departmental appeals on the executive side, the judicial remedy lies only with the prerogative writs, which the superior courts are empowered to issue. Moreover, in the exercise of the prerogative jurisdiction, the courts are eventually reduced to the task of construction of the relevant statute, and may only interfere either by *mandamus* where there has been a clear violation of mandatory provisions by omission or commission, or by *certiorari* where they find that the statutory act was essentially judicial in nature and not a purely executive act. They cannot consider the merits. Whereby the act is within the discretionary field, the courts are ordinarily powerless to interfere.[273] In cases where finding is based on no evidence, ignorance of material evidence, consideration of immaterial evidence, arbitrary exercise of jurisdiction, perversity, or material irregularity in conduct of proceedings causing palpable injustice, constitutional jurisdiction of high court can be invoked to rectify wrong and injustice occasioned thereby.[274]

(II) Certiorari and prohibition

Writs of *certiorari* and prohibition are generally treated together because both are used to control excess of jurisdiction committed by bodies which are entrusted with power to determine the rights of individuals in a judicial manner.[275] Writ of prohibition prohibits a person from doing something in excess of his authority and writ of *certiorari* has the effect of declaring that something done by him is without lawful authority and of no legal effect. The rationale of prohibition is that prevention is better than cure and it, therefore, comes into play at an earlier stage than *certiorari*. The latter is applied to a decision which is *fait accompli*; prohibition seeks to prevent the *fait* from becoming *accompli*.

Like Britain, *certiorari* and prohibition in the Indo-Pakistan subcontinent have been regarded as remedies in respect of judicial or quasi-judicial acts but not of administrative acts. *Besant* v. *Advocate General of Madras*[276] was an earlier case on the point. There a magistrate ordered under a statute that the dispensation of a deposit be cancelled and a fresh deposit made. On an application for *certiorari* by the printer and publisher of the newspaper on the grounds that the order was made in breach of the principle of *audi altrem partem*, the judicial Committee of the Privy Council held (on appeal) that *certiorari* did not lie; the order in question being an administrative and not a judicial one. This decision continues to guide and shape the judicial policy in India. Pakistan, on the other hand, has abandoned the distinction between judicial and administrative acts for the purpose of judicial control in general and *certiorari* in particular. Where an import registration certificate was suspended without giving opportunity of a hearing to the applicant, the Supreme Court held that *certiorari* lies in respect of judicial and administrative acts alike.[277] This position has been affirmed in successive decisions of the Supreme Court.[278]

Certiorari jurisdiction is based on the principle that the superior courts have to examine if jurisdiction is correctly exercised by an inferior court or tribunal and in accordance with law. In cases of abuse or excess of jurisdiction, the orders passed are liable to be corrected by the high court in exercise of judicial review and the constitutional jurisdiction. In other words, the high court, as a delegatee of superior judicial authority, is responsible for keeping inferior courts or bodies exercising judicial or quasi-judicial powers within the limits of their jurisdiction.[279] Even where the law attaches finality to the decision of an inferior tribunal, but the order made by the tribunal is without jurisdiction or beyond the sphere allotted to it, the high court can interfere in the exercise of its writ jurisdiction, though such orders may not be questioned before another tribunal in collateral proceedings.[280] The exercise of *certiorari* jurisdiction draws no distinction between the person performing judicial or quasi-judicial functions.[281] It gives the high court jurisdiction to interfere in all cases of excess of jurisdiction, whether the person exceeding jurisdiction is a court, a judicial or a quasi-judicial body or a purely executive or administrative tribunal or officer.[282] Where a statute requires public enquiry, but besides public enquiry, private enquiry is also held, the order based on such an enquiry can be set aside.[283] However, if the court feels that questions have been left undecided or that a question has to be decided after the taking of fresh evidence, the case should be returned to the inferior tribunal for a fresh decision in accordance with law after quashing the order complained against.[284] However, it is no function of the court to tell the inferior tribunal how to decide the matter after it has been remanded to it to decide according to law.[285]

Where a defect of jurisdiction is apparent on the face of the record, a prohibition will lie if an order, void for want of jurisdiction, is about to be executed.[286] Similarly, if a tribunal having become *functus officio*, assumes jurisdiction to do so something further, a prohibition will lie.[287] A prohibition is justified only where there is unlawful assumption of jurisdiction as distinguished from an erroneous and improper exercise of it.[288] Moreover, prohibition is a right where an excess of jurisdiction is made out and the tribunal is under a duty to act judicially.[289] Where the absence of jurisdiction is apparent on the face of the record, prohibition may be claimed as of right despite acquiescence in the exercise of jurisdiction, the reason being that if prohibition were not to issue, the case might become a precedent if allowed to stand without impeachment.[290] The 'person' includes any body politic or corporate against whom prohibition may issue and includes, the Water and Power Development Authority (WAPDA),[291] the Election Commissioner[292] or a University.[293]

In Pakistan, *certiorari* process has been used against every conceivable kind of statutory functionary or department, e.g. administrative authorities and tribunals, army, boards of education, boards of revenue, border area authorities, capital development authority, carriage authorities, civil courts, claims authorities, coast guards, cooperative societies, court of wards, criminal courts, custodian of evacuee property, district boards, economic reforms authorities, educational authorities, educational institutions, election commission, election tribunals, federal and provincial governments, immigration authorities, industrial tribunals, labour tribunals, land acquisition authorities, land colonisation authorities, land customs authorities, land reforms authorities, licensing authorities, local bodies, medical council, motor and transport authorities, municipalities, railways, police, post office authorities, power development authorities, professional bodies, public service commission, public sector development corporations, quota allotment authorities, rent collectors, sea customs authorities, settlement and rehabilitation authorities, small causes court, statutory banks, taxation authorities, the *auqaf* authorities, the frontier authorities, the State Bank, universities, urban administrators, urban building control authorities, urban development authorities, urban improvement trusts, etc.

The case of *Gobindrao* v. *State of Madhya Pradesh*[294] was in appeal from the full bench decision of the Madras High Court which dismissed an application for *certiorari* to quash an order of the state government rejecting a claim for pension. On appeal, the Supreme Court not only set aside the order, but also directed the state government to dispose of the case in the light of its judgment. The direction in a prayer for *certiorari* amounts to *mandamus*.

In a case where the applicant seeks, and the court grants, not only the quashing of the impugned decision, but also some positive act, the appropriate procedure is to apply for the grant of *certiorari* as well as *mandamus*.[295] The courts in Pakistan, as in England, have combined *certiorari* and *mandamus* in such a case. In fact, this has been done in cases of *ultra vires*[296] as well as error of law apparent on the fact of the record.[297]

(III) MANDAMUS

Writ of *mandamus* is a judicial remedy issued in the form of an order or direction from the Supreme Court or a high court to any constitutional, statutory or non-statutory agency or body to do some specified act which the agency or body is obliged to do under the law and which is in the nature of a public duty or a statutory duty. The question whether, and if so how far, it goes to compel the exercise of discretion is difficult to answer. The court usually issues *mandamus* where a tribunal has refused to exercise a discretion when it has a duty to do so.[298] But *mandamus* cannot be used to enforce the manner in which the discretion has to be exercised. *Mandamus* is a positive command to perform a certain act (i.e. duty of public nature) and has no negative function which is peculiar province of *certiorari* and prohibition.

A writ of *mandamus* is a command issuing from the high court, directing a person to do any particular act therein specified, which appertains to his office and is in the nature of a public duty. It issues to the end that justice may be done in all cases where there is a specific legal right and no specific legal remedy for enforcing such right, it may issue in cases where, although there is an alternative legal remedy, such mode of redress is less convenient, beneficial and effectual.[299]

The command may issue to a purely administrative body.[300] However, it is not one of the purposes of *mandamus* to obtain expedition in the matter of orders by government upon an administrative matter of which it is seized.[301] On the other hand, a *mandamus* can issue to restore a person to office, where he has been dismissed contrary to a rule having a statutory force.[302] In fact, *mandamus* has been employed to restore to office persons wrongfully removed,[303] or to admit to public office persons duly elected or appointed[304] or to direct an election to a public office.[305] However, the office to which a person prays for restoration by *mandamus* must be a corporate, elective or municipal office.[306] To be entitled to *mandamus*, the applicant must have a legal right to demand the performance of a legal duty.[307] The mere fact of a person being interested in proper performance of a duty by a public functionary is not enough for granting writ of *mandamus*. A person seeking writ of *mandamus* must show right of interest in him to compel performance of a legal duty through court's interference.[308] On the other hand, a *mandamus* will not issue where no duty of a public nature is involved and the right claimed is merely a private right as for instance, where there is a dispute between two rival groups of the share-holders of a company,[309] or between parties to a private contract.[310] A writ of *mandamus* may be issued in a negative form.

In Pakistan and India, however, *mandamus* is used in both positive and negative forms.[311] Thus the courts have used it to restrain the authorities from imposing or authorising the imposition of a tax,[312] to prevent them from enforcing a certain order cancelling a licence[313] to direct them not to enforce bye-laws,[314] to stop take-over orders,[315] to command the authorities not to carry out police inspection of private houses[316] and to restrain government officials from enforcing the provisions of void statutes.[317] The writ of *mandamus* has also been issued in a positive form. Thus, *mandamus* may issue against the government directing it to pay the leave salary[318] allowance[319] or future salary[320] or to forward to the president a competent appeal of a government official.[321] A writ of *mandamus* may be issued to a purely administrative authority.[322]

In India and Pakistan, there has emerged what is known as *certiorarified mandamus,* which covers practically the whole ground of *certiorari*. This development again has its parallel in American administrative law, where *certiorari* floundered off the rock of 6 administrative and judicial issues, leaving *mandamus* to sail through.[323] The following decisions illustrate the point. In *State of Bihar* v. *D.N. Ganguly*[324] where a certain notification of the government to cancel its previous order of reference to an industrial tribunal was sought to be quashed on the grounds that it was *ultra vires,* the high court granted *certiorari*. On appeal, the Supreme Court confirmed the finding of the high court that the notification was *ultra vires,* but finding that the order in question was administrative and, therefore, not amenable to *certiorari*, granted *mandamus*. In *Rameshzvar Prasad* v. *District Magistrate*,[325] an order of refusal to renew a licence on irrelevant considerations was quashed, not by *certiorari*, as it was an administrative, but under the wider powers of Article 226 of the Constitution, and *mandamus* was granted to direct the District Magistrate to consider the application for renewal on merits. In the case of *Commissioner 565 of Police, Bombay* v. *Gordhandas*,[326] where a licence was cancelled by an authority other than the one which had the power to grant or refuse it, *mandamus*, it was held, lies to the appropriate authority ordering it decide the issue.

In Pakistan also, in earlier cases where *certiorari* was held inappropriate against the administrative authorities, *mandamus* was the instrument for reviewing the actions of public authorities on the grounds of *ultra vires*. *S M Giribala* v. *East Bengal Evacuee Property Management Committee*,[327] was a case where the East Bengal Evacuee Property Management Committee, having no jurisdiction to take over the management of certain property, did not. It was held that, although *certiorari* does not lie against administrative authorities, *mandamus* would issue. Since then the distinction between administrative and judicial acts as regards *certiorari* has been discarded,[328] but *mandamus* has retained its position. *Inayat Lillah* v. *M.A. Khan*[329] was a case that came before the Supreme Court. There, the manager of a mosque imposed a ban on the holding of a certain gathering in the mosque. It was held that he exceeded his powers and a direction issued that the gathering be permitted.

5.6.3 RESTRICTIONS ON THE EXERCISE OF WRIT JURISDICTION

The constitutions of Pakistan and India and the courts in the two countries have laid down certain principles of exercise of writ jurisdiction. These principles have the tendency to limit or restrict the exercise of writ jurisdiction on the grounds of *locus standi*, adequate alternative remedies available, discretion, acquiescence, laches, equity etc. However, where the jurisdiction of the court is ousted by the constitution itself, it will be for the court to interpret the ousting provisions.[330] Nevertheless, the jurisdiction of high courts is not barred from reviewing acts, actions or proceedings that suffer from want of jurisdiction, or are *coram nonjudice* or are *mala fide*.[331] Some of these principles restricting the writ jurisdiction are examined below.

(i) PERSONS AGAINST WHOM WRIT CAN BE ISSUED

Authorities amenable to the writ jurisdiction, in the nature of prohibition, *mandamus*, and *certiorari* are restricted to central and provincial governments and local authorities or persons performing functions in connection with the affairs of the federation, a province or a local authority.[332] The courts have interpreted these bodies and their officials to include government, semi-government, autonomous, and statutory bodies. Writs lie against administrative authorities and tribunals, criminal courts, licensing authorities, boards of education and examiners, board of revenue, educational authorities, cooperative societies, court of wards, custodian of evacuee property, claims commissioner, settlement and rehabilitation authority, border area committees, district boards, election tribunals, excise authorities, taxing authorities, industrial tribunals, labour tribunals, land acquisition authorities, land reforms commissioner, medical council, motor and transport authorities, sea customs authorities, universities, government controlled development corporations, *auqaf* development, licensing authorities etc.

(ii) ADEQUATE ALTERNATIVE REMEDY

Writ petition does not lie where there is an adequate alternative remedy available to the party. In the United States of America, the prematurity of the application for a writ is a well recognised barrier to judicial review of administrative orders.[333] Where an order is subject to appeal or revision, writ of *certiorari* does not lie against such order. Where the right which the petitioner for a writ claims to vest in him is entirely the creation of a statute, it is all the more imperative on him to exhaust the remedies provided by the statute before he comes to the high court. He cannot be permitted to say that while he would have one or all the benefits of the statute, he would comply with some of its remedial processes.[334] The alternative remedy, however, should be specific, adequate, prompt and efficacious. Where a petitioner alleged his forced and illegal eviction from a plot of land by an administrative authority or a local body, his writ of *mandamus* was dismissed because he had failed to approach the authority concerned for relief before approaching the high court in writ jurisdiction.[335] The remedy of a suit,[336] amendment of the suit,[337] an appeal[338] or some other step to be taken before a specially constituted authority such as an election tribunal[339] or an ordinary criminal court[340] have been held adequate alternative remedy by the superior courts in Pakistan. A mere representation,[341] revision[342] or review[343] is not an adequate remedy. Under the general law governing them, certain writs, e.g. prohibition and *certiorari*, cannot be refused on the grounds that an alternative is available,[344] or where the error is apparent on the face of the record[345] or the constitutionality of an act is challenged or some principle of natural justice has been violated.[346]

In Pakistan, the high court, if satisfied that no other adequate remedy is provided by law, can on application of party judicially review actions of administrative tribunals. The factor of assuming jurisdiction will be judicial satisfaction of high court as regards adequacy of other remedy. Normally, the high court will not entertain constitutional petition when other appropriate or suitable remedy is available under the law. The question of adequacy, however, is not a rule of law, barring or limiting jurisdiction of high court, rather it controls and regulates the same. Mere availability of alternate remedy will not *ipso facto* debar a party from evoking constitutional jurisdiction of high court. Where order, act or omission of a functionary appears to be autocratic, capricious, or tends to defy mandatory pre-condition for exercise of authority or suffers from total lack of jurisdiction or indicates exercise of assumption of authority which evidently does not vest in it or reflects patent illegality whereby alternate remedy does not seem to be effective or efficacious, constitutional jurisdiction can be legitimately exercised.[347] In the past, existence of an alternative adequate remedy did not affect the court's jurisdiction to issue a writ though it is an important factor to be considered while exercising this discretionary jurisdiction.[348]

In India, while the existence of an effective alternative remedy such as a right of appeal is a bar to obtaining *certiorari* and prohibition,[349] a writ petition cannot be dismissed solely on the grounds of the availability[350] of an alternative remedy. The rule requiring the exhaustion of alternative remedies is a rule of convenience rather than a rule of law.[351]

(III) REQUIREMENT OF AGGRIEVED PARTY

Writ petitions in nature of prohibition, *mandamus* or *certiorari* can only be issued on the application of an aggrieved party. A party who stands to lose or gain an advantage by observance or non-observance of law is an aggrieved party.[352] A person aggrieved must be a person who has suffered a legal grievance, or a person against whom a decision has been pronounced which has wrongfully deprived him of something, or wrongfully refused him something or wrongfully affected his title to something.[353] The person seeking *mandamus* must show that he has a personal interest in the performance of a legal duty which if not performed, could result in the loss of some personal advantage.[354] Superior courts, in the exercise of writ jurisdiction, do not go into academic controversies. While exercising writ jurisdiction, the court has to consider as first question whether the petitioner has *locus standi* to invoke the constitutional jurisdiction of the court and it is a basic principle that a person seeking judicial review of an administrative or quasi-judicial action must show that he has a direct personal interest in the act which he challenges before his prayer for review is entertained. Thus a petitioner does not have a standing to seek judicial review unless he is interested in and affected adversely by the decision of which he seeks review, and his interest must be of a personal and not an official nature.[355]

A person in order to qualify as an 'aggrieved party' may not have a right in strict sense, but he can nevertheless maintain a constitutional petition if his interests are prejudicially affected. For instance, petitioners who though do not have their properties situated in the close neighbourhood of the site of an intended building but also reside in the same area, can also maintain the constitutional petition against the proposed construction in case of infraction of any building regulation which prejudicially affects them. The deprivation of any amenity confers a right on the residents of the locality to maintain a constitutional petition in circumstances.[356] In the same way as regards conditions of service of employee of statutory body, if governed by statutory rules, any action prejudicially taken against such employee in derogation or in violation of the said rules can be set aside by writ petition. However, terms and conditions of employee, if not governed by statutory rules, but only by regulation, instructions or directions which the institution or body in which he is employed has issued for its internal use, any violation thereof, will not normally be enforced through writ petition.[357] For instance, in a statutory auction, an intending bidder is an aggrieved party, if statutory provisions have not been observed; but a mere intending candidate for election has no immediate interest to give him a *locus standi* to question the validity of an election law.[358] Hence, in the case of two 'Bell Helicopters' by government, where, of the two bids for the purchase of such helicopters, government accepted a bid which was higher, constitutional petition as found to be maintainable, controversy raised therein was capable of being reviewed by court.[359] In a case of a person detained under a wholly illegal order, the son would be an aggrieved party.[360] Similarly, a person moving a petition in her capacity as the wife of one of the detenus and as acting chairman of a political party to which all detenus belong, though not alleging contravention of her own fundamental rights, is an aggrieved person.[361] All these cases clearly show a trend in Pakistan to relax the stringent conditions of *locus standi* and aggrieved person.

(IV) WRIT—A DISCRETIONARY REMEDY

Relief of *certiorari*, prohibition or *mandamus*, being a discretionary relief, cannot be claimed as a matter of right or course.[362] The relief may be refused on the ground of laches (inordinate delay) or some other conduct of the applicant[363] e.g. acquiescence in illegal assumption of jurisdiction or other irregularity in procedure.[364] Writ petitions are not issued where the applicant has been guilty of suppression of material facts or of other fraudulent or unconscionable or contumacious conduct.[365] Writ jurisdiction is not to be used in aid of injustice[366] or in favour of a person in possession of ill-gotten gains or who comes to court with sullied hands.[367] A writ petition is dismissed if petitioner is proved to have acquiesced in the impugned administrative directions voluntarily.[368] Where a petitioner had the right to seek the remedy but he did not insist at proper stage for the determination of his rights, the same cannot be granted to him because of inordinate delay on his part in approaching the court on the ground of laches.[369]

(V) JUDICIAL RESTRAINT IN POLICY MATTERS

It is settled law that in the areas of economics and commerce, there is far greater latitude available to the executive than in other matters. The Court cannot sit in judgment over the wisdom of the policy of the legislature or the executive. Economic and fiscal regulatory measures are a field where Judges should encroach upon very warily as Judges are not experts in these matters. The impugned policy parameters were fixed by experts in the Central Government, and it is not ordinarily open to the Supreme Court to sit in appeal over the decision of these experts.

The power to lay down policy by executive decisions or by legislation includes power to withdraw the same unless it is by *mala fide* exercise of power, or the decision or action taken is in abuse of power. The court leaves the authority to decide its full range of choice within the executive or legislative power. In matters of economic policy, the court gives a large leeway to the executive and the legislature. Granting licences for import or export is an executive or legislative policy. The Government would take diverse factors into account for formulating the policy in the overall larger interest of the economy of the country. When the the Government is satisfied that change in the policy was necessary in the public interest it would be entitled to revise the policy and lay down a new policy.

There should be judicial restraint in fiscal and economic regulatory measure. The State should not be hampered by the Court in such measures unless they are clearly illegal or unconstitutional. All administrative decisions in economic and social spheres are essentially *ad hoc* and experimental. Since economic matters are extremely complicated this inevitably entails special treatment for distinct social phenomena. The State must therefore be left with wide latitude in devising ways and means of imposing fiscal regulatory measures, and the Court should not, unless compelled by the statute or by the Constitution, encroach into this field. It does not make any difference whether the policy has been framed by the legislature or the executive and in either case there should be judicial restraint. The Court can invalidate an executive policy only when it is clearly violative of some provisions of the statute or Constitution or is shockingly arbitrary but not otherwise.[370]

(VI) PRESUMPTION OF VALIDITY OF PUBLIC ACTS

The acts of public authorities are not to be lightly interfered with in writ jurisdiction because the presumption is in favour of the validity of the order. The superior courts must explore every possible explanation for the validity and it is only after examining every possible aspect that they may interfere in writ jurisdiction if they come to the conclusion that the order before them was without jurisdiction.[371] Thus, before striking down an order passed by a public authority, court must examine the entire field of powers conferred on the authority by which the impugned order has been passed and all efforts should be made to uphold it.[372] Writ jurisdiction is not to be used in aid of injustice,[373] or in favour of a person in possession of ill-gotten gains or who comes to court with sullied hands.[374]

(VII) PROCEDURE FOR EXERCISE OF WRIT JURISDICTION

The high courts frame their own rules regulating their practice and procedure but principles of the Civil Procedure Code have been held to apply to writ petitions, e.g. provisions relating to review,[375] *res judicata*,[376] remand,[377] abatement,[378] restoration of applications for default,[379] bringing on record legal representatives, and adding parties[380] etc. Despite the limitation and restrictions on the exercise of writ jurisdiction discussed above, the writs of prohibition, *mandamus*, and *certiorari* have proved speedy and efficacious remedies available to the aggrieved parties for the redress of wrongs done or the judicial, quasi-judicial review of these acts and orders specially in Pakistan and India. Superior courts in these countries have extensively used these remedies as instruments of judicial review of administrative actions.

(VIII) CONCLUSION

The experience of the various remedies used in Indian and Pakistani administrative law reveals a system in which the good ones do not necessarily drive the bad ones out of circulation; the bad ones adapt themselves to the new situation. The process of transformation and adaptation has led to the overlapping of remedies, particularly in the case of the prerogative remedies: *mandamus* has assumed the shape of *certiorari*, prohibition, injunction, and declaration; *certiorari* has acquired the form of *mandamus* and declaration; and so on. The net result of this process has been the introduction of an element of flexibility even into the prerogative writs, which have been stratified into rigid forms in English common law through centuries. While in the Anglo-American experience they failed to reform themselves to suit the exigencies of the present era, in the Indian Subcontinent they have achieved this impossible feat. The 'administrative' rock is no longer impervious to *certiorari*. If a rough and readymade distinction can be made between the prerogative remedies and the ordinary law remedies, the former, it seems, will lead the way, leaving the latter to keep the rearguard in future administrative law in India and Pakistan.

5.7 JUDICIAL REVIEW OF ADMINISTRATIVE ACTIONS IN AUSTRALIA

In Australia, the Administrative Decisions (Judicial Review) Act was passed by both Houses of Parliament in May 1977. Broadly, the Act provides for judicial review of administrative decisions by the Federal Court of Australia. It applies to decisions of an administrative character made, proposed to be made, or required to be made (whether in the exercise of a discretion or not) under an enactment, other than decisions made by the Governor General.[381]

The making of a decision is very widely defined to include: the making, giving or issuing, suspending, revoking, or refusing to make, give or issue an order, award, determination, certificate, direction, approval, consent, permission or licence; imposing a condition or restriction, making a declaration, demand or requirement; retaining, or refusing to deliver up an article; or doing or refusing to do any other act or thing.[382] A report or recommendation required to be made before a decision is reached may be deemed to be a decision for the purposes of the Act.[383] A failure to make a decision includes a refusal to make that decision, and attracts review.[384]

A person who is aggrieved by a decision[385] or by conduct for the purpose of making a decision[386] may seek an order for review. A person aggrieved includes a person whose interests are adversely affected by a decision, or would be so affected if a decision was made, or not made, in accordance with a report or recommendation, or by conduct for the purpose of making a decision, or by a failure to make a decision.[387] Persons interested in a decision, conduct for the purpose of making, or in a failure to make a decision may apply to be made parties to any application made for an order for review. The application may be granted conditionally, or refused.[388] Application for an order for review is to be made in such manner as is prescribed by Rules of Court and it must set out the grounds of the application.[389] Provisions about time limits for applications are rather complex[390] but broadly the intention is that applications should be lodged within 28 days after the applicant has received adequate reasons for decision. In some cases (e.g. where there was no decision in writing) no period is prescribed and an application must be made within a reasonable time after the decision was made. If it is not so made the court may refuse to entertain an application.[391]

It will no longer be possible for administrators to shield themselves from judicial review by refusing to give reasons for particular decisions. Section 13 provides that any person entitled to make an application under the Act may, by notice in writing given to the person who made the decision, request him 'to furnish a statement in writing setting out the findings on material questions of fact, referring to the evidence or other material on which those findings were based and giving the reasons for decision'.[392] Additional statements may be ordered by the court to give 'further and better particulars'.[393] The statement of reasons must ordinarily be furnished within 14 days[394] but provision is made for review of the request for reasons and a request may be refused if not made within a reasonable time.[395] The attorney general may certify that disclosure of information concerning a specified matter would be contrary to the public interest by reason that it would prejudice the security, defence or international relations of Australia, or involve disclosure of cabinet deliberations or decisions, or would justify a claim of Crown privilege.[396] But this does not affect the inherent power of the court to order disclosure.[397] Statements of reasons may, of course, be refused or modified to take account of the attorney general's certificate.

It is important to note that the jurisdiction of the state courts to review federal decisions to which the Act applies is wholly excluded except for review by *habeas corpus*.[398] Also the rights conferred by the Act[399] are declared to be in addition to any other rights to seek review 'whether by the court, by another court, or by another tribunal, authority or person'.[400] The federal court or any other court, may in its discretion, refuse to review a decision for the reason that review is being sought elsewhere and that review is adequate.[401]

The core of the Act which sets out the grounds on which an order for review may be made are Sections 5, 6, and 7. Section 7 provides that an applicant may seek review where there has been a failure to make a decision or unreasonable delay in making a decision. 'Unreasonable delay' is a new ground for review and it may prove to be extremely important. Section 5 is set out *verbatim* below. Section 6 varies in wording only to the extent made necessary by the fact that it deals with 'conduct for the purpose of making a decision'.

5. (1) A person who is aggrieved by a decision to which this Act applies that is made after the commencement of this Act may apply to the Court for an order of review in respect of the decision on any one or more of the following grounds:

   (a) that a breach of the rules of natural justice occurred in connection with the making of the decision;
   (b) that procedures that were required by law to be observed in connection with the making of the decision were not observed;
   (c) that the person who purported to make the decision did not have jurisdiction to make the decision;
   (d) that the decision was not authorised by the enactment in pursuance of which it was purported to be made;
   (e) that the making of the decision was an improper exercise of the power conferred by the enactment in pursuance of which it was purported to be made;
   (f) that the decision involved an error of law, whether or not the error appears on the record of the decision;
   (g) that the decision was induced or affected by fraud;
   (h) that there was no evidence or other material to justify the making of the decision;
   (i) that the decision was otherwise contrary to law.

   (2) The reference in Paragraph (1)(e) to an improper exercise of a power shall be construed as including a reference to:

(a) taking an irrelevant consideration into account in the exercise of a power;

(b) failing to take a relevant consideration into account in the exercise of a power;

(c) an exercise of a power for a purpose other than a purpose for which the power is conferred;

(d) an exercise of a discretionary power in bad faith;

(e) an exercise of a personal discretionary power at the direction or behest of another person;

(f) an exercise of a discretionary power in accordance with a rule or policy without regard to the merits of the particular case;

(g) an exercise of a power that is so unreasonable that no reasonable person could have so exercised the power;

(h) an exercise of a power in such a way that the result of the exercise of the power is uncertain; and

(j) any other exercise of a power in a way that constitutes abuse of the power.

(3) The ground specified in Paragraph (1)(h) shall not be taken to be made out unless:

(a) the person who made the decision was required by law to reach that decision only if a particular matter was established and there was no evidence or other material (including facts of which he was entitled to take notice) from which he could reasonably be satisfied that the matter was established; or

(b) the person who made the decision based the decision on the existence of a particular fact, and that fact did not exist.

Furthermore Section (2)(j) permits development of the concept of abuse of discretion. Some tentative comments may be made at this stage although judicial interpretation may invalidate them. The provision about 'natural justice'[402] may exclude the concept of 'fairness' except as a synonym for 'natural justice'. Review for error of law is available whether or not the error appears on record of the decision[403] and this may completely obliterate the doubtful distinction between jurisdictional and non-jurisdictional error. Paragraphs dealing with 'policy rules'[404] and 'uncertainty'[405] do clearly modify the common law. One of the most interesting provisions is the ground 'that there was no evidence or other material to justify the making of the decision'.[406] This appears to introduce the United States 'substantial evidence' ground for review and also gives statutory support for a developing English line of decisions.

Orders which may be made by the courts are set out in Section 16 as follows:

16. (1) On an application for an order of review in respect of a decision, the Court may, in its discretion, make all or any of the following orders:

   (a) an order quashing or setting aside the decision, or a part of the decision, with effect from the date of the order or from such earlier or later date as the Court specifies;

   (b) an order referring the matter to which the decision relates to the person who made the decision for further consideration, subject to such directions as the Court thinks fit;

   (c) an order declaring the rights of the parties in respect of any matter to which the decision relates;

   (d) an order directing any of the parties to do, or to refrain from doing, any act or thing the doing, or the refraining from the doing, of which the Court considers necessary to do justice between the parties.

(2) On an application for an order of review in respect of conduct that has been, is being, or is proposed to be, engaged in for the purpose of the making of a decision, the Court may, in its discretion make either or both of the following orders:

   (a) an order declaring the rights of the parties in respect of any matter to which the conduct relates;

   (b) an order directing any of the parties to do, or to refrain from doing, any act or thing the doing, or the refraining from the doing, of which the Court considers necessary to do justice between the parties.

(3) On an application for an order of review in respect of a failure to make a decision, or in respect of a failure to make a decision within the period within which the decision was required to be made, the Court may, in its discretion, make all or any of the following orders:

   (a) an order directing the making of the decision;

    (b) an order declaring the rights of the parties in relation to the making of the decision;

    (c) an order directing any of the parties to do, or to refrain from doing, any act or thing the doing, or the refraining from the doing, of which the Court considers necessary to do justice between the parties.

(4) The Court may at any time, of its own motion or on the application of any party, revoke, vary, or suspend the operation of, any order made by it under this section.

Some significant changes from the common law are embodied in the section. Orders may be prospective or retrospective. Part of a decision may be invalidated. An order may be made referring the matter back to the original decision maker. Orders may be 'shaped' to do justice between the parties. It should be noted also that an application for review does not 'stay' a decision, but the court on application or of its own motion may order a stay of proceedings.[407]

Finally, under the provisions of the Act, it is provided that the attorney general may intervene in proceedings on behalf of the Commonwealth and shall be deemed a party to the proceedings.[408] Regulations may be made excluding a class or classes of decisions from judicial view under the Act.[409]

Although it is routinely insisted that the review provided for by the Act is 'supervisory review' and not review on the merits (a jurisdiction which *may* be given to the administrative appeals tribunal) there can be no doubt that penetration to the merits is possible—as indeed it is possible at common law. The powers of the court are extremely wide and no judge would find great difficulty in discovering suitable grounds for review if he wanted to invalidate, or refer back, a particular decision. In this situation there are some dangers. One danger is that judges will intervene in the administrative process far too readily. This danger can be averted only by the practice of wise judicial restraint. It is not desirable that the judge should intervene thoughtlessly in areas of administrative expertise.[410]

It is noticeable that Australia has incorporated in a statute the principles of judicial control of administrative actions that have been developed by the superior courts in UK, USA, Pakistan, and India over a long period of time through precedents and case law. This is something unique about the Australian statute which is worth mentioning in this book.

5.8 Contribution of Judicial Review to the Development of Administrative Law

The study of administrative law is broadly divided into four categories. The first deals with composition and powers of organs of administration; the second refers to the limits on the powers of administrative authorities. The third refers to the procedures used in exercising those powers. Evolving of fair procedures in the way of minimising the abuse of vast discretionary powers conferred on administration is an essential part of the study of administrative law. The fourth refers to the control of administration through judicial or other means.

5.8.1 Judicial control of administrative action as a means of development of administrative law

The primary purpose of administrative law is to keep the powers of government within their legal bounds, so as to protect the citizen against their abuse.[411] The individual is in the weakest defensive position against the mighty power of the administration. It is, therefore, the important function of the administrative law to ensure that government powers are exercised according to law, on proper legal principles, according to the rules of reason and justice, and not on the mere caprice or whim of the administrative officers, and that the individual has adequate remedies when his rights are infringed by the administration.

The abuse of governmental powers do not necessarily carry any innuendo of malice or bad faith. Government departments may misunderstand their legal position as easily as many other people, and the law which they have to administer is frequently complex and uncertain. Abuse is, therefore, inevitable, and it is all the more necessary that the law should provide means to check it.[412] The courts are constantly occupied with cases of the kind which are nothing more than the practical application of the rule of law, meaning that the government must have legal warrant for what it does and that if it acts unlawfully, the citizen has an effective legal remedy. On this elementary foundation the courts have erected an intricate and sophisticated structure of rules.

It is also the concern of administrative law to see that public authorities can be compelled to perform their duties if they default in doing so. The courts are called upon in many cases to compel administrative authorities to perform their functions and to exercise their powers in accordance with law and principles of natural justice. The law provides compulsory remedies for such situations, thus dealing with the negative as well as the positive side of maladministration.

The essence of administrative law lies in judge-made doctrines which apply right across the board and which therefore generally set legal standards of conduct for public authorities. The purpose of administrative justice, subject as it is to the vast empires of executive power that have been created, is that the public must be able to rely on the law to ensure that all this power may be used in a way conformable to its ideas of fair dealing and good administration.

5.8.2 Conclusion

From the above discussion, it is clear that not only judicial control of administrative action is one of the organs of administrative law, but by and large it is the most important one. The courts have become final arbiters of the exercise of authority by administration in order to ensure that such authority is exercised in accordance with law and free from abuses like arbitrariness, caprice, perversity and violation of principles of natural justice. In the process of this judicial review, a vast body of principles and procedures has been laid down by the superior courts in Britain, USA, Pakistan, and India. These principles and procedures have become the primary guidelines for administration and administrators in the exercise of their powers and authority. The administrative law is at the crossroads of the principal organs of government, legislature, executive, and judiciary. Legislature frames the laws and rules thereunder for the conduct of administration in a country; the executive carries out its functions in accordance with the laws and rules so framed, and is responsible for the conduct of administration; and the judiciary, through judicial review, keeps administration and administrative authorities within the bounds of laws framed by legislature. The courts have come to perform the ultimate function of check of administrative authorities and protection of common citizens from their excesses by the instrument of judicial review. Thus, judicial review, exercised by the courts over the acts and orders of administrative authorities, has become *sine qua non* for the study of administrative law.

Notes

1. *Syed Abul Ala Maudoodi* v. *Government of West Pakista*n, PLD 1964 SC 673 at p. 709.
2. S.A. de Smith, *Judicial Review of Administrative Action* (4th edn., London: J.M. Evans Stevers and Sons, 1980), 29–30.
3. *Shaukat Ali* v. *Secretary, Industries*, MLD 1995 123; *Ramana Dayaram Shethy* v. *International Airport Authority*, AIR 1979 SC 1628; *Shri Vallabharaya* v. *Davi Hanumancharyulu*, AIR 1985 SC 1147; *Kasturi Lal* v. *State of Jammu*, AIR 1980 SC 1992.
4. W.A. Robson, *Justice and Administrative Law* (1951) 573.
5. M.A. Fazal, *Judicial Control of Administrative Action in India, Pakistan and Bangladesh* (2nd edn., Allahabad: The Law Book Company Ltd, 1990) 10.
6. Denning, *Freedom Under the Law* (1949) 126.
7. Suranjan Chakraverti, *Domestic Tribunals and Administrative Jurisdictions* (Delhi) 3.
8. A.V. Dicey, *The Law of the Constitution* (1885) 180.
9. E.C.S. Wade & C. Godfrey Phillips, *Constitutional and Administrative Law* (1977) 549.
10. U.P.D. Kesari, *Lectures on Administrative Law* (1980) 175.
11. Like James M. Beck in *Our Wonderland of Bureaucracy* (1932).

12. J.M. Landis, *The Administrative Process* (1938) 14.

13. Shri N.C. Chatterjee, 'Control of the Legislative powers of Administration', 1 Journal of the Indian Law Institute (1938–9), 125.

14. *Faridson Ltd.* v. *Government of Pakistan*, PLD 1961 SC 537.

15. *Kamil Khan Mumtaz v. Province of Punjab*, PLD 2016 Lahore 699.

16. *Abdul Wahab v. Habib Bank Ltd.*, 2013 SCMR 1383.

17. W.A. Robson, 'Administrative Law in England 1919–48' in British Government since 1918 (1950) 85–6.

18. Lord Hewart, *Not without Prejudice* (1935), 96.

19. Charles S. Rhyne, *Law and Judicial Systems of Nations* (1978) 241–42.

20. Charles Szladits, *Guide to Foreign Legal Materials: French, German, Swiss* (1959) 18–19.

21. *Muhammad Husain Munir* v. *Sikandar*, PLD 1974 SC 139; *Venkata Giri* v. *HRE Board*, AIR 1949 PC 156; *Joychand* v. *Kamalaksha*, AIR 1949 PC 239.

22. S.A. de Smith, *Judicial Review of Administrative Action* (3rd edn., Stevens and Sons Ltd, 1973) 83.

23. M.A. Fazal, *Judicial Control of Administrative Action in India, Pakistan and Bangladesh* (3rd edn., London: Butterworth, 2000) 91.

24. *Mohammad Ismail* v. *Province of E. Pak*, PLD 1964 SC 475.

25. *Syed Abul Ala Maudoodi* v. *Government of West Pakistan*, PLD 1964 SC 673.

26. Lord Russel, CJ, in *Kruse* v. *Johnson* [1898] 2 QB 91.

27. *Commissioner of Income Tax* v. *Asiatic Industries Ltd*, PLD 1964 Dacca 769; *Provincial Transport Authority* v. *State Industrial Court* [1963] AIR, SC 114.

28. *Nasreen Fatima Awan* v. *Principal*, PLD 1978 Quetta 17.

29. *Safar Ali* v. *Province of East Pakistan*, PLD 1964 Dacca 467.

30. *Akbar Ali* v. *Raziur-ur-Rehman*, PLD 1966 SC 492.

31. Muhammad Munir, *Constitution of the Islamic Republic of Pakistan* (1976) 422.

32. *Simpson Motor Sales (London) Ltd* v. *Hendon Corp.* [1964] AC 1088.

33. *Fawcertt Properties Ltd* v. *C.C. Bucks* [1961] AC 636.

34. *Webb* v. *Ministry of Housing and Local Government* [1965] 2 All ER 193 (CA).

35. *Nybucuoak Council of Sydney* v. *Campbell* [1925] AC 338.

36. *Hanson* v. *Radcliffe* [1922] UDC 2 Ch 490.

37. [1905] AC 426.

38. *Safdar Ali* v. *Province of EP*, PLD 1964 Dacca 467; *Shyam Behari* v. *State of MP*, AIR 1965 SC 427; *Girdharil* v. *State of Gujrat*, AIR 1966 SC 1408.

39. *Zafar-ul-Ahsan* v. *The Republic of Pakistan*, PLD 1960 SC 113.

40. *Abdur Rauf* v. *Abdul Hamid Khan*, PLD 1965 SC 671.

41. *Federation of Pakistan* v. *Saeed Ahmad*, PLD 1974 SC 151.

42. *Muhammad Jamil Asghar* v. *The Improvement Trust, Rawalpindi*, PLD 1965 SC 698.

43. *Mohammad Bachal Memon* v. *Government of Sind*, PLD 1987 Karachi 296.
44. *Government of West Pakistan* v. *Shorish Kashmiri*, PLD 1969 SC 14.
45. *Associated Provincial Picture House Ltd* v. *Wednesbury Corp.* [1948] 1 KB 223.
46. *Deputy Director of Consolidation* v. *Deen Bandhu*, AIR 1965 SC 484.
47. *S.V. Sivaswami* v. *State of Madhya Pradesh*, AIR 1991 SC 911.
48. *B. Rajagopala* v. *STA Tribunal*, AIR 1964 SC 1573.
49. *Noor Mohammad* v. *District Magistrate*, PLD 1976 Lahore 233.
50. *Mohammad Tufail* v. *Province of Punjab*, PLD 1978 Lahore 87.
51. *Ghulam Mohiuddin* v. *Chief Settlement Commissioner*, PLD 1964 SC 829.
52. *Hamid Javed* v. *Dean, Faculty of Engineering*, PLD 1964 Lahore 483.
53. *Muhammad Tufail* v. *Province of Punjab*, PLD 1978 Lahore 87.
54. [1942] AC 206.
55. *Mohammad Akram* v. *C.A. Saeed*, PLD 1965 Lahore 703; *Ghulam Jilani* v. *Government of W. Pakistan*, PLD 1967 SC 373.
56. *Nasim Fatima* v. *Government of W. Pakistan*, PLD 1967 Lahore 103.
57. *Southend-on-Sea Corp* v. *Hodgson on (Wickford) Ltd* [1962] 1 QB 416: A contrary line of reasoning adopted by Denning, J, in *Robertson* v. *Ministry of Pensions* [1949] 1 KB 227 was rejected by the House of Lords in *Howell* v. *Falmouth Boat Construction Co. Ltd* [1951] AC 837 at 845, 849.
58. PLD 1964 SC 438.
59. AIR 1991 SC 818.
60. *Barium Chemicals Ltd* v. *Company Law Board*, AIR 1967 SC 295; [1966] 1 SCA 74; [1066] Supp SCR 311 [1976] 2 SCWR 567; [1966] 2 SCJ 623; [1966] 36 Com Cas 639; *Ghulam Quadir* v. *Ahmed Shafi*, PLD 1967 Lah. 68; *Mohd Bux* v. *State of Rajasthan*, AIR 1993 Raj. 211 (FB); *K.K. Krishnan Nair* v. *Scrutiny Committee, Secretary, RTA Malaya Puram*, AIR 1993 Ker. 313; *Shaukat Ali* v. *Government of the Punjab*, PLD 1992 Lah. 277.
61. *National Buildings Construction Corporation* v. *S. Ragunthan*, (1998)7 SCC 66.
62. Province of Punjab v. Malik Shah Nawaz, 2012 MLD 1045.
63. Vol 1(1), 4th edn. para 81, pp 151-2.
64. (1985) 3 All ER 300.
65. (1993) 3 SCC 499.
66. *Regarding Pensionary Benefits of the Judges of Superior Courts*, PLD 2013 S.C. 829.
67. [1955] 3 All ER 48; [1956] AC 14.
68. S.P. Sathe, *Administrative Law* (3rd edn., N.M. TripathiPvt Ltd, 1979) 154.
69. S.A. de Smith, *Judicial Review of Administrative Action* (1973) Supra Note 20, 112.
70. C.T. Carr, *Concerning English Administrative Law* (1941) 108.
71. *Province of E. Pakistan* v. *Kushti Dhar Roy*, PLD 1964 SC 636; *Sales Tax Officer* v. *Shiv Ratan*, AIR 1966 SC 142.

72. *Imtiaz Ahmad* v. *Ghulam Ali*, PLD 1963 SC 382; *Nagendraw Nath Bora* v. *Commissioner of Hills Div.*, AIR 1958 SC 398; *Kareshalya Devi* v. *Bachittar Singh*, AIR 1960 SC 1168.

73. *State of Madras* v. *G. Sundram*, AIR 1965 SC 1103; *State of AP* v. *Sree Rama Rao*, AIR 1963 SC 1723; *State of Orissa* v. *Murlidhar*, AIR 1963 SC 404.

74. *Saburur Rehman* v. *Government of Sind*, PLD 1996 SC 801.

75. *Muhammad Yaqub* v. *Zahir Alam*, PLD 1976 Quetta 77.

76. *Kamran Industries v. Collector of Customs*, PLD 1996 Karachi 68; *Sabur Rahman v. Government of Sindh*, PLD 1989 Karachi 572; *Alam Zeb Khan* v. *Election Commission*, PLD 1989 Peshawar 231; *Muhammad Soomar* v. *Provincial Election Authority*, PLD 1988 Karachi 75; *Dad Khan* v. *Abdul Rahim*, PLD 1986 Quetta 93.

77. *R.* v. *Board of Control, ex p. Pretty* [1956] 2 QB 109, *R.* v. *Norfolk Justice, ex p. Wagland Union* [1909] 1 KB 463.

78. *Banbury* v. *Fuller*, 9 Exch. 111, 140 [1853].

79. *Cromwell* v. *Benson* [1932] 285 US 22.

80. Act XIV of 1882.

81. *Raghunath Das* v. *Sundar*, AIR 1914 PC 129.

82. *Newspaper Ltd.* v. *State Industrial Tribunal*, AIR 1957 SC 532.

83. *Akhtar Ali Parvez* v. *Altafur Rehman*, PLD 1963 Lahore 390.

84. *Muhammad Jamil Asghar* v. *Improvement Trust*, PLD 1965 SC 695.

85. *Muller & Phillips* v. *District Magistrate*, PLD 1974 Karachi 261; *Latifan* v. *Muhammad Ishaq*, PLD 1974 Lahore 65.

86. *Mehr Dad* v. *Settlement & Rehabilitation Commissioner*, PLD 1974 SC 193.

87. Supra Note 21, p. 181.

88. *R.* v. *Galway Justice* [1906] 2 IR 446; *R.* v. *Nat Bell Liquors Ltd* [1922] 2 AC 128; *R.* v. *Makony* [1910] 2 IR 695.

89. *Imtiaz Ahmad* v. *Ghulam Ali*, PLD 1963 SC 382; *Tofazzal Hosain* v. *Province of E. Pakistan*, PLD 1963 SC 251; *Province of E. Pakistan* v. *Kushti Dhar Roy*, PLD 1964 SC 636; *Kaushalya Devi* v. *Bachittar Singh*, AIR 1960 SC 1168; *State of Orissa* v. *Murlidhar*, AIR 1963 SC 404.

90. *R.* v. *Smith* [1800] STR 588.

91. *Ashbridge Investment Ltd* v. *Minister of Housing and Local Government* [1965] IWLR 1320 (CA).

92. *Golam Mohiuddin* v. *State of W. Bengal*, AIR 1964 Calcutta 503.

93. *Union of India* v. *H.C. Goel*, AIR 1964 SC 364.

94. *Subal Chandra* v. *I.M.S. Huq*, PLD 1960 Dacca 606.

95. *Abul A'la Maudoodi* v. *Government of W. Pakistan*, PLD 1964 SC 673.

96. H.W.R. Wade, *Administrative Law*.

97. *Heesab* v. *Election Authority*, PLD 1986 Karachi.

98. *Syed Yakoob* v. *Radha Krishnan*, AIR 1964 SC 477.

99. *Nawaza* v. *Additional Settlement and Rehabilitation Commissioner*, PLD 1970 SC 39; *Noor* v. *Settlement and Rehabilitation Commissioner* [1969] SCMR

51; *Eastern Express Co. Ltd* v. *Fifth Sind Labour Court*, PLD 1977 Karachi 168; *Muhammad Yousaf* v. *Fourth Sind Labour Court*, PLD 1977 Karachi 711; *Jan Textile Mills Karachi* v. *Sind Labour Appellate Tribunal*, PLD 1977 Karachi 836.

100. *State of Madras* v. *G. Sundram*, AIR 1965 SC 1103; *State of Orissa* v. *Murlidhar*, AIR 1963 SC 404; *State of AP* v. *Sree Rama Rao*, AIR 1963 SC 1723.

101. *Ismat Khanum* v. *Rao Riaz Ali Khan* [1978] SCMR 335.

102. *Armah* v. *Government of Ghana* [1966] 3 All ER 177.

103. *Muhammd Ibrahim* v. *Secretary to the Government of Pakistan*, PLD 1993 Karachi 478. *Province of E. Pakistan* v. *Abdus Sobhan Sowdagar*, PLD 1964 SC 1.

104. *Tata Cellular* v. *Union of India*, AIR 1996 S.C.11; (1994) 6 SCC 651.

105. *Asif Fasihuddin Vardag* v *Government of Pakistan*, 2014 SCMR 676; *Sterling Computers Ltd.* v. *Messrs M & N Publications Ltd.*, AIR 1996 S.C.51.

106. *Iqbal Haider* v. *Capital Development Authority*, PLD 2006 SC 394, *Matters of Privatization of Pakistan Steel Mills*, PLD 2010 SC 759, *HRC No. 4688/06*, PLD 2001 SC 619, *In the matter of: Alleged Corruption in Rental Power Plants*, 2012 SCMR 773. *Ramana Dayaram Shetty* v. *International Airport Authority of India*, AIR 1979 S.C. 1628; (1979)3 SCC 489; *Tata Cellular* v. *Union of India*, AIR 1996 S.C. 11, (1994) 6 SCC 651; *Raunaq International Ltd.* v. *I.V.R. Construction Ltd.* AIR 1999 S.C. 393, (1999) 1 SCC 492.; *Air India Ltd.* v. *Cochin International Airport Ltd.* AIR 2000 S.C. 801, (2000) 2 SCC 617 and *Reliance Energy Ltd.* v. *Maharashtra State Road Development Corporation Ltd.* (2007) 8 SCC 1.

107. *Messrs Airport Support Services* v. *The Airport Manager, Quaid-e-Azam Internatioal Airport, Karachi* 1998 SCMR 2268; *Messrs Ramna Pipe and General Mills (Pvt.) Ltd.* v. *Messrs Sui Northern Gas Pipe Lines (Pvt.) Ltd.* 2004 SCMR 1274 and *In re: Action regarding huge loss to public exchequer in awarding LNG Contract.* PLD 2010 SC 731.

108. H.W.R. Wade, *Administrative Law* (4th edn., Oxford: Clarendon Press, 1977) 45.

109. *R.* v. *Northumberland Compensation Appeal Tribunal* [1952] IKB 338.

110. *Tata Iron & Steel Co.* v. *S.R. Sarkar*, AIR 1961 SC 65.

111. *Chief Land Commissioner, Punjab* v. *Nazar Hussain Shah* [1975] SCMR 352.

112. [1969] 2 AC 147.

113. *R.* v *Greater Manchester Cornor, ex p. Tal* [1984] 3 All ER 204.

114. *Municipal Board* v. *Imperial Tobacco of India Ltd* [1999] 1 SCC 566.

115. *Principal, Patna College* v. *K.S. Raman*, AIR 1966 SC 707; *Amrik Singh* v. *B.S. Malik*, AIR 1966 Punjab 344.

116. *Armah* v. *Government of Ghana*, (1966) 3 All ER 177.

117. *Gray* v. *Powell*, (1941) 314 U.S. 402.

118. *Halsbury's Laws of England, Vol. 1(1), 4th edn. Para.* 78.

119. Administrative Law by H.W.R. Wade and C.F. Forsyth, 11th edn. 2014) p. 306

120. *Judicial Review of Administrative Action*, 8th edn. pp. 636-641.

121. *Sabir Iqbal v. Cantonment Board, Peshawar*, PLD 2019 S.C.189

122. *Hombe Gowda Educational Trust v. State of Karnataka*, (2006) 1 SCC 430.

123. H.W.R. Wade, Administrative Law (1977) Supra Note 96, 395.

124. S.A. de Smith, Judicial Review of Administrative Action (1973) Supra Note 20, 134.

125. Article 4 of the Constitution of 1973, reads as under:

(1) To enjoy the protection of law and to be treated in accordance with law is the inalienable right of every citizen, wherever he may be, and of every other person for the time being within Pakistan;

(2) In particular—

(a) no action detrimental to the life, liberty, body and reputation or property of any person shall be taken except in accordance with law;

(b) no person shall be prevented from or be hindered in doing that which is not prohibited by law; and

(c) no person shall be compelled to do that which the law does not require him to do.

126. *Abdus Saboor Khan* v. *Karachi University*, PLD 1966 SC 536; *University of Dacca* v. *Zakir Ahmad*, PLD 1965 SC 90; *Abul A'la Maudoodi* v. *Government of W. Pakistan*, PLD 1964 SC 673.

127. *Ghulam Mohammad* v. *Collector*, PLD 1973 Lah. 528; *Nawaz Khan* v. *Central Record Officer*, PLD 1967 Lah. 42; *Rehmatullah Khan* v. *The State*, PLD 1965 Pesh. 162; *Abul Al'a Maudoodi* v. *Government of W. Pakistan*, PLD 1964 SC 673.

128. *Abdul Sabur Khan* v. *University of Karachi*, PLD 1966 SC 536; *University of Dacca* v. *Zakir Ahmad*, PLD 1965 SC90; *Hafeezuddin* v. *Khadim Husein*, PLD 1965 Lah. 439; *Asifa Sultana Begum* v. *Chief Settlement & Rehabilitation Commissioner* PLD 1964 Pesh.114.

129. *Pakistan* v. *Abdul Ghani*, PLD 1964 SC 68.

130. *Irshad Ali* v. *Government of Pakistan*, PLD 1965 Lah.7; *Mohammad Siddiq Javed Chaudhary* v. *Superintendent of Police*, PLD 1974 SC 393.

131. *Rehmatullah Khan* v. *The State*, PLD 1965 Pesh. 162.

132. *Ajit Kumar Nag v. General Manager*, (2005) 7 SCC 764.

133. *Dimes* v. *Grand Junction Canal Proprietors*, (1852), 3 HLC 759.

134. [1948] AC 87.

135. *Venkatachelam Iyer* v. *State of Madras*, AIR 1957 Madras 623.

136. *Nageswara Rao* v. *APSRT Corporation*, AIR 1959 SC 308.

137. *Nages Wararao* v. *State of AP*, AIR 1959 SC 1376; *Narayanappa* v. *State of Mysore*, AIR 1960 SC 1073.

138. S.A. de Smith, Judicial Review of Administrative Action (1973) Supra Note 20, 232–7.

139. *R.* v. *Sussex Justices Exparte McCarthy* (1924) IKB 256; *Anwar* v. *The Crown*, PLD 1955 FC 185.
140. *R.* v. *Camborne Justices* (1955) 1 QB 41; *R.* v. *Barnsby Licensing Justices*, (1960) 2 QB 167.
141. PLD 1972 SC 139.
142. AIR 1975 AP 138.
143. [1968] 3 All ER 304 (CA).
144. Although his view of it was whether a reasonable man would think there was a real likelihood of bias—a view adopted by Lord Widgery in *R.* v. *Altrincham JJ, ex p. Pennington* [1975] QB 549.
145. [1979] QB 674.
146. [1979] QB 674.
147. [1983] 1 All ER 490 (QBD).
148. *Metropolitan Properties Ltd* v. *Lannon* [1969] 1 QB 577.
149. *R.* v. *Barnsley Metropolitan BC ex p.* Hook [1976] 3 All ER 452.
150. *R.* v. *LCC ex p.* Akkersdyk [1892] 1 QB 190; *Hannam* v. *Bradford City Council* [1970] 2 All ER 690.
151. *Cooper* v. *Wilson* [1937] 2 KB 309; *R.* v. *Salford Assessment Committee ex p.* Ogden [1937] 2 KB 1; *R.* v. *Assessment Committee for N E Surrey, ex p. F W Woolworth & Co. Ltd* [1933] 1 KB 776.
152. *R.* v. *Kent Police Authority, ex p. Godden* [1971] 2 QB 662; *R.* v. *Leicestershire Fire Authority ex p.* Thompson [1878] 77 LGR 373.
153. *National Labour Relations Board* v. *Pittsburgh S.S. Co.* [1949] 337 US 656.
154. *Mohammad Mohsin Siddiqi* v. *Government of W. Pakistan*, PLD 1964 SC 64.
155. *Arjun Chanbey* v. *India*, AIR 1984 SC 1356.
156. *Ashok Kumar Yadav* v. *Haryana* [1985] 4 SCC 417.
157. *Pratap Singh* v. *State of Punjab*, AIR 1964 SC 72.
158. *APSRT Corp.* v. *S. Transport*, AIR 1965 SC 1303; *C.S. Rowjee* v. *State of AP*, AIR 1964 SC 963.
159. *Manak Lal* v. *Prem Chand Singhvi*, PLD 1957 SC (Ind) 346, AIR 1957 SC 425.
160. *Krishna* v. *Rukhmini*, AIR 1980 Kant 7.
161. *Dimes* v. *Grand Junction Canal Proprietors* [1852] 3 HLC 759; *R.* v. *Sunderland Justices* [1901] 2 KB 357.
162. *R.* v. *Barnsby Licensing Justices* [1960] 2 QB 167.
163. *Tumey* v. *Ohio*, 273 US 510 [1927].
165. Ibid.
165. [1895] ILR 20 Bombay 502.
166. *Manak Lal* v. *Prem Chand*, PLD 1957 SC (Ind) 346.
167. Gurdev Narayan v. State of Bihar, AIR 1955 Patna 131.
168. *R.* v. *Nailsworth Licensing Justices* [1953] 2 All ER 652.
169. *R.* v. *Comptroller-General of Patents* [1953] 1 All ER 862.

170. PLD 1951 FC 62.

171. PLD 1960 SC 301.

172. *R.* v. *Cheltenham Commissioners* [1841] 1 QB 467; *R.* v. *Williams ex p. Philips* [1914] 1 KB 608.

173. *Moore* v. *Gamgee* [1890] 25 QBD 244; *Farqubarson* v. *Morgan* [1894] 1 QB 552.

174. *Moore* v. *Gamgee* [1890] 25 SBD 244; *Zainab Tiwana* v. *Aziz Ahmad Waraich*, PLD 1967 Lahore 977.

175. [1723] 1 Strange 557. Cited in M.A. Fazal, Judicial Control of Administrative Action in India and Pakistan (1969) 187.

176. H.H. Marshall, Natural Justice (1959) 18.

177. *Protector* v. *Town of Colchester* [1655] style 447.

178. [1964] AC 40.

179. [1967] 2 All ER 152

180. *Muhammad Siddique Malik* v. *Dr Miss Zubeda*, PLD 1957 Karachi 194.

181. *Abdul Latif* v. *Government of West Pakistan*, PLD 1962 SC 384.

182. *Abdul Nabi* v. *Commissioner, FCR Quetta*, PLD 1962 Quetta 1.

183. *Faridsons Ltd.* v. *Government of Pakistan*, PLD 1961 SC 537.

184. *Abul A'la Maudoodi* v. *Government of W. Pakistan*, PLD 1964 SC 673; *Waheed-ud-din Khan* v. *Deputy Commissioner, Kohat*, PLD 1964 Peshawar 104.

185. *Corporation* v. *Fahmida Begum*, PLD 1952 Lahore 258; *Syed Shah* v. *Khuda Bakhsh*, PLD 1954 Lahore 606; *Abdul Hakim* v. *Karam Dad*, PLD 1966 Lahore 16.

186. *Chief Commissioner Karachi* v. *Mrs Sohrab Katrak*, PLD 1959 SC (Pak) 45.

187. *Commissioner of Income Tax* v. *Sayeedur Rehman*, PLD 1964 SC 410.

188. *Chief Commissioner* v. *Mrs Dina Sohrab Katrak*, PLD 1959 SC 45.

189. *University of Dacca* v. *Zakir Ahmad*, PLD 1965 SC90.

190. *Abdul Latif* v. *Government of West Pakistan*, PLD 1962 SC 384.

191. *Qadir Bux* v. *Commissioner* (FCR), PLD 1965 Quetta 6; *Abdul Nabi* v. *Commissioner (FCR)*, PLD 1962 Quetta 1.

192. *Farid Sons Ltd* v. *Government of Pakistan*, PLD 1961 SC 537.

193. *Hopkins* v. *Smethwick Local Board* [1889] 24 QB 712; *Russel* v. *Russel* [1880] 14 Ch. D. 471.

194. *Irshad Ali* v. *Government of Pakistan*, PLD 1965 Lah. 7.

195. *The General Discipline* Rules of University of Engineering & Technology, Lahore (revised), Clause 5(h).

196. *Ahmed* v. *University of Engineering & Technology*, PLD 1981 SC 464; *Shahid Javed Malik* v. *Board of Intermediate & Secondary Education*, PLD 1980 Lah. 176; *Board of Intermediate & Secondary Education* v. *Mohammad Yaqub*, PLD 1977 SC 69; *Ghulam Hyder* v. *Board of Intermediate & Secondary Education*, PLD 1971 Lah. 952; *Malik Abdul Majid* v. *University of the*

Punjab, PLD 1970 Lah. 416; *Abdul Sabur Khan* v. *University of Karachi*, PLD 1966 SC 536; *University of Dacca* v. *Zakir Ahmed*, PLD 1965 SC 90.

197. *Re National Carbon Co.*, AIR 1934 Calcutta 725.

198. AIR 1950 SC 222.

199. AIR 1962 SC 1110 at 1113.

200. *Raghunath Thakur* v. *Bihar* [1989] 1 SCC 229.

201. *Maharaja Dharmander Prasad Singh* v. *India* [1989] 2 SCC 505.

202. *Ridge* v. *Baldwin* [1964] AC 40.

203. *Abdus Saboor Khan* v. *Karachi University*, PLD 1966 SC 536; *University of Dacca* v. *Zakir Ahmad*, PLD 1964 SC 90.

204. [1954] 52 LGR 304.

205. *Lord Luke* v. *Minister of Housing and Local Government*, [1967] 2 All ER 1066.

206. *Promod Chandra* v. *State of Orissa*, AIR 1962 SC 1288.

207. *Nuruzzaman Chowdhry* v. *Secretary, Education Dept.*, PLD 1967 Dacca 179.

208. *Ridge* v. *Baldwin* [1964] AC 40; *Vidyodaya University of Ceylon* v. *Silva* [1964] 3 All ER 865.

209. *Chairman, E. Pakistan Development Corp.* v. *Rustom Ali*, PLD 1966 SC 848.

210. M. Munir, *Constitution of Islamic Republic of Pakistan* (1976) 431.

211. PLD 1960 Karachi 500.

212. *Rehmatulla* v. *State*, PLD 1965 Peshawar 162; *Anil Kumar* v. *Presiding Officer*, AIR 1985 SC 1121.

213. S.P. Sathe, *Administrative Law* (1979) Supra Note 60, 191.

214. *Express Newspapers* v. *Union of India*, AIR 1958 SC 578.

215. *Govindrao* v. *State of MP*, AIR 1963 SC 1222.

216. *Mahabir Prasad* v. *State of UP*, AIR 1970 SC 1302.

217. *Mollah Ejahar Ali* v. *Government of East Pakistan*, PLD 1970 SC 173.

218. *Dost Mohammad Cotton Mills Ltd* v. *Pakistan*, PLD 1976 Karachi 1078.

219. *Maharashtra* v. *Salem Hasan Khan* (1989) 2 SCC 316.

220. O. Hood Phillips, *Constitutional and Administrative Law* (1967) 662.

221. *David* v. *Abdul Cader* [1963] WLR 834.

222. [1964] AC 1129.

223. *Agra Municipality* v. *Manglilal*, AIR 1952 Allahabad 554.

224. *Chellu* v. *Palghat Municipality*, AIR 1955 Madras 562.

225. *Brijbala* v. *Patna Municipal Corp.*, AIR 1959 Patna 273.

226. *Mathura Municipality* v. *Gopi Nath*, AIR 1962 Allahabad 211.

227. *Muhammadi Steamship Co. Ltd* v. *Federation of Pakistan*, PLD 1959 Karachi 232.

228. *Government of Pakistan* v. *Mohammad Ali*, PLD 1965 Karachi 1.

229. *Pakistan* v. *Muhammad Yaqoob Butt*, PLD 1963 SC 627.

230. *Ramiz Ahmad* v. *Punjab Province*, PLD 1964 Lahore 736.

231. AIR 1997 SC 1886.

232. Griffith and Street, *Principles of Administrative Law* (4th edn., London: Sir Isaac Pitman and Sons Ltd, 1967) 245.
233. M.V. Home Office [1994] 1 AC 377.
234. Factortamo (No.2) [1991] 1 AC 603.
235. Section 54 of Specific Relief Act, 1877.
236. Section 53 of Specific Relief Act, 1877.
237. Section 55 of the Specific Relief Act, 1877.
238. *Walsh Degree College* v. *Laxmi Narrain*, AIR 1976 SC 888.
239. Section 56 of the Specific Relief Act, 1877.
240. *Noor Mohammad* v. *Ghulam Masih Gill*, PLD 1965 Baghdad-ul-Jadid 1.
241. *Malik Khizar Hayat Khan Tiwana* v. *Punjab Province*, PLD 1955 Lahore 88.
242. AIR 1963 All 449.
243. Section 56(d) provides: An injunction cannot be granted: (d) to interfere with the public duties of any department of the government.
244. *S.A. Abbasi* v. *Chairman, District Council, Gulshan-e-Iqbal*, PLD 1985 Kar. 400; Section 55 of the Specific Relief Act 1877 (now Section 39, Specific Relief Act 1963), provides for mandatory injunctions.
245. *Ghulam Rasool* v. *State of J&K*, AIR 1983 SC 1188; *Jamil Ahmed* v. *Provincial Government of W. Pakistan*, PLD 1982 Lah. 49. In Pakistan, prior notice is not necessary for injunctions alone but it is necessary for declarations: *Mohd. Ryas Hussain* v. *Cantonment Board, Rawalpindi*, PLD 1976 SC 785.
246. *Att-Gen* v. *Harris* [1961] 1 QB 74 (ordering removal of caravans placed on the defendant's land in breaches of planning control). *Hoffman-la Roche and Co.* v. *Secretary of State for Trade and Industry* [1975] AC 295 (to restrain charging of higher prices for drugs contrary to a statutory order); *Stafford B C* v. *Elkenford* [1977] 2 All ER 519; *Att-Gen* v. *Chandry* [1971] 3 All ER 938.
247. S.A. de Smith, *Judicial Review of Administration Action* (1973) Supra Note 426.
248. Supra Note 21, p. 517.
249. Section 42 of the Specific Relief Act, 1877.
250. *Monmohan Roy* v. *Commissioner of Chandpur Municipality*, PLD 1958 Dacca 47; *Abdur Rahman Bhuiya* v. *Commissioner of Narayanganj Municipality*, PLD 1959 Dacca 5.
251. *Muhammad Nawab v. Province of Punjab*, PLJ 2014 Lahore 542.
252. *Aftab Ali Khan* v. *Akbar Ali Khan* [1929] Allahabad LJ 794.
253. *Budhu Singh* v. *Board of Revenue*, AIR 1957 Allahabad 719; *Muhammad Ismail* v. *Patna Municipality*, AIR 1943 Patna 34.
254. *SI Syndicate* v. *Union of India*, AIR 1975 SC 460.
255. Code of Civil Procedure (Amendment) Ordinance, 1962.

256. *Krishnaveni Ammal* v. *Soundarajan* AIR 1945 Mad. 53; *Ramakrishna* v. *Narayana* 39 ILR 1914 Mad 80; *Ramachandra Rao* v. *Secretary of State* 39 ILR 1915 Mad. 808; *Andhra University* v. *Durgah Lukshmi* AIR 1951 Mad. 870; *Secretary of State* v. *Subba Rao* 56 ILR 1933 Mad. 749.

257. *Mohammad Hasan* v. *Gajadhar Prasad* AIR 1937 All. 585; *Sri Krishna* v. *Mailabir* AIR 1933 All. 488 (FB).

258. 43 ILR 1916 Cal. 694 (PC) at 704. In this case, the judicial committee was dealing with a suit to revoke probate, after the will had been affirmed by a court of appropriate jurisdiction. It held that once the will had been affirmed by a court of appropriate jurisdiction, its decision could not be impugned by a court exercising a different jurisdiction.

259. *Secretary of State for India* v. *Subba Rao*, 56 ILR 1933 Mad. 749.

260. *Snow-white Food Products Ltd* v. *Punjab Vanaspati Supply Co*, 49 CWN 172; *Narawanprosad* v. *Indian Iron & Steel Co. Ltd*, AIR 1953 Cal. 695; *Mohd. Manjurul Hug* v. *BissessTvar Banerjee*, AIR 1943 Cal 361.

261. *Maulavi Muhammad Fahimul Hug* v. *Jagat Balla Ghrosh*, 2 ILR 1922 Pat. 391. *Bai Shri Vaktuba* v. *Agarsinghji*, 34 ILR 1910 Bom. 676 (680).

262. *Kishore Lal* v. *Beg Raj*, AIR 1952 NI 387.

263. Pollock and Mulla, *Indian Contract and Specific Relief*.

264. *Ramaraghava Reddy* v. *Seshu Reddy*, AIR 1967 SC 436

265. PLD 1954 Sind 107.

266. PLD 1959 Lah. 429.

267. PLR (1959) Dac. 477.

268. 26 IA 16.

269. 40 IA 182.

270. H.W.R. Wade, *Administrative Law* (1977) Supra Note 96, 519.

271. *Shyabudinsab* v. *Municipality*, AIR 1955 SC 314; *Muhammad Sadeque* v. *Rafiq Ali*, PLD 1965 Dacca 330.

272. S.A. de Smith, *Judicial Review of Administrative Action* (1973) Supra Note 20, 337.

273. *Faridsons Ltd* v. *Government of Pakistan*, PLD 1961 SC537.

274. *Lal Mohammad* v. *Gul Bibi*, PLD 1986 Quetta 185; *Abdul Rahim* v. *Shahida Khan*, PLD 1984 SC 329; *Nasreen Fatima Awan* v. *Bolan Medical College*, PLD 1978 Quetta 17; *Rahim Shah* v. *Chief Election Commissioner*, PLD 1973 SC 24; *Nawaza* v. *Additional Settlement Commissioner & Rehabilitation Commissioner*, PLD 1970 SC 39.

275. *R.* v. *Electricity Commissioners* [1924] IKB 171.

276. [1919] 46 IA 176.

277. *Faridsons Ltd.* v. *Government of Pakistan*, PLD 1961 SC 537.

278. *Abul A'la Maudoodi* v. *Government of West Pakistan*, PLD 1964 SC 637; *University of Dacca* v. *Zakir Ahmad*, PLD 1965 SC 90; *Muhammad Siddique* v. *Chief Settlement Commissioner*, PLD 1965 SC 123.

279. *Royts of Garabando* v. *Zamindan*, AIR 1943 PC 164.

280. *Nawab Syed Raunaq Ali* v. *Chief Settlement Commissioner*, PLD 1973 SC 236.

281. *Shaukat Ali* v. *Commissioner*, PLD 1963 Lahore 127.

282. *Abdul Razzaq* v. *WAPDA*, PLD 1973 Lahore 188; *Province of West Pakistan* v. *Mehboob*, PLD 1962 SC 433.

283. *Errington* v. *Minister of Health* (1935) 1 KB 249.

284. *Azmat Ali* v. *Chief Settlement Commissioner*, PLD 1964 SC 260.

285. *Mohammad Tufail* v. *Settlement Commissioner*, PLD 1967 Karachi 258.

286. *R.* v. *Edmudsbury* [1974] 2 All ER 170; *Estate & Trust Agencies* v. *Singapore Improvement Trust* [1937] AC 898; R. v. North [1927] 1 KB 491.

287. *R.* v. *Campbell* [1953] 1 All ER 684.

288. *East & West Steamship Co.* v. *Pakistan*, PLD 1958 SC (Pak) 41.

289. *Tariq Transport Co.* v. *Sargodha-Bhera Bus Service*, PLD 1958 SC (Pak) 437.

290. *Mohammad Tufail* v. *Abdul Ghafoor*, PLD 1958 SC (Pak) 201.

291. *Iftikharul Haq* v. *WAPDA*, PLD 1974 Lahore 82.

292. *Asghar Husain* v. *Election Commissioner*, PLD 1968 SC387; *Presiding Officer* v. *Sadruddin Ansari*, PLD 1967 SC 569.

293. *University of Dacca* v. *Zakir Ahmad*, PLD 1965 SC90.

294. AIR 1965 SC 1222.

295. Per Lord J. Denning in *Baldwin & Francis Ltd* v. *Patents Appeal Tribunal* [1959] 2 All ER 433 (447) HL; *R* v. *Northumberland Compensation Appeal Tribunal, ex parte Shaw* [1951] 1 KB 711 and on appeal [1952] 1 KB 338.

296. *Afzal Phan Begum* v. *Chief Settlement and Rehabilitation Commissioner*, PLD 1962 Lah. 970; *Doreen Barkat Ram* v. *Custodian, Evacuee Property*, PLD 1962 Lah. 424.

297. *Mohd. Anwar* v. *Govt. of Pakistan*, PLD 1962 Lah 443.

298. *Padfield* v. *Minister of Agriculture, Fisheries and Food*, (1968 1 All E.R. 694; *R.* v. *Metropolitan Police Comm., Ex p. Blackburn* (1968) 1 All E.R. 763.

299. *The King* v. *Archbishop of Canterbury* [1812] 15 East 117, 136. Halsbury's *Laws of England* (3rd edn., London: Butterworths, 1955) Vol. XI, para. 200.

300. *District Magistrate* v. *Raza Kazim*, PLD 1961 SC 178; *Bubna More & Co. Ltd* v. *Modern Trading Co. Ltd*, PLD 1960 Dacca 768.

301. *M.A. Mohammad Ather* v. *Pakistan*, PLD 1962 SC 367.

302. *Abdul Hafeez* v. *Lahore Municipal Corporation*, PLD 1967 Lah. 1251.

303. *R.* v. *Blooer* (1760) 2 Burr. 1043.

304. *R.* v. *Bishop* [1916] 1 KB 466.

305. *Re Barnes Corp.* [1933] 1 KB 668.

306. *Faiz Ahmed* v. *Registrar of Cooperative Societies*, PLD 1962 SC 315; *Pakistan* v. *Nasim Ahmed*, PLD 1961 SC 445.

307. *Mohammad Yunus* v. *Islamic Republic of Pakistan*, PLD 1972 Lah. 847; *Zainul Abiddin* v. *Multan Central Cooperative Bank*, PLD 1966 SC 445.

308. *Chaudhary Zahoor Elahi* v. *Anti-Corruption Establishment*, PLD 1975 Lah. 532.

309. *Gujrat Punjab Bus Ltd* v. *Mohammad Ashraf Paganwalla*, PLD 1960 Lah. 609.

310. *Ashraf Ali* v. *Abdul Awal*, PLD 1968 Dacca 962; *Amin Ahmed* v. *Khairman*, PLD 1968 Dacca 217; *East Pakistan Industrial Development Corporation* v. *Rustam Ali*, PLD 1966 SC 848; *AFM Abdul Fateh* v. *Province of East Pakistan*, PLD 1966 Dacca 178; *Mustafa Ansari* v. *Deputy Commissioner*, PLD 1966 Dacca 576.

311. *M. Dalmia Cement Ltd.* v. *Superintendent*, PLD 1964 Karachi 203; *Siddiq Wahab* v. *Corporation*, PLD 1957 Karachi 175.

312. *Himmatlal* v. *State of MP* [1954] SCR 1122.

313. *Dwankar Prasad* v. *State of UP* [1954] SCR 803.

314. *Shyam Lal* v. *Ferozabad Municipality*, AIR 1956 Allahabad 185.

315. *S.M. Giribala* v. *East Bengal Evacuee Property Management Committee*, PLD 1960 Dacca 768.

316. *Kharak Sing* v. *State of UP*, AIR 1963 SC 1295.

317. *Saifuddin Saheb* v. *State of Bombay*, AIR 1962 SC 853.

318. *Ghulam Mustafa Shah* v. *Pakistan*, PLD 1963 SC 268.

319. *Qazi Khan* v. *State of Pakistan*, PLD 1963 Peshawar 41

320. *Wasi Haider* v. *Province of W. Pakistan*, PLD 1963 Karachi 458.

321. *Province of West Pakistan* v. *S.I. Mahboob*, PLD 1962 SC 433.

322. *District Magistrate, Lahore* v. *Raza Kazim*, PLD 1961 SC 178; *S.M. Giribala Basu* v. *East Bengal*, PLD 1960 Dacca 768.

323. The expression was used in American administrative law: Kleps, *Certiorarified Mandamus*, 2 Stanford LR [1950] 285.

324. AIR 1958 SC 1018.

325. AIR 1954 All 144.

326. [1952] SCR 135.

327. PLD 1960 Dac. 768.

328. *Faridson Ltd* v. *Government of Pakistan*, PLD 1961 SC 537.

329. PLD 1964 SC 126.

330. *Federation of Pakistan* v. *Saeed Ahmad Khan*, PLD 1974 SC 151.

331. *Saburur Rehman* v. *Government of Sind*, PLD 1996 SC 801; *Saburur Rehman* v. *Government of Sind*, PLD 1989 Kar. 572; *Federation of Pakistan* v. *Ghulam Mustafa Khar*, PLD 1988 SC 26; *Mohammad Bachal Memon* v. *Government of Sind*, PLD 1987 Kar. 296; *Fauji Foundation* v. *Shamimur Rehman*, PLD 1983 SC 457; *F.B. Ali* v. *The State*, PLD 1975 SC 566; *Federation of Pakistan* v. *Saeed Ahmed Khan*, PLD 1974 SC 151.

332. Article 199 of the Constitution of Islamic Republic of Pakistan, 1973.

333. *Columbia Broadcasting System* v. *US*, 316 US 407.

334. *Tariq Transport Company* v. *Sargodha-Bhera Buss Service*, PLD 1958 SC (Pak) 437.

335. *Asif Ali* v. *KMC*, 1995 CLC 1659, relying upon *District Magistrate* v. *Syed Raza Kazim*, PLD 1961 SC 178.

336. *Muhammad Idris* v. *EP Timber Merchants*, PLD 1968 SC 412.
337. Ghani v. Mahmud, PLD 1966 SC 802.
338. *Nizamuddin Ahmad* v. *Commissioner of Sales Tax*, 1971 SCMR 68.
339. *The Presiding Officer* v. *Sadruddin*, PLD 1967 SC 569.
340. *Wasimul Haque* v. *Government of Sind*, PLD 1975 Karachi 1.
341. *Abdul Hamid Khan* v. *D.M. Larkana*, PLD 1973 Karachi 344.
342. *Abdul Baqi* v. *Superintendent of Central Prison*, PLD 1957 Karachi 694.
343. *Hajra* v. *Additional Commissioner*, PLD 1971 Karachi 563.
344. *Murree Brewery Company Ltd.* v. *Pakistan*, PLD 1972 SC279; *Premier Cloth Mills Ltd.* v. *Sales Tax Officer*, 1972 SCMR 257; *Muhammad Afzal* v. *Board of Revenue*, PLD 1967 SC 314.
345. *Syed Ali Abbas* v. *Vishansingh*, PLD 1967, SC 294.
346. *Rehmatullah Khan* v. *State*, PLD 1965 Peshawar 162; *State of UP* v. *Muhammad Nooh*, AIR 1958 SC 86.
347. *Allah Dost* v. *Mohammad Alam*, PLD 1987 Quetta 235; *Abid Hussein* v. *Government of Sind*, PLD 1984 Kar. 269; *Sher Shah Industries Ltd.* v. *Government of Pakistan*, PLD 1982 Kar. 653; *Salooka Steels Ltd* v. *Pakistan Coast Guards*, PLD 1981 Quetta 1; *Sind Employee's Social Security Institution* v. *Mumtaz Ali*, PLD 1975 SC 475; *Murree Brewery Co. Ltd* v. *Government of Pakistan*, PLD 1972 SC 279; *Anjumane Ahmadya* v. *Deputy Commissioner,* PLD 1966 SC 639; *Nagina Silk Mills* v. *Income Tax Officer*, PLD 1963 SC 322; *Jalal Din* v. *Mohammad Akram Khan*, PLD 1963 Lah. 595.
348. *Nagina Silk Mills* v. *Income Tax Officer*, PLD 1963 SC 322; *Pakistan* v. *Ziauddin*, PLD 1962 SC440; *Nawabzada Mohammad Amir Khan* v. *Controller of Estate Duty*, PLD 1961 SC 119.
349. *Titaghar Paper Mills Co. Ltd* v. *State of Orissa*, AIR 1983 SC 603.
350. *V. Vellaswami* v. *Inspector-General of Police, Madras*, AIR 1982 SC 82.
351. *Ram and Shyam Co.* v. *State of Haryana*, AIR 1985 SC 1147.
352. *Begum Nazir Abdul Hamid* v. *Pakistan*, PLD 1974 Lahore 7; *Muhammad Ashraf* v. *Board of Revenue*, PLD 1968 Lahore 1155.
353. *Salam Muhammad Abdul* v. *Chairman*, PLD 1965 Dacca 231
354. *Irshad Ali* v. *Pakistan*, PLD 1975 Lahore 7.
355. *Managing Committee* v. *Settlement Commissioner*, PLD 1972 Lahore 245; *Tariq Transport Co. Lahore* v. *Sargodha-Bhera Bus Service*, PLD 1958 SC (Pak) 437; *Mian Fazal Din* v. *LIT*, PLD 1969 SC 223.
356. *Ardeshir Cowasjee* v. *Multiline Associates*, PLD 1993 Karachi 237.
357. *Kohat Cadet College* v. *Mohammad Shoaib Qureshi*, PLD 1984 SC 172.
358. *A.K. Fazlul Qadir Chaudhry* v. *Government of Pakistan*, PLD 1957 Dacca 342.
359. *Pacific Multi-National (Pvt) Ltd* v. *Inspector General of Police*, PLD 1992 Karachi 283.
360. *Province of West Pakistan* v. *Hira Lall Aaggarwala*, PLD 1970 SC 399.
361. *Nusrat Bhutto* v. *Chief of Army Staff*, PLD 1977 SC 657.

362. *Mahmud ul Haque* v. *SDO*, PLD 1963 SC233; *Muhammad Athar* v. *Pakistan*, PLD 1962 SC 367.

363. *Muhammad Athar* v. *Pakistan*, PLD 1962 SC 367.

364. *Shamsul Hasnain Haider* v. *Ghulam Ali Khan Talpur*, PLD 1963 Karachi 588.

365. *Zaitun* v. *Farzand Ali*, 1970 SCMR 149; *Saleh Shah* v. *Custodian*, 1971 SCMR 543.

366. *Tufail Muhammad* v. *Muhammad Ziaullah Khan*, PLD 1965 SC 269.

367. *Wali Muhammad* v. *Sakhi Muhammad*, PLD 1974 SC 106.

368. *Inamur Rehman* v. *Federation of Pakistan*, PLD 1977 Karachi 524.

369. *Dil Shah* v. *Mussarat Nazir*, PLD 1991 SC 779.

370. *Bajaj Hindustan Ltd. v. Sir Shadi Lal Enterprises Ltd.*, (2011) 1 SCC 640, *Aravili Golf Club v. Chander Hass*, (2008) 1 SCC 783; *Shri Sitaram Sugar Co. Ltd. v. Union of India*, (1990) 3 SCC 223; *Prag Ice and Oil Mills v. Union of India*, (1978) 3 SCC 459.

371. *Lahore Improvement Trust* v. *Custodian of Evacuee Property*, PLD 1971 SC 811; *Chairman, E. Pakistan Railway Board* v. *Abdul Majid*, PLD 1966 SC 725; *Liaquat Rashid* v. *Commissioner*, 1993 CLC 558.

372. *Ahmad Tariq Rahim* v. *Federation of Pakistan*, PLD 1991 Lahore 78.

373. *Tufail Mohammad* v. *Mohammad Ziaullah Khan*, PLD 1965 SC 269.

374. *Tufail Mohammad* v. *Sakhi Mohammad*, PLD 1974 SC 106; *Wali Mohammad* v. *Government of Baluchistan*, PLD 1972 Quetta 33; *Mohammad Yaqub* v. *Lyallpur Municipal Committee*, PLD 1971 Lah. 664; *Abdul Hamid* v. *Province of East Pakistan*, 1971 DLC 839; *Liaqat Hussein Khan* v. *Secretary* 1971 DLC 176; *Ayam Ali* v. *Custodian of Evacuee Property*, PLD 1968 Lah. 148; *Amir Abdullah* v. *Mohammad Yaqub*, PLD 1967 Lah. 722.

375. *Qaim Hussein* v. *Anjuman-e-Islamia*, PLD 1974 Lah. 346; *Husain Bakhsh* v. *Settlement Commissioner*, PLD 1970 SC1; *Hyder* v. *Pakistan*, PLD 1967 Lah. 882.

376. *Fazal Din* v. *Custodian of Evacuee Property*, PLD 1971 SC 779; *Barkat Ali* v. *Ghulam Mohammad*, PLD 1970 Quetta 10; *Ahmed Khan* v. *Chief Justice and Judges of the High Court of West Pakistan*, PLD 1968 SC 171; *Barkat Ali* v. *Zaman*, PLD 1968 Lah. 770; *Ahmed Khan* v. *Board of Revenue*, PLD 1967 Lah. 1030; *Tamizuddin Munshey* v. *Election Tribunal*, PLD 1967 Dacca 303; *Nasim Fatima* v. *Government of West Pakistan*, PLD 1967 Lah. 103; *Dildar Mohammad* v. *Heeman*, PLD 1967 Lah. 18; *Mirza Mohammad Yaqub* v. *Chief Settlement Commissioner*, PLD 1965 SC 254; *Mohammad Khan* v. *Lahore Cantonment Board*, PLD 1964 Lah. 125.

377. *Abdul Jabbar* v. *Abdul Wahid*, PLD 1974 SC 331; *Ibrahim* v. *Bashir Ahmad*, PLD 1971 SC 31; *Mohammad Tufail* v. *Chief Settlement & Rehabilitation Commissioner*, PLD 1971 Lah. 257; *B.H. Syed Begum* v. *Afzal Jahan Begum*, PLD 1970 SC 29.

378. *Sirajul Hassan* v. *Settlement Commissioner,* PLD 1974 Lahore 285.
379. *Tolomal* v. *Deputy Commissioner,* PLD 1972 Kar. 116; *Tufail Mohammad Khan* v. *Abdul Hamid,* PLD 1967 Lah. 1058; *Abdul Rehman* v. *Rafiq,* PLD 1966 Lah. 550.
380. *Sirajul Hassan* v. *Settlement Commissioner,* PLD 1974 Lahore 285; *Nabi Bux* v. *Mohammad Akram,* PLD 1969 Lah. 880; *Mohammad Ibrahim* v. *Chief Settlement & Rehabilitation Commissioner,* PLD 1966 Lah. 396.
381. Section 3(1). In practice, most decisions made by the Governor General are of little administrative significance. Presumably, the exception is seen as a 'safety-valve'.
382. Section 3(2)
383. Section 3(3)
384. Sections 3(1) and 7.
385. Section 5.
386. Section 6.
387. Section 3(4).
388. Section 12.
389. Section 11. Review is not confined to those grounds: Section 11(6).
390. See Section 11(3)
391. Section 11(4) and (5).
392. Section 13(1).
393. Section 13(7)
394. Section 13(2).
395. See Section 13(4), (5), and (6).
396. Section 14(1).
397. Section 14(4).
398. Section 9.
399. In Sections 5, 6, and 7.
400. Section 10.
401. Section 10(2) and (3).
402. Section 5(1)(a).
403. Section 5(1)(f)
404. Section 5(2)(f).
405. Section 5(2)(h).
406. Section 5(1)(h). And see the modification in ss.(3).
407. Section 15.
408. Section 18.
409. Section 19.
410. Harry Whitemore and Mark Aronson, *Review of Administrative Action* (1978 edn., Sydney: The Law Book Company Ltd) 15–19.
411. H.W.R. Wade, *Administrative Law* (1977) Supra Note 96, 5.
412. Ibid.

CHAPTER VI

Administrative Tribunals

6.1 INTRODUCTION

6.1.1 THE GROWTH OF TRIBUNALS

Outside the ordinary courts of law there is a host of special statutory tribunals with jurisdiction to decide legal disputes. They are one of the by-products of the present age of intensive government, and they particularly multiply in a welfare state. The movement of progressive society nowadays might be said to be from social contract to social status. Fewer people are left to rely on personal transactions enforced by the ordinary law courts, and more people are subjected to regulatory schemes like national insurance, the health service, state education, agricultural control, rent control, and many other similar schemes which are administered under elaborate Acts of the parliament. These have become a new source of social friction, and have given rise to many disputes. What benefit may A claim under the insurance scheme? Whether Dr B ought to be removed from the health service? Is C entitled to a reduction of rent before his eviction? Should D be allowed to give notice to his farm tenant?

To add all this work to the tasks of the ordinary courts would not only cause a breakdown of the court system, it would also in many cases be wrong in principle. The court process is generally elaborate, slow, and costly. Its defects are also of its merits if the object is to dispense high standard of justice and indeed the litigant has to pay for it. But in administering social services the aim is different. Disputes have to be disposed of smoothly, quickly, and cheaply. The object is to dispense justice consistent with efficient administration. Many of these disputes are better decided by administrative bodies on which technical experts can sit. Special forms of tribunals have therefore been devised, and the contrast between them and the ordinary courts is obvious. A new system for the dispensation of justice has grown side by side with the old one. National insurance tribunals, rent tribunals, transport tribunals, and health service tribunals, together with many others, have come to play a vital role in the life of the ordinary citizen which is (assuming the ordinary citizen to be law-abiding) likely to be of more direct concern to him than that of the courts of law.

The total number of the tribunals falling within the scope of the Tribunals and Inquiries Act 1958 now come to about 2000, when all their local subdivisions are included.

The various kinds of tribunals are constituted and identified by express provisions in various Acts of the parliament. It is very rare that the parliament would give delegated power to set up a new kind of tribunal by ministerial order. Power, nevertheless, is given to ministers to provide membership, organisation, and proceedings of the tribunals which have been constituted under the statutes.

Such bodies are often called 'administrative tribunals', but this does not mean that their decisions are necessarily administrative. In a large number of cases, the decisions are judicial in nature, in the sense that the tribunals have to decide facts and apply rules to them impartially and without at times considering executive policy. Such tribunals are in substance courts of law. They are designated 'administrative' because the reasons for preferring them to the ordinary courts of law are administrative in nature. An administrative tribunal is, in fact a part of a scheme of administration of some statutory service or system of control for which, as a whole, a minister is responsible to the parliament. When, for example, unemployment benefit is awarded by a national insurance local tribunal, its decision is as objective as that of any court of law. Basically two elements form part of a decision: the facts as they are proved, and the statutory rules which have to be applied to them. The rules would generally give the tribunal a measure of discretion. But discretion given is required to be used objectively, and does no more alter the nature of the decision than does the 'judicial discretion' which is familiar in courts of law. These tribunals, therefore, have the character of courts but they are enmeshed in the administrative machinery of the state, and are ultimately subject to some control by the courts.[1]

6.1.2 DISTINCTION BETWEEN TRIBUNALS AND INQUIRIES

There is a clear contrast between a statutory tribunal and a statutory inquiry. The tribunal finds facts and decides the case by applying legal rules thereto. The inquiry finds facts and makes recommendations to a minister who would then take a decision which may include a large element of policy. A tribunal may go no further than the facts and the law, because the issue before it is self-contained. The inquiry is concerned only with the local aspects of what may be a larger issue. Tribunals are generally used where individual cases have to be decided and the minister in charge of the scheme would not want to be responsible for the decisions. Inquiries are used where the minister wants to be responsible for the decision, but wants to be properly informed before he makes it. In other words, tribunals make judicial decisions and inquiries constitute preliminary steps to administrative decisions.

The British Parliament has experimented with many different bodies and procedures and has in some cases set up tribunals where one would expect to find inquiries and vice versa. Transport licensing, in particular, has been affected by the tradition of employing independent tribunals for deciding what are really questions of policy. The Railway Commission (1873), the Railway and Canal Commission (1888), the Railway Rates Tribunal (1921), and the Transport Tribunal (1947) were successively empowered to control railway rates and charges. This was essentially a commercial and political matter, yet an independent tribunal was employed. Rate control for railways generally has now been found unnecessary, but the Transport Tribunal still controls passenger fares in London. Similarly the licensing of commercial road services is entrusted to tribunals, the traffic commissioners; appeals lie from them to the Transport Tribunal in respect of goods and services and to the Minister of Transport in respect of passenger services. The logic of these arrangements is not evident, but they work well and have survived several investigations.[2] Air transport licensing, which was introduced in 1960 to control the allocation of routes and the scales of charges, is assigned to the Air Transport Licensing Board, from which, however, appeal lies to the minister. This curious system at least recognises that ultimately the decision is one of policy.

Where the decision has to be taken by a minister, he must necessarily appoint someone to hear the case and then advise him how to decide it. The procedure is therefore that of an inquiry, and the Tribunals and Inquiries Acts will apply accordingly, even though the subject matter seems more suitable for a tribunal. This is the situation where ministers have to decide questions of fact and law, for example under the national insurance scheme where certain important questions in claims for benefit are 'minister's questions', subject to a right of appeal to the court on a point of law.[3] Similarly appeal from the decision of a district auditor lies to the minister in some cases, even though the only question may be the legality of the local authority's expenditure, thus raising only issues of fact and law. Sometimes appeal lies to the minister from a fully formed tribunal, as in the case of air transport licensing mentioned above, and as in the case of appeals to the Minister of Health by doctors found guilty of default by the National Health Service Tribunal or a local executive council. In some of these situations, the minister's function may be explained as a kind of prerogative of mercy or as an ultimate political appeal, but in others it defies logical analysis. We are here in an area where tribunal and inquiry procedures are strangely intermixed.

6.1.3 COURTS AND ADMINISTRATIVE TRIBUNALS

It has not been an easy task to distinguish between the Courts and the Administrative Tribunals performing judicial or quasi-judicial functions. The true question in the case of such tribunals always is whether the act which is being complained of is a judicial act and whether the procedure adopted by the tribunal is judicial or quasi-judicial or whether the dominant or general aspect of the tribunal is that of a judicial, quasi-judicial or administrative body.[4] In the case of *Mehram Ali v. Federation of Pakistan*,[5] it has been held that Constitution recognizes only such specific Tribunals to share judicial powers with the Courts, established under Article 175 of the Constitution, which have been specifically provided by the Constitution itself, namely, Federal Shariat Court under

Chapter 3A, Tribunals under Article 212, Election Tribunals under Article 225 of the Constitution. The same view was reiterated with approval by this Court in the case of *Liaqat Hussain v. Federation of Pakistan*.[6]

The Supreme Court discussed this aspect in a number of cases and concluded as follows:-

According to the dictionary meaning, the following three elements are essential for understanding the concept by a Court:-

(1) Time when judicial functions may be exercised.

(2) A place for the exercise of judicial functions.

(3) A person or persons exercising judicial functions.

Thus, the judicial functions are the common characteristic of each element. The term 'judicial function' has also not been clearly spelt out either in any dictionary or in any other book. However, Griffith, C.J. in *Huddart Parker* case[7] has defined the term as, "the words 'judicial power' as used in section 71 of the Constitution to mean the power which every sovereign authority must of necessity have to decide controversies between its subjects, or between itself and its subjects, whether the rights relate to life, liberty, or property. The exercise of this power does not come into being until some tribunal which has power to give binding and authoritative decision (whether subject to appeal or not) is called upon to take action." The same definition has been quoted with approval in *Shell Co. of Australia Limited v. Federal Commissioner of Taxation*[8] and *United Engineering Workers' Union v. Uevanayagam*[9] From the detailed analysis of above case-law it is clear that the exercise of judicial power is considered to be an essential feature of a Court, and it distinguishes a Court from an administrative tribunal.[10]

Elaborating further the Supreme Court held that the determining factor is always the nature of the dispute to be resolved by a Tribunal. When the Tribunal has to determine a dispute relating to a right or liability, recognized by the Constitution or law and was under an obligation to discover the relevant facts, in the presence of the parties, in the light of the evidence produced before them; it acted judicially. Whenever judicial power was vested in a forum, be it called a court or a tribunal, for all intents and purposes, it was a court. Exercise of judicial power is considered to be essential feature of a court, and it distinguished a court from an administrative tribunal. Since the Service Tribunals exercised judicial powers, therefore, they are included in the term 'Court' mentioned in Article 175 of the Constitution.[11]

In order to ensure that the Service Tribunals function independently as judicial bodies, it was directed that as a prerequisite for making appointments of the Chairman and Members of Service Tribunals independent it was held necessary to make their appointments with a meaningful consultation of the Chief Justice. Such consulation has to be of the Chief Justice of Pakistan in case of appointment of the Chairman and Members of Federal Service Tribunal. For such appointments in Provincial Service Tribunals, the consulation would be that of the Chief Justice of the respective provincial High Court. Furthermore, to ensure independence, the tenure of office of Chairman and members would not exceed three years and would not be extendable.[12]

6.1.4 COMPOSITION AND OPERATION

The common feature of all statutory tribunals, as opposed to inquiries, is that they make their own decisions independently and are free from political influence. In abnormal cases where appeal lies to a minister, the minister's policy may indirectly influence them. But from direct political control they are as free as are the courts of law, and this independence is jealously preserved.

Tribunals are, therefore, as a rule staffed by independent persons, not by civil servants. Even if in a sense they are people's courts, they have at least their full share of judicial independence. People at times do not give them credit for their impartiality which is often because of minor factors that arouse suspicion. For instance, a pensions appeal tribunal or a national assistance appeal tribunal would usually have a civil servant as its clerk, who would tell the appellant how to proceed and would require him to fill up forms emanating from his department. The tribunal may sit in the department's premises, and the part played by the official representing the department before the tribunal, as well as the position of the clerk itself, may give an impression of being under influence. But the truth may be to the contrary. A typical tribunal (especially if it is an appeal tribunal) would consist of three persons. The chairman would, in many cases, be a practising lawyer, perhaps a local solicitor, who provides his services part-time. The other two members would be chosen from a panel of people willing to serve, none of whom would be in the employment of the department. In many cases they might represent certain interests, such as landlords and tenants in the case of Agricultural Land Tribunals, and employers and employed in the case of National Insurance Local Tribunals. The tribunal would thus consist of an independent chairman, and one person chosen from each of the panels of names put forward by the employers and the trade unions respectively (or as the case may be). The chairman is usually paid, but the members would often be unpaid, and might regard the work as public service. In other cases members may have expert qualifications, as, for example, members of Pensions Appeal Tribunals, some of whom must be medical practitioners, and in that case they are normally paid. One special case is the Patents Appeal Tribunal, which consists of a high court judge. Some of the important adjudicators, such as the national insurance commissioner (who hears appeals from the local tribunals), are paid at least as much as county court judges, or equivalent rates for part-time. At the other end of the scale, the chairmen and members of Rent Tribunals receive little more than token payments. These differences reflect—though by no means always faithfully—the wide variation in the type of work, which may range from highly skilled full-time employment of a most responsible kind to relatively petty adjudications undertaken voluntarily (like the work of a justice of the peace) as a service to the community. Tribunals' clerks are also subject to a variety of arrangements. For the most part they are civil servants, and form the one substantial link between the departments and the tribunals.

But rent tribunals appoint and employ their own clerks, who accordingly do not have civil service status.

The Special Commissioners of Income Tax are exceptional among tribunals in that they consist wholly of officials. But they are acknowledged in practice to be independent and their decisions are subject to appeal to the high court on points of law.

6.1.5 APPEALS

There is great diversity also in the arrangements for appeals. Sometimes there is a two- or three-tier structure, as with claims to benefits under national insurance. These claims are first determined by the local insurance officer, who is not a tribunal but an official of the ministry. From his decision there is an appeal to the local tribunal, consisting of an independent legal chairman appointed by the minister and two other members (not officials) representing employers and employees respectively. From the local tribunal a final appeal lies with the National Insurance Commissioner, who must be a barrister of at least ten years' standing. These authorities also adjudicate claims arising from industrial injuries,[13] which previously went to industrial injuries tribunals. The National Health Service has an elaborate appeal structure for the benefit of doctors and others against whom complaints are made by patients.[14] If the complaint is upheld by the initial tribunal (the local executive council) the doctor may appeal to the National Health Service Tribunal and thence further to the minister if threatened with removal from the health service. If threatened with lesser penalties he may appeal to the minister directly.

The above are cases where the appeal consists of a full re-hearing of the case on its merits. From many tribunals there is no such general right of appeal, but there is then usually a right of appeal to the courts on any question of law. Decisions of the Lands Tribunal and of the Transport Tribunal, for example, are subject to a right of appeal on a point of law to the Court of Appeals. Similar appeals lie to the high court from many other tribunals, either under specific statutes[15] or under the general provision of the Tribunals and Inquiries Act 1958. The latter statute gives an appeal on a point of law from rent tribunals, independent schools tribunals, compensation appeal tribunals and many others, including new tribunals such as industrial tribunals and rent assessment committees to which its provisions are extended by ministerial order.

In a few cases there is no appeal of any kind; some examples are supplementary benefit appeal tribunals, betting levy appeal tribunals, and compensation appeal tribunals. In others there is an appeal to a higher tribunal and therefore no appeal to the courts. For example, there is no appeal to the courts from the National Insurance Commissioner, the highest judicial authority in the hierarchy of tribunals dealing with national insurance and industrial injuries. But here it is important to remember that the court can intervene in case of error on the face of the record, so that these tribunals have become subject to a wider measure of judicial control that was contemplated when they were created.

6.2 Constitutional Developments Regarding Service Laws until 1973

Immediately before Independence, the territories which now constitute Pakistan were governed as part of India under the Government of India Act 1935, which was the constitutional document then in force.[16] Under the Indian Independence Act, 1947, the Indian Subcontinent was declared independent and two independent dominions, namely Pakistan and India, were created by partitioning the former British India. Under Section 9 of this Act of 1947, the governor generals of both the dominions till 31 March 1948 had the power to make by order such provisions as appeared to them to be necessary, inter alia, to bring the provision of that Act (of 1947) into effective operation and to make necessary adaptations of the Government of India Act, 1935, in its application to their respective dominions. In exercise of the authority thus conferred on him, the Governor General of Pakistan promulgated the Pakistan (Provisional Constitution) Order,

1947.[17] In this way, the Government of India Act, 1935—with slight modifications and necessary adaptations—became the first (although provisional) Constitution of Pakistan and continued as such until 1956 when the regular Constitution of 1956, providing for the parliamentary form of government, was enacted.

The Constitution of 1956 was annulled by the proclamation dated 7 October 1958 by President Iskander Mirza who imposed Martial Law throughout the country. However, three days later, the President promulgated the Laws (Continuance in Force) Order which in effect restored laws in force before the proclamation including those regulating the jurisdiction of all courts, including the Supreme Court and the high courts, and of all other judicial authorities. The order allowed all persons in the service of Pakistan to continue in office and directed further that the country would be governed as nearly as may be in accordance with the late Constitution of 1956. The question of the validity of the Laws (Continuance in Force) Order came up before the Supreme Court of Pakistan in *State* v. *Dosso*[18] wherein it was upheld as valid. A constitutional commission was set up to make recommendations as to the future constitution of the country. The commission recommended presidential form of government as being most suitable to the conditions in Pakistan and also made a number of other recommendations as to the future Constitution of the country. The other recommendations were generally rejected but the one relating to the presidential form of government was accepted.[19] President Mohammad Ayub Khan promulgated the Constitution of 1962 on 1 March 1962, providing for presidential form of government which came into force on 8 June 1962 on which date Martial Law was lifted.

The Constitution of 1962 and the regime of President Ayub lasted until 25 March 1969 when he relinquished his office as President. He handed over his powers to General Agha Muhammad Yahya Khan, then Commander-in-Chief of the Pakistan Army, who through a proclamation assumed the office of President, abrogated the Constitution of 1962 and imposed Martial Law throughout the country appointing himself Chief Martial Law Administrator as well. By another proclamation, dated 31 March 1969, he promulgated the Provisional Constitution Order which came into force immediately and directed that notwithstanding the abrogation of the constitution, the state would be governed in accordance with the Constitution of 1962 but subject to any contrary provision in the Provisional Constitutional Order or any regulation or order made from time to time by him as the Chief Martial Law Administrator or as President. The persons who were in the service of Pakistan before the proclamation continued in office. The regime of General Yahya lasted until 20 December 1971 when he handed over power to the leader of the majority in the National Assembly from West Pakistan in the general elections held in December 1970, Mr Zulfiqar Ali Bhutto, who assumed the office of President and Chief Martial Law Administrator. The Supreme Court of Pakistan, in the case of *Asma Jilani* v. *Government of the Punjab*[20] held General Yahya usurper and invalidated the Martial Law imposed by him. Consequently, Martial Law was lifted and the Interim Constitution of 1972 was enforced. The Interim Constitution of 1972 was replaced by the permanent Constitution of the Islamic Republic of Pakistan, 1973 which came into force on 14 August 1973.

6.2.1 CONSTITUTIONAL PROTECTION PROVIDED TO THE PUBLIC SERVANTS

As discussed above, the Government of India Act, 1935, duly modified and adapted, served as Provisional Constitution of Pakistan from 1947 to 1956. Section 240 of the Act made provisions for the terms and conditions of service of persons who were members of the Civil Service of Pakistan or were holding any civil posts in Pakistan. Broadly speaking, the civil servants in Pakistan were extended the following protections:

    (i) Any person serving in the affairs of the federation appointed by the secretary of state for India or the secretary of state in council, would not be dismissed from the service by any authority subordinate to the governor general.

(ii) Any such person serving in the affairs of a province would not be dismissed from the service by any authority subordinate to the governor of that province.

(iii) Any civil servant, not falling in the above categories, would not be dismissed from service by any authority subordinate to one by which he was appointed.

(iv) Any civil servant as aforesaid would not be dismissed or reduced in rank until he was given a reasonable opportunity of showing cause against the action proposed to be taken in regard to him. However, this protection was not extended to persons dismissed or reduced in rank on the grounds of conduct leading to their conviction on a criminal charge. An authority empowered to dismiss or reduce in rank could waive the requirement of opportunity of showing cause if he considered it not reasonably practicable for any reason to be recorded in writing.

The Constitution of 1956 also provided constitutional protection to civil servants in similar terms. The constitution extended protection to a civil servant against dismissal from service by an authority subordinate to one who had appointed him or was authorised to appoint him. In the same way, requirement of reasonable opportunity of showing cause was extended against dismissal from service, removal from service or reduction in rank.[21] The constitution also provided for the same exceptions against the requirement of reasonable opportunity of showing cause against the proposed action with the condition that the president or the governor, as the case may be, were empowered to dispense with such opportunity, for reasons to be recorded, in the interest of the security of Pakistan or any part thereof.[22] The Constitution of 1956 also extended constitutional protection to civil servants in matters of terms and conditions of their service other than disciplinary matters. It was also provided that conditions of service of civil servants serving in connection with the affairs of the federation would be prescribed by the rules made by the President or by some person authorised by the president in this behalf.[23] In the same way, it was provided that conditions of service of civil servants serving in connection with the affairs of a province would be prescribed by the rules made by the governor of the province or by some person authorised by the governor for the purpose.[24] It was further provided that rules to be framed would not vary the tenure and conditions of service of any civil servant to his disadvantage.[25] A right of appeal was also provided to a civil servant against orders punishing or formally censuring him, altering or interpreting to his disadvantage any rule affecting his conditions of service, or terminating his employment otherwise than upon his reaching the age fixed for superannuation.[26] In case any such order was passed by the president or a governor, the civil servant aggrieved could apply for review of that order. However, civil servants employed on temporary basis were not extended such protection and their employment was made terminable on one month's notice or less.[27]

The Constitution of 1962 made identical provisions regarding dismissal or removal from service or reduction in rank and guaranteed reasonable opportunity of showing cause against the proposed action.[28] Rule-making powers of the president and governors of provinces were restricted to conform with such guarantees and restrictions were placed against varying the terms and conditions of a civil servant to his disadvantage with the difference that such restriction was confined only to those terms and conditions which relate to remuneration or age fixed for superannuation. Similarly, right of appeal, or to apply for review in case of orders of the president or a governor, was provided against orders punishing or formally censuring a civil servant, or altering or interpreting to his disadvantage any rule affecting his terms and conditions of service, or terminating his employment otherwise than upon his reaching the age fixed for superannuation.[29] However, under this constitution, the president or a governor of a province were empowered to order retirement of those civil servants who had completed twenty-five years of service in the public interest and to make rules for retirement of civil servants at any time after they had completed fifty-five years of age.[30] These protections were not extended to civil servants who were in temporary employment and the president and governors of the provinces were authorised to make rules for regulating temporary employment.[31]

The Interim Constitution of 1972 made provisions identical to the Constitution of 1962.[32] However, the authority to retire a civil servant in the public interest on the completion of twenty-five years of service was extended to 'competent authority', which was defined as 'authority competent to make appointment to the post concerned'.[33]

6.2.2 SERVICE LAWS AS INTERPRETED BY THE SUPERIOR COURTS

The constitutional protection extended to civil servants in Pakistan was liberally construed by the Superior Courts in Pakistan. Constitutional provisions providing for protection against arbitrary dismissal or removal from service, reduction in rank or taking of such action by an authority inferior to the appointing authority were held to be mandatory and overriding.[34] The requirement for 'reasonable opportunity of showing cause against proposed action' was discussed and elaborated by the superior courts with the result that constitutional guarantees against dismissal or removal from service or reduction in rank were crystallised in the following requirements:

(i) A civil servant who is proceeded against should be informed of charges against him and should be allowed reasonable time to submit his reply thereto.[35]

(ii) A fair and impartial departmental enquiry should be held against the accused civil servant according to principles of natural justice.[36]

(iii) After the conclusion of the departmental enquiry and on receipt of an enquiry report from the enquiry officer, the punishing authority, after deciding upon provisional punishment, was then required to serve a second show cause notice on the accused civil servant clearly mentioning the penalty or penalties he intended to impose.[37]

(iv) The punishing officer ought to supply a copy of the enquiry report, or substantial portion thereof, with the second show cause notice in order to enable the accused civil servant to effectively submit his reply to the show cause notice.[38]

(v) The punishing authority should allow an opportunity of personal hearing to the accused civil servant if so requested by the latter.[39]

These requirements were extended to the civil servants who were employed on temporary basis.[40] The rights of the temporary government servants were abridged by the first proviso to Clause (2) of Article 182 of the 1956 Constitution which made their employment terminable on one month's notice or less. The Constitution of 1962 also separately provided for government servants employed on temporary basis under its Article 179 and the president and governors of the provinces were empowered to frame rules for regulating their temporary employment. However, temporary government servants could not be removed from service by notice simpliciter when such termination was in fact being effected on account of his undesirable character and conduct in which case opportunity to show cause was legally necessary.[41] The superior courts even extended the constitutional protection to civil servants on probation who could not be removed by an officer of the rank lower than that of the appointing officer[42] and could not be removed on the grounds of misconduct without being served with a show cause notice and without holding a proper inquiry.[43] Constitutional protection was also extended to government servants having officiating appointments if they were for an indefinite period of time.[44] On promulgation of the first constitution in 1956, constitutional jurisdiction of the high courts (also called writ jurisdiction) was frequently exercised to afford relief to the aggrieved civil servants against violation of their legal and constitutional protection.[45]

6.3 INTRODUCTION OF SERVICE TRIBUNALS UNDER THE 1973 CONSTITUTION

6.3.1 HISTORICAL BASIS FOR THE CHANGE

Pakistan, on independence, inherited its bureaucratic set up from British India. Bureaucracy had been developed as a powerful institution by the British colonial masters who ruled India with iron hands through the bureaucrats who were fully loyal to their British masters regardless of the political currents in the country. This institution also developed its own internal unity, fraternity, and cohesion. At times it acted in a concerted manner in the face of other institutions and persons including the politicians. It was due to its internal organisation, cohesion, and unity that Pakistan's history of its early days is chequered with frequent interference from the bureaucrats. The bureaucracy became so powerful and confident that it nearly undermined the political process in the country and took over the task itself of governing the country at the highest level. Several bureaucrats turned themselves as successful politicians and from among their ranks emerged two of Pakistan's governor generals, namely Ghulam Mohammad and Iskander Mirza (who also became the first president of Pakistan under the Constitution of 1956) and one prime minister, namely, Chaudhry Muhammad Ali.

There are few who dispute that incalculable harm was done to the constitutional, legal and political framework in Pakistan by the aforesaid governor generals. Ghulam Mohammad created the first constitutional crisis in Pakistan by dismissing the first Constituent Assembly in the year 1954, thus leading to court battles which culminated in the judgements of the Federal Court in the cases of Maulvi Tamizuddin Khan,[46] Usif Patel,[47] and Governor General's Reference.[48] Iskander Mirza freely meddled with parliamentary politics by involving himself in political intrigues, thus destabilising successive governments to serve his own interest and to perpetuate his hold on power. As if all that was not enough for him, he abrogated the first constitution of Pakistan in October 1958 and imposed Martial Law throughout the country. This led to another constitutional crisis. The Supreme Court was called upon to examine the validity of the Martial Law which it upheld in *State* v. *Dosso*[49] on the rationale that victorious revolution or a successful coup d'état is a recognised legal method of changing a constitution.

During the Martial Law years of 1958 to 1962, the bureaucracy gained further powers as it was not accountable to the people of Pakistan. The Martial Law administration was totally dependent upon civil bureaucracy for its day-to-day business of running the country and the citizens fell completely into the merciless clutches of bureaucracy unfettered by any political checks and balances. government machinery under the Constitution of 1962 hardly brought any change in this situation and the bureaucracy continued to grow more and more powerful, arrogant, and indifferent to the needs of the common man. To put it in the words of Mr Bhutto, bureaucracy became 'a class of Brahmans or Mandarians unrivalled in its snobbery and arrogance, isolated from the life of the people and incapable of identifying itself with them'[50] It was only obvious that there would be an outcry from the people at large against this institution. Political agitation against President Ayub's regime from November 1968 to March 1969 brought to the forefront deep seated public resentment against the bureaucrats.

In the general elections held in Pakistan in December 1970, Mr Bhutto, as leader of the Pakistan Peoples Party, included bureaucratic and administrative reforms in his election manifesto. He promised extensive administrative reforms to cut down the power and privileges of the bureaucrats. When he became President of Pakistan, in his first speech delivered to the nation on 20 December 1971, he depreciated bureaucracy as 'nursed and brought up on the traditions and concepts of colonialism'. He stressed the need for bureaucracy 'with a liberal outlook, dynamic in its working, and motivated with a desire to serve the nation'. A high powered committee was appointed to address itself to the task of overhauling the bureaucracy. The committee was required to take stock of the existing position, to review the recommendations of various experts, commissions and committees made from time to time and to chalk out a programme of administrative reforms in the light of new requirements. This committee after examining various issues: including revision of the services structure, the eradication of corruption, creation of a more scientific and effective machinery, and the establishment of a sound and rational training programme submitted its recommendations. Most of the recommendations of the committee, as accepted by the government, may not be relevant for the purpose of the present study but the following two matters are worth mentioning:

(i) Constitutional safeguards and guarantees were to be abolished and terms and conditions of service of civil servants were to be brought under the legislatures' control through ordinary legislation; and

(ii) Administrative tribunals were to be set up as forums where governmental officials could get their grievances redressed.

6.3.2 PROVISIONS REGARDING CIVIL SERVANTS UNDER THE 1973 CONSTITUTION

In keeping with the aforementioned recommendations of the committee, the 1973 Constitution made clear departure from all the previous constitutions in respect of provisions regarding guarantees to the civil servants against arbitrary and wrongful dismissal or removal from service or reduction in rank. The constitution made no mention of any guarantees extended to government servants under previous constitutions and the matter of determination of their conditions of service was relegated to the realm of ordinary laws as enacted from time to time by the parliament or the provincial assemblies, as the case may be.[51] The parliament and the provincial assemblies were also empowered to enact laws for the establishment of one or more administrative courts or tribunals to exercise exclusive jurisdiction in respect of the following matters:[52]

(i) Terms and conditions of persons in the service of Pakistan, including disciplinary matters;

(ii) Claims arising from tortious acts of the government or its servants while acting in exercise of their duties, or of any local or other authority empowered to levy any tax or cess; or

(iii) The acquisition, administration and disposal of enemy property under any law.

The jurisdiction of such administrative courts and tribunals was made entirely exclusive and, on their establishment, no other court could grant an injunction, make any order or entertain any proceedings in respect of matters within their jurisdiction.[53] Provisions of Clause (2) of Article 212 were not applicable to an administrative court and tribunal established under an Act of provincial assembly unless at the request of that assembly made in the form of a resolution, Parliament by law extending these provisions to such a court or tribunal.[54] At the request of the provincial assemblies of the North West Frontier Province (NWFP),[55] the Punjab, and Sind, the Parliament by statute extended the provisions of Article 212 (2) of the Constitution with effect from 6 May 1974, to the service tribunals established by the three provinces.[56] Similarly at the request of the provincial assembly of Baluchistan, the parliament by statute extended the provisions of Article 212 (2) of the constitution with effect from 19th May 1976 to the service tribunal established for Baluchistan.[57] Appeal was provided to the Supreme Court against the decisions of the administrative courts or tribunals only if the Supreme Court grants leave to appeal on a substantial question of law of public importance.[58]

6.3.3 NEW CIVIL SERVICE LAWS AND ESTABLISHMENT OF SERVICE TRIBUNALS

In keeping with the address of Prime Minister Z.A. Bhutto on 20 August 1973,[59] legislation was passed introducing new service structure and laying down terms and conditions of civil servants. The most important federal law passed in this behalf was Civil Servants Ordinance[60] which was later replaced by an Act of

Parliament containing identical provisions.[61] This law defined a 'federal civil servant' as somebody who is a member of an All-Pakistan Service or of civil service of the federation, or who holds a civil post in connection with the affairs of the federation, including any post connected with defence. However, a person on deputation from any province, employed on contract or work charge basis or being 'worker' or 'workman' as defined in the Factories Act or the Workmen's Compensation Act, was not to be included in such definition.[62] This law broadly laid down terms and conditions of the service of federal civil servants regarding their tenure, appointment, probation, confirmation, seniority, promotion, posting and transfer, termination from service, reduction in rank, retirement, conduct, discipline, pay, leave, pension, gratuity, provident fund, benevolent fund, and group insurance.[63] It also provided for right of appeal, representation or review to a civil servant aggrieved against an order relating to the terms and conditions of his service.[64]

In accordance with Article 212 of the constitution, legislation was passed establishing administrative tribunals in respect of matters relating to the terms and conditions of civil servants, including their disciplinary matters.[65] No administrative courts or tribunals were created in regard to matters relating to claims arising from tortious acts of government or its employees or in respect of matters relating to the acquisition, administration and disposal of enemy property. Consequently, in these matters adjudication continued under the jurisdiction of ordinary courts. The president was empowered to establish one or more service tribunals through notification specifying therein their territorial limits within which their jurisdiction would extend.[66]

Following the federal legislation, provincial legislation was also undertaken on similar lines. All the four provinces in Pakistan enacted laws:

(i) Laying down the terms and conditions of civil servants serving in their respective provinces;[67] and

(ii) Establishing service tribunals for their respective provinces for determination of any disputes pertaining to the terms and conditions of the service of their civil servants including their disciplinary matters.[68]

All these provincial statutes follow federal statute on the subject with very few modifications here and there but there are no material differences worthy of mention. With the establishment of the federal and provincial service tribunals at the centre and the provinces under their respective enactments, all the proceedings (in respect of matters within the exclusive jurisdiction of these tribunals), before courts including the high courts of the provinces stood abated.[69] However, the statutes, providing for the establishment of service tribunals, allowed parties to the abated proceedings to prefer an appeal to the appropriate tribunal in respect of the matter in issue in such abated proceedings within ninety days of the commencement of the statute concerned or the establishment of the appropriate tribunals.[70] Subsequently, the appeals pending before the Supreme Court were saved through a constitutional amendment.[71]

6.3.4 CONSTITUTION OF THE SERVICE TRIBUNALS

The federal service tribunal consisted of a chairman and two members to be appointed by the President of Pakistan.[72] The number of members was enhanced by an amendment in the law to not more than three.[73] Originally, the chairman and the members were required to sit and hold the hearings as a full court but by an amendment, the chairman was empowered to constitute benches consisting of not less than two members, including the chairman.[74] In case of difference of opinion among the members of a bench, the decision of the majority prevails.[75] If the members are equally divided and the chairman of the tribunal is himself a member of the bench, the opinion of the chairman prevails and the decision of the tribunal is expressed in terms of his opinion.[76] If the members are equally divided and the chairman of the tribunal is not himself a member of the bench, the case is referred to the chairman and the decision of the tribunal is expressed in terms of the opinion of the chairman.[77]

The chairman of a tribunal is required to be a person with legal training and experience and is to be selected from among persons who are or have been judges of high courts or are qualified to be judges of high courts.[78] A person can be appointed as a judge of a high court if he is not less than forty years of age and has been an advocate of a high court for not less than ten years or has been a member of a civil service for not less than ten years having served for at least three years as a district judge in Pakistan or has held a judicial office in Pakistan for not less than ten years.[79] No statutory qualifications are prescribed for members. The president has full discretion to appoint members having qualifications prescribed by rules framed by the president.[80]

Service tribunals for the provinces were also constituted on the same lines. Each service tribunal consisted of a chairman and two members[81] appointed by the governor of the province concerned. In the provinces of NWFP and the Punjab, the chairmen of the service tribunals have been empowered to constitute benches consisting of the chairman alone, or one member only, or two members without the chairman; or the chairman with more than one member.[82] In the case of a difference of opinion among the members of a bench, its decision is expressed in terms of the view of the majority. Where members are equally divided, the matter may be referred to the member, not on the bench, by the chairman in order to break the tie.[83] If for some reason the matter cannot be referred to the chairman or the member (who did not sit on the bench equally divided in opinion), then the decision of the tribunal is expressed in terms of the opinion of the senior member of the bench.[84]

The chairmen of provincial service tribunals are required to have the same qualifications as are prescribed for the chairman of the federal service tribunals. Members of provincial tribunals are required to be civil servants who have held Class I or equivalent posts under the federal government or a provincial government. However, the minimum length of service required to qualify for appointment as a member of a provincial service tribunal varies from province to province.[85]

6.3.5 JURISDICTION OF SERVICE TRIBUNALS

Prior to promulgation of the Constitution of 1973, civil service tribunals were introduced in West Pakistan through ordinary legislation with their jurisdiction limited to hearing appeals against orders regarding fixation of seniority of government servants in the service of West Pakistan.[86] On the dissolution of the province of West Pakistan, this law was adopted as such in the provinces of Baluchistan and Sind. In the province of NWFP, a new law was promulgated on the subject with effect from 30 April 1971, repealing the West Pakistan statute.[87] Similarly, in the province of the Punjab, a new law was promulgated on the subject with effect from 27 October 1970, repealing the West Pakistan statute.[88] However, the repealing statutes in these two provinces saved the actions and orders passed under the repealed statute and all the appeals pending before the previous tribunal under the West Pakistan law in relation to the territories forming part of these two provinces were transferred to the tribunals formed under the new statutes.[89] The jurisdiction under the new statutes was also limited to the matters of seniority of government servants. The West Pakistan statute barred the jurisdiction of all courts in the matters within the exclusive jurisdiction of the tribunal.[90] The statutes of NWFP and the Punjab expressly extended this barring clause to the high courts as well.[91] Since there was no constitutional provision prior to the Constitution of 1973 for establishment of administrative courts and tribunals and barring the jurisdiction of courts in the matters within the exclusive jurisdiction of such courts and tribunals, therefore the provision in these statutes barring the jurisdiction of the high courts did not extend to their constitutional jurisdiction. The high courts could and did entertain constitutional petitions (writ petitions) against the decisions of the tribunals (constituted under the said statutes) provided that the order challenged was without lawful authority or wholly without jurisdiction.[92]

The jurisdiction of federal service tribunal extends to those government servants who fall within the definition of 'civil servant' as defined in the Civil Servants Act, 1973.[93] The Service Tribunals Act 1973 adopted the same definition.[94] In the beginning a difficulty arose in the matter of those persons who were dismissed or removed from service, compulsorily retired as a result of disciplinary action or otherwise, and also in the case of pensioners. The question was whether those persons, who had ceased to be civil servants, could seek redress from service tribunal. This difficulty was removed by an amendment[95] in the Service Tribunals Act, thus extending the jurisdiction of the service tribunal to those persons as well who had been formerly civil servants. The laws of civil servants in the provinces adopted definitions of 'civil servant' similar to those in the federal law. The definition of 'civil servant' in the four provinces is nearly identical. A 'civil servant' is defined as a person who is a member of a civil service of the province concerned or who holds a civil post in connection with the affairs of the province but does not include a person who is:

(i) on deputation to the province concerned from the federation or from other province or other authority (like autonomous bodies); or

(ii) employed on contract, or on work charged basis, or who is paid from contingencies; or

(iii) a 'worker', or 'workman' as defined in the Factories Act, 1934 (Act XXV of 1934) or the Workmen's Compensation Act, 1923 (Act VIII of 1923).[96]

This definition was adopted by the laws about service tribunals in the four provinces for the purpose of jurisdiction.[97] The difficulty discussed above, in relation to the federal service tribunal, also arose initially in the provinces and it was similarly resolved through amendments in the laws concerned.[98] It is thus self-evident that all government servants employed by the federal government or any provincial government, with the exception of those on deputation or work-charged basis, fall within the jurisdiction of the service tribunals. The exception on the basis of the Factories Act and the Workmen's Compensation Act only relates to a certain category of government employees primarily working in the railways department, or working in factories managed by the government, or employed by an autonomous corporation even if it is under the complete control of the government.[99] But where an employee in the railways department, who otherwise fell within the definition of 'workman', but at the relevant time he was performing functions which took him temporarily outside such definition, it was held that he was subject to the jurisdiction of service tribunal.[100] Employees of the federal or a provincial government can be declared by statute to be in the service of Pakistan and be deemed to be civil servants for purposes of the laws of service tribunals. Employees of Water and Power Development Authority (WAPDA), an autonomous statutory corporation under the federal government, were so declared[101] and its employees have been seeking redress from the federal service tribunal. Employees of corporations or institutions set up, established, managed or controlled by the federal government were declared to be in the service of Pakistan and persons, employed in such corporations who are removed from service or reverted to a lower post or grade, could seek redress from the federal service tribunal.[102] However, not all matters relating to the terms and conditions of service of such employees could be agitated before the service tribunal and even in the matter of removal from service or reduction in rank, only actions taken under Section 3 of the Corporation Employees' (Special Powers) Ordinance 1978 fell within the jurisdiction of the service tribunal.[103] Jurisdiction of the service tribunal does not extend to the employees of the Election Commission of Pakistan because they are governed by Article 221 of the constitution and rules framed thereunder and not under Article 240 of the constitution under which various legislation regarding civil servants has been passed.[104]

The persons locally employed by the Pakistani Missions abroad on temporary/contract employment are not civil servants. Such persons may be holding civil posts in connection with the affairs of the Federation but since they were not employed on regular basis through the usual procedure as prescribed for the appointment of civil servants under the Civil Servants Act, 1973 and the Rules framed thereunder, therefore such persons were not entitled to invoke the jurisdiction of the Federal Service Tribunal.[105]

Now the jurisdiction of the Federal Service Tribunal has been extended to the employees of all corporations or statutory bodies under any federal law.[106] This amendment was challenged before the Supreme Court which held the newly added Section 2A in Service Tribunal Act (STA) as *ultra vires* of Articles 240 and 260 of the constitution. The Supreme Court held as under:[107]

> Under Article 260 of the Constitution, a person can be declared to be in service of Pakistan if his duties have a nexus with the affairs of the Federation, meaning thereby that a person who is playing an active role in the performance of sovereign functions of the State and exercises public powers can legitimately claim to be in the service of Pakistan . . . Parliament, undoubtedly can declare any service to be a service of Pakistan but subject to the condition that such declaration should not be based on legal fiction, as done in Section 2-A, Service Tribunals Act, 1973 whereby through a deeming clause, a person of a government controlled corporation in terms of Section 2-A Service Tribunals Act, 1973 has been declared to be in 'Service of Pakistan' and for such reason he shall be deemed to be a civil servant; secondly, conditions under Article 260 of the Constitution with regard to having nexus/connection with the affairs of the Federation have not been fulfilled.

> By means of a legal fiction, such status has been conferred upon them notwithstanding the fact that stately their cases are not covered by the definition of a 'civil servant' and on account of this legal fiction a discrimination has been created between persons who have been excluded from the definition of civil servant as per section 2(1)(b) of the Civil Servants Act, 1973, whereas the persons in the employment of government controlled corporations, either created by or under a statute, most of them incorporated under the Companies Ordinance 1984, have been declared to be in the service of Pakistan and deemed

to be civil servants. Thus, it has created a classification which does not seem to be reasonable.

It is therefore held:

(1) Section 2-A of the STA, 1973 is partially *ultra vires* of Articles 240 and 260 of the constitution to the extent of the category of employees, whose terms and conditions of service have not been determined by the federal legislature and by a deeming clause they cannot be treated civil servants as defined under Section 2(1)(b) of the CSA, 1973 and they are not engaged in the affairs of the federation.

(2) Section 2-A of the STA, 1973 cannot be enforced in the absence of amendment in the definition of the civil servant under Section 2(1)(b) of the CSA, 1973.

(3) The cases of employees under Section 2-A, STA, 1973, who do not fall within the definition of a civil servant as defined in Section 2(1)(b) of the CSA shall have no remedy before the service tribunal, functioning under Article 212 of the constitution and they would be free to avail an appropriate remedy.

Service tribunals were given exclusive jurisdiction in respect of matters relating to terms and conditions of service of civil servants, including disciplinary matters.[108] Any civil servant aggrieved by any final order, original or appellate, made by a departmental authority in respect of any of the terms and conditions of his service, can prefer an appeal within six months of the establishment of the tribunal or within thirty days of the communication of such order to him, whichever is later.[109] 'Departmental authority' is defined as an authority competent to make an order in respect of any of the terms and conditions of civil servants. Where appeal, review or representation is provided to the civil servant under any law or rules framed thereunder against a final order of a departmental authority, to a higher departmental authority or the same departmental authority (in case of review), then no appeal to the tribunal lies unless decision has been finally taken on such departmental appeal, review or representation or at least a period of ninety days has elapsed from the date of institution of such departmental appeal, review or representation. There was initially some confusion about the period of limitation for filing of appeal before the service tribunals which has since been settled by the Supreme Court and it has been held that a civil servant may institute a departmental appeal or application for review or representation, as the case may be, within thirty days of the communication of the order to him and wait for ninety days from the date of such institution. He then has thirty days (from the expiry of the ninety days) to file appeal before the tribunal.[110] No appeal lies with the tribunals if an order or decision of a departmental authority was made before the 1 July 1969.[111] Appeal also does not lie with a tribunal against an order or decision of a departmental authority determining the fitness or otherwise of a person to be appointed to or hold a particular post or to be promoted to a higher grade. A High Court could entertain constitutional petition involving question of fitness of civil servant for promotion.[112] Although a Tribunal could not go into the fitness of civil servant for promotion, yet it can go into the question of eligibility of civil servant for promotion because eligibility is a right and part of terms and conditions of service.[113] The right to appeal before the services tribunal is available against the original as well as appellate order of departmental authority. This right cannot be abridged to only original order and not appellate order.[114]

6.3.6 SERVICE TRIBUNALS FOR SUBORDINATE JUDICIARY

Service Tribunals were set up for judicial officers in the subordinate judiciary under the provincial laws. Such a Tribunal was set up in the Punjab under Punjab Subordinate Judiciary Service Tribunal Act, 1991. Similar tribunals were set up in other provinces under Khyber Pakhtoonkhwa Subordinate Judiciary Service Act, 1991 and Balochistan Subordinate Judiciary Service Act, 1989. The Tribunals constituted under these laws consist of senior judges of the respective High Courts. After the Islamabad High Court was set up, a tribunal has been constituted under Islamabad Subordinate Judiciary Service Tribunal Act, 2016. In the province of Sindh, no separate law for constitution of such tribunal was passed. However the Sindh Subordinate Judiciary Service Tribunal (Procedure)

Rules were framed under the Sindh Service Tribunal Act, 1973. Under these procedure rules, a Tribunal consisting of judges of the High Court of Sindh has been constituted to deal with terms and conditions of the judges of subordinate judiciary in Sindh.

The Supreme Cout held that an informant as complainant against a judicial officer need not be made a party in the proceedings before a Tribunal. Disciplinary proceedings against a judicial officers, which are essentially between an employer and employee cannot be made contentious by an outsider.[115] Since the Tribunal has been conferred the power of civil courts under the law therefore, it can pass any appropriate order including the order of sending the case back to the departmental authority for decision afresh after *de novo* enquiry.[116] A judicial officer cannot be removed from service even during the period of probation without assigning any reason. Inclusion of "no reason clause" in the appointment letter did not mean that the authority had been entrusted with unfettered authority to terminate any judicial officer without any material on the record.[117]

6.3.7 REACTION TO SERVICE TRIBUNALS

The introduction of service tribunals was not initially welcomed especially by civil servants. After all, they were accustomed to constitutional protection ever since the independence of Pakistan. They considered themselves as a secure and privileged class and suspected that Mr Z.A. Bhutto's promise for bringing administrative reforms was in fact a political gimmick with the underlying object to subjugate the bureaucracy to his arbitrary will, stripped of constitutional protection and jurisdiction of ordinary courts. Civil servants regarded these tribunals as an affront to their independence and spared no effort to avoid their jurisdiction. The fact that these tribunals had civil servants as members, who had no security of tenure and that the executive branch of the government dealt with their appointments, transfers and removal further fuelled their suspicion and distrust. There was a clear tendency on the part of civil servants to invoke the constitutional jurisdiction of high courts in matters relating to disciplinary actions and other terms and conditions of their service. This state of affairs obviously necessitated determination of the question of jurisdiction of these tribunals.

The legal battle that ensued over the question of jurisdiction of the service tribunals stands more or less concluded. Their jurisdiction was vehemently contested by the civil servants and, with the assistance of some of the ablest lawyers in Pakistan, they put forward the proposition that these tribunals are of limited jurisdiction and that their establishment has not fettered, in any way, the constitutional jurisdiction[118] of high courts. This proposition, raised repeatedly before Supreme Court of Pakistan and provincial high courts, was generally based upon the following rationale:

(i) These tribunals are, in their nature, quasi judicial bodies meant to go into the questions of fact only and could not go into the questions of law.

(ii) These tribunals cannot go into questions of *vires* of a statute or rules framed thereunder.

(iii) The constitutional jurisdiction of the High Courts can be exercised where an order is passed *mala fide*, without jurisdiction or is in the nature of *coram non judice* or *ab initio void*.

(iv) These tribunals, being creation of ordinary laws, cannot oust the constitutional jurisdiction of the high courts.

These propositions have not found favour with Supreme Court of Pakistan. However, where any Service Tribunal is not in existence or not functional due to vacancy in the office of its Chairman, the constitutional jurisdiction of a High Court can be invoked because litigants could not be left in vacuum for an indefinite period. The court recognized the applications of the principle of *"ubi jus ibi remedium* (where there is a right there is a remedy) being applicable under Articles 4 and 10A of the Constitution.[119]

6.4 COURT BATTLES OVER THE JURISDICTION OF THE SERVICE TRIBUNALS

6.4.1 DETERMINATION OF THEIR JURISDICTION

The Supreme Court of Pakistan and the high courts, after detailed consideration of the above arguments, have repelled them. It has been held that the constitutional jurisdiction of the high court is completely ousted regarding matters falling within the ambit of jurisdiction conferred on these tribunals,[120] and the disputes relating to the terms and conditions of service of the civil servants were held to be in the exclusive jurisdiction of the service tribunals.[121] The scope of the jurisdiction of these tribunals in relation to the terms and conditions of service of civil servants have been held much wider than the constitutional jurisdiction of the High Courts.[122] The service tribunals have jurisdiction rather obligation to decide all questions of law and facts raised before them.[123] They are competent to go into all issues of law and can strike down any piece of subordinate legislation found *ultra vires* of any law.[124] They have jurisdiction to decide the questions of *mala fide*, without jurisdiction, *coram non judice* and *void ab initio*.[125] Baluchistan High Court, after analysing provisions of Article 212 of the Constitution of 1973 and provisions of laws of the service tribunals, arrived at the conclusion that an appeal does not lie before a tribunal in the following cases:[126]

(i) when the impugned order was passed before 1 July 1969;[127]

(ii) when the civil servant punished is not a 'civil servant' for the reason of his exclusion from the definition of 'civil servant' in Section 2(1)(b) of Civil Servants Act;[128]

(iii) when the order is not a final order;[129]

(iv) when the punishment is other than the punishment of dismissal, removal, compulsory retirement, reduction to a lower post or time scale;[130]

(v) when the impugned order relates to a person's fitness to hold a post or to be appointed to such post or to be promoted to a high post or grade;[131] and

(vi) when the order is not passed by a competent departmental authority and is for such reason void.[132]

Appeal before the service tribunal has been held invalid if it has been filed without exhausting the department remedies of appeal, review or representation, as provided under a law or rules framed thereunder, against the order challenged.[133] When the constitution requires particular kind of controversy to be decided by exclusive forum, the mandate of the constitution could not be allowed to be defeated by merely choosing to approach different forum.[134]

It has been consistently held by the Supreme Court and the high courts that the service tribunals are courts of exclusive jurisdiction and are fully competent to decide all questions of law and fact that arise in the controversies before them including the questions of *coram non judice, mala fide, void ab initio* and without jurisdiction.

6.5 HOW INDEPENDENT ARE SERVICE TRIBUNALS?

The service tribunals in Pakistan have been functioning for more than twenty-five years and have assumed an important role in the judicial systems of Pakistan. However, their independence as judicial bodies has never been beyond question as they are yet to attain the respect, prestige and credibility of independent judicial bodies. Some of the factors that are important in determining independence of judicial bodies are enumerated below:

(i) Provisions regarding appointment and removal of judges;
(ii) Security of tenure of office of judges;
(iii) Independence from the control and influence of the executive; and
(iv) Control over execution of the orders passed.

The chairman and members of the federal service tribunal are appointed by the president of Pakistan on such terms and conditions that he may determine.[135] The law does not provide for tenure of office of the chairman and members and no procedure for their removal has been prescribed. It is, thus, clear that the federal executive, acting through the president, has complete discretion to remove the chairman or any member of the tribunal at any time without any cause. There are no provisions empowering the tribunal to ensure the execution of its orders and it has no power to punish any person for contempt of court for disobeying or disregarding its orders. It has been commonly noticed that orders of the tribunal, when they are to the distaste of the government, any of the government departments or their functionaries, remain unimplemented for years together. For the last some years, a liaison officer in the establishment division of the federal government has been appointed to assist in the execution of the orders of the tribunal but improvement brought about is not very significant.

The chairman and members of a provincial tribunal are appointed by the governor of the province concerned. In Baluchistan and NWFP, the terms and conditions are to be determined by the governor concerned.[136] In Punjab, the law originally provided that the term of office of chairman and a member of a tribunal would be four years. The chairman or a member could be removed from office earlier than the expiry of his term by the governor on the recommendation of a committee of three persons (one of whom to be a judge of a high court and two civil servants not below the rank of deputy secretary to the provincial development). Such removal could only be effective if the finding of the committee would be that the chairman, or as the case may be, the member was incapable of performing the duties of office by reason of physical and mental incapacity or had been guilty of misconduct.[137] These provisions did not last very long and, in less than a year's time, were substituted by an amendment in the law, bringing the provisions in accordance with those of the federal law and provincial laws of Baluchistan and NWFP on the subject.[138] The terms and conditions of the appointment and removal of the chairman and members are to be determined by the Governor without any statutory guidelines or controls.[139] In Sind, the history of the law in this respect has been just the opposite to that of the Punjab. In the original law,[140] the provisions for appointment and removal of the chairman and members of the tribunal were more or less identical to provisions in federal law and provincial laws of

Baluchistan, NWFP, and Punjab (as it stands after the amendment of 1975). The terms and conditions of appointment (and removal) of the chairman and members were to be determined by the provincial government without any statutory control or guidelines. However, an amendment was brought about in the original law in 1974 and term of office of chairman and members was fixed at three years and the government is empowered to extend the same for such further period as it may deem fit.[141] The removal of chairman or members before the expiry of their terms of office, was made subject to certain statutory requirements.[142] Where the provincial government considers that chairman or member of the tribunal is unable to perform his duties because of physical or mental incapacity or is guilty of misconduct, it can appoint a committee consisting of three persons headed by a person who is qualified to be appointed as chairman of tribunal, to enquire into the matter.[143] The committee, which has powers of a civil court for purpose of such enquiry, is required to hold a thorough enquiry and submit report to the government.[144] In case the committee is of the view that the chairman or, as the case may be, a member is incapable of performing his functions or is guilty of misconduct,[145] the government can remove such chairman or member before the expiry of his terms of office.[146] The provincial government, through an amendment, was temporarily empowered until 31 December 1977 to curtail the term of office of chairman or of any member.[147]

It can therefore be concluded that the chairman and members of the tribunals (with the exception of Sind) can be removed from office on free will of the executive. They are, therefore, not free from control and influence of the executive. They are without powers to ensure execution of their orders. In these circumstances, these tribunals cannot be deemed to be independent judicial bodies.

6.6 APPEAL AGAINST DECISIONS OF TRIBUNALS

Appeals lie to the Supreme Court of Pakistan from the decisions of administrative tribunals not as a matter of right but on leave only if a case involves a substantial question of law of public importance.[148] The Supreme Court does not interfere in appeal against order passed by a service tribunal in exercise of discretion vested in it like condonation of delay in filing an appeal before the tribunal,[149] provided that the view taken by a tribunal, in circumstances of a case, is not found to be arbitrary or perverse so as to be an abuse of its jurisdiction. The Supreme Court does not interfere with it in the exercise of its appellate jurisdiction.[150] Similarly, decisions of service tribunals on questions of fact are not interfered with.[151] Where an order of tribunal is fairly detailed, showing consideration of every aspect of the case and pleas taken by the parties, such order is not normally interfered with.[152] The decisions of tribunals, therefore, are final on questions of fact. On questions of law as well, the decisions of tribunals are final unless the Supreme Court is satisfied that, in the first place, the question of law raised is of substantial nature and, secondly, that it is of public importance at the same time. These two conditions are rarely met and, therefore, chances of grant of leave to appeal by the Supreme Court are rather rare in actual practice. Another reason is that the Supreme Court, being at the top of the hierarchy of courts and tribunals in Pakistan, does not have time for controversies raised by individuals unless such controversies are likely to affect a large number of cases which call for authoritative pronouncement at the highest judicial level. The result is that grievances of persons against wrong findings of fact (howsoever perverse) and findings on questions of law (which is neither substantial nor of public importance), remains generally unredressed.[153] A new plea cannot be allowed to be raised for the first time in a petition for leave to appeal before the Supreme Court.[154] Point neither taken by the appellant in memorandum of appeal before tribunal nor taken in appeal before the departmental appellate authority cannot be agitated at belated stage in appeal before the Supreme Court.[155] No appeal can be entertained by the Supreme Court against interlocutory orders passed by the service tribunal.[156]

6.7 Experience with Tribunals

Experience with service tribunals over a quarter century can best be described as mixed. On the one hand, civil servants have been extended the opportunity to agitate all questions of law and fact against orders they are aggrieved of, which was not the case previously because the constitutional jurisdiction of high courts was restricted to the actions taken illegally and without lawful authority. A finding of fact was not interfered with. The tribunals, in some cases, have given liberal legal interpretations which have widened the scope of relief available to civil servants.[157] There are a large number of cases in which relief has been provided by these tribunals to civil servants who had been wronged.

Although certain chairmen and members of the tribunals have shown strong tendency to grant relief liberally and to base their decisions on recognised principles of law, yet factors like lack of security of tenure of office and want of independence from the executive have hampered their functioning and undermined their credibility, effectiveness, authority and prestige. In one instance, the federal government reacted very strongly to the decisions of a bench of federal service tribunal consisting of two members, namely Dr A.Q.K. Afghan and Mr N.A. Chaudhry, who passed orders striking down orders of dismissal or removal of certain government servants under Removal from Service (Special provisions) Regulation (Martial Law Regulation 58 of 1970) and ordered their reinstatement.[158] Through an amendment in the provisional constitution, all orders and actions under Martial Law Regulation 58 of 1970, which were set aside by service tribunals, were validated, all proceedings pending before the tribunal or any other court in relation to the said regulation were held to have abated and decisions already given by tribunals were declared null and void and of no effect whatsoever.[159] The matter did not stop there. The two aforementioned members, being senior civil servants themselves, were abruptly removed from service tribunal, and transferred to unimportant posts.[160] One of them, Dr A.Q.K. Afghan, was later removed from service without any show cause notice.[161] However,

Dr Afghan had the audacity to file an appeal before service tribunal against order of his own removal from service, which was also heard by a bench of two members (one who had apparently replaced him and Mr Chaudhry). These members had of course grown wiser and thought it safe for themselves to dismiss the appeal of the erstwhile member of the tribunal.[162] It was argued on behalf of Dr Afghan that since the law does not provide any fixed tenure of office of the chairman and members of tribunal, therefore, their tenure of office is indefinite and they could not be transferred or removed from office. This argument was rejected in the strongest terms as unreasonable, anomalous and absurd.[163] In another instance, the chairman of the Punjab Service Tribunal, who gave certain decisions to the distaste of the provincial government in the Punjab, was abruptly removed.[164] It is, therefore, clear, that the chairman and members of the tribunals should stay on the right side of the government in power and should avoid offending government, particularly in sensitive matters.

As discussed above, except for chairmen of the tribunals, members are drawn from among senior civil servants who do not have any legal training. Some of the appointees had some exposure to quasi-judicial offices at some stage of their careers as civil servants while others lacked even such minimal exposure. Their lack of knowledge and experience in principles of law is generally reflected in the quality of judgments produced by them. After amendments in laws for service tribunals allowing for formation of benches, it is frequently found that a bench is formed consisting of two members only with both of whom having no legal education and training. Although some of the judgments of these tribunals can be happily compared with the judgments of the superior courts but others are not very presentable. At times, tenor of the judgment is more like a bureaucrat's note rather than a judicial pronouncement. Misunderstanding and misconception of principles of law as laid down in statutes and precedents of superior courts are easily noticeable. The federal service tribunal, in one of its judgments affecting a large number of cases, held that it could not exercise its jurisdiction because the law,[165] under which the orders challenged were passed, was subsequently validated by constitutional provisions.[166] The tribunal failed to notice or properly construe the leading judgment of the Supreme Court of Pakistan concerning these constitutional provisions.[167] The federal service tribunal, in its judgment passed on 20 November 1977, did not consider the leading judgments of the Supreme Court given in 1973 and 1974.[168] In another case, a member of the federal service tribunal recorded his dissent against the majority view of the chairman and another member (which was based upon proper application of recognised principles of law) and proceeded to write his opinion on his own notions of law (based upon his self-assumed better understanding of the English language assisted by some English dictionaries) but in total ignorance of recognised principles of law.[169] There are many other instances of poor or sub-standard judgments of these tribunals especially from members without judicial or legal experience or training.

6.8 NEED FOR REFORMS

It cannot be denied that the performance of service tribunals in Pakistan leaves much to be desired and reforms are urgently needed. Before any reforms are suggested, it would be necessary to identify specific areas of the law where action is needed immediately. No proposal can be deemed final for the reason that problems will keep cropping up from time to time and the recommendations at this point in time can at best be based upon the experience with these tribunals over more than a decade. Some of the principal problems with the tribunals can be identified and discussed below.

6.8.1 COMPOSITION OF TRIBUNALS

As discussed above, all the tribunals have chairmen who are required to have legal or judicial training. Members, however, are to be drawn from among civil servants with little or no legal or judicial training. No efforts have been made to find civil servants with legal acumen and exposure to judicial training.[170] Sometimes, a judicial member is appointed to service tribunal, in addition to the chairman, but such practice has not been consistently followed.[171] Each tribunal has either two or three members on it. The result is that a professional judge, that is the chairman, is outnumbered by lay judges, i.e. the members. Consequently, quality of judgments suffers and confidence of the litigants before these tribunals is further eroded.

Recently, it has become common practice to appoint retired civil servants to the federal service tribunal. This has caused further deterioration in the standard and quality of proceedings and judgments of the tribunals which has further undermined the confidence of civil servants in these tribunals. It is generally believed that retired civil servants who are appointed to the tribunals are interested in saving their jobs rather than doing justice to civil servants litigating before them. In one of the laws, Service Tribunals Act, 1973, it was provided that where there was difference of opinion between the chairman and a member of the Tribunal, the opinion of the chairman would prevail. This provision was held invalid by the Federal Shariat Court holding that the law, granting double weight to the opinion of the Chairman and to let him decide the fate of a judicial matter solely on his strength was repugnant to the Injunction of Holy Quran. It was also held that such a law was also invalid because it violates the concept of equality because equality among human beings was enshrined In the Holy Quran and Sunnah of the Holy Prophet (PBUH).[172]

6.8.2 SECURITY OF TENURE OF OFFICE FOR CHAIRMAN AND MEMBERS

It has already been discussed that with the exception of Sind, laws relating to these tribunals do not provide for a fixed tenure of office for the chairman and members of these tribunals. There is no statutory guarantee against their removal or premature retirement and they serve at the pleasure of the executive of federation and provinces. Their sense of insecurity is sometimes reflected in their judgments.[173] It cannot be over emphasised that if these tribunals are to be allowed to administer justice fearlessly, then a fixed term of office with guarantee against arbitrary removal during such term should be provided in the laws relating to these tribunals.

6.8.3 INDEPENDENCE OF TRIBUNALS FROM THE EXECUTIVE

The service tribunals have not so far developed into independent judicial bodies. The appointment and removal of the chairman and members of these tribunals are entirely in the hands of the executive of the federation or provinces, as the case may be. The executive has virtually unrestricted and unlimited choice in the matter of appointment of chairmen and members of tribunals, and such choice has frequently been exercised in a fanciful manner.[174] Some of the important causes of lack of independence of these tribunals are the want of a fixed period of office and absence of statutory guarantees against arbitrary removal.

6.8.4 POWER TO PASS INTERIM ORDERS

It has been provided in all the statutes, federal as well as provincial relating to service tribunals that appeals before a service tribunal can only be filed after exhausting remedies provided before the department concerned by way of appeal, review or representation. After initiation of departmental remedy, the aggrieved person is bound to wait for 90 days before he may approach a service tribunal unless the departmental authority takes a decision earlier than that on departmental appeal, review or representation, as the case may be. In that case, appeal before tribunal can be filed on receipt of the decision of departmental authority. Appeals filed before such expiry of time or receipt of departmental order are premature.[175] Initiation of departmental remedy does not suspend *ipso facto* the challenged administrative act or order and there is hardly any instance that the departmental authority or appellate departmental authority has suspended such act or order. The net result is that departmental authority concerned gets ample opportunity to implement its administrative act or order, howsoever illegal and unsustainable it may be. One of the common reasons for invoking constitutional jurisdiction of high courts is the possibility of obtaining interim order of suspension of challenged administrative act or order provided the high court agrees to exercise its constitutional jurisdiction. Although there is no specific provision in any of the laws relating to service tribunals regarding passing of interim or interlocutory orders, yet interlocutory orders suspending the challenged order or act have been passed on the basis of the legal principle that the court that has jurisdiction to pass a final order in a matter can also pass any incidental or supplemental order in the proceedings pending before it.[176] However, the statutory requirement to wait for ninety days after filing departmental remedy before approaching service tribunal has rendered the exercise of such jurisdiction as redundant in most cases. The result is that injury, although temporary, is caused to the aggrieved person and, at times, such injury is substantial to the terms and conditions of his service. This situation requires to be remedied.

6.8.5 INEFFECTIVE DEPARTMENTAL REMEDIES

The law requires that a civil servant cannot approach a service tribunal unless he avails himself of departmental remedies provided by law or rules applicable to him before higher departmental authority and that 90 days should elapse from the date of initiation of such a remedy. This provision was apparently well intentioned and the purpose was to resolve a dispute or satisfy a grievance within the administrative machinery without having to go into contentious litigation before the service tribunal. But unfortunately, this provision has been severely abused. This provision has been used by departmental authorities to delay the matter so the order under challenge becomes operative. Naturally the aggrieved person is frustrated by inaction on the part of the departmental authorities. An action against a civil servant whether of disciplinary nature or concerning some other terms and conditions of his service, is supposed to be taken by the competent authority under applicable rules on its own but in reality such action is only taken after due consultation with the higher authorities, who are to ultimately hear departmental appeals. Hence higher departmental authority has, in most cases, already made up its mind and there is no possibility of obtaining any relief from it. It is also frequently noticed that such higher departmental authorities are so remote or indifferent that they do not find or even care to find time to apply their independent mind to the case so as to decide objectively. That is the reason why more than 90 per cent of departmental appeals are not decided within the 90 days allowed for the purpose and the departmental remedies have just been turned into a frustrating waiting game. In majority of decisions that are taken, mostly the higher departmental authorities do not apply their minds and ask for comments from their subordinates who have already taken the decision under challenge. In such cases, a note is put up from below which is obviously adverse to the applicant and tends to justify the decision already taken. The appellate authority does not generally take the trouble to differ with the note and an order rejecting the departmental appeal is communicated in very brief and mechanical terms, without assigning reasons for the same. The only time an applicant gets any relief is when he happens to personally approach such appellate authority who is favourably pre-disposed towards him through personal recommendations or, may be at times for some other consideration.

6.8.6 LACK OF AUTHORITY FOR EXECUTION OF ORDERS

As discussed above, service tribunals have not been vested with authority to execute their own orders. They have no power to punish for contempt of court. Consequently, their orders are frequently ignored or are at times, flouted blatantly. This weakness has greatly undermined the authority, prestige, and public confidence in these tribunals. Reforms are required in this respect as well.

6.8.7 RIGHT OF APPEAL AND REVIEW

As discussed above, laws relating to the service tribunals create only one service tribunal for federal civil servants and one service tribunal for each province. No hierarchy of tribunals providing for appeals or revision against orders of the lower tribunal to higher tribunal has been set up. Even power to review their own orders has not been conferred on these tribunals.[177] The appeal provided against decisions of service tribunals is restricted to substantial questions of law of public importance. It lies in the Supreme Court of Pakistan only on grant of special leave and not as a matter of right. The Supreme Court, being the highest court in the country for all jurisdictions, is already overburdened and chances of grant of leave to appeal is minimum. Resultantly, there is at times, practically no remedy by way of appeal against or review of erroneous, illegal, and fanciful orders of tribunals. Reforms are urgently needed for providing real and meaningful right of appeal and review.

6.9 Administrative Tribunals for Civil Servants in India

6.9.1 Constitutional provision for creation of administrative tribunals

Originally, in the Constitution of India, there was no provision similar to Article 212 of the 1973 Constitution of Pakistan until 1976. Therefore, all disputes concerning recruitment and conditions of service of persons in government service central, state or local were adjudicated upon by the ordinary courts. However, in 1976, by the Constitution (Forty-second Amendment) Act 1976, Part XIV-A was added to the constitution containing Articles 323-A and 323-B authorising the parliament and state legislatures to constitute administrative tribunals for service matters and for certain other matters. Article 323-A deals with the creation of tribunals for civil servants. The justification of Article 323-A lies in the fact that massive case law had been generated in India in relation to service matters and too much time of the courts was being consumed in such type of litigation.[178]

This constitutional amendment was passed during the period of state of emergency during the government of Indira Gandhi. After the defeat of Indira Gandhi's Congress Party in the Lok Sabha elections of 1977, an effort was made to omit Articles 323-A and 323-B through the 45th Amendment Bill, 1978 but it did not succeed because of opposition in the Rajya Sabha (the Upper House).[179]

These two Articles, however, are not self executory, but require legislation to implement them. These are only enabling provisions that provide for broad framework for the establishment of the tribunals. An interesting aspect of Article 323-A is that the parliament has been given power to establish service tribunals not only for central government employees but also for employees of the state, local governments and government corporations. This is quite a drastic change in the existing system where each of these units (states, local governments, and government corporations) has control over disciplinary proceedings relating to its employees.[180] Other features of Article 323-A can be described as follows:

(i) A law made by the parliament in this regard can provide for the establishment of an administrative tribunal for the Union and a separate administrative tribunal for each state or for two or more states.[181]

(ii) Such law may specify the jurisdiction, powers (including the power to punish for contempt) and authority which may be exercised by each of such tribunals.[182]

(iii) Such law may provide for the procedure including provisions as to limitation and rules of evidence to be followed by such tribunals.[183]

(iv) Such law may exclude the jurisdiction of all courts, except the jurisdiction of the Supreme Court under Article 136, to hear appeals through special tribunals, with respect to the dispute or complaints within the jurisdiction of such tribunals.[184]

(v) Such law may provide for the transfer to such tribunals cases which are pending before a court or other authority at the time of establishment of each tribunal.[185]

(vi) Incidental provisions for the effective functioning of such tribunals may be included in such laws.[186]

(vii) The provisions of this article override any provision in the constitution or any other law, to the contrary.[187]

Article 323-B has the same features, as described above for Article 323-A, with the following differences:

(i) Legislative power is divided between the union and state legislatures in the matter of establishment of tribunals according to their respective legislative competence over each of the subjects.[188]

(ii) Matters which mean adjudication or trial by such tribunals of any disputes, complaints or offences are: taxation, foreign exchange, customs, labour disputes, land reforms, elections, essential goods, and urban property. Their jurisdiction may also include offences and matters incidental to such matters.[189]

(iii) Appropriate legislature is empowered to establish a hierarchy of tribunals relating to each subject enumerated in Clause (2) of Article 323-B. This is in clear contrast to Article 323-A which provides for only one tribunal and no hierarchy for the Union and one tribunal for each state or two or more states together.

6.10 Law of Administrative Tribunals

Despite the constitutional amendment in 1976, nothing was done in this regard till 1985.[190] In 1985, the parliament passed the Administrative Tribunals Act (No. 13 of 1985). This law has been passed under Article 323-A of the constitution because it deals exclusively with tribunals for adjudication of service disputes and not for other matters specified under Article 323-B. This law can be discussed from the aspects of establishment of tribunals, their composition and benches, terms and conditions of office of their chairmen, vice chairmen, and members, and their jurisdiction and procedure. These aspects are separately discussed below:

6.10.1 ESTABLISHMENT OF TRIBUNALS

The Act provides for the establishment of a central administrative tribunal, state administrative tribunals, and joint administrative tribunals. The central government has been empowered to establish a central administrative tribunal by notification.[191] The central government on request from a state government may, by notification, establish an administrative tribunal for the state.[192] Two or more states are allowed to enter into an agreement to have a joint administrative tribunal and, on approval of such agreement by the central government, establish a joint administrative tribunal for such states. Such agreement is required to contain provisions in regard to participation of the signatory states in making appointment of the chairman, vice chairman, and members of the tribunal, places of sitting of the benches thereof, and apportionment of expenditure.[193]

6.10.2 COMPOSITION AND BENCHES OF TRIBUNALS

Each tribunal is to consist of a chairman and such number of vice chairmen and other members as the appropriate government may deem fit.[194] 'Appropriate government' means the central government in relation to the central administrative tribunal or a joint administrative tribunal and the state government in relation to a state administrative tribunal.[195] The jurisdiction, powers and authority of a tribunal can be exercised by benches thereof.[196] A bench is to be presided by the chairman, or in his absence, by a vice chairman and consist of at least two other members.[197] The bench, presided over by the chairman, is to be the principal bench and the other benches are known as additional benches.[198] The principal bench would be exercising concurrent jurisdiction with additional benches and is not contemplated to be an appellate bench. The chairman may also act as the chairman of any additional bench, may transfer the vice chairman of any additional bench, may transfer the vice chairman or other members from one bench to another bench, and may authorise the vice chairman or other member appointed to one bench to discharge also the functions of the vice chairman or other member of another bench.[199] A bench can function in the absence of its chairman or a member. In the absence of its chairman, the senior member would preside the bench.[200] The chairman or a member, on authorisation from the chairman, can function as an additional bench consisting of a single member and exercise the jurisdiction, powers and authority of the tribunal in respect of cases or classes of cases as specified by the chairman by general or special order.[201] The chairman has the authority to withdraw any case pending with a bench of single member and transfer it to a bench of three members.[202] The appropriate government is to specify the places of sitting of the principal bench and other benches.[203]

6.10.3 QUALIFICATIONS FOR APPOINTMENT AS CHAIRMAN, VICE CHAIRMAN, AND MEMBERS OF THE TRIBUNALS

A person who is, or has been, a judge of a high court; or has, for at least two years, held office of vice chairman; or has, for at least two years, held the post of a secretary to the Government of India or any other post under the central or a state government carrying a scale of pay not less than that of a secretary to the Government of India can be appointed as chairman of a tribunal.[204] A person who is, or has been, a judge of a high court, or has, for at least two years, held the post of a secretary to the Government of India or any other post under the central or a state government carrying a scale of pay not less than that of a secretary to the Government of India, or has, for a period of not less than three years, held office as a member, can be appointed as vice chairman.[205] A person who is, or has been, or is qualified to be, a judge of a high court; or has, for at least two years, held the post of an additional secretary to the Government of India or any other post under the central or a state government carrying a scale of pay not less than that of an additional secretary to the Government of India; or has for at least three years, held the post of joint secretary to the Government of India or any other post under the central or a state government carrying a scale of pay not less than that of a joint secretary to the Government of India, can be appointed as a member.[206] The president of India appoints the chairman, vice chairman and members of the central administrative tribunal, a state administrative tribunal (after consultation with the governor of the concerned state) and a joint administrative tribunal (subject to the terms of the agreement between the participating state governments) and after consultation with the governors of the concerned states.[207] In the absence of the chairman, due to his death, resignation, illness or otherwise, the vice chairman or in case there are two or more, then the one notified by the appropriate government, would discharge functions of the chairman until the date the chairman resumes his duty or is appointed.[208]

6.10.4 TERMS AND CONDITIONS OF OFFICE OF THE CHAIRMAN, VICE CHAIRMAN, AND MEMBERS OF THE TRIBUNALS

The chairman, vice chairman or members of tribunals hold office for a term of five years or until they attain the age of superannuation which is 65 years, in the case of chairman or vice chairman, and 62 years, in the case of a member, whichever occurs earlier.[209] The chairman, vice chairman or any member cannot be removed from office except by an order made by the president on the ground of proven misbehaviour or incapacity after an inquiry made by a judge of the Supreme Court in which such chairman, vice chairman or other member had been informed of the charges against him and given a reasonable opportunity of being heard in respect of those charges.[210]

The chairman of the central administrative tribunal is ineligible for further appointment either under the Government of India or under the government of a state.[211] The chairman of a state administrative tribunal or a joint administrative tribunal can be appointed as the chairman, or vice chairman or member of the central administrative tribunal or as the chairman of any other state administrative tribunal or joint administrative tribunal, but not for any other employment either under the Government of India or under the government of a state.[212] The vice chairman of the central administrative tribunal can be appointed as the chairman of that tribunal or as the chairman or vice chairman of any state administrative tribunal or joint administrative tribunal, but not for any other employment either under the Government of India or under the government of a state.[213] The vice chairman of a state administrative tribunal or a joint administrative tribunal can be appointed as the chairman of that tribunal or as the chairman or vice chairman of the central administrative tribunal or of any other state administrative tribunal or joint administrative tribunal, but not for any other employment either under the Government of India or under the government of a state.[214] A member of any tribunal can be appointed as the chairman or vice chairman of such tribunal or as the chairman, vice chairman or member of any other tribunal, but not for any other employment either under the Government of India or under the government of a state.[215] The chairman, vice chairman or member, is not allowed to appear, act or plead before any tribunal of which he was chairman, vice chairman or other member.[216]

6.10.5 JURISDICTION OF ADMINISTRATIVE TRIBUNALS

Jurisdiction of administrative tribunals extends to 'service matters' which, in relation to a person, means all matters relating to conditions of his service in connection with affairs of the Union or of any state or of any local or other authority within the territory of India or under control of the Government of India, or of any corporation owned or controlled by the government. These matters include remuneration (including allowances), pension, and other retirement benefits; tenure including confirmation, seniority, promotion, reversion, premature retirement, and superannuation; leave of any kind; disciplinary matters; or any other matter whatsoever.[217] Persons who are subject to such jurisdiction of central administrative tribunal are members of any All-India Service; or persons appointed to any civil service of the Union or any civil posts under the Union, or civilians appointed to any defence services or posts connected with defence; or person whose services have been placed by a state government with any local or other authority or any corporation or other body, at the disposal of the central government for such appointment; or persons in the employment of any corporation as notified by the central government, owned or controlled by the central government.[218] The jurisdiction of central administrative tribunal also extends to recruitment, and matters concerning recruitment of the categories of the government employees mentioned before.[219] The jurisdiction of the central administrative tribunal could also extend to matters enumerated above in relation to employees of any local or other authority within the territory of India or corporation owned or controlled by the central government through notification by the central government and such jurisdiction would apply with effect from the date specified in such notification.[220] Similar provisions have been made regarding administrative tribunal for a state in relation to members of the civil service of that state or those holding civil posts under that state.[221] A state government can also extend, by notification, jurisdiction of its administrative tribunal to such matters in relation to the employees of local or other authorities and corporations controlled or owned by the state government.[222] A joint administrative tribunal would exercise the jurisdiction, powers and authority exercisable by the administrative tribunal for such states.[223]

The tribunals, central as well as state or joint, in their respective spheres, have been vested with all the jurisdiction, powers and authority exercisable earlier by all courts except the Supreme Court under Article 136 of the constitution.[224] This may mean that the tribunals have the power to issue writs, orders or directions for the enforcement of fundamental rights, under Article 32 of the constitution and for any other purpose under Article 226.[225] Under Article 32(3), the parliament is authorised to empower by law any other court to exercise all or any of the powers exercisable by the Supreme Court under Article 32 of the constitution. It will have to be judicially determined if these administrative tribunals fall within the definition of the word 'court' as used in Article 32(3).[226] The law of administrative tribunals is of recent origin and it will take some time before the Supreme Court of

India is called upon to make authoritative pronouncement upon the standing of such tribunals as 'courts' or otherwise. Naturally, there are other important issues which will have to be resolved by the Supreme Court in this behalf. Those issues may be: whether the law of administrative tribunals is against the basic structure of the constitution for taking away the power of judicial review? Whether constitutional jurisdiction of high courts under Article 226 can be invoked when such tribunals act without jurisdiction or exceed their jurisdiction? Whether creation of classification of civil servants separate from ordinary citizens and creation of separate tribunals to deal with their matters is violative of 'equality before the law' and 'equal protection' clauses as contained in Article 14 of the constitution? Only time will tell how these issues are resolved through judicial pronouncements. It can, however, be argued that classification of civil servants separately from all other citizens is not per se invidious or unreasonable and can be sustained under Article 14 of the constitution.

The tribunal has inherited the jurisdiction of the High Court in service matters, therefore, in exercise of its power of judicial review, it cannot interfere with the penalty imposed by the disciplinary authority on the ground that it is disproportionate to the proved misconduct, if the findings as to misconduct are supported by legal evidence.[227]

The Act does not provide for any appeal or review of the order of the tribunal except that a person aggrieved may file a special leave petition before the Supreme Court. However, after the decision of the Supreme Court in *L. Chandra Kumar v. Union of India*[228] service tribunals have been brought under the jurisdiction of High Courts and their decision now would be appealable before the High Courts also.

6.10.6 PROCEDURE OF ADMINISTRATIVE TRIBUNALS

It has been provided that a person aggrieved by any order pertaining to any matter within the jurisdiction of a tribunal may make an application to the tribunal for the redressal of his grievance.[229] The order concerned should of course emanate from the government, or a local or other authority or corporation or an officer, committee or other body or agency acting on behalf of such government, or local or other authority or corporation.[230] Tribunals are not expected to admit an application unless they are satisfied that the applicant had availed of all the remedies available to him under the relevant service rules.[231] It does not mean that the party will have no right to make an application to a tribunal till the competent authority finally disposes of the matter. If such authority sleeps over the matter, then the aggrieved person can move the tribunal after the expiry of six months from the date of initiation of such departmental remedy.[232] Submission of a memorandum to the president or the governor of a state or to any other functionary does not fall within the meaning of remedies available to an aggrieved person.[233] A tribunal, on receipt of such application may admit it if it is satisfied that the requirements under the Act are complied with or otherwise may reject the application summarily.[234] When an application is admitted by a tribunal, then all other proceedings pending under the relevant service rules for the redressal of grievances in relation to the subject matter of such application abate and no appeal or representation in this behalf can be entertained.[235] Limitation for entertainment of application before a tribunal is one year from the final order made by the competent authority on the appeal or representation filed by an aggrieved person under the relevant service rules and in case no such final order is made, then one year after the expiry of six months from the date of initiation of a remedy under the relevant rules.[236] Tribunals have the power to condone delay in filing of applications before them for sufficient cause to be shown by the applicant.[237] Tribunals have the power to regulate their own procedures and are not bound by the procedure laid down in the Code of Civil Procedure but are required to be guided by the principles of natural justice.[238] A tribunal has all the powers of a civil court under the Code of Civil Procedure in respect of summoning of witnesses; discovery, production, and requisitioning of documents including public record; receiving evidence on affidavits; issuing commissions for examination of witnesses or documents; reviewing its decisions; dismissing an application for default or deciding it *ex parte*; and setting aside dismissal in default or *ex parte* order.[239] A tribunal is expected to decide every application before it as expeditiously as possible and to decide after perusal of documents and written representations and after hearing of oral arguments.[240]

A tribunal has the authority to make interim orders on an application subject to the condition that copies of such application are furnished to the opposite party or parties and opportunity is given to such opposing party or parties to be heard in the matter before making interim orders. In exceptional circumstances, a tribunal can dispense with these requirements in order to avoid irreparable loss or injury to the applicant.[241] An order of a tribunal is to be executed in the same manner in which an order of a higher departmental authority, deciding an appeal or representation against the order challenged under the service rules, is to be executed.[242] Administrative tribunals have been vested with the same authority to punish for contempt of court as can be exercised by a high court.[243] This authority to punish for contempt of court can prove a useful tool for effective execution of orders of tribunals.

Appropriate government is required to make provisions, by notification, for the distribution of business amongst the principal bench and the additional bench or additional benches and specify matters which are to be dealt with by each bench.[244] In case of any ambiguity about any matter falling within the purview of any bench of a tribunal, the decision of the chairman would be final.[245] The chairman of a tribunal has the authority to withdraw any case from an additional bench to the principal bench or to transfer any case from any bench to any other bench.[246] The decision of a bench on any point required to be expressed in accordance with the opinion of the majority and in case members of a bench are equally divided, then a statement of the case setting forth point or points of differences would be submitted to the chairman who may constitute special bench of one or more members to decide on the point or points of differences and the decision would be expressed in terms of the opinion of the majority of members of the original as well as special benches.[247]

6.10.7 DELEGATED LEGISLATION

The central government has been delegated power to frame rules for carrying out provisions of the Act.[248] The rules are supposed to provide for classification of cases to be decided by a bench of more than three members; procedure for the investigation of misbehaviour or incapacity of chairman, vice chairman or other member; the salaries and allowances payable to, and the other terms and conditions of the chairman, vice chairman, and other members; the form of application, the documents, and other evidence that would accompany such application and fees payable with such application; and the rules of procedure for a tribunal.[249] Rules framed by the central government are required to be laid before each house of parliament and both houses of parliament can agree on making modifications of or omission from these rules and such rules can only become effective subject to such modifications or omissions.[250] In the same way, the appropriate government can, by notification, make rules to provide for the financial and administrative powers of the chairman of a tribunal, and salaries, allowances, and conditions of service of the employees of a tribunal.[251] Where such rules are made by a state government, they are required to be laid before the state legislature which can make any modifications or omissions that it deems necessary.[252] The central government has accordingly framed procedure rules for the central administrative tribunal which are called Central Administrative Tribunal (Procedure) Rules, 1985 which came into force on the 2nd of September 1985.[253]

6.11 LATER DEVELOPMENTS IN RESPECT OF ADMINISTRATIVE TRIBUNALS

6.11.1 HISTORICAL BACKGROUND

As discussed above, the primary reason given for establishment of administrative tribunals for civil servants was the pendency in the high courts of a large number of service cases of civil servants. Due to such pendency, the Indian Parliament's attention was drawn to the pressing problem of backlog of cases in the high courts. The central and state governments started looking for ways and means to relieve high courts of this load. In 1969, a committee was set up by the central government under the chairmanship of Mr Justice Shah of the Supreme Court of India to make recommendations suggesting ways and means for effective and expeditious disposal of matters relating to service disputes of government servants, as it was found that a sizable portion of litigation pending in the high courts related to this category. This committee recommended setting up of an independent tribunal to handle pending cases before the Supreme Court and the high courts. While this report was being considered by the government, Administrative Reforms Commission also took note of the situation and recommended the setting up of civil service tribunals to deal with appeals of government servants in disciplinary matters. It was in the light of such concern and recommendations that the 42nd amendment of the constitution introduced Article 323-A for the establishment of administrative tribunals for civil servants in employment of central as well as state governments. Consequently, under this constitutional provision, the Administrative Tribunals Act of 1985 was enacted and enforced.[254]

6.11.2 COMMENCEMENT OF THE LAW AND THE ESTABLISHMENT OF ADMINISTRATIVE TRIBUNALS

The Central Government of India, by notification, appointed 1 July 1985 as the date on which provisions of the Act, in so far as they relate to the central administrative tribunal would come into effect.[255] The central government established central administrative tribunal with effect from 1 November 1985.[256] The central government, for purposes of central administrative tribunal, specified Delhi as the place for its principal bench and Allahabad, Banglore, Bombay, Calcutta, Gauhati, Madras, and Nagpur as places for its additional benches.[257]

Since the law of administrative tribunals was passed in 1985, some important developments have taken place which deserve mention at this stage.

6.11.3 LAW OF ADMINISTRATIVE TRIBUNALS JUDICIALLY REVIEWED

It did not take too long before the *vires* of the Administrative Tribunals Act 1985 was challenged before the Supreme Court of India. An Application under Article 32 of the constitution was filed before the Supreme Court in which the following questions were raised:

(i) Judicial review is a fundamental aspect of the basic structure of the Indian Constitution and, therefore, the bar of the jurisdiction of the high courts, under Articles 226 and 227 of the constitution as contained in Section 28 of the said Act of 1985, could not be sustained.

(ii) Even if the bar of jurisdiction is upheld, the tribunal being a substitute for the high courts, its constitution and set-up should be such that it would in fact function as such substitute and become an institution in which the parties could repose faith and trust.

(iii) Benches of the tribunal should not only be established at the seat of every high court but should be available at every place where the high courts have permanent benches.

(iv) So far as the tribunals to be set up by the central or state governments are concerned, they should have no jurisdiction over the employees of the Supreme Court or members of the subordinate judiciary and employees working in such establishment, inasmuch as exercise of jurisdiction of the tribunal would interfere with the control absolutely vested in the respective high courts in regard to the judiciary and other subordinate officers under Article 235 of the constitution.[258]

During pendency of this case, an Act amending the Administrative Tribunals Act 1985 was passed. This amending Act, known as the Administrative Tribunals (Amendment) Act 1986, made extensive amendments in the original Act and some of the objections raised before the Supreme Court were met. Section 2 (b) was omitted retroactively with effect from 1 November 1985, as a result of which officers and servants in the employment of the Supreme Court and members and staff of the subordinate judiciaries were excluded from the purview of the Act of 1985.[259] Section 28 of the Act of 1985 was also amended and the entire jurisdiction of Supreme Court under the constitution was saved.[260] This was clearly a departure from the original text wherein the jurisdiction of the Supreme Court was also excluded, except under Article 136 of the constitution which provides for entertaining appeals against decisions on grant of special leave only. With this amendment, writ jurisdiction of Supreme Court under Article 32 has also been left untouched. Hence power of judicial review by the Supreme Court is still available. The Attorney General of India also undertook on behalf of the central government to arrange for sittings of the benches of the tribunal at the seat or seats of each high court on the basis that sittings would include 'circuit sitting' and details thereof would be worked out by the chairman or vice chairman concerned. Hence, two of the objections raised before the Supreme Court were allowed through such amendments and undertaking.

The Supreme Court then considered the question of bar of jurisdiction of high courts and upheld as valid and proper the exclusion of jurisdiction of the high courts in service matters. It was also observed that since the judicial review by the Supreme Court has been left unaffected after the 1986 amendment and matters of importance and grave injustice could always be brought before the Supreme Court for determination or rectification, and therefore, exclusion of the jurisdiction of high courts does not totally bar judicial review.[261] Nevertheless, the Supreme Court held that the administrative tribunal, which has been introduced as a substitute of the high court, must be a worthy successor of the high court in all respects. In order to make administrative tribunal as efficacious as high courts, the Supreme Court gave certain directions and recommendations which are as follows:

(i) Since the questions likely to be adjudicated upon by administrative tribunals would involve interpretation and applicability of Articles of constitution, therefore, they would not only require judicial approach but also knowledge and expertise in constitutional law. It is, therefore, necessary that those who adjudicate upon these questions should have some modicum of legal training and judicial experience. It was therefore recommended that qualifications for appointment as chairman of tribunal should not include those persons who have merely been secretaries to the Government of India and did not have proper judicial or legal training. Similarly, qualification for appointment as vice chairman of tribunal should not include persons who had been secretaries or additional secretaries to the Government of India without any judicial and legal experience and training. It was suggested that a district judge or an advocate qualified to be a judge of high court should be eligible for being vice chairman of administrative tribunal.

(ii) The government should not have unfettered discretion to appoint chairman, vice chairman, and administrative members of administrative tribunal. It was, therefore, recommended that chairman, vice chairman, and administrative members should be appointed by the concerned government either after consultation with the Chief Justice of India, or after consultation with a high-powered selection committee headed by the Chief Justice of India, or a sitting judge of Supreme Court or concerned Chief Justice of high court nominated by the Chief Justice of India. It was observed that only appointments made in either of the two modes suggested would ensure independence of administrative tribunals as judicial bodies duly insulated from all forms of interference from executive branches of the government.

(iii) The government should set up a permanent bench and, if it is not feasible having regard to the volume of work, then at least a circuit bench of administrative tribunal be set up wherever there is a seat of high court.

In order to give teeth to these suggestions and recommendations, it was held that the amendments suggested above should be carried out on or before 31 March 1987, otherwise the Administrative Tribunals Act 1985 would be declared invalid. The recommendations about the manner of appointment of chairman, vice chairman or administrative members were made operative prospectively and the appointments already made prior to the judgment were not declared invalid. However, future appointments were made subject to one of the two modes suggested by the Supreme Court.[262]

The Indian Parliament responded to the recommendations made by the Supreme Court of India in the case of Sampath Kumar by passing the Administrative Tribunals (Amendment) Act 1987, amending the Administrative Tribunals Act 1985. Although all the recommendations of the Supreme Court have not been accepted and incorporated, yet the following amendments have been made keeping in mind the said judgment.

(i) Officers or servants of the Supreme Court or of any high court had been excluded from the jurisdiction of administrative tribunals. By this amendment, this provision has been extended to officers or servants of courts subordinate to high courts. This provision completely separates judiciary, superior as well as subordinate, from administrative tribunal, thus extending complete control to the judiciary over its officers and servants.

(ii) Qualifications for appointment as chairman of a tribunal have been amended. After this amendment, only a sitting or a retired judge of a high court or a vice chairman of a tribunal with at least two years standing is eligible for appointment as chairman of a tribunal. Provision about eligibility of a central secretary to the Government of India for appointment as chairman has been omitted.

(iii) Qualifications for appointment as vice chairman of a tribunal have been amended and apart from sitting or retired judges of high courts, persons who are qualified for appointment as such judges have also been made eligible for appointment as vice chairman of a tribunal.

(iv) The appointment of chairman, vice chairman or member of any tribunal has been made subject to consultation with the Chief Justice of India.

(v) The chairman, vice chairman, or members of a tribunal are made eligible for re-appointment for another term of five years after completion of the first term of five years. This is subject to the proviso that, in case of chairman or vice chairmen, they have not attained the age of sixty-five years and, in case of members, they have not attained the age of sixty-two years.

(vi) All the cases, pending before a tribunal immediately before the amendment of 1987, in which tribunals have ceased to have jurisdiction, stand transferred to the courts having requisite jurisdiction. This provision has been apparently made in view of the amendment excluding officers or servants of subordinate courts from the jurisdiction of the tribunals.

The whole question of constitutionality of the Administrative Service Tribunals Act, 1985 once again came under the scrutiny of the Supreme Court in the pace-setting case of *L. Chandra Kumar*[263]. The court, in this case, held that *Sampath Kumar* was decided against the background and that the litigation before the High Courts had exploded in an unprecedented manner and, therefore, an alternative inquisitional mechanism was necessary to remedy the situation. But it is self-evident and widely acknowledged truth that tribunals have not performed well, hence drastic measures were necessary to elevate their standard ensuring that they stand up to constitutional scrutiny. The court further held that because the constitutional safeguards, which ensure the independence of the judges of the Supreme Court and the High Courts, are not available to the members of the tribunals, hence, they cannot be considered full and effective substitute for the superior judiciary in discharging the function of constitutional interpretation. Against this backdrop, the court came to the conclusion that administrative tribunals cannot perform a substitutional role to the High Court, it can only be supplemental. Therefore, clause 2(d) of Article 323-A and clause 3(d) of Article 323-B of the Constitution, to the extent they exclude the jurisdiction of the High Courts and the Supreme Court under Articles 226, 227 and 32 of the Constitution, were held unconstitutional; and for the same reason Section 28 of the Administrative Tribunals Act, 1985 which contains the "exclusion of jurisdiction" clause, was also held unconstitutional. It was further observed by the court that the power of judicial review of the constitutional courts is a part of the inviolable basic structure of the Constitution which cannot be ousted. However, service tribunals should continue to be the courts of first instance in service matters, and no writ can be directly filed in the writ courts on matters within the jurisdiction of tribunals. Though the two-judge Bench, one of whom must be a judicial member, of the tribunal can determine the constitutionality of any statutory provision, yet it cannot determine the constitutionality of the Administrative Tribunal Act, 1985. But the exercise of this power should be subject to the scrutiny by the Division Bench of the High Court within whose jurisdiction the tribunal is situated. By bringing back the tribunals within the jurisdiction of the High Courts, the court served two purposes. While saving the power of judicial review of legislative action vested in the High Courts under Articles 226 and 227 of the Constitution, it would ensure that frivolous claims are filtered out through the process of adjudication by the tribunal. The High Court would also have the benefit of a reasoned decision on merits which would be of use to it in finally deciding the matter. In view of this decision, the existing provision of direct appeals to the Supreme Court under Article 136 of the Constitution also stands modified. Now the aggrieved party would be entitled to move the High Court and from the decision of the Division Bench of the High Court, he can move the Supreme Court under Article 136 of the Constitution. The court saved the constitutionality of Section 5(b) by providing that whenever a question involving the constitutionality of any provision arises, it shall be referred to a two-member Bench, one of whom must be a judicial member.[264]

Through this important case, the court has, in one sense, tried to save the jurisdiction of constitutional courts from encroachment by the legislature by invoking the doctrine of "basic features of the Constitution"[265]

6.11.4 OTHER AMENDMENTS MADE IN THE ADMINISTRATIVE TRIBUNALS ACT 1985

The Administrative Tribunals (Amendment) Act 1986, in addition to the amendments discussed above, introduced some other amendments which are discussed below:

(i) Members of the tribunal were divided into 'administrative members' and 'judicial members'. Qualification for a judicial member is that he is or has been or is qualified to be judge of high court or a member of Indian Legal Service and has held a post in Grade I of that service for at least 3 years. The qualification for appointment as an administrative member is that he has been holding the post of additional secretary to the Government of India for at least 2 years, or the post of joint secretary to the Government of India for at least 3 years.[266] As a result of this division of the members into judicial and administrative members, every bench of the administrative tribunal can have the service of a person legally and judicially trained. It has also been provided that a bench of tribunal would consist of one judicial member and one administrative member.[267]

(ii) The provisions of the Administrative Tribunals Act 1985 have been extended to societies owned or controlled by the government as well.

(iii) Appeal has been provided against decree or orders made or passed by any court, other than a high court, in any suit or proceedings before the establishment of tribunal, in matters falling within the jurisdiction of tribunal, to central administrative tribunal or to any other concerned tribunal.[268]

(iv) Rule-making power under the Administrative Tribunals Act, 1985 has been made retrospective but the same cannot affect interests of any person retrospectively.[269]

6.11.5 CONCLUSION

The Supreme Court of India has been instrumental in bringing about important and fundamental reforms in the law of Administrative tribunals. As a result of amendments carried out either during the pendency of Sampath Kumar's case, or as a result of the recommendations made by the Supreme Court in the said case, administrative tribunal has been elevated to the position of a proper judicial body. The chairman, vice chairman, and judicial members of the tribunal are now to be persons who are legally and judicially trained and their mode of appointment has been made very similar to that of judges of superior courts in India. This ensures independence of tribunals and enhances confidence of persons litigating before them. All actions and orders of administrative tribunals are subject to judicial review by the Supreme Court. The Supreme Court has also liberally interpreted the jurisdiction of administrative tribunals and has upheld the order of the central administrative tribunal striking down as constitutionally invalid a rule framed by the President of India as being violative of certain fundamental rights provided under the constitution.[270] The rationale given by the Supreme Court is that administrative tribunal being substitute of the high court, had the necessary jurisdictional power and authority to adjudicate upon all disputes relating to service matters including power to deal with all questions pertaining to constitutional validity or otherwise of such law when they are offending against fundamental rights guaranteed by the constitution. In this way, administrative tribunals have been conferred jurisdiction to judicially review law and rules framed thereunder and to declare such laws or rules invalid if found repugnant to provisions of the constitution.

There are two categories of service tribunals, one constituted by the States under their own legislations and the other constituted under the Central legislation, Administrative Tribunals Act, 1985. There was a third category in which a service tribunal had been established in Andhra Pradesh through the amendment of the Constitution in 1976 which was abolished in 1989. While the States of Uttar Pradesh, Rajasthan, Gujarat and Assam have established service tribunals under their own laws, the States of Orissa, Himachal Pradesh, Karnataka, Madhya Pradesh, Tamil Nadu and Maharashtra have established tribunals for their employees under the Central legislation. Central Administrative Tribunal (CAT) has also been established for Central Government employees. This tribunal works in 18 places through its Benches. Besides these, Circuit Benches are also held at other places particularly where the seat of High Court is located. The basic purpose behind the establishment of these tribunals was to provide expeditious justice to the civil servants who were not available through the traditional system. How far this purpose has been achieved is a moot question. However the trend which was discouraging in the beginning is now showing some encouraging trends.[271]

6.12 STATUTORY TRIBUNALS

An intensive form of government is responsible for entrusting administration with adjudicatory powers. For the exercise of this power, a tribunal is a very efficacious instrumentality which, from a functional point of view, is somewhere in between a court and the government department exercising adjudicatory powers.

The dictionary meaning of the word 'tribunal' is 'seat of a judge' and, if used in this sense, it is a wide expression which includes within it 'court' also. But in administrative law, the term 'tribunal' is used in a special sense and refers to adjudicatory bodies outside the sphere of ordinary courts of the land. Under the Indian Constitution, Articles 136, 226, and 227, refer to terms 'court' and 'tribunal' which have been used to mean two different things.[272] Therefore, a tribunal may possess some but not all trappings of a court.[273] A body in order to be designated as a 'tribunal' must be one which is invested with the judicial powers to adjudicate on questions of law or fact affecting the rights of citizens in a judicial manner. In *Bharat Bank* v. *Employees*,[274] while deciding whether an Industrial Tribunal set up under the Industrial Disputes Act, 1947 is a 'tribunal' or not for the purpose of Article 136, the Supreme Court laid down that a 'tribunal' must possess the following characteristics:

(i) The proceedings before it must commence on an application which is in the nature of a plaint.

(ii) It must have the powers of a court relating to discovery, inspection and taking of evidence.

(iii) It must allow examination and cross-examination of witnesses.

(iv) It must allow legal representation.

(v) It must decide on the basis of the evidence before it and according to the provisions of the statute.

(vi) The members constituting a tribunal must be qualified to be judges.

Later decisions of the Supreme Court added a few more characteristics to this list:

(i) It must be required to hold sittings in public.[275]

(ii) It must be capable of giving determinative judgment or award affecting the rights and obligations of the parties.[276]

(iii) It must be invested with the state's inherent judicial power, meaning thereby that its constitution and the power to decide disputes must be derived from the statute.[277]

The Supreme Court of Pakistan has discussed the nature and functions of administrative tribunals in the following words:[278]

A tribunal is not always furnished with the trappings of a Court, nor will such trappings make its action judicial. The character of the action taken in a given case and the nature of the right on which it operates must determine whether the action is judicial, ministerial or legislative or whether it is simply the act of a public agent. A tribunal acts judicially in the full sense of the term if:

(1) it has to determine a dispute;
(2) the dispute relates to a right or liability which, whatever its immediate aspect, is ultimately referable to some right or liability, recognised by the Constitution or statute or by custom or equity which the domestic law has declared to be a rule of decision;
(3) since every right or liability depends upon facts the tribunal is under an obligation to discover the relevant facts;
(4) the ascertainment of the fact is in the presence of the parties either of whom is entitled to produce evidence in support of its respective case and to question the truth of the evidence produced by his opponent; and
(5) after an investigation of the facts and hearing legal arguments the tribunal renders a judgment which so far as the tribunal is concerned terminates the dispute.

In the case of an administrative tribunal, however, the emphasis is on policy, expediency and discretion to enable it to achieve the object with which it was set up. In the case of such a tribunal, the approach in determining the relevant facts is therefore often subjective and not objective, there being generally no lis before it in which the parties arrayed against each other for the enforcement of a private right or liability and who for that purpose are entitled to produce evidence and adduce legal argument. The word 'quasi' as prefixed to the world 'judicial' may either indicate that the tribunal is not acting purely administratively or that it is acting in a manner in which a judicial tribunal is expected to act.

The use of the statutory tribunal as a mode of deciding disputes is on the increase because it has all the benefits of a court without suffering from its limitations. Tribunals are equipped to function in an independent manner, with speed and without the technical procedural requirements which made the courts to grind so slow. It is with this advantage in mind that Article 212 was introduced in the 1973 Constitution of Pakistan and Part XIV-A has been inserted in the Indian Constitution by the Forty-second Amendment Act, 1976 giving power to the parliament and the provincial legislatures to establish tribunals to deal with specified subjects.

Article 323-B provides that the appropriate legislature may, by law, provide for the adjudication or trial by tribunals of any disputes, complaints, or offences with respect to all or any of the matters enumerated below with respect to which such legislature has power to make laws:

(i) Levy, assessment, collection, and enforcement of any tax.

(ii) Foreign exchange, import, and export across customs frontiers.

(iii) Industrial and labour disputes.

(iv) Land reforms by way of acquisition, by the state of any estate or any right or the extinguishment or modification of any such rights or by way of ceiling on agricultural land or in any other way.

(v) Ceiling on urban property.

(vi) Elections to either house of parliament or the house or either house of the legislature of a state.

(vii) Production, procurement, supply, and distribution of foodstuffs (including edible oilseeds and oils) and such other goods as the president may, by public notification, declare to be essential goods for the purpose of Article 323-B and the control of prices of such goods.

(viii) Offences against laws with respect to any of the matters specified in the above categories.

(ix) Any matter incidental to any of the matters specified above.

A law made under this article may:

(i) provide for the establishment of a hierarchy of tribunals;

(ii) specify the jurisdiction, powers (including the power to punish for contempt), and authority which may be exercised by each of the said tribunals;

(iii) provide for the procedure (including provisions as to limitation and rules of evidence) to be followed by such tribunal;

(iv) exclude the jurisdiction of all courts except the jurisdiction of the Supreme Court under Article 136 with respect to all or any of the matters falling within the jurisdiction of the said tribunals;

(v) provide for the transfer to each such tribunal of any cases pending before any court or any other authority;

(vi) contain such supplemental, incidental and consequential provisions (including provision as to fee) as may be necessary for the effective functioning of such tribunals.

These provisions of the constitution would introduce a new era of tribunals. No exhaustive list of the tribunals already working can be prepared as they appear under various names. However, the following important tribunals are at work in various fields:

(i) Industrial Tribunals established under the Industrial Disputes Act, 1947.

(ii) Railway Rates Tribunal established under the India Railways Act, 1890.

(iii) Income Tax Appellate Tribunal, established under the Income Tax Act, 1961.

(iv) Employees' Insurance Court, established under the Employees' State Insurance Act, 1948.

(v) Court of Survey, established under the Merchant Shipping Act, 1958.

(vi) Copyright Board established under the Copyright Act, 1958.

(vii) Unlawful Activities Tribunal established under the Unlawful Activities (Prevention) Act, 1967.

(viii) The Press and Registration Appellate Board established under the Press and Registration of Books Act, 1867.

(ix) Foreigners Tribunal established under the Foreigners Act, 1946.

    (x) Compensation Tribunals established under the various Zamindari Abolition Acts, Slum Clearance and Planning laws, Air Corporation Act, Life Insurance Corporation Act etc.

   (xi) Claims Tribunals established under the Motor Vehicles Act, 1939.

In India, these tribunals do not follow any formal procedure. The procedure is sometimes laid down in the statute and sometimes the tribunal is left free to develop its own procedure. The procedure for Copyright Board is given in the Copyright Act, while Tax Appellate Tribunal is left free to decide its own procedure. However, as a matter of general practice the tribunals exercise the powers of a civil court relating to examination, discovery, inspection, production of documents, compelling attendance of witnesses, and issuing commissions. Their proceedings are considered as judicial proceedings for purposes of Sections 193, 195, and 226 of the Indian Penal Code and they are deemed to be civil courts for purposes of Sections 480 and 482 of the Criminal Procedure Code. In the interest of flexibility and adaptability, the technical rules of the Indian Evidence Act do not apply to tribunals. However, the rules of procedure of the tribunals should not violate the requirements of fair procedure and they must conduct themselves with openness, fairness, and impartiality.

It is not possible to discuss all the statutory tribunals functioning in Pakistan and India in various spheres. Hence, as an illustrative measure, details of the Income Tax Appellate Tribunal may be noted. This tribunal functions under the Income Tax Ordinance, 1979 and Income Tax Act, 1961 in Pakistan and India respectively, as a second appellate authority to hear appeals in cases relating to income tax, wealth tax, and estate duty. They consist of as many judicial and accountant members as the government may deem fit to appoint. Any person may be appointed as a judicial member with judicial or legal experience. A chartered accountant or departmental official can be appointed as accountant members. Ordinarily, a bench consists of one judicial member and one accountant member. A special bench consisting of three or more members may also be constituted. Decisions are given by majority and in case of equal division the case is referred to one or more other members. The hearing before such Tribunal is oral and it exercises the powers of a civil court relating to examination, discovery, inspection, production of documents, compelling attendance of witnesses, and issuing commissions. Decisions of the tribunal are final on questions of fact[279] but a reference may be made to the high court or the Supreme Court on questions of law. Decision of the high court on a reference is appealable before the Supreme Court if the high court certifies it a fit case for appeal. The Law Commission and the Direct Taxes Administration Committee in India have reviewed the functioning of the tribunal and made various recommendations regarding appointment of its members, appeal, and procedures to improve its functioning.[280]

If statutory tribunals are to develop in Pakistan and India as a system for the administration of justice and not as mere administrative expedients, it is necessary that their functioning be properly supervised. With this end in view, a Council on Tribunals was constituted under the Tribunals and Enquiries Act, 1958 in Britain. The membership of this committee is sixteen. Except five legal members, the rest are lay persons. This constitution introduces the elements of public opinion and flexibility in the functioning of the council. The parliamentary commissioner (ombudsman) is also an ex-officio member. Except for the parliamentary commissioner, all the members are appointed by the Lord Chancellor and the Secretary of State for Scotland acting jointly. The council has only advisory jurisdiction. Its main function is to deal with the problems of tribunals and inquiries and for this purpose it is in constant negotiation with the government regarding new proposals for legislation, rules and procedure, organisational problems, quality of members, individual complaints, etc. Therefore, right from the proposal stage to the final establishment of a tribunal, the council is in the picture to help administrative justice to develop as an organised system. The council is empowered to receive complaints against the functioning of tribunals and inquiries. After investigation, it can publish its views to create public opinion for reform in the system.

To supervise the working of administrative agencies exercising adjudicatory powers in the USA, the Congress passed a legislation in 1964 for the establishment of an Administrative Conference, which came into existence in 1968. Its membership is 83. The conference has three components: chairman, council, and general assembly. The chairman is appointed by the president for a period of five years. The council consists of ten members appointed by the president for three-year terms. The general assembly of members is chosen by different federal agencies. A few public men are also chosen by the chairman with the approval of the council for a term of two years. The conference is entirely a recommendatory body and its main function is to put forward recommendations to improve the efficiency, adequacy, and fairness of the legal procedure of federal administrative agencies exercising adjudicatory and rule-making powers. More recent recommendations of the conference have dealt with procedural refinement, i.e. recruitment and status of hearing examiners, summary decisions, discovery, sovereign immunity, etc.

In Pakistan and India, there is an undeniable need for such an agency which could supervise the functioning of decision-making and rule-making administrative agencies. Such an agency would help in the development of administrative justice as a system.

6.13 Domestic Tribunals

The term 'domestic tribunal' refers to those administrative agencies which are designed to regulate professional conduct and to enforce discipline among the members by exercising investigatory and adjudicatory powers. Such agencies may be contractual or statutory. Contractual domestic tribunals are those which exercise jurisdiction arising not out of any statute but from an agreement between the parties. An agency constituted by a private club to decide disputes between its members is a contractual domestic tribunal. Such a tribunal is not subject to the writ jurisdiction of the court but in certain situations remedy by way of injunction, declaration or damages may be available.

Statutory domestic tribunals are those which derive power and authority from a statute and exercise regulatory and disciplinary jurisdiction over its members. Such tribunals have been established under the Legal Practitioners and Bar Councils Act, 1973, Advocates Act, 1961, Chartered Accountant Act, 1949, Medical Councils Act, 1945, Press Council Act, 1965, and the Engineering Council Act, 1976. The list is merely illustrative and not exhaustive. Such tribunals are free to develop their procedure but in every case they are bound to follow the principles of natural justice. Decisions of statutory domestic tribunals are subject to the writ jurisdiction of the Supreme Court and high courts in the same manner as any other statutory tribunal. However, the scope of judicial review in case of domestic tribunals is highly limited because the essential function of a domestic tribunal is discipline among its members. This seems to be the thrust of the Supreme Court decision in *State of Haryana* v. *Rattan Singh*.[281] In this case, Rattan Singh who was a conductor of Haryana Road Transport was dismissed. On the Palwal route, his bus was taken over by the flying squad. The inspector found eleven passengers without tickets though they had paid the fare. An inquiry was held on the report of the inspector and the services of the conductor was terminated. A suit for declaration that the services have been illegally terminated was filed by the conductor. The court granted the declaration and on appeal the high court sustained the decision on the grounds that:

(i) none of the eleven witnesses was examined by the domestic tribunal;

(ii) the inspector did not record the statement of the eleven passengers which was necessary as per the rules.

On appeal, the Supreme Court disagreed with the high court and observed that the simple point involved in the case is whether there was some evidence or was there no evidence—not in the technical sense governing the regular court proceedings but in a fair common sense way as a man of understanding and worldly wisdom would accept. Viewed this way, sufficiency of evidence in proof of findings of a domestic tribunal is beyond scrutiny.

As an illustrative measure the constitution and the functioning of the domestic adjudicatory authority constituted under the Legal Practitioners and Bar Councils Act, 1973 to regulate and to enforce discipline in the legal profession may be noted. This Act makes provisions for the creation of the Pakistan Bar Council and provincial bar councils. These bar councils are empowered by the Act to enforce discipline in the legal profession. The task of deciding cases of professional misconduct is entrusted to a discipline committee and disciplinary tribunal. The bar council, either on its own initiative or on an application by any other person, can refer the matter of alleged professional misconduct by a lawyer to the discipline tribunal. For the conduct of business before it, the committee or tribunal exercise the powers of a civil court relating to examination, discovery, inspection, production of documents, compelling attendance of witnesses, and issuing commissions. Its proceedings are deemed to be judicial proceedings within the meaning of Sections 193 and 228 of the Indian Penal Code. The committee has the power either to reprimand or suspend or remove the name of the lawyer from its rolls. The decisions of the committee/tribunal of provincial bar councils are appealable before the Pakistan Bar Council. From the orders of the Pakistan Bar Council, a further appeal lies to the Supreme Court.

Besides tribunals, there exists a whole multitude of administrative officers and agencies exercising adjudicatory powers in varied forms. No systematic research has so far been undertaken in Pakistan and India regarding the manner of functioning of these officers and agencies.[282]

Notes

1. H.W.R. Wade, *Administrative Law* (3rd edn., Oxford: Oxford University Press, 1971) 254–255.

2. Franks Committee's Report, Cmnd. 218 (1957), para. 229.
3. National Insurance Act 1965 Sections 64, 65; National Insurance (Industrial Injuries) Act 1965, Section 35. Cf. *Healey* v. *Minister of Health* [1955] 1 QB 221 (Minister's power to decide category of employment).
4. *Tariq Transport Company v. The Sargodha Bhera Bus Service*, PLD 1958 S.C 437.
5. PLD 1998 SC. 1445
6. PLD 1999 SC. 504
7. *Huddart, Parker & Co v. Moorehead*, (1909) 8 CLR 330. It was a case decided by High Court of Australia.
8. (1930) All ER 671
9. (1976) 2 All ER 367
10. *Sh. Riaz-ul-Haq v. Federation of Pakistan*, PLD 2013 S.C. 501
11. Ibid.
12. Ibid.
13. National Insurance Act 1966, Section 8.
14. See *R.* v. *Ministry of Health* [1968] 1 QB 84.
15. For example, from the Special Commissioners of Income Tax and from Mental Health Review Tribunals.
16. M. Munir, *Constitution of the Islamic Republic of Pakistan: A Commentary on the Constitution of Pakistan 1962* (1965 edn.) 12.
17. Ibid., p. 29.
18. PLD 1958 SC (Pak) 533.
19. M. Munir, *Constitution of the Islamic Republic of Pakistan: A Commentary on the Constitution of Pakistan, 1973* (1976 edn.) 47.
20. PLD 1972 SC 139.
21. The Constitution of the Islamic Republic of Pakistan, 1956, Article 181.
22. Ibid., Article 181 (2) (c).
23. Ibid., Article 182 (2) (a).
24. Ibid., Article 182 Clause 1 (2) (b).
25. Ibid., Article 182 Clause 1 (3) (a).
26. Ibid., Article 182 Clause 1 (3) (b).
27. Ibid.
28. The Constitution of the Islamic Republic of Pakistan, 1962, Article 177.
29. Ibid., Article 178 Clauses (2) and (3).
30. Ibid., Article 178 Clauses (4) and (5).
31. Ibid., Article 179.
32. Interim Constitution of the Islamic Republic of Pakistan, 1972, Articles 220–222.
33. Ibid., Article 221, Clause (4).
34. *The High Commissioner of India* v. *I.M. Lall*, PLD 1948 PC 150; *North West Frontier Province* v. *Suraj Narain Anand*, PLD 1949 PC 1; *Ibrahim* v. *Federation of Pakistan*, PLD 1957 Lahore 925; *Muhammad Afzal Khan* v. *Federation of Pakistan*, PLD 1957 Lahore 17; *Imtiaz Ali Khan* v. *The Chief*

Commissioner, PLD 1962 Karachi 144; and *M.G. Hassan* v. *Government of Pakistan,* PLD 1970 Lahore 518.

35. *The High Commissioner of India* v. *I.M. Lall,* PLD 1948 PC 150; *Habib Khan* v. *Federation of Pakistan,* PLD 1954 Sind 199; *A.Q.Y. Sheikh* v. *Pakistan,* PLD 1963 Karachi 660.

36. *Muhammad Munir Khan* v. *Province of Punjab,* PLD 1954 Lahore 299; *Noor-ul-Hassan* v. *Federation of Pakistan,* PLD 1955 Sind 200; *Muhammad Muhsin Siddiqi* v. *Government of West Pakistan,* PLD 1964 SC 64; *Naseem Jahan Naim* v. *The General Manager,* PLD 1968 SC 112.

37. *The High Commissioner of India* v. *I.M. Lall,* PLD 1948 PC 150; *Muhammad Munir Khan* v. *Province of Punjab,* PLD 1954 Lahore 299; *Ibrahim* v. *Federation of Pakistan,* PLD 1957 Lahore 925. *Imtiaz Ali Khan* v. *Chief Commissioner,* PLD 1962 Karachi 144.

38. *Khadim Hussain* v. *Federation of Pakistan,* PLD 1955 Sind 250; *Federation of Pakistan* v. *Murad Ali,* PLD 1961 Karachi 285.

39. *Abdul Hamid* v. *Province of West Pakistan,* PLD 1963 SC 460.

40. *Yusuf Ali Khan* v. *Province of Punjab,* PLD 1949 Lahore 219. *Noor-ul-Hassan* v. *Federation of Pakistan,* PLD 1955 Sind 200. *Federation of Pakistan* v. *Mrs A.V. Isaacs,* PLD 1956 SC (Pak) 431. *Noor-ul-Hassan* v. *Federation of Pakistan* PLD 1956 SC (Pak) 331. *Province of Punjab* v. *Akhtar Ali,* PLD 1956 (WP) Lahore 336. *Federation of Pakistan* v. *Shamsul Huda* PLD 1957 Dacca 148. *Pakistan* v. *Golam Moinuddin Ahmad,* PLD 1966 Dacca 570 (DB).

41. *Muhammad Afzal Khan* v. *Federation of Pakistan,* PLD 1957 Lahore 17.

42. *Federation of Pakistan* v. *S. Murad Ali,* PLD 1961 (WP) Karachi 285.

43. *Mohammad Siddique Javaid Chaudhry* v. *Government of West Pakistan,* PLD 1974 SC 393.

44. *Ch. Bashir Ahmad* v. *Province of West Pakistan,* PLD 1958 Lahore 206; *Bashir Ahmad Qureshi* v. *Province of West Pakistan,* PLD 1958 Lahore 299; *Col. K.M. Sana* v. *Government of West Pakistan,* PLD 1962 Lahore 509; *Abdul Majid Sheikh* v. *Mushaffe Ahmad* PLD 1965 SC 208.

45. *Naseem Ahmad* v. *Secretary, Government of Pakistan,* PLD 1960 Karachi 262; *Imtiaz Ali Khan* v. *Chief Commissioner,* PLD 1962 Karachi 144.

46. *Federation of Pakistan* v. *Maulvi Tamizuddin Khan,* PLD 1955 FC 240.

47. *Usif Patel* v. *Crown,* PLD 1955 FC 387.

48. *Re Reference by His Excellency the Governor General,* PLD 1955 FC 435.

49. PLD 1958 SC (Pak) 533.

50. Address of Z.A. Bhutto, then Prime Minister of Pakistan, to the nation on television and radio on 20 August 1973. The text of the speech is reproduced on pages 5 and 8 of *Daily Dawn* (Karachi) in its issue dated 21 August 1973.

51. Constitution of the Islamic Republic of Pakistan, 1973, Article 240.

52. Ibid., Article 212. The Interim Constitution of 1972 included similar provisions in its Article 216 which empowered Federal Legislature to

establish one or more administrative courts or tribunals to exercise exclusive jurisdiction in respect of matters relating to the terms and conditions of persons in the service of Pakistan, including the award of penalties and punishments; matters relating to the imposition, levy and collection of any tax, duty, cess or impost; matters relating to claims arising from tortious action of the government, any person in the service of Pakistan, any local or other authority empowered by law to levy any taxes or cess, and any servant of such authority acting in the discharge of his duties as such servant; matters relating to industrial and labour disputes; and matters relating to the acquisition, administration and disposal of any property which is deemed to be evacuee property or enemy property under any law. There was also a clause in the article ousting the jurisdiction of all other courts in the matters to which the jurisdiction of such administrative court or tribunal extended. It is noticeable that the federal legislature was given greater authority to create administrative courts and tribunals spread over much larger area of administrative activity under the Interim Constitution. Under the Permanent Constitution of 1973, this area of administrative activity of the creation of administrative courts and tribunals was restricted as is clear from the language of its Article 212. Any way, the federal legislature did not pass any law under the Interim Constitution for the creation of any law regarding administrative courts or tribunals and hence Article 216 was not put into effect.

53. Supra Note 42, Article 212, Clause (2).
54. Ibid., Proviso to Clause (2).
55. In April 2010, the 18th Amendment bill became an Act of Parliament, renaming the North West Frontier Province (NWFP) to 'Khyber-Pakhtunkhwa'.
56. Provincial Service Tribunals (Extension of Provision of Constitution) Act, 1974 (Act XXXII of 1974).
57. Provincial Service Tribunals (Extension of Provision of the Constitution) (Amendment) Act, 1976 (Act XXXIV of 1976), amending the Act XXXII of 1974.
58. Article 212, Clause (3).
59. Text reported in *Daily Dawn* of 21 August 1973.
60. Ordinance XIV of 1973.
61. Civil Servant Act, 1973 (Act LXXI of 1973).
62. Ibid., Section 2 (1) (b).
63. Ibid., Sections 3 to 21.
64. Ibid., Section 22.
65. Service Tribunals Ordinance, 1973 (Ordinance XV of 1973), later repealed by Service Tribunals Act, 1973 (Act IXX of 1973).
66. Service Tribunals Act, 1973, Section 3.
67. In the province of Baluchistan, Baluchistan Civil Servants Ordinance, 1973 (Baluchistan Ordinance IX of 1973) was promulgated which came into

force on 15 November 1973. This ordinance was later repealed by an Act of provincial assembly of Baluchistan called Baluchistan Civil Servants Act, 1974 (Baluchistan Act IX of 1974) which came into force on 12 March 1974. In the North West Frontier Province (NWFP), NWFP Civil Servants Ordinance, 1973 (NWFP Ordinance XI of 1973) was promulgated and became effective from 22 October 1973. This ordinance was later repealed by an Act of the provincial assembly of NWFP called NWFP Civil Servants Act (NWFP Act XVIII of 1973) and came into force on 12 November 1973. In the province of Sind, Sind Civil Servants Ordinance, 1973 (Sind Ordinance X of 1973) was promulgated which was later repealed by an Act of provincial assembly of Sind called Sind Civil Servants Act, 1973 (Sind Act XIV of 1973) which came into force on 5 December 1973. In the province of Punjab, Punjab Civil Servants Ordinance, 1974 (Ordinance II of 1974) was promulgated and became effective from 6 March 1974. This ordinance was later repealed by an Act of the provincial assembly of Punjab, called Punjab Civil Servants Act, 1974 (Punjab Act XIII of 1974) which came into force on 4 June 1974.

68. In the province of Baluchistan, provincial assembly passed an Act called Baluchistan Service Tribunal Act, 1974 (Baluchistan Act V of 1974) which came into force on 27 June 1974. In the North West Frontier Province, NWFP Service Tribunals Ordinance, 1973 (NWFP Ordinance I of 1974) was promulgated which was later repealed by an Act of provincial assembly of NWFP called NWFP Service Tribunals Act, 1974 (NWFP Act I of 1974), which came into force on 28 March 1974. In the province of Sind, the Sind Service Tribunals Ordinance, 1973 (Sind Ordinance XI of 1973) was promulgated which was later repealed by an Act of Provincial assembly of Sind, called Sind Service Tribunals Act, 1973 (Sind Act XV of 1973) which came into force on 5 December 1973. In the province of Punjab, Punjab Administrative Tribunals Ordinance, 1974 (Ordinance of 1974) was promulgated which was later repealed by an Act of the provincial assembly of Punjab, called Punjab Administrative Tribunals Act, 1974 (Punjab Act IX of 1974) which came into force on 20 June 1974. The nomenclature of this Act was later changed to Punjab Service Tribunals Act, 1974 through amendment brought about in the original Act by Punjab Administrative Tribunals (Amendment) Act 1975 (Punjab Act XXVI of 1975).

69. Article 212 Clause (2) of the Constitution of 1973 as amended by the Constitution (First Amendment) Act, 1974 (Act XXXIII of 1974).

70. Section 6 of the Service Tribunal Act, 1973; Section 6 of the Baluchistan Service Tribunals Act, 1974; Section 8 of the NWFP Service Tribunals Act, 1974; Section 6 of the Sind Service Tribunals Act, 1973; Section 8 of the Punjab Service Tribunals Act, 1974.

71. Constitution (Fifth Amendment) Act, 1976 (Act LXII of 1976) amending Article 212, Clause (2) of the Constitution.

72. Service Tribunals Act, 1973, Sec. 3.

73. Service Tribunals (Amendment) Ordinance, 1978 (Ordinance IX of 1978) Section 2 amending Section 3 of the Service Tribunals Act, 1973).
74. Ibid., Section 3 introducing Section 3-A in the Service Tribunals Act, 1973.
75. Service Tribunals Act, 1973, Section 3-A Sub-section (2)(a).
76. Ibid., Section 3-A Sub-section (2)(c).
77. Ibid., Section 3-A, Sub-section (2)(b). See also *Muhammad Ashraf Nadeem* vs. *Government of Pakistan*, PLJ 1982 Tribunal Cases (Services) 165.
78. Ibid., Section 3, Sub-section (3)(a).
79. Constitution of Islamic Republic of Pakistan, 1973, Article 193.
80. Service Tribunals Act, 1973, Section 3, Sub-section (3)(b).
81. An exception is North West Frontier Province, where NWFP Service Tribunal Act 1974, Section 3 provides for appointment of not less than two and not more than four members.
82. NWFP Service Tribunal Act 1974, Section 5. Benches were introduced in Punjab by amendment introduced in the Punjab Service Tribunal Act 1974 through Punjab Service Tribunals (Amendment) Ordinance, 1980 (Punjab ordinance II of 1980) adding Section 3-A in the parent Act.
83. NWFP Service Tribunals Act, 1974, Section 5, Sub-section (2).
84. Punjab Service Tribunals Act, 1974, Section 3-A, Sub-section (2).
85. In Baluchistan, NWFP, and Sind, minimum lengths of service required are ten, fifteen, and seventeen years respectively. In Punjab, it is provided that the qualifications of the members would be determined by the rules to be framed by the governor.
86. West Pakistan Civil Services (Appellate Tribunals) Ordinance, 1969 (WP Ordinance XXVIII of 1969).
87. North West Frontier Civil Services (Appellate Tribunals) Ordinance, 1971 (NWFP Ordinance II of 1971).
88. Punjab Civil Servants (Appellate Tribunals) Ordinance 1970 (Punjab Ordinance IV of 1970).
89. NWFP Ordinance II of 1971, Section 18 and Punjab Ordinance IV of 1970, Section 14.
90. West Pakistan Ordinance XXVIII of 1969, Section 9.
91. NWFP Ordinance II of 1971, Section 5 and Punjab Ordinance IV of 1976, Section 4.
92. *Muhammad Elias Dubash* vs. *Civil Service Appellate Tribunal*, PLD 1974 Lahore 90.
93. Definition of 'Civil Servant' given in Section 2(1)(b) of Civil Servants Act 1973.
94. Service Tribunals Act, 1973, Section 2(a).
95. Service Tribunals (Amendment) Act, 1974 (Act XXXI of 1974).
96. Baluchistan Act IX of 1974, Section 2(1)(b); NWFP Act XVIII of 1973, Section 2(1)(b); Punjab Act III of 1974, Section 2(1)(b); Sind Act XIV of 1973, Section 2(1)(b).

97. Baluchistan Act V of 1974, Section 2(a); NWFP Act of 1974, Section 2 (a); Punjab Act IX of 1974, Section 2(a); Sind Act XV of 1974, Section 2(a).

98. Baluchistan Service Tribunals (Amendment) Ordinance 1976 (ordinance VI of 1978), Section 2; NWFP Service Tribunals (Amendment) Act, 1974. Section 2; (Act IX of 1974); Sind Service Tribunals (Amendment) Act, 1974 (Act IX of 1974). In Punjab, in the original Act itself, the definition extended to those persons who have been civil servants.

99. *Sultan Khan* v. *Chairman Pakistan Ordinance Factory* [1983] PLC (CS) 1070; *Gul Hassan* v. *Chairman, Pakistan Railway Board* [1983] PLC (CS) 1164; *Muhammad Rashid* v. *Secretary, Ministry of Defence* [1984] PLC (CS) 1511; *Muhammad Nawaz Sheikh* v. *Secretary Ministry of Communications* [1985] PLC (CS) 395.

100. *Mufti Mushtaq Ahmad* v. *Federation of Pakistan*, PLD 1981 SC 172.

101. West Pakistan Water and Power Development Authority (Amendment) Act, 1975 (Act XXXIV of 1975).

102. Corporation Employees, (Special Powers) Ordinance, 1978 (Ordinance XIII of 1978).

103. *Aftab Ahmad Mirza* v. *Pakistan National Council of the Arts* [1980] PLC (CS) 329, *Zulfiqar* v. *Pakistan Steel Mills Corporation* [1980] PLC (CS) 510.

104. *Muhammad Ashfaq Mallal* v. *Chief Election Commissioner, Islamabad* [1980] PLC (CS) 445.

105. *Federation of Pakistan v. Ali Naseem*, 2016 SCMR 1744.

106. Section 2A of Service Tribunals Act, 1973. Section 2A has been added by Service Tribunal (Amendment) Act, 1997 (Act XVII of 1997).

107. *Muhammad Mubeen-us-Salam* v. *Federation of Pakistan*, PLD 2006 SC 602.

108. Act LXX of 1973, Section 3(2); Baluchistan Act V of 1974, Section 3(2); NWFP Act I of 1974, Section 3(2); Punjab Act IX of 1974, Section 3(2); and Sind Act XV of 1973, Section 3(2).

109. Section 4 of all the Acts above.

110. *Chief Engineer (North)* v. *Saifullah Khan Afridi* [1995] SCMR 776; *Noor Khan Chaudhry* v. *Province of Sind* [1982] SCMR 582.

111. Section 4 of Federal as well as all Provincial Service Tribunal laws.

112. *Muhammad Nadir Khan v. Central Selection Board*, 2014 PLC (CS) 1134 (Peshawar High Court).

113. *Mian Abdul Malik v Dr. Sabir Zameer Siddiqi*, 1991 SCMR 1129; *Ghulam Muhammad Qureshi v. Federation of Pakistan*, SBLR 2014 Tribunal 353 (Federal Service Tribunal).

114. *Firdous Ali* v. *Secretary, Establishment Division* [1997] SCMR 1160. See also [1997] PLC (CS) 579.

115. *Muhammad Inayat Gondal v. Registrar, Lahore High Court*, 2015 SCMR 705

116. *Muhammad Inayat Gondal v. Registrar, Lahore High Court*, 2015 SCMR 821

117. *Ch. Muhammad Hussain Maikan v. Registrar, Lahore High Court*, 2015 PLC (C.S) 307 (Punjab Subordinate Judiciary Service Tribunal).

118. Jurisdiction under Article 199 of the Constitution of 1973.

119. *Sarfraz Saleem v. Federation of Pakistan*, PLD 2014 S.C. 232

120. *Muhammad Aslam Bajwa* v. *Federation of Pakistan*, PLD 1974 Lahore 545; *M.A. Majid* v. *Government of Pakistan* [1976] SCMR 311; *Fazal Elahi Eajaz* v. *Government of Punjab*, PLD 1981 SC 137; *Mian Amanul Mulk* v. *NWFP* PLD 1981 Peshawar 1; *Khalilur Rehman* v. *Government of Pakistan*, PLD 1981 Karachi 750; *Abdul Bari* v. *Government of Pakistan*, PLD 1981 Karachi 290; *Sahrah Butt* v. *Government of Punjab*, PLD 1982 Lahore 42; *Ch. Ghulam Rasul* v. *Province of Punjab*, PLD 1982 Lahore 264; *Farid Ahmad* v. *Karachi Shipyard & Engineering Works Ltd*, PLD 1983 Karachi 576.

121. *M.A. Majid* v. *Government of Pakistan* 1976 SCMR 311; *Muhammad Hashim Khan* v. *Province of Baluchistan*, PLD 1976 Quetta 59; *Fazal Elahi Ejaz* v. *Government of Punjab*, PLD 1977 Lahore 549; *Muttaqi Husain Rizvi* v. *Province of Sind*, PLD 1978 Karachi 703; *Muktada Karim* v. *Government of Pakistan*, PLD 1981 Lahore 359; *Islamic Republic of Pakistan* v. *Dr Safdar Mahmood*, PLD 1983 SC 100.

122. *Muhammad Aslam Bajwa* v. *Federation of Pakistan*, PLD 1974 Lahore 545.

123. *M. Yamin Qureshi* v. *Islamic Republic of Pakistan* PLD 1980 SC 22.

124. *Iqan Ahmad Khurram* v. *Government of Pakistan*, PLD 1980 SC 153; *Muhammad Hashim Khan* v. *Province of Baluchistan*, PLD 1976 Quetta 59; *Fazal Elahi Ejaz* v. *Government of Punjab*, PLD 1977 Lahore 549; *Abdul Bari* v. *Government of Pakistan*, PLD 1981 Karachi 290; *Kalilur Rehman* v. *Government of Pakistan*, PLD 1981 Karachi 750.

125. *Muhammad Aslam Bajwa* v. *Federation of Pakistan*, PLD 1974 Lahore 545; *Muhammad Hashim Khan* v. *Province of Baluchistan*, PLD 1976 Quetta 59; *Fazal Elahi Ejaz* v. *Government of Punjab*, PLD 1977 Lahore 549; *Dr Raja Manzoor Elahi* v. *NWFP*, PLD 1980 Peshawar 81; *Khalilur Rehman* v. *Government of Pakistan*, PLD 1981 Karachi 750; *Abdul Bari* v. *Government of Pakistan*, PLD 1981 Karachi 290; *Mian Amanul Mulk* v. *NWFP*, PLD 1981 Peshawar 1.
    See also *Afzal Husain Syed* v. *Government of Punjab*, PLD 1980 Lahore 697 and *Raja Mohammad Sadiq* v. *Water and Power Development Authority*, PLD 1978 Lahore 738, wherein it was held that the high court can intervene if the order impugned is without lawful authority, *void ab initio* or *coram non judice* on the face of the record. This view does not hold good due to the later judgements expressing view to the contrary.

126. *Mujeebullah Aijaz* v. *Director General, T&T Department*, PLD 1980 Quetta 58.

127. The same view was expressed by the Supreme Court in *Islamic Republic of Pakistan* v. *Amjad Ali Mirza*, PLD 1977 SC 182.

128. Jurisdiction of the tribunals extends to those persons also who have been civil servants if the controversy involved pertains to their terms and conditions of service including disciplinary matters.

129. A final order, it is held, has the distinction of determining the rights of the parties concluding the controversy so far as particular authority or forum is concerned. *S.H.M. Rizvi* v. *Maqsood Ahmad*, PLD 1981 SC 612. See also *Saiful Haque Hashmi* v. *Government of Sind*, PLD 1979 Karachi 298, where it has been held that jurisdiction of the service tribunal can not be circumvented by filing constitutional petition before the competent authority has passed a final order. See also *Khalilur Rahman* v. *Government of Pakistan*, PLD 1981 Karachi 750 in which it is held that jurisdiction of high courts is barred even in relation to interlocutory orders where such orders are eventually to merge in final orders capable of being brought before service tribunals in appeal.

130. Also *Mohibullah* v. *Federation of Pakistan*, PLD 1975 Lahore 813. But see *Khalilur Rahman* v. *Government of Pakistan* PLD 1981 Karachi 750, and *Abdul Bari* v. *Government of Pakistan*, PLD 1981 Karachi 290, in which it has been held that order of retirement simpliciter passed on the completion of 25 years of service does not fall outside the purview of the service tribunals and they can adjudicate in such matters. The same view is held in *Muktada Karim* v. *Government of Pakistan*, PLD 1981 Lahore 359.

131. Also *Saghir Ahmad* v. *Federation of Pakistan*, PLD 1976 Lahore 287. But the expression fitness or otherwise of a person to be appointed to or hold a particular post has been interpreted as limited in application to cases of persons seeking appointments to posts for first time or outside their cadre or to appointments to a particular post in same or equivalent cadre. *Muttaqi Hussain Rizvi* v. *Province of Sind*, PLD 1978 Karachi 703.

132. See *Khalilur Rahman* v. *Government of Pakistan*, PLD 1981 Karachi 750, in which it was held that question of competency of authority passing an order, if belonging to the hierarchy of affairs of the department concerned, is subject to the jurisdiction of service tribunals. The view of the Baluchistan High Court in PLD 1980 Quetta 58 does not appear to hold good on account of later several judgements of the superior courts as mentioned in Note 109 above.

133. *S. Ali Reza Shah Naqvi* v. *Government of Sind*, PLD 1979 SC 856.

134. *Muhammad Anis* v. *Abdul Haseeb*, PLD 1994 SC 539; *Dil Murad* v. *Federation of Pakistan* [1998] PLC (CS) 378; *Abdul Bari* v. *Government of Pakistan*, PLD 1981 Karachi 290.

135. Service Tribunals Act 1973, Section 3(4).

136. Baluchistan Service Tribunal Act, 1974, Section 3(4); NWFP Service Tribunals Act, 1974, Section 3(4).

137. Punjab Administrative Tribunals Act, 1974, Section 3 (unamended).

138. Punjab Administrative Tribunals (Amendment) Act, 1975 substituted Section 3 of the Original Act with new Section 3.

139. New Section 3(4) of Punjab Act of 1974.

140. Sind Service Tribunal Act, 1973, Section 3(4) (unamended).

141. Sind Service Tribunals (Second Amendment) Act, 1974, substituting Sub-section (4) of Section 3 in the original Act of 1973.

142. Ibid., New Section 3-A regarding removal of chairman or members added to the original Act.

143. New Section 3-A, Sub-section (1).

144. Ibid., Sub-section (3).

145. 'Misconduct' means a conduct prejudicial to the good order of service discipline or contrary to the Government Servants (Conduct) Rules or unbecoming of an officer or a gentleman and includes any act on the part of the chairman or a member, to bring or attempt to bring, political or other outside influence, directly or indirectly, to bear on the government or any governmental officer, in respect of any matter relating to his retention as such chairman or member, punishment, retirement or other conditions of his service, and includes:

   (i) Conviction of an offence involving moral turpitude;

   (ii) Active participation in sectarian, communal or political controversies;

   (iii) Persistent disregard of the Rules of Business, relating to the conduct of affairs of the tribunal; or

   (iv) Assuming a style of living beyond his legitimate means. See Explanation to Sub-section (2) of Section 3-A of Sind Service Tribunals Act, 1973.

146. Sub-Section (2) of Section 3A of Sind Service Tribunals Act, 1973.

147. Sind Service Tribunals (Amendment) Ordinance, 1977 adding Sub-section (4-A) in Section 3 of the Original Act of 1973.

148. Constitution of Islamic Republic of Pakistan, 1973, Article 212 Clause (3); *Muhammad Yousaf* v. *Province of Punjab* [1992] SCMR 1748; *M.A. Majid* v. *Government of Pakistan* [1976] SCMR 311.

149. *Pakistan State Oil Co.* v. *Muhammad Tahir Khan,* PLD 2001 SC 980; *Sh. Masud Ahmad* v. *Pakistan,* PLD 1976 SC 195.

150. *Babur Gul* v. *Sohail Ahmad Sheikh* [2002] SCMR 581; *Ali Hassn Rizvi* v. *Islamic Republic of Pakistan* [1986] SCMR 1084; *Islamic Republic of Pakistan* v. *Dr Safdar Mahmood,* PLD 1983 SC 100.

151. Ibid.

152. *Muhammad Hussain Kazi* v. *Government of the Punjab,* PLD 1983 SC 187.

153. *Iftikhar* v. *Khadim Husain,* PLD 2002 SC 607; *Muhammad Sharif* v. *Abdul Majid* [1986] SCMR 190.

154. *Capt (R) Muhammad Naseem Hijazi* v. *Province of Punjab, 2000* PLC (CS) 1310 (SC). See also *Muhammad Feroze* v. *Muhammad Jamaat Ali* [2006] SCMR 1304; *Naheed Rasheed* v. *Federation of Pakistan,* PLD 2002 SC 371.

155. *Muhammad Ashraf Kayani* v. *Azad Kashmir Government* [1995] PLC (CS) 969.

156. *Mustafa Nawaz Khokhar* v. *Federal Board,* PLD 2003 SC 154; *Kh. Abdul Waheed* v. *WAPDA* [1986] SCMR 1534.

157. Some of the examples are: *M.A. Ghafoor* v. *Secretary Establishment Division* [1982] PLC (CS) 547, *Abdul Rashid Bhatti* v. *Secretary Establishment*

Division [1982] PLC (CS) 668, *Syed Imtiaz Ali Naqvi* v. *Managing Director* [1984] PLC (CS) 1606, *Manzoor Hussain Shah* v. *Government of the Punjab.* In these cases, it has been held that an employee should not be denied the pay of the post in which he is required to work even through he may not be formally promoted to the grade of that post or he was appointed against a higher post with the orders that he would continue to draw pay in the lower pay and scale. See also *Jameel Ahmad Bhutto* v. *Federation of Pakistan* [1980] PLC (CS) 10, *Dost Muhammad* v. *Deputy Commissioner* [1980] PLC (CS) 611; *Mubarik Ahmad Malik* v. *Federation of Pakistan* [1980] PLC (CS) 418; *Naeem Akhtar* v. *Secretary Ministry of Planning* [1983] PLC (CS) 727, *Khadim Ali Tahir* v. *Chairman, POF Wah Cantt* [1983] PLC (CS) 243; *Muhammad Iqbal* v. *Commissioner, Sargodha Division* [1983] PLC (CS) 467; *Basharatullah Khan* v. *Secretary, Ministry of Finance* [1984] PLC (CS) 610; *Muhammad Ashraf* v. *The Commissioner, Lahore Division* [1984] PLC (CS) 1147; *M. Mobin Khan* v. *Collector of Customs* [1985] PLC (CS) 523; *Muhammad Afzal* v. *Superintendent of Police* [1985] PLC (CS) 882; wherein it was held that discretion to dispense with departmental enquiries cannot be exercised arbitrarily or capriciously and must be based on sound reasons and where the allegations give rise to disputed or complicated questions of facts, a departmental enquiry should be held. See also *Abdul Karim Sheikh* v. *Post Master General* [1982] PLC (CS) 795; *Zakir Ali* v. *Commissioner of Income Tax* [1980] PLD (CS) 273 wherein it has been held that 'Authority' (who can only impose minor penalties) cannot be the same persons and each case of major penalty should be scrutinised by two persons at different levels.

158. *W.A. Shaikh* v. *Pakistan,* 1981 PLC (CS) 363; *Qazi Muhammad Anwar Barlas* v. *Secretary Establishment Division* [1981] PLC (CS) 330; *M.H. Shamim* v. *Secretary Establishment Division,* [1981] PLC (CS) 337.

159. Provisional Constitution (Second Amendment) Order 1982 (CMLA Order 3 of 1982).

160. Both the members were appointed as Officers on Special Duty.

161. It is noticeable that the decisions in the cases of W.A. Shaikh, Qazi Muhammad Anwar Barlas, and M.H. Shamim were announced on 26 February 1981, 28 February 1981, and 28 February 1981 respectively and Dr Afghan was removed from service through a notification dated 9 March 1981.

162. *Dr A.Q.K. Afghan* v. *Secretary Establishment Division* [1982] PLC (CS) 214.

163. Ibid.

164. This happened in November 1980.

165. Removal from Service (Special Provisions) Regulation (MLR 58 of 1969).

166. Constitution of Islamic Republic of Pakistan, 1973, Article 270; Interim Constitution of Islamic Republic of Pakistan, 1972, Article 281.

167. *The State* v. *Zia-ur-Rehman,* PLD 1973 SC 49, wherein it was held that notwithstanding the validation provision (Article 281 of the Interim Constitution 1972), the courts could review acts done, orders made or

proceedings taken without jurisdiction, *mala fide* or *coram non judice*. The other case was *Federation of Pakistan* v. *Saeed Ahmad Khan*, PLD 1974 SC 151 in which it was held that Martial Law Regulation No. 58 has not been saved under Article 270(1) of the Constitution of 1973 by the Parliament under the Validation of Laws Act LXIII of 1975 and hence courts can review orders passed under the said Regulation.

168. See *M. Yamin Qureshi* v. *Islamic Republic of Pakistan*, PLD 1980 SC 22.
169. See *Abdul Karim Shaikh* v. *Post Master General* [1982] PLC (CS) 795.
170. It is interesting to note that a retired Brigadier (Abdul Rashid) from the Army was taken as a member of the Federal Service Tribunal and served as such for more than two years. A retired Major General (Abdur Rahman) also served as a member of the Federal Service Tribunal. Similarly, persons who have served in the Agriculture or Information Departments of the government, or who have been professional engineers or accountants or have been in the postal Service of Pakistan, have served or are serving as members of the Tribunals. Such persons have obviously not been exposed to any legal or judicial training.
171. Mr B.G.N. Kazi (who later became a Judge of Sind High Court) and Mr Jamal-ud-Din Abro served as members of the Federal Service Tribunal for some period of time. They were both drawn from the judicial service and had served as District and Sessions Judges for considerable period of time. From 1982 to 1988, no member of the said tribunal was drawn from judicial service. In 1988, a retired Sessions Judge, Mr Hasan Nawaz, was appointed as a member of this tribunal.
172. *Capt* * *Mukhtar Ahmad Shaikh* v. *Federation of Pakistan*, PLD 2014 FSC 23.
173. See *Mohammad Ashraf Nadeem* v. *Government of Pakistan* PLJ 1983 (Tr. Cases) 165. In this case, the Chairman of the Federal Service Tribunal after striking down the challenged administrative order as *mala fide*, ventured into adding the last two paragraphs about the reduction of arrears of pay and suggesting that action similar to the quashed action could then be taken under a law that came on the statute books after original order. These paragraphs are clearly irrelevant to the case before the tribunal but explains the insecure state of the mind of the chairman.
174. See Note 151 above.
175. *S. Ali Raza Shah Naqvi* v. *Government of Sind*, PLD 1979 SC 856; *Mufti Mushtaq Ahmad* v. *Federation of Pakistan*, PLD 1981 SC 172.
176. *Ch. Zafarullah Khan* v. *Pakistan*, PLD 1975 SC 15.
177. It has been held by Federal Service Tribunal that it has no jurisdiction to review its own judgements on merits. It can only correct mathematical or clerical errors in such judgements. *Muhammad Ali* v. *Post Master General* [1982] PLC (CS) 757; *Malik Mushtaq Hussain* v. *Secretary to the Government of Pakistan* [1982] PLC (CS) 342. Punjab Service Tribunal has also expressed the same view in *Khalid Parvez* v. *Director General* [1985] PLC (CS) 768, and *Nazar Mohammad Khan* v. *The Secretary to Government of*

Punjab [1980] PLC (CS) 79. In the latter case, Punjab Service Tribunal has expressed its opinion in favour of conferment of power of review in the Service Tribunals. NWFP Service Tribunal however has taken the contrary view and exercised review jurisdiction in *Abdul Rashid* v. *Government of NWFP*, PLJ 1976 Tribunal Cases (Service) 338.
178. M.P. Jain, *Indian Constitutional Law* (3rd edn., 1978) 635.
179. Durga Das Basu, *Shorter Constitution of India* (9th edn., 1984) 787.
180. M.P. Jain, Supra Note 160.
181. The Constitution of India, Article 323-A, Clause (2)(a).
182. Clause (2)(b).
183. Clause (2)(c).
184. Clause (2)(d).
185. Clause (2)(e).
186. Clauses (2)(f) and (g).
187. Clause (3).
188. Article 323 B.
189. Clause (2).
190. V.S. Chauhan, 'Justice by Tribunal: A Brief Comment on the Administrative Tribunals Act, 1985', AIR 1986 Journal 56.
191. The Administrative Tribunals Act, 1985, Section 4(1).
192. Section 4(2).
193. Section 4(3) and (4).
194. Section 5(1).
195. Section 3(d).
196. Section 5(1).
197. Section 5(2).
198. Section 5(3).
199. Section 5(4)(a), (b), and (c).
200. Section 5(5).
201. Section 5(6).
202. Section 5(6) Proviso.
203. Section 5(7).
204. Section 6(1).
205. Section 6(2).
206. Section 6(3).
207. Section 6(4), (5), and (6).
208. Section 7.
209. Section 8.
210. Section 9(2).
211. Section 11(a).
212. Section 11(b).
213. Section 11(c).
214. Section 11(d).
215. Section 11(e).

216. Section 11(f).
217. Section 3(q).
218. Section 14(1)(b) & (c).
219. Section 14(1)(a).
220. Section 14(2) and (3).
221. Section 15(1).
222. Section 15(2) and (3).
223. Section 16.
224. See Sections 14(1) and 15(1).
225. V.S. Chauhan, Supra Note 172, p. 58.
226. The main test laid down by the Supreme Court of India for determination of a tribunal is that the body or authority has been constituted by the state and has been clothed with the state's inherent judicial power to deal with disputes between parties and determine them on the merits fairly and objectively. It has been conceded that it is really not possible to describe exhaustively the features which are common to the tribunals and the courts and features which are distinct and separate. *All Party Hill Traders' Conference* v. *Captain W.A. Sangma*, AIR 1977 SC 2155 and *Associated Cement Companies Ltd* v. *P.N. Sharma*, AIR 1965 SC 1595. Applying this test, administrative tribunals are tribunals for the purpose of Article 136 of the Constitution but the question still remains as to whether they are 'courts' within the meaning of Article 32(3). Construing the word 'tribunal' literally as used in Article 323-A and Administrative Tribunals Act, 1985, it can be said that not being a 'court', it cannot exercise the powers exercisable by the Supreme Court under Article 32.
227. *Union of India* v. *Parma Nanda*, AIR 1989 SC 1185; (1989) 2 SCC 177.
228. AIR 1997 SC 1125; (1997) 3 SCC 261.
229. Administrative Tribunals Act, 1985, Section 19(1).
230. Explanation to Section 19(1).
231. Section 20(1).
232. Section 20(2)(b).
233. Section 20(3).
234. Section 19(3).
235. Section 19(4).
236. Section 21(1).
237. Section 23(3).
238. Section 22(1).
239. Section 22(3).
240. Section 22(4).
241. Section 24.
242. Section 27.
243. Section 17.
244. Section 18(1).
245. Section 18(2).

246. Section 25.
247. Section 26.
248. Section 35(1).
249. Section 35 (2).
250. Section 37(1).
251. Section 36.
252. Section 37(2).
253. Ministry of Home Affairs Notification No. GSR 713 dated 26 July 1985 published in the Gazette of India, Part II, Section 3 (1), dated 3 August 1985, pp. 1835–41.
254. Lall, *Remedies of Government Servants in Service Matters under the Administrative Tribunals Act 1985*, revised by Justice K.B. Asthana (2nd edn., 1987), Preface, v–vi.
255. Ministry of Personnel and Training, Administrative Reforms, and Public Grievances and Pension (Department of Personnel and Training), Notification No. GSR 527(E), dated 1 July 1985, published in the Gazette of India, Extra., Part II, Section 3(i) dated 1 July 1985, p. 2.
256. Ministry of Personnel and Training, Administrative Reforms, and Public Grievances and Pension (Department of Personnel and Training), Notification No. GSR 764 (E), dated 1 July 1985, published in the Gazette of India, Extra., Part II, Section 3(i) dated 26 September 1985, p. 2.
257. Ministry of Personnel and Training, Administrative Reforms, and Public Grievances and Pension (Department of Personnel and Training), Notification No. GSR 609(E) dated 26 July 1985, published in the Gazette of India, Extra., Part II, Section 3(i), p. 1.
258. *S.P. Sampath Kumar* v. *Union of India*, AIR 1987 SC 386.
259. The Administrative Tribunals (Amendment) Act 1986, Section 3.
260. Ibid., Section 19.
261. Supra Note 237.
262. Ibid.
263. AIR 1997 S.C. 1125; (1997) 3 SCC 261.
264. I.P. Massey, *Administrative Law*, Ninth Edition 2017, Eastern Book Company Lukhnow/New Delhi, pp. 616-7
265. Ibid, p. 617
266. Supra Note 209, Section 7.
267. Ibid., Section 6.
268. Ibid., Section 29-A.
269. Section 36 A inserted by the Administrative Tribunals (Amendment) Act, 1987 (Act No. 51 of 1987).
270. *J.B. Chopra & others* v. *Union of India*, AIR 1987 SC 357.
271. I.P. Massey, Supra Note 264, pp. 618-9.
272. *Harinagar Sugar Mills* v. *Shyam Sunder*, AIR 1961 SC 1669.
273. *ACC* v. *P.N. Sharma*, AIR 1965 SC 1595.
274. AIR 1950 SC 188.

275. *Jaswant Sugar Mills* v. *Lakshmi Chand*, AIR 1963 SC 677, applying the test the court held that a conciliation officer exercising power under Clause 29 of the Order of the Governor issued under the UP Industrial Disputes Act is not a tribunal.
276. Ibid.
277. *Engineering Mazdoor Sabha* v. *Hind Cycles Ltd*, AIR 1963 SC 874, held Arbitrator appointed under Section 10 of the Industrial Disputes Act, 1947 is not a tribunal.
278. *Tariq Transport Company* v. *Sargodha Bhera Bus Service*, PLD 1958 SC (Pak.) 437 at p. 455.
279. *Karam Chand Thapar* v. *CIT* [1972] 4 SCC 124; AIR 1971 SC 1590.
280. See Law Commission of India Report on Income Tax Act, 1922 (Twelfth Report) 48 (1958) and the Report of the Direct Taxes Administration Committee, at 81–86 (1958–59).
281. [1977] 2 SCC 491.
282. For a detailed study see S.N. Jain, *Administrative Tribunals in India* (Indian Law Institute, 1977); Balram K. Gupta, 'Administrative Tribunals and Judicial Review: A Comment on Forty-second Amendment' in *Indian Constitution: Trends and Issues* (Indian Law Institute, 1978) 401; Jain and Jain, *Principles of Administrative Law*, Chapter V, 129–171; S.P. Sathe, 'Forty-fourth Constitutional Amendment', *Economic and Political Weekly*, Vol. XI No. 43, 23 October 1976; U. Baxi, 'Constitutional Changes; An Analysis of the Swarn Singh Committee Report' [1976] 2 SCC (Journal) 17–28; I.P. Massey, 'Constitution Amended', *Secular Democracy Journal*, 11 December 1976, 13.

CHAPTER VII

The Citizen and Maladministration

7.1 Ombudsman

Justitio Ombudsman, commonly called Ombudsman, is variously described as the Parliamentary Supervisory Official for Civil Affairs in Sweden, Inspector-General of Administration in Finland, the *Folketingets* Commissioner in Denmark, and the Parliamentary Commissioner in New Zealand. Its East European counterpart is Procurator General.[1] Swedish in origin, the office of Ombudsman[2] (literally an officer or a commissioner) was adopted, and established in Finland in 1919, in Denmark in 1958, and in New Zealand in 1962. The unique importance and usefulness of this office for imparting functional efficiency, responsibility and integrity in the administration has already attracted attention of the informed people in a number of countries, for instance the United States of America and Commonwealth countries of Canada, Britain, India, and Singapore besides Bangladesh, Ghana, and New Zealand.

7.1.1 Development of the concept of Ombudsman

(i) Sweden

First established in 1809, the office of ombudsman is considered very important in Sweden in view of its proven utility as a potent instrument for the redressal of citizens' grievances against the administration, and is by now endowed with rich constitutional conventions, tradition and experience attached to it. Finland adopted it in 1919 and Norway in 1963.[3] An ombudsman is appointed by the Swedish Parliament, for a four-year term at a time. A person is selected for this high office mainly for reasons of high integrity, character, and established reputation for competence. His main duty is to act as an authorised agency of the parliament for maintaining a constant vigil over and scrutiny of the discharge of administrative and judicial functions by the government and other authorities. He hears complaints of individual against the administration; inquires into individual complaints of maladministration, abuse of administrative discretion or administrative inefficiency; and takes appropriate action for the redressal of grievances against the government departments, public officials, and authorities. He is intended to keep a watch over government departments, administrative agencies, authorities, and officers; to receive individual complaints against them; and to inquire into acts of the administration contrary to law; misuse of administrative processes; and acts which are unreasonable, unjust, arbitrary, oppressive, improper or wrong. He also audits administrative procedure and problems becoming apparent in the course of investigation of complaints of individuals. He is not supposed to be a terror to administrative officials, but merely provides a machinery to look into the discharge of administrative action, and to conduct an informal review of improper administrative orders, determinations, and decisions. He establishes informal contacts with administration, points out instances of improper exercise of authority, draws attention to instances of abuse of discretion, or negligence in the discharge of duties by the administrative personnel. He can act as a responsible critic of administrative misconduct. He can suggest appropriate intra departmental action against a refractory authority or delinquent officer. In case any individual public servant is guilty of gross misconduct or violation of official duties, he can recommend disciplinary proceedings. While discharging his function properly, the ombudsman renders a not so easily available service to the private individual citizen. He helps him get redress where the ordinary parliamentary and judicial modes of redressal are wholly ineffective, inadequate, or unavailable. He is effective in areas in which the common administrative law remedies too are, as they are generally understood, largely inadequate. He submits a report to the parliament which helps it to act as the grand inquest of the nation.

(II) DENMARK

Under a Danish law passed in 1954, provision was made for the *Folketingets* Commissioner with an office similar to that of an ombudsman in Sweden. After every general election the Danish Parliament (*Folkelingets*) appoints a person possessed of legal qualifications and known for good reputation from amongst persons who are non-members as the *Folketingets* Commissioner. He holds office at the pleasure of the parliament, and occupies his office so long as he enjoys the confidence of that body. During his term of office he is paid a salary at the maximum rate in the scale of a judge of the Supreme Court, is given a personal allowance and waiting money (compensation payable to government servants who are out of office); and is assured of a pension after his retirement. He cannot hold any other office whether public or private, except with the consent of a parliament committee appointed to consider matters pertaining to his office. The functions of the office of *Folketingets* Commissioner include:

(a) supervision of the civil and military government, and administration;

(b) keeping a watch over unlawful, arbitrary or unreasonable decisions of public authorities and abuse, or misuse of powers vested in them; and

(c) gathering information relating to acts of negligence and mistakes of civil servants and all other persons including ministers, but not judges in the performance of their official duties.

He has a general jurisdiction over the administration, members of civil and military services, and other persons holding public offices, except the judges. He can conduct examination by request or *suo motu* into any civil action performed in the service of the state and coming within the jurisdiction of public authorities and the state agencies, and investigate an administrative order on an allegation of official misconduct, abuse of public duties and discretion. He can also advise institution of departmental proceeding, or the prosecution of a civil servant for proved irregularities, or abuse of official position, and express his view on matters of administrative problems and defect in existing laws or administrative regulations coming to his notice. He can place his views before the cabinet and the parliament.

The Danish Parliament prescribes the general procedure and rules for the functioning of the office of the commissioner. Any person having sufficient reason for grievance against any governmental agency can lodge a written complaint within a year from the date on which the subject matter of the complaint is committed. The complaint should bear the complainant's name and is accompanied with his evidence. If the complaint is not filed too late in the day and does not otherwise fall outside its jurisdiction, the commissioner inquires into it. He observes secrecy in the matter brought before him while investigating the truth of the complaint. He can reject unfounded, vexatious, infructuous, insignificant, or false complaints. In the course of the inquiry he can communicate with the appropriate department, the concerned officer through the normal channel, and demand from them a statement on the complaint. All administrative authorities must cooperate with him by supplying 'such information . . . documents and records as he may demand.' Every year he submits an annual report to the parliament. The report is printed, published and made available to the public.

(III) NEW ZEALAND

The ombudsman idea caught the imagination of people in New Zealand after the Kandy (Sri Lanka) Seminar held in 1959 under the aegis of the United Nations in which New Zealand was represented by her attorney-general who was also the Minister of Justice in the government of his country. It was earlier to the publication of the Whyatt Report in Britain. In fact, the New Zealand Parliament was already considering the Parliamentary Commissioner for Investigations Bill which had been introduced in it on 19 August 1960. The bill was finally passed as the New Zealand Parliamentary Commissioner (Ombudsman) Act, 1962. A study of this law is, particularly, fruitful as under it provision is made for the establishment of the office of ombudsman for the first time in a country practising the system of parliamentary government of the British model in vogue in most of the countries of the Commonwealth of Nations. Under the New Zealand law, the governor-general appoints the ombudsman on recommendation of the House of Representatives. Though the governor-general formally appoints him, yet he neither selects him, nor appoints him in accordance with the normal practice of parliamentary constitutional government of acting on the advice of the ministers. Still, it must be appreciated that the commendation of the House by a majority is conditioned by the mechanics of party system, and therefore, the choice cannot fall on a person who will not be approved by the government.

Nevertheless, the provision that the person should be selected by the House and recommended for appointment creates a psychology and institutional difference placing the parliamentary commissioner in a special position. He owes 'special responsibilities to the parliament and not the government.' This position is re-enforced by the provision that he is an officer of the parliament, and does not hold his office during the pleasure of Her Majesty. He is not deemed to be employed in the service of Her Majesty for purposes of public service legislation and the law of superannuation. His tenure corresponds with the life of the House of one single parliament. During a parliamentary term he is given no security of tenure, and can be removed on the initiative of the House of Representatives. He must enjoy full and complete confidence of the House. The formal order removing him from office can be passed by the governor-general upon an address of the House. The grounds of removal may include his disability, bankruptcy, neglect of duty, or misconduct. When the parliament is not sitting, the governor-general on his own can, if necessary, suspend him after satisfying himself of the grounds till the end of the next ensuing parliamentary session. He cannot take up any appointment under the government; and cannot also engage himself elsewhere earning any reward 'outside the duties of his office'. He can resign his office by writing to that effect to the Speaker of the House of Representatives; and if the latter is not available, to the prime minister. He is paid a salary fixed on the recommendation of a Royal Commission appointed by the governor-general under Section 27 of the Civil List Law. His salary is made a charge on the consolidated fund, and so cannot be reduced. He is entitled to allowances payable to a member of a statutory board. Described as an officer of the parliament, the commissioner is administered an oath of office and an oath of secrecy by the speaker, or on his authorisation by the clerk of the House of Representatives. He is obliged to act faithfully and impartially. He is given under the statute a general power and wide jurisdiction over the government departments.

Without prejudice to the generality of the jurisdictional authority a long schedular list of sixty-five departments is given in the Act over which he exercises his supervision and control. The reach of his authority does not extend to matters relating to the armed forces, or decisions of the government. He can look into only operational as distinguished from planning determinations of administration. The ministers of the government are excluded from his jurisdiction for reasons of their direct and immediate responsibility to the parliament according to the well established rules and conventions of the parliamentary government. The statutory corporations are autonomous in character, and therefore, are not considered part of the government administration. Functionally speaking, the commissioner has wide jurisdictional authority of investigation over a wide range of matters, except policy matters, questions of legality of governmental acts and cases in which a right of appeal to a law court or a tribunal exists, even if such right is not availed of. He has the authority to investigate the grounds and basis of any decision, recommendation made, or any act done or omission made relating to any matter of administration and affecting any person or body of persons in his personal capacity.[4]

He not only enquires into acts of maladministration, but also oversees the exercise of administrative discretion and processes of administrative decision-making. When properly approached, he establishes contact with the appropriate department or authority informally asking it to remove the grievance of the complainant. If it becomes necessary for him to undertake an investigation in any matter, he is given access to all records and files. The concerned department and the authority cannot withhold from him relevant papers and records on the plea of an injury by its disclosure. This places him in a more advantageous position as compared to a law court which is handicapped by the decision in the Thetis Case[5] on privileged documents. However, he cannot insist on production of any paper or giving of any testimony, if its production might prejudice maintenance of relations with foreign states, or secrecy of deliberations and proceedings of the cabinet. Subject to the statutory provisions and rules framed in this respect by the House of Representatives, the commissioner is given discretion to regulate the procedure of his office 'in such manner as he thinks fit'. He has control over his staff which he himself appoints. However, the number of persons of his staff is fixed by the prime minister, and salary fixation requires the approval of the Finance Ministry. Members of his staff are not deemed to be governed by the Public Services Act, 1912, and the Superannuation Act, 1956. Their duty is specially stated to assist the commissioner in 'the efficient carrying out of functions and not to divulge any information' outside their duties. After having received a complaint he conducts the investigation in camera. He can give a hearing to the departmental representative likely to be affected adversely, and can also summon any person including the complainant who, in his opinion, is able to give information, produce document or papers which relate to the matter under investigation. He cannot, however, compel an official to give any testimony if the latter is bound to maintain secrecy under the State Services and Official Secrets Act, 1951.

Since after its establishment the ombudsman has proved to be an effective agency to tackle administrative corruption and maladministration cases, it takes up allegations of administrative muddle, error and red tape. He seems to create a new administrative morality and equality by insisting upon fairness, courtesy and reasonableness.[6]

(IV) THE UNITED STATES OF AMERICA

In the United States of America the reception of the idea of an ombudsman has encountered strong constitutional and other practical difficulties. Because of the established constitutional position originally founded on the doctrine of separation of powers, the idea of accountability of the administration to the Congress is opposed to the known constitutional jurisprudence of the country. It is doubtful if the president's administration would ever submit to any supervisory jurisdiction of an officer appointed by and responsible to Congress at any foreseeable time. Nevertheless, arrangements for making the administration responsive to the grievances of the public have been proposed, discussed and often adopted. The Attorney-General's Committee on Administrative Procedure (1941), the Benjamin Report in the State of New York (1942), the Hoover Commission's task force on Regulatory Commissions (1949), the President's Conference on Administrative Procedure (1953) and the recommendations of the American Bar Association (1956) are some of the notable steps in the direction. In 1953, the president established an Office of Administrative Procedure in the Department of Justice 'to carry on continual studies of the adequacy of the procedure by which the federal agencies determine the rights, duties, and privileges of persons', and directed it to 'collect and publish facts and statistics concerning the procedure of the agencies. In 1957, the House of Representatives formed a 'Committee on Legislative Oversight' to investigate the administration and enforcement of the law by the government departments and the agencies. In 1959, the Senate too appointed a sub-committee for the purpose which reported in 1961 and recommended the establishment of an Office of Administration and Reorganisation in the White House charged with the duty of compilation of statistics and investigation of the trouble spots in the administration.

(v) OTHER COUNTRIES

The International Commission of Jurists set up a Committee (Committee III) to discuss the need for an ombudsman in the Asian and Pacific region. They recommended the establishment of this institution under a statute for dealing with complaints against the administration, as also to take up matters brought to its notice otherwise. It should have both accusatorial and inquisitorial functions. The head of state and judges should not be within its jurisdiction.

An Ombudsman has since been appointed in a number of countries of Africa and Asia. The Constitution of the Republic of Ghana (1969) made provisions for the appointment and functions of the Ombudsman in accordance with the law. The President of Ghana would appoint the Ombudsman in consultation with the Council of State notwithstanding the general position requiring him to act with the advice of the cabinet, or a minister along with the general authority of the cabinet. The Ombudsman would investigate any action taken in exercise of the administrative functions of any department or ministry of state, any statutory corporation or any member of the public services. The specific categories of 'matters which can be subjected to investigation' were specified by law. The procedure for lodging of citizens' complaints, investigations and redressal of grievances too was enabling him to perform his functions of disposal of grievances of the citizens. These purposes would include:

(a) to enforce information production;
(b) to enforce attendance of witnesses and their examination;
(c) to institute civil proceedings; and
(d) to make recommendations in respect of appropriate remedies.

In each session of the parliament, a report of Ombudsman giving a summary of matters investigated and action taken by him during the preceding session of the parliament is required to be presented.

7.2 OMBUDSMAN (PARLIAMENTARY COMMISSIONER) IN BRITAIN

Like any other country with an intensive form of government, in Britain also, the grip of the parliament and the courts over the ever-widening fronts of the administration started showing signs of weakness. The resultant discontentment due to administrative faults also started mounting, and ultimately erupted in the Crichel

Down episode in 1954. This case, though it had little legal content, focused attention on the maladministration of the government in dealing with a citizen's grievance. In this case, the government had acquired a piece of land for use as a bombing range during the war. After the war was over, the owner desired to repurchase it. The claim of the owner was considered by various officials with the usual impersonal attitude and callous indifference. Ultimately, the land was given to the Agriculture Ministry to be used as a model farm. The public criticism and heat which this episode generated led to the appointment of Franks Committee and on its recommendations the Tribunals and Inquiries Act, 1958 was passed. It was followed by the Parliamentary Commissioner Act in 1967.

The parliamentary commissioner envisaged under the Act is a permanent appointee with the security of service like that of a high court judge. He is appointed by the Crown on the advice of the prime minister. His salary is charged on the consolidated fund and holds office during good behaviour, subject to the retiring age of sixty-five. He can only be removed on addresses from both Houses of Parliament. He has the power to appoint his own staff subject to the Treasury approval. He does not receive complaints directly from the citizens but through members of parliament. This is done to reconcile the notion of ministerial responsibility with the concept of this institution. He has no other power except to investigate and report. The report is made to the Select Committee of the House of Commons which examines it and proposes action. Ministers are not outside the purview of this jurisdiction. One of the characteristic features of this institution is its non-lawyer character and, therefore, proceeds with the work in an informal manner without obsession with legal technicalities. However, for legal advice it can always use the office of the Treasury Solicitor. There is no set prescribed procedure of inquiry, but the commissioner has adequate powers to investigate a complaint thoroughly. The investigations are conducted in private and the officials implicated are given reasonable opportunity to defend themselves. He can administer oath and compel the attendance of witnesses and the production of documents. He has powers of contempt of court. His reports on investigations, and communications with members of parliament on the subject matter of complaint, are protected by absolute privilege in the law of defamation.[7] Irrespective of the Official Secrets Acts and the law relating to Crown privilege, he is entitled to access any relevant document except the one relating to the proceedings of the cabinet and its Committees.[8] However, 'Crown privilege' may be asserted to prevent the commissioner or any member of his staff from disclosing information obtained during his investigation.[9] Official Secret Acts may also be used to prevent disclosures for purposes other than investigation and report.[10] The commissioner is prohibited from investigating an action in respect of which the person has a remedy in a court or tribunal by way of appeal, reference or review, unless he is of the opinion that such remedy would not be adequate.

The jurisdiction of the commissioner extends to departments given in the Second Schedule of the Act. The Third Schedule lays down the departments which are excluded from his jurisdiction. External relations, crime investigation, judicial proceedings, prerogative of mercy, governmental, contractual and commercial transactions, award of honours; granting of royal charters;, national health service, local government, police and personnel matters in armed forces, and the civil services are excluded from this jurisdiction. This exclusion is the subject of much criticism in Britain. Jurisdiction of investigation extends to the case of 'injustice in consequence of maladministration'.[11] However, the terms, 'injustice' and 'maladministration' have been deliberately left undefined to make the boundaries of jurisdiction flexible. Nevertheless, 'injustice' includes cases of hardship and a sense of grievance, besides legally redressable damage. Maladministration covers a multitude of administrative fault of commission and omission, corruption, bias, unfair discrimination, harshness, misleading a member of public as to his rights, failing to notify him properly of his rights or to explain the reason for a decision, general highhandedness, using power for a wrong purpose, failing to consider relevant material, taking irrelevant material into account, losing or failing to reply to correspondence, delaying unreasonably before making a tax refund or presenting a tax demand or dealing with an application for a grant or licence and so on.[12]

The Barlow Clowes Affair

The Parliamentary Commissioner's success in securing some £150 million compensation to those who had lost money in the Barlow Clowes affair has been his most spectacular single achievement thus far, and deserves to be separately considered.

Barlow Clowes was a brokerage business selling gilt-based investments under a 'bond washing' scheme which transmuted highly taxed income into lowly taxed capital. When the tax loophole was closed in 1985, funds were diverted from the UK firm to associated firms in Gibraltar and Jersey and were put into highly speculative investments and high living for the fund managers, and interest was paid out of capital. Eventually the firms' liabilities greatly exceeded their assets and many investors lost their life savings. The Department of Trade and Industry (DTI), which was responsible for the regulation of the financial services industry, was accused of having persistently disregarded evidence of serious malpractices and having known for several years that the UK firm was trading without the *necessary* licence, but only in late 1987 did they appoint statutory inspectors. Calls for compensation from the government fell upon deaf ears. But then the Parliamentary Commissioner, in response to a reference from Mr Alf Morris MP (the first of 159 MPs to refer cases to him), took up the case.

The Commissioner identified five areas in which there had been significant maladministration by the DTI. First, the DTI had given erroneous advice to Barlow Clowes in 1975 that the firm did not need a DTI licence. Secondly, the DTI ought to have realised in 1984 that there was a separate Barlow Clowes partnership established in Jersey (which contradicted several of the representations made by the UK firm). This should have alerted the DTI that something untoward was happening. Thirdly, when alerted the DTI eventually decided to grant a retrospective licence in 1985; that decision had been taken maladministratively' in that too much regard was paid to the fact that such a licence would shield the DTI from criticism and too little to whether the grant of such a licence would be in the interests of the investors. Fourthly, the DTI, concerned that the capital of the fund was being eroded, had sought reassurances from accountants but these reassurances were too narrow to be satisfactory. Fifthly, there had been several months' delay in acting after warnings that all was not well from the Stock Exchange.

However, the important question was whether the maladministration identified had caused the losses to the investors. The Commissioner concluded that this was the case particularly in regard to the Jersey partnership. Had the significance of this been appreciated the Barlow Clowes operations would have been brought to a halt before most of the losses were incurred, Hence, he recommended that compensation should be paid.[13]

THE SPREAD OF THE OMBUDSMAN PRINCIPLE

One of the many proofs of the success of the ombudsman principle is its continual extension into new areas. Having been instituted in Britain for the central government, it has now been extended to the National Health Service and local government. Every year there are new extensions of the principle in other countries. Few indeed are the constitutional innovations for which such widespread success can be claimed.

The principle has spread outside the sphere of government into that of business and finance. Voluntary ombudsman systems have been established successfully in the insurance and banking industries. There is a Financial Services Ombudsman with a wide jurisdiction over persons 'authorised' to provide regulated financial services. A Legal Services Ombudsman ensures that the professional bodies that exercise disciplinary functions over the various forms of legal professional (including licensed conveyancers) deal with complaints about misconduct properly.'" Prisoners have recourse to a non-statutory Independent Complaints Adjudicator. There is an independent Housing Ombudsman. The so-called Pensions Ombudsman, who has power to determine as well as to investigate complaints of maladininistration in occupational or personal pension schemes, is in reality a statutory tribunal. His awards are legally enforceable and are subject to a right of appeal to the High Court on a point of law.

As this last example makes plain several of these more recently created 'ombudsmen' are strictly speaking not ombudsmen in the sense generally used. They often have the power to give directions rather than simply make recommendations; and they are often concerned with the resolution of private disputes (with judicial review being used as an appeal against an ombudsman's award) rather than with holding government to account for maladmin-istration. They might more properly be termed adjudicators or tribunals. But a cavil over a name should not divert attention from their success and usefulness.[14]

7.3 OMBUDSMAN (*LOKPAL* AND *LOKAYUKTA*) IN INDIA

In its report dated 20 October 1966, the Indian Administrative Reforms Commission advocated the adoption of an institution like that of the Ombudsman for redress of citizens' grievances.[15] The Commission felt that the redressal of citizens' grievances would be basic to the functioning of democratic governments, would strengthen the hands of the government in administering the laws of the land and would enable the governments to go up in public faith and confidence, without which progress would not be possible.

The scheme propounded drew largely from the experiences of other countries. However, in many respects, it contained a number of peculiar features of its own to meet the special circumstances of India. Some of these circumstances mentioned by the Commission were:[16]

(i) The experience of countries like Sweden, Norway, Denmark, and New Zealand, having small areas and population, cannot necessarily be a precedent for India with such a vast area and huge population.

(ii) Whereas Norway, Sweden, Denmark, New Zealand, and the United Kingdom have centralised administrations, India is a federation based on division of functions between the centre and the states. This would raise the problem of separate jurisdictions for Ombudsman and he would have to deal with so many different authorities.

(iii) India has a parliamentary form of government with ministerial responsibility. Therefore the ministers are responsible to their respective legislatures for the acts of permanent officials serving under them. Even when commissions are appointed to investigate into the conduct of ministers, it is the respective legislature which becomes seized of the matter and would be the final authority which would take action or to which action would be reported.

(iv) The question of the right of a citizen to have access to the Ombudsman would come in conflict with the rights of a parliament or state legislature wherein the same issue could be raised by various means such as interpellations, adjournment motions, etc., or investigation by the committee on petitions.

(v) The courts in India have extensive powers to correct actions of the administrative authorities through constitutional writs and this would have to be taken into account and the provisions in this behalf should avoid any conflict of jurisdiction between the Ombudsman and the courts and that suitable procedures should be devised for the purpose.

(vi) There is a likelihood that interested persons might misuse the institution of Ombudsman to make false or baseless charges against the administration either to discredit it or delay or halt the implementation of various measures that might be undertaken in pursuance of government policies and programmes.

The commission suggested that the special circumstances relating to India can be fully met by providing for two special institutions for the redress of citizens' grievances. One of these may be designated as *Lokpal* and he should deal with complaints against the administrative acts of ministers or secretaries to the government at the centre and in the states. There should be another authority in each state and at the centre to be designated as *Lokayukta* for dealing with complaints against the administrative acts of other officials.

In working out other details pertaining to the offices of the *Lokpal* and *Lokayukta*, the Commission sought to achieve the following objectives:

(i)   that these offices should be demonstrably independent of the executive, legislature and the judiciary, and thus be impartial;

(ii) that their investigations and proceedings should be conducted in private and should be informal in character;

(iii) that their appointment, as far as possible, should be non-political, and that their status should be comparable with the highest judicial functionaries in the country;

(iv) that they should deal with matters in a discretionary field involving acts of injustice, corruption or favouritism;

(v)   that their proceedings should not be subject to judicial interference and they should have the maximum latitude and powers in obtaining information relevant to their duties; and

(vi) that they should not look forward to any benefit or pecuniary advantage from the executive government.[17]

The *Lokpal* would be appointed by the president on the advice of the prime minister which would be tendered by him after consultation with the Chief Justice of India and the leader of the opposition in the *Lok Sabha*. The *Lokpal* would have the same status as the Chief Justice of India. His tenure would be five years subject to his eligibility for reappointment for another term of five years in accordance with the same procedure. He could resign his office by writing to the president. He would not be removable from his office except in the manner prescribed in the constitution for the removal of a Judge of the Supreme Court, i.e. when a resolution passed by each House of Parliament, by absolute majority of the membership in each House and by a majority of not less than two-thirds of the members of that House present and voting, on grounds of proved misbehaviour and incapacity is presented to the president. The salary and other emoluments of the *Lokpal* would be the same as those of the Chief Justice of India.

The *Lokpal* would be free to choose his own staff, but their number, categories and conditions of service would be subject to the approval of the president. His budget would be subject to the control of parliament. Generally speaking, the *Lokpal* would have the power to investigate an administrative act done by or with the approval of a minister or a secretary to government at the centre or in the state, if a complaint were to be made against such an act by a person who was affected by it and who claimed to have suffered an injustice on that account. In this context, an 'act' would include a 'failure to take action'.

The following matters would be excluded from the purview of the *Lokpal*:

   (i) Action taken in a matter certified by a Minister as affecting the relations or dealings between the Government of India and any foreign Government or any international organisation of states or governments.

   (ii) Actions taken under the Extradition Act, 1962 or the Foreigners Act, 1946.

   (iii) Action taken for the purpose of investigation of crime or protecting the security of the State including action taken with respect to passports.

   (iv) Action taken in the exercise of power in relation to the determination as to whether the matter should go to a court or not.

   (v) Action taken in matters which arise out of the terms of contract governing purely commercial relations of administration with customers or suppliers except complaints of harassment or delays in the performance of contractual obligations.

(vi) Action taken in respect of appointments, removals, pay, disciple, superannuation or other personnel matters.

(vii) Grants of honours and awards.

(viii) A decision made in exercise of discretion by an administrative authority unless the elements involved in the exercise of discretion are absent to such an extent that no discretion ought to have been exercised at all.

(ix) Any action in respect of which the person aggrieved has or had the right of appeal, reference or review before a tribunal constituted by or under any statute.

(x) Any action in respect of which a person aggrieved has or had a remedy by way of proceedings in any court of law. The *Lokpal* may, however, look into such a matter if he is satisfied that in the particular circumstances it is not reasonable to expect the complainant to take or to have taken proceedings in a court of law.

(xi) An administrative action which was taken more than twelve months before the date of the complaint.

So far as the *Lokayukta* was concerned, it was envisaged that he would be concerned with problems similar to those which the *Lokpal* would face in respect of ministers and secretaries of a state. However, in respect of action taken at subordinate levels of official hierarchy, he would, in many cases, have to refer complainants to competent higher levels. His powers, functions and procedures could be prescribed *mutatis mutandis* with those which had been suggested for the *Lokpal*. His status, position, emoluments, etc. were, however, to be analogous to those of a chief justice of a high court and he should be entitled to have free access to the secretary to the government concerned or to the Head of the Department with whom he would mostly have to deal to secure justice in deserving cases. Where he was dissatisfied with the action taken by the department concerned, he should be in a position to seek a quick corrective action from the Minister or the Secretary concerned, failing which he should be able to draw the personal attention of the Prime Minister or the Chief Minister as the case may be. The procedure proposed to be followed by the *Lokpal* would apply *mutatis mutandis* to investigations taken up by the *Lokayukta*.

7.3.1 BILLS FOR ESTABLISHMENT OF THE OFFICES OF *LOKPAL* AND *LOKAYUKTAS*

The Government of India accepted the recommendations of the commission. The government took the definitive step towards the creation of the Ombudsman System in India when, in 1969, *the Lok Sabha* drafted the *Lokpal* and *Lokayuktas* Bill, 1968. By and large, the bill followed the model suggested by the commission with a few deviations. One major deviation made by the bill was to confine the jurisdiction of the Ombudsman to the centre sphere only leaving the states out of its purview whereas the commission had suggested one comprehensive scheme covering the centre-state administration as a whole. But because of the objections raised by many states against a central functionary interfering with their administrative affairs, the idea of bringing the state administration within the purview of the *Lokpal* was dropped. It was left to the states to establish their own Ombudsman.

The chief feature of the bill was to enable the *Lokpal* to initiate an investigation when a person made a complaint that he had suffered injustice in consequence of maladministration or corruption. Complaints about maladministration were characterised as 'grievance' and a complaint about corruption was termed as 'allegation'.

Another bill was introduced in 1971 which referred only to the central administration and not to state administration. The bill provided for the appointment, by the president of one *Lokpal* and one or more *Lokayuktas*. The *Lokpal* was to be appointed after consultation with the Chief Justice of India and the Leader of the Opposition in the *Lok Sabha*. If there was no such leader, a person elected by the members of the Opposition in the *Lok Sabha* for this purpose was to be consulted. The *Lokayuktas* were to be appointed after consultation with the *Lokpal*. Presumably, the president would have acted in this matter, as he does in other matters, on the advice of the prime minister in keeping with the theory of parliamentary form of government.[18]

Another bill was introduced in 1977 which completely negated the western idea of Ombudsman. The jurisdiction of the Central *Lokpal* was confined only to 'public men' which term included central ministers (including the Prime Minister), members of parliament, members of the legislative assemblies for the Union Territories and a few other categories of elected functionaries.[19] The government servants as such were to be beyond the purview of the *Lokpal*. However, the *Lokpal* could inquire into the conduct of any other person only to the extent necessary to inquire into any allegation of misconduct against a public man. Secondly, the proposed *Lokpal* was not to be concerned with cases of maladministration but only with cases involving corruption.

Another bill in this behalf was introduced in 1985, in the *Lok Sabha*. The bill closely followed the model of the *Lokpal* Bill, 1977 which lapsed because of the dissolution of the *Lok Sabha*. The new bill, like its 1977 counterpart, covered only allegations of misconduct. Grievances were excluded from *Lokpal*'s jurisdiction. The bill provided for an institutionalised framework for inquiry into charges of corruption in high places. The bill did not provide for a mechanism for redressal of grievances against the Administration which is usually the most important function assigned to the Ombudsman in other countries.[20]

Again, another *Lokpal* bill was sought to be introduced in *Lok Sabha* in 1989. This bill made *Lokpal* a three-member body, and even the Prime Minister was brought within the jurisdiction of the *Lokpal*. The bill lapsed with the dissolution of the ninth *Lok Sabha*. Thereafter, the *Lokpal* Bill, 1996, was introduced in the eleventh *Lok Sabha* on 13 September 1996. But this bill also lapsed with the dissolution of the *Lok Sabha*. The *Lokpal* Bill, 1998 was introduced in the Lok Sabha on 3 August 1998 but before the bill could be enacted, the *Lok Sabha* was dissolved and, consequently, the bill lapsed. Again, the *Lokpal* Bill, 2001 was introduced by the central government in *Lok Sabha* in August 2001. Some of the provisions contained in the bill were quite different from the provisions made in the previous bills.[21]

It appears from the history of the bills for establishment of the office of *Lokpal* that the Indian governments were never serious about enacting a law in this behalf. The succeeding prime ministers and central ministers have been averse to any interference in their functions by an authority like the Ombudsman. They deliberately allowed the succeeding bills to lapse.

7.3.2 STATE *LOKAYUKTA*

While the idea of establishing an Ombudsman at the central level has proved abortive, several states have however adopted the system. These states include Orissa,[22] Maharashtra,[23] Rajasthan,[24] Bihar,[25] Uttar Pradesh,[26] Andhra Pradesh,[27] Karnataka,[28] Madhya Pradesh,[29] Gujarat,[30] and Delhi.[31]

The State Acts do not follow any uniform pattern. In some of the states, the task assigned to the *Lokayuktas* is to look into cases of corruption as well as maladministration. These Acts follow the model of the Central Bill of 1971. In other states, the task assigned to the *Lokayuktas* is confined only to allegations of corruption involving ministers (other than the chief minister) and government servants.

To narrate briefly the main features of the system in Andhra Pradesh, the Governor appoints the *Lokayukta* after consultation with the Chief Justice. Only a judge or a retired chief justice of a high court can be appointed to this office. The governor also appoints one or more *Upa-Lokayukta* from amongst the district judges. The term of office for each is five years but any of them can be removed from office by the governor for misbehaviour or incapacity after an inquiry by a Supreme Court judge or the chief justice of a high court.

The function of the *Lokayukta* is to investigate any action taken by, or with the approval of, or at the behest of (a) a minister or a secretary; (b) a member of the state legislature; or (c) a mayor of a municipal corporation. All other public servants in the states fall under the purview of the *Upa-Lokayukta*. The chief minister does not come within the purview of the *Lokayukta*. The emphasis of the system is on investigation of 'allegations', i.e. complaints of corruption by public servants and not on maladministration. The competent authority is bound to take action on the report of the *Lokayukta* or *Upa-Lokayukta* within three months.

The Karnataka system closely follows the Andhra Pradesh model but with some differences. In Karnataka, the Chief Minister falls within the purview of the *Lokayukta*. In appointing him, the Governor is to have more pervasive consultation, i.e., he has to consult with the chief justice of the high court, the chairman of the legislative council, the speaker of the assembly and the leaders of opposition in both the council and the assembly. Like Andhra Pradesh, in Karnataka as well, provision is made for the appointment of *Upa-lokayuktas* and only allegations (i.e. charges of corruption) are to be investigated by the *Lokayukta* and not those of maladministration. In both the Acts, the statutory corporation owned or controlled by the government: government companies, universities, and even co-operative societies under the contrail of the government fall within the purview of the *Upalokayukta*.

Under the Delhi *Lokayukta* and *Upa-lokayukta* Act, 1995, the *Lokayukta* takes cognizance of 'allegations' only. Allegation is defined so as to mean that a public functionary:

   (i) has failed to act in accordance with the norms of integrity and conduct 'which ought to be followed by public functionaries or the class to which he belongs';

  (ii) has abused or misused his position to obtain any gain or favour to himself or to any other person or to cause loss or undue harm or hardship to any other person;

(iii) was actuated in the discharge of his functions as such public functionary by improper or corrupt motives or personal interest;

(iv) is or has at any time during the period of his office been in possession of pecuniary resources or property disproportionate to his known resources of income.

'Public functionary' has been defined by Section 2(m) as a person who is or has been at any time:

(i) chief minister or a minister;

(ii) a member of the state legislative assembly (but not speaker or dy. speaker);

(iii) a person having the rank of a minister, or

(iv) chairman, vice-chairman, managing director or a member of the board of directors of a co-operative society subject to the control of the government, a government company, local authority, corporation or a member of the municipal corporation.

In *Ram Nagina Singh* v. *S.V. Sohni*,[32] the appointment of the *Loktyukta* in Bihar was challenged through a writ petition for *quo warranto* under Article 226 of the Indian Constitution. Dismissing the petition, the high court made an important point that when a statute confers power on the governor to appoint the *Lokayukta*, the governor is to exercise the power on the advice of the Council of Ministers.

The fact remains, however, that the *Lokayukata* institution in the states has not been very successful so far. The reason is that each state government seeks to install the system for cosmetic purposes, as a populist measure, to give a sense of confidence to the public that corruption is being fought or that one can have redress against maladministration. However, in practice, the government does not take the institution seriously. Its reports are not implemented. The reasons are primarily political; the ruling party does not wish to mar its image by accepting the fact that there has been any corruption or maladministration while it remained in office. Examples abound when no action has been taken even when the *Lokayuktas* have revealed specific instances of corruption or maladministration.[33]

7.3.3 *Lokpal* and *Lokayuktas* Act, 2013

The demand for setting up the institution of *Lokpal* and *Lokayukta* was given a new impetus recently when social activist Anna Hazare went on fast unto death to push for the "Jan Lokpal Bill" proposed by the civil society in India in view of all pervasive governance deficit in the country. Salient features of the proposed Bill included constitutional position for *Lokpal* and *Lokayukta*, i.e *Lokpal* would be independent from executive and political control, completion of investigation within one year and trial within the next year, financial and criminal liability of the guilty, recovery of financial loss to the exchequer from the corrupt person, and compensation to the complainant from the fine imposed. Regarding appointment, the Bill proposes a transparent and participatory process through a selection committee consisting of judges, constitutional authorities and civil society. Bill also proposes a merger of anti-corruption agencies like Central Vigilance Commission (CVC), vigilance departments and anti-corruption branch of the Central Bureau of Investigation (CBI) with the *Lokpal*. Its jurisdiction would extend to all public officers, politicians and judges and others found guilty of corrupting them. It's jurisdiction will cover cases of misconduct of functionaries and grievances of the people. Though Lokpal would not have judicial powers, but would have power to grant stay and to launch prosecution. It's orders would be subject to review by the High Courts and the Supreme Court. Members of the *Lokpal* could be removed for misconduct by a five-member Bench of the Supreme Court. Selection committee would consist of the Vice-President of India, *Lok Sabha* Speaker, *Rajya Sabha* Chairman, Comptroller and Auditor General, Chief Election Commissioner, two senior most judges of the Supreme Court, two senior most judges of the High Court, Chairman of the National Human Rights Commission and the outgoing members of the *Lokpal*. Government constituted a joint committee consisting of members of the civil society and the government to give a final shape to the Bill.[34]

However, the *Lokpal* and *Lokayuktas* Bill, 2011 was passed by *Lok Sobha* on 27 December 2011. It was tabled In *Rajya Sabha* on 29 December 2011 where it remained pending for a long time and was passed on 17 December 2013. The *Lokpal* body was not given the Constitutional status as the Constitutional Amendment Bill, which could provide for making the *Lokpal* a Constitutional body, and was described by the Prime Minister as 'disappointment'. The Bill passed by the Parliament deleted the provision that gave the presiding officers the power to act against ministers and MPs, even before trial. It excluded armed forces and coast guards from the purview of the Act. The *Lokpal* would take complaints against the Prime Minister after consent of two-thirds of *Lokpal* panel. The consent of State governments is mandatory for the notification to set up *Lokayuktas* in the states, but the setting up of them in the States was made mandatory. The appointment panel is loaded in favour of the government.

Pinaki Chandra Ghose, a retired Supreme Court judge, was appointed as the first *Lokpal* of India by a Committeee consisting of Prime Minister Narindra Modi and Chief Justice of the Supreme Court of India, Ranjan Gogoi and Lok Sabha speaker Sumitra Mahajan and eminent jurist, Mukul Rohatgi on 17 March 2019.

7.3.4 OMBUDSMAN FOR LOCAL SELF-GOVERNMENT BODIES

The State of Kerala has created a very interesting institution, i.e. Ombudsman for Local Self-Government (LSG) bodies. The object of the Ombudsman is 'to conduct a detailed inquiry regarding any proceedings of the local self-government bodies and the public servants holding office thereunder concerning corruption, maladministration or defects in the administration and settle such complaints.'

The authority has been created under the Kerala Panchayat Raj Act. 1994 as amended in 1999. The authority known as Ombudsman is to consist of seven persons as follows: (a) a person who is or has been a high court judge as chairman; (b) two district judges; (c) two government officials not below the rank of government secretary; and (d) two 'honest and respectable' social service workers. Adequate provisions have been made to ensure their independence and objectivity. Appointments are to be made by the state governor on the advice of the chief minister.

The institution has been created on the recommendation of the Sen Committee. The committee suggested that while tribunals would adjudicate upon appeals from decisions taken in exercise of regulatory authority, there should be an institution 'to investigate the field of administrative activity, i.e. to investigate independently complaints from individuals and groups and even the government relating to defective administration by the local bodies.'[35]

7.4 OMBUDSMAN (*WAFAQI MOHTASIB*) AND PROVINCIAL OMBUDSMAN IN PAKISTAN

7.4.1 LAW OF OMBUDSMAN IN PAKISTAN

In Pakistan the desirability of establishment of an institution in the nature of Ombudsman was practically felt for a long time. This institution was practically important due to the manner in which the bureaucracy in Pakistan has dealt with the affairs of the common man. On Independence, the government that was formed declared that the development of the country and bringing about social justice in accordance with the teaching of Islam and the aspiration of free people would be the major objectives of the new nation. These objectives called for complete restructuring and reorientation of the administrative machinery. During the period of over 40 years, some visible efforts were made to reform the administrative machinery in order to make it more responsive to the needs of an independent country where the objective of the administrative machinery would be to bring about welfare of the common man. These efforts, however, largely failed to make a dent in the overall structure and orientation of the administrative machinery. There were several reasons for this failure. The most important one is lack of political commitment. There has been no political will to completely restructure and reorient the administrative machinery to make it responsive to the needs of the people. Another significant factor has been that efforts to reform the administrative machinery were shaped and formulated by the very people who had themselves been part of the administrative machinery for many years and had imbibed the old philosophy of administration. Even in respect of inadequate proposals for reform that have emerged from this framework, serious hurdles were placed in their way by the very administrative machinery which these proposals were meant to reform.

It is, however, surprising that the step towards the establishment of the office of Ombudsman was taken by none other than the Martial Law Regime of General Zia ul Haq. He established the office of Federal Ombudsman (*Wafaqi Mohtasib*) through President's Order I of 1983.[36] The objectives of *Wafaqi Mohtasib* have, however, been spelt out in the Preamble to the President's Order as follows:

> Whereas it is expedient to provide for the appointment of *Wafaqi Mohtasib* (Ombudsman) to diagnose, investigate, redress and rectify any injustice done to a person through maladministration.

The institution of *Wafaqi Mohtasib* is primarily concerned with the diagnosis, investigation, redress, and rectification of any injustice done to a person through maladministration of a federal government Agency. The Pakistani law of the Ombudsman is largely based on the Parliamentary Commissioner for Administration Act, 1967 of the UK although there are some differences in details like the provision in the UK Law that complaints can only be entertained when received through a member of the parliament and complaints directly received from the public cannot be investigated by the commissioner. Besides, there is no definition of the term 'maladministration' in English Law. In the President's Order No. I of 1983 the term 'maladministration' has, however, been defined as follows:

'Maladministration' includes:

(i) a decision, process, recommendation, act of omission or commission which:

    (a) is contrary to law, rules or regulations or is a departure from established practice or procedure unless it is bona fide and for valid reasons; or

    (b) is perverse, arbitrary or unreasonable, unjust, biased, oppressive, or discriminatory; or

    (c) is based on irrelevant grounds; or

    (d) involves the exercise of power, or the failure or refusal to do so, for corrupt or improper motives, such as, bribery, jobbery, favouritism, nepotism and administrative excess; and

(ii) neglect, inattention, delay, incompetence, inefficiency, and inaptitude in the administration or discharge of duties and responsibilities.

Another very important aspect of the law of Ombudsman is the definition of 'agency as follows:

'Agency' means a Ministry, Division, Department, Commission or office of the Federal Government or a statutory corporation or other institution established or controlled by the Federal Government but does not include the Supreme Court, the Supreme Judicial Council, the Federal Shariat Court or a High Court.

It is obvious from the above that the jurisdiction of the Ombudsman is restricted to those federal organisations which would fall within the meaning of agency as defined above.

The dictionary meaning of the term "maladministration" is "to handle a matter inefficiently or improperly". The Urdu definition, refers to various types of malpractices which are opposed to law, fair play and principles of equity and justice. In common parlance, the introduction of the office of the Ombudsman and conferment of power upon it was meant to check administrative excesses and abuses of bureaucracy.[37]

The Ombudsman is appointed by the President of Pakistan for a period of four years and is not eligible for extension of tenure or for re-appointment as *Mohtasib* under any circumstances.[38] He cannot hold any office of profit in the service of Pakistan or occupy any other position carrying the right of remuneration for rendering of services.[39] His salary, allowances and privileges, and other terms and conditions of service are determined by the President. He can be removed from the office on the grounds of misconduct or incapability of performance of duties of his office by reason of physical or mental incapacity. However, the Ombudsman can request an open public evidentiary hearing before the Supreme Judicial Council. If such hearing is not held within 30 days of the receipt of such request, or not concluded within 90 days of its receipt, the Ombudsman would be absolved of any stigma whatever. In such circumstances, the Ombudsman may choose to leave his office.[40] It appears from the provisions that if he is absolved then he can choose to continue in office till the expiry of his tenure.

The Ombudsman can assume jurisdiction on the complaint by an aggrieved person or on a reference by the president, the parliament or on the motion of the Supreme Court or high court during the course of any proceedings before it. The Ombudsman can undertake any investigation into any allegation of maladministration on the part of any agency or any of its officers or employees.[41] However, he has no jurisdiction to investigate or enquire into any matters which are subjudice before a court of competent jurisdiction, relates to the external affairs of Pakistan or relates to or is connected with the defence of Pakistan or any part thereof. Thus, the Military, Naval, and Air Force of Pakistan and matters covered by law relating to these forces would fall outside the jurisdiction and powers of the Ombudsman. His jurisdiction does not extend to determination of the terms and conditions of government servants.

The Ombudsman has the same powers as are vested in a civil court in respect of summoning and enforcement of attendance of any person and examination made on oath, compelling the production of documents, receiving evidence on affidavits and issuing Commission for the examination of witnesses.[42] The

Ombudsman or any member of the staff authorised in this behalf can enter any premises for purposes of any inspection or investigation where he has reason to believe that any article, book of account or any other document relating to the subject matter of inspection or investigation would be found. He or his delegatee could search premises, inspect any such article, book of accounts or other documents, take extracts or copies, impound or seal them or make inventories of the same therefrom.[43] He can also constitute an inspection team for the purpose of any of his functions. He can establish a standing or advisory committee with specified jurisdiction for the performance of such of his functions as are assigned to them from time to time. He can also delegate, by order in writing such of his powers as may specify in the order to any member of his staff or such delegatee are required to submit their reports to the Ombudsman with their recommendations for appropriate action.[44] If, after due investigation or inquiry, the Ombudsman reaches certain conclusions and findings, he may communicate them to the agency concerned:

(i) to consider the matter further;
(ii) to modify or cancel the decision, process, recommendation, act or omission;
(iii) to explain more fully the act or decision in question;
(iv) to take disciplinary action against any public servant of any Agency under the relevant laws applicable to him;
(v) to dispose of the matter or case within a specified time;
(vi) to take action on his findings and recommendation to improve the working and efficiency of the Agency within a specified time; or
(vii) to take any other step specified by the Ombudsman.

The Agency concerned after receipt of such recommendations would take action accordingly or in the alternative inform the Ombudsman the reasons for not complying with the same. If he comes to the conclusion that an injustice has been caused in consequence of maladministration which is not being deliberately remedied by the agency concerned he may, if he thinks fit, lay a special report on the case before the President. Failure to comply would constitute 'defiance of recommendations' and the President may, in his discretion, direct the agency concerned to implement the recommendations and inform the Ombudsman accordingly.[45] In order to lend teeth it has been provided that in the instance of defiance of recommendations the report by the Ombudsman would become a part of the personal file or Character Role of the public servant primarily responsible for the defiance provided that the public servant concerned is granted an opportunity to be heard in the matter. The Ombudsman can also refer the case of any person guilty of maladministration to the concerned authority for appropriate, corrective or/and disciplinary action.[46] The Ombudsman has the same powers as the Supreme Court to punish any person for its contempt who abuses, interferes with, impedes, imperils or obstruct the process of the Ombudsman in any way or disobeys any of his orders or scandalises the Ombudsman or brings him, his staff or nominees or delegatee into hatred, ridicule or contempt.[47]

The Ombudsman is required to submit an annual report to the President and can make public any of his study, research conclusions, recommendations, ideas or suggestions in respect of any matters dealt with by his office.[48] No court or other authority has jurisdiction to question the validity of any action taken or intended to be taken or order made or anything done or any grant of injunction or stay or any other interim order in relation to any proceedings before the Ombudsman.[49] No suit, prosecution or other legal proceedings would lie against the Ombudsman, his staff or any of his delegatee or advisor for anything which is in good faith done or intended to be done.[50] Any person aggrieved by a decision or order of the Ombudsman may, within 30 days of the decision or the order, make a representation to the President who may pass any order he deems fit.[51] The provisions of the law regarding Ombudsman would override other laws and would have effect notwithstanding anything contained in any other law for the time being in force.[52]

7.4.2 EXPERIENCE WITH OMBUDSMAN IN PAKISTAN

One distinguishing feature of the institution of Ombudsman (*Wafaqi Mohtasib*) in Pakistan has been the large number of complaints handled by it. Whereas most of such institutions in sixty or so countries of the world handle only a few hundred cases a year each, including the Parliamentary Commissioner of the UK, the institution of *Wafaqi Mohtasib* in Pakistan has been inundated with thousands of public complaints. In the first five months of its existence in 1983, the institution received 7,814 complaints about half of which pertained to provincial Agencies and did not fall within its jurisdiction.[53] In 1984, the number of complaints rose to 38,030; out of these 18,509 complaints pertained to provincial Agencies.[54] In the third year of its existence (1985), the institution received 34,939 complaints, out of which 15,391 pertained to provincial Agencies.[55] In the fourth year (1986), the number of complaints received by the institution increased to 42,744, out of which 16,331 pertained to the provincial Agencies.[56] In 1987, the number of complaints further rose to 44,323, out of which only 36 per cent pertained to provincial Agencies and out of the remaining 28,415 complaints relief was provided in 52 per cent cases.[57] A large number of complaints which are handled by the *Wafaqi Mohtasib* in Pakistan are normally handled by the internal complaint handling machineries of the government agencies in the advanced countries. The glaring disparity between the number of cases handled by the institution of *Wafaqi Mohtasib* in Pakistan and similar institutions elsewhere in the world, however, put it in a different category altogether. The main reason why there is such a large number of complaints filed with the institution in Pakistan compared with similar institutions elsewhere is the insensitivity of bureaucracy to the aspirations and needs of the common man.[58]

Although the office of Ombudsman is a creature of the executive in Pakistan yet successive governments after its creation have been averse to the orders of the Ombudsman when they go against any agency of the government. There is a clear tendency of the government officials not to implement his orders. Either steps are taken to delay implementation of his orders or the representations filed before the president by the federal government against the order of Ombudsman are indefinitely delayed. Once representation is filed, the matter goes into cold storage because the president does not decide the representation on his own but waits for the advice of the prime minister, the cabinet or, practically speaking, the Law Ministry. None of these authorities is in any hurry to render such advice and, in any case, if at all any such advice is rendered, it is bound to go in favour of the government. Thus, it is noticeable that representations filed by the federal government are generally accepted by the President.

Nevertheless, delay in disposing of the representation is worse than decision in favour of the government. The aggrieved party can at least seek judicial review of the order of the President. There have been instances where representations before the president have remained undecided for more than five years. The government assumes that after it files a representation before the President, the order of the Ombudsman stands suspended and every effort is then made to keep such representations in cold storage. Actually, these representations languish in the Ministry of Law for a long time and are not sent to the Presidency for consideration of the President.

The Supreme Court of Pakistan, in a case, took serious notice of this practice and issued a *suo moto* notice to the federal government as to why a direction is not issued for disposal of the representations (under Article 32 of the office of *Wafaqi Mohtasib* (Ombudsman) Order) as expeditiously as possible but ordinarily not later than 90 days of the receipt of a representation by the President.[59] The Supreme Court proceeded to determine this matter under Article 37 of the Constitution which makes it incumbent upon the state to ensure inexpensive and expeditious justice. The court eventually decided the *suo moto* review petition on 1 July 1999 holding that the President should decide a representation within 90 days from its receipt.

Another aspect which was taken notice of by the Supreme Court was that such representations were not being decided by the president by application of his own mind. The decision of the president on such representations has been brief either accepting or rejecting the representation. No reasons were assigned by the president for arriving at the conclusion. Generally, the president acted on the advice of the Law Ministry which used to opine in favour of the government.

In the face of this situation, the Supreme Court held that recording of valid reasons in writing is mandatory while disposing of such representations by the president. The court held that the words 'as he may deem fit' used in Article 32 clearly signify that the president has full and complete powers to arrive at a conclusion in order to do justice but in exercise of such powers, he must act justly and fairly and if the recommendations made or findings recorded by the *Mohtasib* (Ombudsman) are intended to be interfered with, in the interest of justice, valid reasons must be assigned.[60] No arbitrary orders can be passed under the said Article and it is wholly immaterial whether in such cases he acts independently or on the advice of the prime minister. The court repelled the argument on behalf of the federal government that while disposing of a representation, the President can pass any order without assigning reasons. The court held that the statute of the Ombudsman is a self-contained code and provides methodology and manner of enforcement of the findings recorded and the recommendations made by the *Mohtasib* on complaints lodged by any person against maladministration and injustices suffered by him.

7.4.3 JUDICIAL REVIEW OF THE ORDERS OF OMBUDSMAN

Although there is a bar of jurisdiction under the Ombudsman statute against any court or other authority from questioning the validity of any action taken or order passed by the Ombudsman under the statute or from granting any injunction or stay or from making any interim order in relation to any proceedings being held before the Ombudsman or under his authority.[61] However, the superior courts in Pakistan have generally interpreted such ouster of jurisdiction clause as ineffective and inapplicable to the exercise of constitutional/writ jurisdiction by the high courts. Thus the high courts and the Supreme Court have reviewed the orders passed by the Ombudsman or by the President in representation against orders of Ombudsman.

In a case where an Ombudsman gave an order to the Federal Public Service Commission to consider a successful appointee for appointment to a post under the federal government and the president did set aside the order of Ombudsman in representation filed by the federal government, the Lahore High Court reviewed and set aside the order of the president in exercise of the constitutional jurisdiction and upheld the order of the Ombudsman.[62] The Supreme Court upheld the judgment of the Lahore High Court and held that the President should assign reasons in his order so that the aggrieved may challenge the same before the high court in exercise of constitutional jurisdiction.[63]

Exercising judicial review of an order of the Ombudsman, Sindh High Court held that the jurisdiction of the Ombudsman is expressly excluded in case of personal grievances of public servants or functionaries serving in any government department or federal Agency as defined in the Ombudsman Order.[64] In another case, the Lahore High Court held that the Lahore Stock Exchange did not fall within the scope of the expression 'Agency' so as to extend power and jurisdiction of the Ombudsman to deal with complaints of maladministration in relation to its internal affairs.[65] However, the Sindh Industrial Trading Estate was held to be an 'Agency' under the Provincial Ombudsman law.[66] In another case, it was held that *Wafaqi Mohtasib* (Ombudsman) was not empowered to recommend termination of services of a public servant.[67] However, the mere fact that the Ombudsman has recommended the appointment of a public servant does not debar the jurisdiction of the Ombudsman. The bar under Article 9(2) is only against a public servant from filing a complaint in respect of any personal grievance relating to his service. If a complainant is not a public servant at the time of filing of the complaint and seeks appointment as a public servant, the jurisdiction of the Ombudsman is not ousted under Article 9(2).[68]

Wafaqi Mohtasib has no jurisdiction to interfere in matters relating to terms and conditions of employees of financial institutions controlled by the government.[69] He has no jurisdiction to entertain matters relating to terms and conditions of service. Where the Ombudsman failed to show that he had the jurisdiction to entertain the complaint and he had passed the order which was without jurisdiction, such order passed by the Ombudsman was void and without jurisdiction. A petitioner having failed to show whether the Ombudsman had the authority or powers to adjudicate upon matters relating to terms and conditions of service, the high court declined to interfere with the orders passed by the Authorities. A constitutional petition was dismissed in circumstances.[70]

However, in another case, the *Wafaqi Mohtasib* directed the Authority to pay a civil servant his arrears of pay. Authority challenged such directions in Constitutional jurisdiction of high court. Authority's Constitutional petition as also its *intra* Court Appeal against order of the *Wafaqi Mohtasib* were dismissed. Thereafter petition for grant of leave to appeal was lodged before the Supreme Court. While refusing to grant leave to appeal, it was held by the Supreme Court, 'Impugned order appeared to be fair and proper on the face of record to meet the ends of justice.' Direction having been issued by the high court to the authority to pay arrears to the civil servant was fully warranted in law and facts of case. The high court, through its impugned order, had done substantial justice which did not at all call for interference. There being no substance in petition for leave to appeal, same was not maintainable.[71]

The high courts have generally refused exercise of judicial review against the order of Ombudsman where a person files writ petition without availing the remedy of representation before the President of Pakistan. It has been held that since the writ jurisdiction is a discretionary remedy, therefore, the courts are not inclined to exercise it in the cases where statutory remedy of representation before the President has not been availed.[72] However, orders passed by Ombudsman, a sub-constitutional tribunal, though binding on the administration, are not equivalent to declaration of law by the superior courts as envisaged in the constitution.[73]

In a case, where the President of Pakistan had set aside the order of the Ombudsman/*Mohtasib* for the reason that it related to contractual obligation, the Supreme Court held that the action of the President in setting aside the findings and recommendations of the *Mohtasib* only because the matter related to contractual dispute was no reason or ground for justifying interference with the findings and recommendations of the Ombudsman. The only matters which were kept out of his jurisdiction were matters subjudice before some court or Tribunal of competent jurisdiction or those relating to external affairs or defence. All other matters irrespective of the fact whether they stemmed out of contractual obligations or otherwise were well within the powers of the Ombudsman.[74] Similarly, State Life Insurance Corporation was directed by Ombudsman to vacate the land it was occupying and illegally claiming that it belonged to a rightful owner.[75]

Where *Wafaqi Mohtasib* entertained complaint of a civil servant about pensionary benefits, it was held that *Mohtasib* had no jurisdiction in the matter because it related to the terms and conditions of service of a civil servant.[76]

Certain persons filed applications before the *Wafaqi Mohtasib* to appoint them in the company after relaxing the conditions for the 20 per cent quota, reserved for the children of Water and Power Development Authority (WAPDA) deceased or retired employees, and employees who died during service. Thereafter, the *Wafaqi Mohtasib* made recommendations for their appointments after relaxing the prescribed conditions. Not only that, the *Wafaqi Mohtasib* also issued notices to the Electric Supply Company for implementation of such recommendations. Contention of Electric Supply Company was that neither the *Wafaqi Mohtasib* had the power to order and recommend any appointment in a public sector company, nor could he implement the recruitment policy of the company, in view of bar contained under Article 9 of the Establishment of the Office of *Wafaqi Mohtasib* (Ombudsman)

Order, 1983 {"the Order") Appointment and/or recruitment in a public sector company like the Electric Supply Company in the said case was an executive function and such function could not be performed by the *Wafaqi Mohtasib* under Article 9 of the Order which excluded his jurisdiction to entertain a complaint of the nature.

It was held that Jurisdiction of *Wafaqi Mohtasib* was limited as provided under Article 9 of the Order and he could not order and or recommend appointment of a person in the Electric Supply Company, which power rested with the executive authorities.[77]

7.4.4 OMBUDSMAN AND THE GOVERNMENTS IN PAKISTAN

Although the federal government in 1983 was responsible for the creation of the office of Ombudsman, particularly when there was no parliament in the country at that time, yet successive governments in Pakistan have tried to undermine its authority and frustrate its functioning. The governments have generally been appointing such retired judges of the superior courts as Ombudsmen who were regarded as predisposed towards the government in power. The governments do not like interference by the Ombudsman in their affairs and the bureaucracy has done everything within its power to frustrate the orders of the Ombudsman. It is noticeable that on two occasions the incumbent judges of the Supreme Court have been appointed as Acting Ombudsman.[78] In other words, the office of Ombudsman is an additional charge for a Supreme Court judge appointed as such. Obviously, the government which makes such an arrangement is not serious about the office of Ombudsman and it does not desire any devoted or dedicated person to hold the office of Ombudsman and entirely focus on the duties as Ombudsman. Thus, the governments have tried to present the Ombudsman as a showpiece rather than with substantive role in the affairs of Pakistan.

7.4.5 SPECIALISED OMBUDSMAN

The appointment of a specialised Ombudsman is a growing trend throughout the world. Such appointments are made in the departments of revenue, banking, insurance, police, health services, education, army, judiciary, and others. In keeping with the trend, the office of federal tax Ombudsman was established in 2000 under Establishment of Office of Federal Tax Ombudsman Ordinance, 2000.[79] The Federal Tax Ombudsman is appointed by the President for a period of five years and he cannot be reappointed.[80] No qualifications are laid down for such appointment but so far two retired judges of the Supreme Court of Pakistan have been so appointed. The Ombudsman cannot hold any office of profit in the service of Pakistan during such appointment and even for two years after the expiry of his tenure.[81] The Tax Ombudsman, on the complaint of an aggrieved person, or on a reference by the President or a House of Parliament, or a motion of the Supreme Court or a high court on its own motion or during the proceedings before them, investigates any allegation of maladministration on the part of Revenue Department or any tax employer.[82] During the first three years, 5,000 complaints of maladministration were received by the Tax Ombudsman. In a large number of cases, maladministration was established and besides granting relief, disciplinary action and systematic reforms were recommended by the Tax Ombudsman. Majority of such recommendations were implemented but the main hurdle remains to be the mindset of Tax employers which needs to be reformed, reoriented and refreshed.[83]

Where the Federal Tax Ombudsman identified a loss of revenue of Rs.55 billion and the Federal Board of Revenue (FBR) did not recover more than a few millions, the Supreme Court directed the Chairman, FBR to implement the report of Tax Ombudsman and recover the loss caused to the Public Exchequer.[84] The Supreme Court while discussing Sections 14 (Review jurisdiction) and 32 (Representation to President) of Establishment of office of Federal Tax Ombudsman Ordinance, 2000, that the Revenue Division or any person aggrieved of a recommendation made by Tax

Ombudsman may file a representation to the President within 30 days of such recommendation. However, there are three kinds of decisions that can be reviewed by the Federal Tax Ombudsman (1) the findings communicated in terms of Section 11; (2) a recommendation made by him or (3) any other order passed by him. It was also held that in case the Tax Ombudsman makes a new recommendation in exercise of his review jurisdiction, the right to make a representation would be available against such new recommendation before the President.[85]

7.4.6 PROVINCIAL OMBUDSMAN

It has been discussed above that a very high percentage of applications received by the Federal Ombudsman (*Wafaqi Mohtasib*) in the initial years (1983 to 1987) pertained to provincial government departments or agencies which did not fall within the jurisdiction of the Federal Ombudsman. It is also a fact that most of the provincial government departments, particularly the Police and the Revenue Departments and agencies connected therewith have the most interaction with the common man. The common citizen in Pakistan is generally a victim of highhandedness of the police and revenue establishment against whom he has no remedy. This was the main argument in support of the establishment of the office of the Provincial Ombudsman so that it should deal with the complaints against the provincial government departments and agencies.

It was the province of Sindh which took the first step. It established the office of the Provincial Ombudsman under the Sindh Ordinance IX of 1991[86]. This Ordinance was followed by an Act of Provincial Assembly of Sindh which is known as 'Establishment of the office of Ombudsman for the Province of Sindh Act 1991.'[87] This was followed in the Punjab though much later. The first Ordinance establishing the office of Provincial Ombudsman in Punjab was passed on 3 September 1996 through the Punjab Ordinance XI of 1996.[88] It was followed by two other Ordinances i.e. the Punjab Ordinance IV of 1997 and the Punjab Ordinance XIV of 1997.[89]

Finally an Act was passed by the Provincial Assembly of the Punjab in 1997 known as 'the Punjab office of Ombudsman Act 1997.'[90]

The aforesaid Acts and Ordinances in Sindh and the Punjab establishing the office of the Ombudsman have provisions identical to the provisions of the 'Establishment of the office of the *Wafaqi Mohtasib* (Ombudsman) Order 1983'. However, the definition of the agencies applies to provincial departments/commissions/offices/ statutory corporations/institutions. Representation under these provincial laws is provided before the governor of the concerned province though the provisions again are identical. It is, therefore, obvious that the provisions regarding representation under the federal law and its disposal within 90 days as ordered by the Supreme Court of Pakistan, would apply *mutatis mutandis* to the representations under the provincial laws to the governors of the provinces.

It is too early to make any assessment of the performance of the office of the Provincial Ombudsmen but so far no significant progress appears to have been made in the matter of providing redress to the common man against the provincial government departments. The police and the revenue administrations in both the provinces continue to be as harsh and highhanded as they have ever been towards the common man. It appears that although in two provinces the office of the Ombudsmen have been established, the provincial governments are not serious in making the office effective and conducive to good governance.

7.4.7 CONCLUDING REMARKS

From the above discussion it is evident that the office of the Ombudsman is to go a long way before it discovers its true role in the socio politico economic context of Pakistan. Even persons who have held such office have not been able to steer a clear course which would create certainty and uniformity in its law and its execution. Nevertheless, the establishment of such an office at the federal and the provincial levels is a step in the right direction. If appointments to the office are made of such persons who have a clean record of public service, the forum of the Ombudsman may provide redress and succour to the common man. Otherwise such an office would only be a white elephant with a big budget but without any effect on improving the lot and alleviating the sufferings of the common man.

Notes

1. Procurator-General of the USSR or other East European countries used to be appointed and dismissed by and was responsible to the legislature, except in Yugoslavia, since 1954. Broadly speaking, his duty consisted of ensuring respect for legality. He supervised the administrative acts, but could not annul or modify administrative decisions. He could act *proprio motu*, and if in the course of investigation of a grievance he discovered some further violations of the law, he was free to take action. He received complaints in letters or through other communications, or orally in interviews held by him. He was not required to be formal in performing his duties. He could call for documents and other information from administrative authorities as also from individual citizens involved in any breach of the law. He could conduct on-the-spot investigation and could visit prisons. In case he found that a violation of the law had taken place, he could raise the matter with the appropriate administrative authority, or could institute an action in the civil or criminal court.

2. Wade and Forsyth, *Administrative Law* (7th edn., Oxford: Clarendon Press, 1994) 81.

3. M.P. Jain and S.N. Jain, *Principles of Administrative Law* (4th edn., Nagpur: Wadhwa and Company) 916.

4. Ibid., pp. 923–4.

5. *Duncan* v. *Cammel & Laird & Co.* [1924] AC 624, applied in *New Zealand in Hinton* v. *Comtellers* [1953] NZLR 573. See also *State of Punjab* v. *Sukhdev Singh*, AIR 1961 SC 493.

6. See the New Zealand Ombudsman Report, 1961; Ganz G., *Public Law* (1964), 3–8.

7. Section 10(5) of the Parliamentary Commissioner Act, 1967.

8. Section 8.

9. Section 11(3).

10. Section 11(1) and (2).

11. Sections 4, 5(i) and Schedule II of Parliamentary Commissioner Act, 1967.

12. S.A. de Smith, *Constitutional and Administrative Law* (3rd edn.) 618.

13. Wade & Forsyth, Administrative Law (Eleventh edn. 2014, OUP, Oxford), pp. 79-80

14. Ibid, pp. 87-8

15. Administrative Reforms Commission's Interim Report (1966), para. 7.
16. Ibid., para. 17.
17. Ibid.
18. M.P. Jain and S.N. Jain, *Principles of Administrative Law* (6th edn., 2007, Nagpur: Wadhwa and Company) 2467.
19. The bill as originally introduced in the parliament had included a state chief minister within the purview of the *Lokpal*. However, the Joint Committee of the Parliament recommended the deletion of this provision as the chief minister was primarily answerable to his legislative assembly. An amendment moved by the government on 10 May 1979 restored the original position. Ibid., p. 2471.
20. Ibid., p. 2473.
21. Ibid., p. 2474.
22. The Orissa Lokpal and Lokayaktas Act, 1970.
23. The Maharashtra Lokayukta and Upa-Lokayuktas Act, 1971
24. The Rajasthan Lokayukta and Upa-Lokayuktas Act, 1973
25. The Bihar Lokayuktas Act, 1973
26. The UP Lokayukta and Upa-Lokayuktas Act, 1973
27. The AP Lokayukta and Upa-Lokayuktas Act, 1983
28. The Karnataka Lokayukta Act, 1984.
29. The Madhya Pradesh State Legislature passed the law in 1975.
30. The Gujrat Lokpal and Lokayukta Act, 1975.
31. Delhi Lokayukta and Upa-Lokayukta Act, 1995
32. AIR 1971 Patna 36.
33. Supra Note 13, p. 2491. One such typical case has been reported in the press. Several senior officials wee allegedly involved in the land grab scandal in Bhopal which was unearthed in 1982. The Madhya Pradesh *Lokayukta* brought out this matter in his report submitted to the government. He said in his report that the evidence available gave rise to the suspicion that the normal rules for the allotment of land had been violated by the Revenue Department. He therefore suggested departmental inquiry against certain officials. But the Madhya Pradesh government did not take any action in the matter. *The Overseas Hindustan Times*, 20 April 1985, p. 11 has been quoted.
34. I.P. Massey, Administrative Law, Ninth Edition 2017, Eastern Book Company, Lukhnow/Delhi, pp 555-6.
35. Ibid., p. 2487.
36. Establishment of the office of *Wafaqi Mohtasib* (Ombudsman) Order 1983.
37. *Peshawar Electric Supply Co Ltd. v. Wafaqi Mohtasib*, PLD 2016 S.C. 940.
38. Articles 3 and 4.
39. Article 5.
40. Article 6.
41. Article 9
42. Article 14.

43. Article 15.
44. Articles 17, 18, and 19.
45. Articles 11 and 12.
46. Article 13.
47. Article 16.
48. Article 28.
49. Article 29.
50. Article 30.
51. Article 32.
52. Article 37.
53. *Wafaqi Mohtasib* (Ombudsman's) Annual Report, 1983.
54. *Wafaqi Mohtasib* (Ombudsman's) Annual Report, 1984.
55. *Wafaqi Mohtasib* (Ombudsman's) Annual Report, 1985.
56. *Wafaqi Mohtasib* (Ombudsman's) Annual Report, 1986.
57. *Wafaqi Mohtasib* (Ombudsman's) Annual Report, 1987.
58. Ross Masud, *Wafaqi Mohtasib* (Ombudsman) and Bureaucracy in Pakistan, PLD 1989 Journal 10.
59. *Federation of Pakistan* v. *Muhammad Tariq Pirzada* [1999] SCMR 2189.
60. *Federation of Pakistan* v. *Muhammad Tariq Pirzada* [1999] SCMR 2744.
61. Article 29 of Establishment of the office of Wafaqi Mohtasib (Ombudsman) Order, 1983.
62. *Muhammad Tariq Pirzada* v. *Government of Pakistan*, PLJ 1999 Lahore 45.
63. *Federation of Pakistan* v. *Muhammad Tariq Pirzada* [1999] SCMR 2744.
64. *Pakistan International Airlines Corporation* v. *Wafaqi Mohtasib*, NLR 1998 Civil 372.
65. *Tariq Majeed Chaudhry* v. *Lahore Stock Exchange* NLR 1996 Civil 55.
66. *Sindh Industrial Trading Estate* v. *Provincial Ombudsman* [1993] SCMR 948.
67. *Muhammad Aslam Khan* v. *Acting Wafaqi Mohtasib*, NLR 1994 Civil 138.
68. *Pakistan International Airlines Corporation* v. *Wafaqi Mohtasib* [1994] MLD 244.
69. *Muslim Commercial Bank* v. *Momin Khan* [2002] SCMR 958; *Pakistan International Airlines* v. *Captain M.S.K. Lodhi* [2002] SCMR 1004.
70. *Muhammad Aslam Zia* v. *Administrator* [2002] PLC (CS) 606.
71. *Pakistan Railways* v. *Muhammad Ala-ud-Din Babri* [1998] SCMR 1605.
72. *Water and Power Development Authority* v. *Commissioner Hazara Division* [1992] SCMR 2102.
73. *AM Trading Corporation* v. *Central Board of Revenue* [1990] ALD 139.
74. *Capital Development Authority* v. *Raja Muhammad Zaman Khan*, PLD 2007 S.C. 121.
75. *State Life Insurance Corporation* v. *Mst. Nusrat Imtiaz*, 2004 SCMR 376.
76. *Federation of Pakistan* v. *Brig (R) Zulfiqar Ahmad Khan*, 2007 SCMR 1313.
77. *Peshawar Electric Supply Co. Ltd.* v. *Wafaqi Mohtasib*, PLD 2016 S.C. 940.

78. Justice Shafi ur Rehman while he was still a judge of the Supreme Court, was given additional charge as Ombudsman. Similarly Justice Khalil ur Rehman Khan of the Supreme Court was appointed Additional Ombudsmen on the retirement of Justice (Rtd.) A.S. Salam.
79. Ordinance XXXV of 2000, PLD 2001 Central Statutes 31.
80. Ibid., Sections 3 and 4.
81. Ibid., Section 5.
82. Ibid., Section 9.
83. *Justice (R) Saleem Akhtar,* 'Role of Ombudsman in safeguarding Civil Rights', PLD 2004 Journal 81.
84. *In re: Federal Board of Revenue,* 2013 SCMR 634.
85. *Federation of Pakistan v. Sahib Jee,* PLD 2017 S.C. 139.
86. Establishment of the office of Ombudsman for the Province of Sindh Ordinance 1991.
87. Sindh Act I of 1992
88. Punjab Office of the Ombudsman Ordinance 1996
89. Punjab Office of the Ombudsman Ordinance 1997.
90. Punjab Act X of 1997.

Bibliography

Administrative Reforms Commission's Interim Report (1966).

Akhter, Justice (retd.) Saleem, *'Role of Ombudsman in safeguarding Civil Rights'*, PLD 2004 Journal 81.

Allan, C.K., *The Citizen and the Administration*, (London, 1962).

Allen, C.K., *Law and Order* (3rd edn, London, 1965).

Baker, Warren E., *'Policy by Rule or Ad Hoc Approach: Which should it be?'* (1957).

Basu, Durga Das, *Shorter Constitution of India*, (9th edn, New Delhi, 1984).

Brown, J. Neville, and Garner, J.F., *French Administrative Law*, (London, 1973).

Byse, C., *'The Federal Administrative Procedure Act'* [1958].

Carr, C.T., *Concerning English Administrative Law*, 130th Canadian Journal of Economics and Political Science, (New York, 1941).

Chakraverti, Suranjan, *Domestic Tribunals and Administrative Jurisdictions* (London, 1965).

Chatterjee, Shri N.C., *'Control of the Legislative Powers of Administration'*, 1 Journal of the Indian Law Institute (1938–9).

Crawford's *Statutory Construction* (edn.1940).

Cushman, Robert F., ed., *Cases in Constitutional Law*, (4th edn, New Jersey, 1975).

David, Rene, *Droit Administratif in France* (9th edn, London, 1939)

Davis, K.C., *Administrative Law*, (New York, 1971).

Davis, Kenneth C., *Discretionary Justice: A Preliminary Inquiry* (Lousiana,1969).

de Smith, S.A. and Brazier, Rodney, *Constitutional and Administrative Law*, (7th edn, London, 1994).

de Smith S.A., *Judicial Review of Administrative Action* (2nd edn, London, 1968).

_____, *Judicial Review of Administrative Action* (3rd edn, London, 1973).

————, *Judicial Review of Administrative Action* (4th edn, London, 1980).

Denning, Alfred, *Freedom Under the Law,*(London, 1949).

Desai, A.R., *Social Background of Indian Nationalism,* (Delhi 1959).

Dicey, A.V., *The Development of Administrative Law in England,* (1915) 31 LQR 148.

Dicey, A.V., *The Law of the Constitution* (London, 1885).

Dicey, A.V., *The Law of the Constitution* (9th edn, London,1939)

Dil Muhammad, '*Delegated Legislation*', PLJ 1993.

Ehmke, Horst P., '*Delegata Potestas Non Potest Delegari: A maxim of American Constitutional Law*' [1961] 47 Cornell LQ 50.

Evans, J.M., Janisch, H.N. and Mullen, David J., *Administrative Law,* (Toronto, 1985).

Fazal, M.A., *Judicial Control of Administrative Action in India, Pakistan and Bangladesh* (3rd edn, London and Delhi, 2000).

————, *Judicial Control of Administrative Action in India and Pakistan* (Oxford, 1969).

————, *Judicial Control of Administrative Action in India, Pakistan and Bangladesh* (2nd edn, Allahabad, 1990).

Foulkes, David, *Introduction to Administrative Law,* (4th edn, London, 1976).

Friendly, Henry J., *Federal Administrative Agencies: The Need for Better Definition of Standards* (1962), Chapters I and VII.

Gantz David A., *Public Law* (1964).

Garner, J.F., *Administrative Law* (6th edn, London 1985).

Gellhorn, Ernest and Boyer, Barry B, *Administrative Law and Process;* (Minnesota, 1981).

Gellhorn, Walter, Byse, Clark, and Strauss, Peter L., *Administrative Law, Cases and Comments;* (7th Edition, New York,1979).

Griffith, J.A.G., and Street, H., *Principles of Administrative Law,* (5th edn, London, 1973).

————, *Principles of Administrative Law* (4th edn, London, 1967).

Halsbury's Laws of England, Vol. 1(1), (4th edn, Oxford, 1989)

Hamson, C., *Executive Discretion and Judicial Control* (London, 1954).

Hewart, G., *Not without Prejudice* (London, 1935).

Hood, Phillips, *Constitutional and Administrative Law* (3rd edn, London, 2000).

Jaffe, L.L. and Nathanson, Nathaniel L., *Administrative Law: Cases and Materials*, 109–115 (1961).
Jaffe, L.L., *Delegation of Legislative Power. An Essay* [1947] 47 Col. LR 359
Jain, M.P. and Jain, S.N., *Principles of Administrative Law*, (4th edn, Agra,1986).
_____, *Principles of Administrative Law* (3rd edn, Bombay,1979).
Jain, M.P., *Indian Constitutional Law* (3rd edn, Bombay, 1978).
Jones, Harry W., '*The Rule of Law and the Welfare State*' (1958) 58 Col. LR 143.

Kagzi, M.C. Jain, *The Indian Administrative Law;* (6th edn, Delhi, 2002).
Keith, A.B., *A Constitutional History of India, 1600–1935*, (Allahabad, 1937).
Khan, Hamid, *Administrative Tribunals for Civil Servants in Pakistan*, (Lahore, 1990)

Lal's *Remedies of Government Servants in Service: Matters under the Administrative Tribunals Act 1985*, (2nd edn.), (Allahabad, 1987).
Leyland, Peter, and Woods, Jerry, *Text book on Administrative Law*, (3rd edn, London, 1999).

Maitland, F.W., *Constitutional History of England*,(Cambridge, 1908).
Marshall, H.H., *Natural Justice* (London 1959).
Massey, I.P., *Administrative Law*, (9th edn, Delhi 2017).
_____, *Administrative Law* (4th edn, Lucknow, 1980).
Masud, Ross, *Wafaqi Mohtasib (Ombudsman) and Bureaucracy in Pakistan*, PLD 1989 Journal 10.
Munir, Muhammad, *Constitution of the Islamic Republic of Pakistan* (Lahore, 1976).

Northey, J.F., *A Decade of Change in Administrative Law* [1974–5] 6 NZULR 25.

Paterson, D.E., '*First Report of the Public and Administrative Law Reform Committee (1968)*' [1968–69] 3 NZULR 351.

Ramchandran, V.G., *Administrative Law;* (2nd edn, Lucknow 1984).

Report of the Public Inquiry into the Disposal of Land at Crichel Down (Cmd 9176/1954)

Rhyne, Charles S., *Law and Judicial Systems of Nations*, (Cambridge, 1978).

Robson, W.A., *Justice and Administrative Law: A Study of the British Constitution*, (3rd edn, London,1951).

Robson,W.A., *'Administrative Law in England 1919–48'* in *British Government since 1918* (Cambridge,1950).

Salmond, John, *Jurisprudence*, (9th edn, London, 2010).

Sathe, S.P., *Administrative Law* (3rd edn, Bombay, 1979).

———, *Administrative Law,* (2nd edn, Bombay,1974).

Schwartz, Bernard, *An Introduction to American Administrative Law;* (2nd edn, London 1962).

———, *'Legislative Control of Administrative Rules and Regulations: The American Experience'*, [1955] 30 New York University Law Review 1031.

———, *French Administrative Law and the Common Law World,* (Oxford, 1954).

Szladits, Charles, *Guide to Foreign Legal Materials: French, German, Swiss,* (1959).

Taylor, G.D.S., *'Judicial Review of Improper Purposes and Irrelevant Considerations'* [1976] 36 Camb. LJ 272

The Franks Report on Administrative Tribunals and Enquiries of 1957.

The New Zealand Ombudsman Report, 1961.

Wade, E.C.S., and Phillips, C. Godfrey, *Constitutional and Administrative Law,* (9th edn, London, 1977).

Wade, H.W.R, and Forsyth, C., *Administrative Law,* (11th edn, Oxford, 2014).

———, *Administrative Law,* (7th edn, Oxford, 1994).

———, *Administrative Law,* (5th edn, Oxford, 1982).

———, *Administrative Law,* (4th edn, Oxford, 1977).

Whitemore, Harry, and Aronson, Mark, *Review of Administrative Action* (Sydney, 1978).

Wozencraft, F.M., *'The Administrative Conference of the United States'*, [1968–69] Business Lawyer 915, 24.

Index